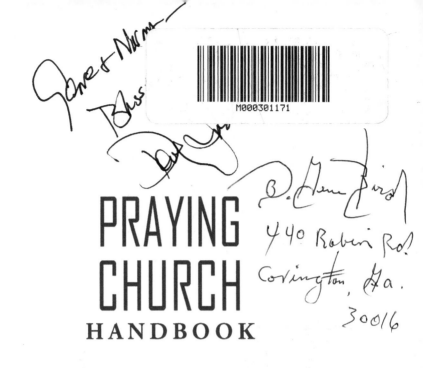

PRAYING CHURCH

HANDBOOK

A Companion to the
Praying Church Resource Guide

VOLUME I
Foundations

Alive Publications
in conjunction with
Church of God Prayer Ministries

Scripture quotations, unless otherwise indicated are taken from the Holy Bible, New King James Version, Copyright – 1979, 1980, 1982, 1990, 1995, Thomas Nelson, Inc., Publishers.

ISBN: 978-0-9820115-8-4

Copyright © 2013 by Alive Publications
Kannapolis, NC 28082
All Rights Reserved
Printed in the USA

Editorial Disclaimer: While this material has been produced with the Church of God and its prayer endeavor, for pastors and prayer leaders, it should be noted that this is in no way an attempt to represent the 'Official' Theology of prayer by the denomination. In this multi-volume set, you will find divergent, at times competing views on prayer. The 20th Century will be referred to as 'the Century of the Holy Spirit,' and it may well be that this century will be called 'the Century of Prayer.' We are still in the Reformation, the Scripture continues to come alive, and the Church is learning the power in sacred privilege of prayer. These chapters are aimed at intensifying the dialogue on prayer.

DEDICATION

This volume is dedicated to Richard Spurling, R.G. Spurling, and John Plemmons who formed a prayer-pact in 1884 that led to the founding of the Christian Union in 1886.

And to those who joined R. G. Spurling after the death of his father - W.F. Bryant, A.J. Tomlinson and M.S. Lemons who are regarded by many as the 'founders' of the Church of God.

Mention should also be made of F. J. Lee, the choir director of First Baptist Church, whose hunger for God in the 1908 Cleveland Revival resulted in his being filled with the Spirit and joining the Church of God. He would become the second General Overseer. Lee University bears his name.

Honorable mention should include Sam Perry, whose regular column in the early issues of the Evangel often centered on prayer. At the 10th General Assembly, in 1914, Perry preached a message on "Intercessory Prayer," one of the first exclusively and specifically on prayer. At the conclusion of his message, "there was a great manifestation of the presence and power of God. Many saw supernatural tongues 'like as of fire' flashed about. People shouted, wept, screamed, danced, prayed, sang and pen cannot describe the scene. Perry seems to have been a key advocate of prayer among the early leaders" – so reads the early history. Perry was appointed as the State Overseer of Kentucky in 1911 and selected as a member of the first Elder's Council in 1917. He went on to publish a paper, "A Call to Prayer" and to establish a "House of Prayer" in Miami.

Special tribute is offered to Edmond and Rebecca Barr, both licensed ministers in the Church of God, our first missionary couple. This dear black brother returned to his native Bahamas with his Florida born wife. Perhaps, as a result of their affirmation, the Church of God continues with a significant black constituency whose influence and contribution to the denomination is priceless. Tribute is also offered to Robert and Ida Evans, along with Carl Padgett, white missionaries to the Bahamas in 1910. And to Lillian Trasher who arrived in Egypt in 1910 and founded an orphanage. Men and women, black and white – thanks for your missionary example bathed in prayer.

Thanks to all the early pioneers – too many to mention. We are borne along by your prayers.

ACKNOWLEDGEMENTS

The Praying Church Handbook has been produced as compendium on prayer and the ministry of prayer for use by pastors and local church prayer leaders. This volume is the first of other volumes to follow.

The Praying Church Handbook is meant as companion to the *The Praying Church Resource Guide,* almost 700 page collection of practical materials for local church prayer leaders. While the 'Resource Guide' is prayer-applied, the 'Handbook' is meant as a more academic companion. We hope you will make both a part of your local church prayer library.

This is a labor of various church leaders in the Church of God to produce serious and substantive materials to ground a well-balanced ministry of prayer in the context of the local church.

I am so grateful to the many contributors – Dr. Raymond Culpepper, General Overseer at the time this project was initiated; Dr. Mark Williams, General Overseer during the time the first volume was completed; Dr. French Arrington, respected and noted Church of God theologian; Dr. James Beaty, Theologian, Educator and Missiologist; Dr. Roland Vaughn, Director of World Missions for two terms, Current Director of the Denomination Unreached People Endeavor; Dr. Grant McClung and his wife Janice, former superintendent to Europe, former Education Director, Author; Dr. David Ramirez, Superintendent of South America; and more – Joann Garzarella, New Jersey Coordinator of Prayer Ministries; David and

Carletta Douglas, Kentucky Coordinator of Prayer Ministries; Mark Hisle, Pastor and Member of the Kentucky Prayer Commission; Kathy Hamon, Coordinator of Prayer Ministries, Minnesota; Ron Lackey, and his wife Margaret – Western North Carolina Prayer Commission; David Nitz, pastor and former Director of Evangelism and Coordinator of Prayer Ministries, Florida; Marc Campbell, Pastor; Mary Rosenberger, Coordinator of Prayer Ministries, Delmarva; Dr. Jacob King, Coordinator of Prayer Ministries, North Georgia.

In addition to the chapters in this volume, which includes a historic review of prayer in the Old and New Testament, subsequent volumes will include a view of prayer through the church ages. Additional materials unique to the Pentecostal perspective on prayer will be offered. The contributions of additional non-Church of God authors will be added, including, Ron Auch (Assembly of God Prayer Leader); Jonathan Graf (Editor, Prayer-Connect Magazine); Dick Eastman (The Jericho Center, International Prayer Leader, Every Home for Christ); Daniel Henderson (Author, Prayer Leader, Acts 6:4 Fellowship Leader), and of course, additional contributions by P. Douglas Small.

P. Douglas Small, Compiler/Editor
Coordinator of Prayer Ministries
Church of God

FOREWORD

By Mark Williams

The Church of God was birthed out of a prayer meeting on the banks of Barney Creek in North Carolina in the 1880s as hungry hearts cried out to God. In the first General Assembly, in 1906, the delegates stated: "It is, therefore, the sense of this assembly that we recommend, advise and urge that each local church hold a prayer meeting at least once a week." Thus, from the earliest days of our movement, we have placed a premium on prayer, understanding that a praying Christian is a powerful Christian. "The effective prayer of a righteous man can accomplish much" (James 5:16 NASB).

Likewise, C. H. Spurgeon, the great preacher of yesteryear, believed greatly in prayer. He said, "Make the most of prayer. . . . Prayer is the master weapon. We should be wise if we used it more, and did so with more specific purpose."

Church growth author Peter Wagner has written, "The more deeply I dig beneath the surface of church growth principles, the more thoroughly convinced I become that the real battle is a spiritual battle and that our principle weapon is prayer."

The Praying Church Handbook began as a project late in the tenure of Dr. Raymond Culpepper. I am happy to see the first volume of what will be a serial compendium on prayer, designed as a more substantive companion to *The Praying Church Resource Manual,* and loaded with practical materials and helps.

This first volume contains a chapter by Dr. Culpepper along

with contributions from Dr. French Arrington and Dr. James Beaty. One special feature of this volume includes snapshots of prayer at our early General Assemblies. Reading these excerpts, I was deeply moved. We began as a movement of prayer, and it is only by a rededication to prayer that we can recapture the pioneer spirit that turned cities upside down with the message of Jesus Christ in the power of the Holy Spirit.

It is my prayer that God will use the *Praying Church Handbook* as the catalyst to fan the flames of renewal throughout our movement and that leaders and congregations will experience the spirit of prayer that pervaded our early days and continues today in places where the Church of God is making notable progress around the world. As we unite in prayer, God will give us a fresh outpouring of His Spirit so that we may experience a great thrust of evangelism and church growth.

God is calling the Church to prayer. Let's pray!

Dr. Mark Williams
General Overseer
Church of God, 2012-

VOLUME I
Foundations

CONTENTS

Introduction - Around the World

FUTURE VOLUMES

Two: Personal and Family Prayer
1. Prayer – the Key to Intimacy with God
2. Effective Personal Prayer – Part I
3. Effective Personal Prayer – Part II
4. Foundations for Family Worship
5. Hearing God
6. Creating a Personal Prayer Room
7. Prayer and the Spiritual Disciplines
8. Prayer and Fasting
9. Praying with the Spirit

The Family and Prayer
10. Power of a Father's Faith
11. The Family Altar
12. The Power of Praying Couples
13. The Missional Family
14. Benefits of Praying Together

Three: The Church at Prayer
1. The 4-Dimensional Model for Prayer Ministries
2. History of Prayer – Part VI (100 AD and Beyond)
3. History of Prayer – Part VII (Post-Reformation)
4. A Praying Pastor
5. Dreaming of a New Day in Pastoral Leadership
6. Prayer in the Corporate Worship Service
7. Effective Prayer Meetings
8. Prayer Ministry and Healing Teams
9. Pastor's Prayer Partner Ministry
10. Managing Prayer Requests

Four: Intercessory Prayer and Missions

1. Am I Really a Watchman?
2. The Pastor's Pit Crew
3. Teaming Intercessors
4. Intercessors: Facts and Feelings
5. Effective Prayer Groups
6. Prophetic Intercession
7. Priestly Intercession
8. Prayer and Care

Prayer and Mission

1. Prayer and the Great Commission
2. Connecting to God's Work in the World
3. Praying with High Global Impact
4. Encouraging and Equipping Missionaries Through Prayer
5. Church Planting and Prayer
6. Spiritual Mapping
7. Giving the Gift of Prayer to Community Leaders
8. Praying for Unreached People Groups

AROUND THE WORLD

Around the world, the cloud of incense is thickening over the earth. The prayer movement may be sputtering and hesitating here in North America, but in other places – it is only gaining momentum. In Indonesia, the largest Muslim nation on the face of the earth, and also the location of the largest Church of God congregation, five million people in stadiums across that nation united for a day of prayer in May 2012! One can almost anticipate the moment, when heaven casts fire into the earth, peals of thunder rumble and the earth trembles.

There are seven notable global prayer trends:

1. *Pastoral Prayer.* A major shift is occurring among pastors.

    For decades, the pastor has been trained as a professional, a church-growth technician, a clinician, rather than a holy man of God. Clergy language has moved from theological terms, to culturally approved psychological language. Now, a fresh wave is emerging, following Acts 6:4, "We will give ourselves to prayer and the word." Daniel Henderson, for years a leader in the pastoral prayer movement along with Brooklyn Tabernacle's Jim Cymbala, are leading a movement of praying pastors - 'The Acts 6:4 Fellowship'.

2. *Academic Training.* In the Post-Reformation era, theological studies mushroomed, differentiating denominations. Controversy trumped consecration in academia. Prayer was

demoted as a focus of theology and quietly relocated to devotional studies. Theology books rarely addressed prayer. The inattention is mysterious, quite stunning, given the centrality of the doctrine, the 'priest-hood of all believers.' Recently, fresh eyes have recognized the importance of prayer theology, prayer training and specifically the inadequate attention given to the development of the prayer life of a potential pastor along with the need of training for prayer leaders.

3. *The 24-7 movement* is gaining momentum everywhere. City-wide prayer centers are becoming common. The movement seeks coordinated prayer in and for a community, 24 hours-a-day, 7-days-a-week. Ceaseless intercession and worship. The movement is spontaneous, and wonderfully out of control.

4. *City-Wide Prayer Movements.* The National Prayer Committee is a constellation of national prayer organizations with different emphases. They sponsor the National Day of Prayer. Recently, they met to consider a grass-roots replication of their association. Locally, agency representatives rarely, if ever, meet together. The 'Prayer Council' movement would synergize national prayer efforts at the local level bringing prayer leaders to the same table. Representatives of national prayer organizations and congregational prayer coordinators would sit at the same table, translating prayer events into a seamless community-wide prayer process. Website: www.pc2ln.org.

5. *Youth and Children's Prayer movements.* It is estimated that as many as two-million children may be intercessors. As young as 5-years-of-age, they pray with passion. They are abundant across South America, Africa and Asia, These kids are not content to pray 'Now I lay me down to sleep ... !' They pray for nations. They weep for the harvest. The phenomenon can only be understood as a move of the Holy Spirit. "Out of the mouths of babes!" The Lord is ordaining prayer and praise. In North America, it is the youth prayer movement that is ablaze. Teens with prayer-fire in their hearts are filling up stadiums. They are buying abandoned warehouses and run-down church facilities

in both large and small cities to create prayer centers. They are systematically prayer walking, driving, targeting prayer to spark a national revival.

6. *The Marketplace*. Nehemiah, it seems, is still alive. An equally stunning movement is emerging among business owners and leaders, CEOs who are serious about uncompromised faith in the marketplace. Movements have arisen to support them. No longer content to be engaged one-day-a-week, their talents and abilities, call and gifts, they now recognize cannot be stuffed into the 'come-to' church they attend weekly. Nor can the 'go ye' gospel that burns within them. In previous generations, they would have answered a call to the pastorate. But now they sense the need to contextualize the gospel in the workplace. Dancing between a faithless culture and legal issues, they are finding creative ways to bring faith into the open square.

7. *Intercessors*. Peter Wagner says that ten-percent of Christians are called to be an intercessor. A more conservative estimate is five-percent. But they are rarely identified, teamed or trained, directed or debriefed. For decades, the emphasis has been on prophetic, not priestly intercession. Intercession and spiritual darkness have almost become synonymous. Now that is beginning to change. New health and balance is coming to intercessory teaching and practice. And ordinary believers are awakening to their intercessory responsibility. Networks of regional and national intercessors are emerging. A culture resistant to the gospel, is surprisingly open to prayer.

Samuel Chadwick argued, "There is no power like that of prevailing prayer – of Abraham pleading for Sodom, Jacob wrestling in the stillness of the night, Moses standing in the breach, Hannah intoxicated with sorrow, David heart-broken with remorse and grief, Jesus in sweat and blood ... always there is the cost of passion unto blood. Such prayer prevails. It turns ordinary mortals into men of power. It brings power. It brings fire. It brings rain. It brings God."

Connect your church to 'The Praying Church Movement' www.praycog.org.

New Resources – *The Praying Church Resource Guide*, a 700-page notebook with practical materials for the local church prayer leader. And *The Praying Church Handbook*, a substantive work on the doctrine of prayer, intercession and prayer as gift to the believer and family. Purchase these resources from the Church of God Prayer Ministries Office.

SECTION ONE

BIBLICAL PERSPECTIVES

CHAPTER ONE

PRAYING TO POSSESS GOD'S PROMISES

A Window Through Time

J. W. Buckalew was one of the most popular and colorful preachers in the early Church of God. He was saved from a rough life – crime and alcohol, a prodigal who spent years running from the police. After he was almost killed, he had a life-changing conversion and an equally radical deliverance experience. He was called to preach – severely mocked and tried, but "he took courage and pressed on for Jesus sake." He and his wife began visiting homes and praying for people. In nearly every home, people were saved, night after night. He rented a small building – and soon quit his mill job. He preached on the streets, in tents, in churches to which he was invited. At times, he slept under the stars. Realizing his need for training, he went to the Pentecostal School in Nashville, TN and found the President in his office on his face praying. Buckalew waited – but President McClurkin was lost in prayer – twenty, twenty-five, thirty minutes. Eventually, he acknowledged Buckalew. "We then knelt and prayed for one another ... I heard him pray ... the Lord made it plain that it was His will for me to be there."

Buckalew had only the money for books – not for board or other needs. Bouts of homesickness would grip him, and McClurkin would then take him on a prayer ministry trip.

He was so poor he was not able to replace his shoes, despite their gaping holes. He blacked his socks, and pleaded with the Lord. A money-order for $2.60 from his wife was the answer. He headed to town to buy new shoes. Full of the joy of the Lord, he began to sing – and suddenly he found himself the center of the attention of several hundred people. So he preached the gospel to them. A bare-footed girl begged him to come and see her mother. "Momma wants you to come over and sing that song for her." He handed out a few more tracts and followed the small girl into a dilapidated one room building. On the filthy and cold floor was a baby. A woman, very sick lay on the bed. Buckalew prayed with her – and they both wept. She told him her story – an alcoholic husband had abandoned her. She had lost hope. Buckalew started singing, *Some Mother's Child*. She wept. He wiped the tears – and kept singing. And then he knelt and prayed for the woman. She clapped her hands and rose from the bed with a glow. He tried to excuse himself, but the Holy Spirit arrested him with the words from James 2:14. He couldn't bless her and depart in peace with her needs unmet. He returned – and gave her the entire $2.60. She had pawned her quilts to buy bread for the children. Again on the street, he started singing. He told the story of the woman's

Realizing his need for training, he went to the Pentecostal School in Nashville, TN and found the President in his office on his face praying. Buckalew waited – but President McClurkin was lost in prayer – twenty, twenty-five, thirty minutes. Eventually, he acknowledged Buckalew. "We then knelt and prayed for one another ... I heard him pray ... the Lord made it plain that it was His will for me to be there."

plight to the gathered crowed, prayed for her and placed his hat down for an offering. He collected $6.25. With that he retrieved her quilts, had coal delivered, connected with some women who agreed to give the woman's place a cleaning. "I shall never forget the change there was in that sad home, the bed and the children looked so nice and clean ... and the room was warm and nice. We all knelt and thanked the Lord."

He looked down at his worn shoes, his money now gone. He could see the side of his foot exposed through the open shoe and felt the biting cold. "Lord, I am willing to go barefooted if I can glorify you in doing so ... You just give me the money to buy some shoes when it pleases you." That Sunday, he put on his worn out shoes, blacked his socks and then headed to the streets to preach before going on to church for the evening service. That night, pacing back and forth in the altar – he felt something in his hand. He looked, thinking it was a dollar bill. It wasn't – it was a ten dollar bill. The next morning there was another in the mail. Twenty-dollars. A ten-fold blessing. He bought his pair of shoes – and other things he needed.†

Later, on his way to Alabama for a revival, he was in a meeting in which a well-dressed and gentile lady stood to testify. She told about reaching the bottom, about abandonment by her husband leaving her and her children homeless and helpless. And she told about a man who came to her little hovel, knelt by her bed and prayed, and how she regained her faith. "I began to mend from that very hour. Now I am well and happy and have work ..." Buckalew walked down the aisle and shook her hand.

Editor's Note: Early Church of God preachers prayed, lived by faith, operated with a profound spirit of compassion – and God used them in mighty ways. They possessed the promises.

†   Lucille Walker, *What To Do When You Pray* (Cleveland, TN: Pathway Press, 1998), 64-68. See also, Incidents in the Life of J. W. Buckalew.

CHAPTER 1

PRAYING TO POSSESS GOD'S PROMISES

Raymond F. Culpepper

*C*onfess your trespasses to one another and pray for one another that you may be healed. The effective fervent prayer of a righteous man avails much. James 5:16-18 NKJV[1]

Elijah was a man with a nature like ours. He prayed earnestly that it would *not* rain, and it did not rain on the land for three years and six months. Later, he prayed again, and the heavens gave rain and the earth produced its fruit.

> *And it came to pass after many days that the word of the Lord came to Elijah, in the third year, saying, "Go, present yourself to Ahab, and I will send rain on the earth." So Elijah went to present himself to Ahab; and there was a severe famine in Samaria.*
>
> *So it was while Jezebel massacred the prophets. . . .*
>
> *Then it happened, when Ahab saw Elijah, that Ahab said to him, "Is that you, O troubler of Israel?"*
>
> *Then Elijah said to Ahab, "Go up, eat and drink; for there is a sound of an abundance of rain." So Ahab went up to eat and drink. And Elijah went up to the top of Carmel; then he bowed down on the ground, and put his face between his knees, and said to his servant, "Go up now, look toward the sea." So he went up and looked, and said, "There is nothing." And seven times he said, "Go again." Then it came to pass the seventh time, that he said, "There is a cloud, as small as a man's hand, rising out of the sea!" So he said,*

---

1   Citations from Scripture in this Chapter are from the *New King James Version* unless otherwise indicated.

"Go up and say to Ahab, 'Prepare your chariot, and go down before the rain stops you'" (I Kings 18:1-2, 4, 17, 41-44).

George Mueller, a man who lived in the 1800's, was one of the greatest prayer warriors of all time. God called George Mueller with a line from Psalms 68:5: "[God would be] a father to the fatherless."And out of that illuminated scripture, George Mueller had a transformation of his life and calling. He began to take care of homeless and orphaned children by providing food and shelter.

George Mueller, according to his biographer, read the Bible through 200 times. He read the Bible through on his knees 100 of the 200 times. His life was limited without social media, Internet, or telephone. But in the 1800s—in the brief span of his life—he ministered and cared for over 2,000 children. It is said by biographers, and found in his journal, that on many occasions there would be no food to feed the children; yet with a bare table, George Mueller would close his eyes, bow his head, and thank God for the food that was about to be set before them. And, time after time, by the conclusion of that prayer of thanksgiving and blessing, somebody, maybe even an angel of the Lord, would come by and leave a miracle. George Mueller's personal journal, when studied by his biographers, indicated that he had literally documented in writing more than 50,000 answers to prayer.

About prayer and the power of a prayer life, George Mueller said: "It is not enough to begin to pray, nor to pray aright; nor is it enough to continue for a time to pray; but we must pray patiently, believing, continuing in prayer until we obtain an answer. We have also to believe that God does hear us and will answer our prayers. Most frequently, we fail in not continuing in prayer until the blessing is obtained and in not expecting the blessing."[2]

2   "George Mueller Quotes." Online. Internet. oChristian.com. © 1999-
      2000.

George Mueller started with the promise of God to be "a father of the fatherless." Have you received a promise from Almighty God to you that is somehow a personal word of God promising you a certain blessing? Has He promised something in your calling, your family, or your church where God has placed you as a shepherd of a flock? Has He promised something in your business, your educational pursuits, or a child to your barren womb? Is there a promise of God that He will heal divisions in a family or a church, or is there a promise of God for a healing?

Elijah—A Man of Prayer

Elijah was a man of like passions as we are, but somehow he was able to internalize the promises of God. Elijah's story in I Kings 18 can help us build a prayer life, and the Holy Spirit can help us to better understand the dynamics that surrounded this great prophet of God.

Someone described Elijah as the meteor of God that went across Israel's dark night with a flash of radiance from the divine. He was, without question, the man of God who got his orders from

---

ACCENT

When J. H. Walker was Superintendent of Education for the Church of God, his appendix ruptured. Dr. Justice Sullivan reported, "I am sorry ... it's too late now. There is nothing that can be done now." He grew weaker and weaker as the poison spread through his body. His eyes were glassy. E. M. Ellis, T. L. McClain and M. P. Cross learned of his situation. They came to visit him - and prayed. "Something has to be done, Brother Walker. Your wife needs a husband and your children need a father!" Brother Walker added, "And God needs a soldier!"

J. H. Walker recalled the moment. They began to pray, and fervently so, and soon Walker recalled, "I ceased to hear them; and a while later ... I saw, as it were, a white, silvery

---

velvet sheet floating down from the top of the room; and as it settled on my bed, I saw what appeared to be a long sword, shining like a neon tube. It came down and pierced my side. My body trembled like a leaf in the wind. I felt the heavenly anointing. I felt rested and a sweet peace thrilled me as I said, 'I'm healed. God has healed me' ... Praise God. I was healed."

The news of the healing of J. H. Walker inspired sermons all across the denomination - "God Needs a Soldier!" J. H. Walker went on to serve as General Overseer for nine years, as Editor in Chief of Church of God Publications, Director of World Missions and President of both Lee and West Coast Bible College.

Lucille Walker, *What To Do When You Pray* (Cleveland, TN: Pathway Press, 1998), 150.

headquarters. His listeners did not need a dictionary to understand what he said. He did not come with apology; he came with the boldness of Almighty God himself. In approximately 850 BC, Elijah burst on the scene in a blaze of heavenly glory; and when he left the scene, he left in another blaze—a chariot of fiery glory. Elijah's arrival came after approximately 50 years of six evil despots ruling Israel. As if this were not bad enough, now there was a seventh one on the throne—his name was Ahab.

James 5:17 tells us that Elijah prayed earnestly. In I Kings 18:1, the chapter opens with the phrase, "after many days." This phrase seems to be connected to the previous chapter, and it could be. However, James 5:16 says, the "effective, fervent prayer of a righteous man avails much." Therefore, "after many days" could mean after many days of effectual, fervent praying. This type of praying is not just a one time explosion of emotion. Matthew 7:7 says, *"Ask, and it will be given to you; seek, and you will find; knock, and it will be opened to you."* Fervent, effectual prayer is about commitment, emotion, involvement, spirit, and voice. We must continue in fervent, effectual prayer; this does not mean going to God on one occasion, and demanding that He grant our request. It is, instead, this holy and humble entrance into the awesome, sovereign presence of the Creator, and there we come to understand the dynamic of prayer.

You don't have to understand everything about prayer, but you do have to understand the partnership of prayer. God is not going to do things for us that we can do for ourselves, and God is not going to do anything for us without us. He is always going to include us in the equation of the solution to the problem. In I Kings 18:1, when it says, "It came to pass after many days that the word of the Lord came to Elijah [saying] 'I will send rain on the earth,'" it was God's promise in response to Elijah's fervent praying.

God gave Elijah a promise of rain, and some of you have been given a promise from God. Somehow, that promise may have died in your spiritual womb. Some of you have been given a promise that perhaps may not have been a promise in the beginning—maybe it was born out of your own desire, or maybe it came from somebody who made a promise to you.

When my father was very ill in 1984, somebody came to visit him and stood over his bedside and prophesied that God would raise Him up from cancer and that it would be to the glory of God. Some in my family hoped that would be the answer from God. But, my father died about two weeks after that promise was given.

Many people have bitterness, hurt, resentment, disappointment, and disillusionment in their lives because they thought God gave them a promise which God did not give them. If He did give a promise to them, it was a promise that took them into His partnership and was not a unilateral guarantee that no matter how they lived or behaved, it would still be done. The following discussion will deal with that process. Eight words will help you to guard your prayer life so that you can possess the promises of God. These words are:

1. Pray   5. Focus
2. Listen   6. Expect
3. Obey   7. Humble
4. Discern   8. Partner

1. Pray

The Bible says Elijah prayed fervently and expectantly, and after many days, the word of the Lord came to him saying, "It is going to rain." Is that a promise from God? Yes, that is a promise from God. So, before doing anything else, we must understand that the promises of God are always preceded with prayer. But if all we ever do is a little "Now I lay me down to sleep," we are going to sleep through the prayer time. If all we ever do is pray before we have a meal, then we will be short of the promises of God. Elijah did not just wake up one morning to hear the Lord saying, "All right, it is going to rain." Instead, for the better part of two to three years, Elijah was saying, "Oh God, please let it rain."

Famine and drought had brought about starvation, and people were dying. Not a drop of rain had fallen in three and one-half years. It was past emergency; it was beyond urgent. It was extreme panic and death in the streets, and somewhere out there an old prophet of God could be heard. One day Elijah was out by the brook Cherith;

another time he was over by Mt. Carmel; another time he was at a widow's house. He felt the pinch himself. He wasn't living in the Marriott having room service. Elijah felt the same pain that the people were feeling. The pain started at the top with King Ahab and Queen Jezebel where judgment was raining down; it was flowing down and hurting all the people. When judgment comes, it often hurts the innocent people as well. Meanwhile, Elijah was praying, "Oh God, let it rain." Day after day after day for three and one-half years, Elijah prayed. It was not a matter of overcoming God's reluctance, or cajoling God to change His mind; it was a matter of God's timing.

Although Elijah had part of the prophetic word in the three and one-half years, he did not know the end from the beginning. Today, God may give you a prophetic word, but that does not mean you know everything in between. Just because God gives you a revelation, does not mean you have the right to go around and give a revelation of your own to everybody else. It begins with PRAYER.

2. Listen

It is one thing to do all the talking, but it is another thing to be quiet and start listening. Prayer is not when you do all the talking. Prayer is where you learn to meditate and be intimate with Him, listening and lying down like a lamb at the feet of the Shepherd. By doing so, your beating heart can somehow align itself with the rhythms of the Holy Spirit, and you can somehow understand what the Spirit is saying to you. We, like Elijah, have to develop the listening side of prayer so we are not doing all the talking. Prayer includes disciplining our spirits, our minds, and our flesh to listen to God.

3. Obey

God not only gave Elijah a promise, but He also gave him a command. In I Kings 18:1, God said, "Go." Usually when we are possessing promises, there will always be a "Go" or something we have to do. Obedience means full and complete obedience. And if we want to possess the promise, we must be willing to obey. It was a terrible thing to have to go show himself to King Ahab when his name was on every post office wall in Israel as Israel's "Most Wanted." It was humiliating when Fox, CNN, and CNBC were highlighting him every night and giving him the name, "Troubler of Israel." But worse than that, it was frightening when the troops were sent out looking for him high and low.

Here was a man with a promise, but now he was asked to obey God. Partial obedience is disobedience. God didn't say to send Ahab a fax; He didn't say to give him a phone call; He didn't say to send him a text; He didn't say that an email would do. He said, "Go." And what He meant was, "Go show yourself to the man who is looking for you." If God gives you a promise, it is not going to be easy to show yourself. That is the reason that some of us let our promises die still in the incubation phase. And that is why some of you are bitter, and some of you are angry, because you feel like God has failed you. If you trace the steps back, you might find there was someplace where God gave you direction. Perhaps, God gave you an order and you said: "I'm not going to apologize; I'm not going to admit that; I'm not going to fast; I'm not going to straighten this out; I'm not going to pray all night. If God wants to do it. . . ." The bottom line is, we must pray, listen, and then obey. If we do not possess the promise, it is not God's failure; it is our failure. So we pray; we listen; we obey.

4. Discern

We have to discern one of three different kinds of promises: (1) universal promises; (2) conditional promises; and (3) personal, private promises.

What are universal promises? They are statements like, "I am God; I change not." "I am the way, the truth, and the life." "If I go, I will come again." These are universal promises! It doesn't matter who is living on earth or who is in heaven, when God states that kind of promise, neither you nor I nor the devil nor anybody else is going to stop it. It's God's word.

The second kind of promise is a conditional promise. For example, God told Naaman to go dip in the Jordan River seven times, and he would be healed of leprosy. If he had not dipped seven times, he would not have been healed. When Jesus made a poultice of spittle and dirt and put it on the man's eyes and told him to go wash it out—that was conditional. If you don't obey, you won't be healed. God often makes conditional promises to us.

The third kind of promise is a personal promise. Personal promises are always conditional. What are the requirements of a personal promise? First of all, you must have faith. Nothing happens when faith is not present. Second, there must be obedience. And, third, there must be steadfastness.

We must be discerning about the promises of God.

I have had people in my church who would get all excited and say, "Pastor, God made me a promise that He is going to bless my business, and He wants me to give my house to the church." That sounded good to me. I would never turn down a house or a car if you said God told you to give it. But as a pastor, I had to help people walk through that. I have had to ask, "Are you sure? Because, before you sign everything over, I just want you to know that I do not doubt your integrity; I doubt your antennae. I want to be sure that you had plenty of cell coverage when you heard God say that." Because, if they gave the church their house, then what happens if God didn't tell them? What happens if they just got excited? It is good to get excited, but it doesn't mean that is a promise of God.

We have emotions and then we have desires. We must be able to discern the difference.

Shortly after Peggy and I were married (we were just children), I bought a car—a 1970 Toronado. I didn't have any money. I didn't make much money, but they sold me this car anyway.

Peggy said to me, "Honey, are you sure?"
And I said, "I have just prayed about it, Sweetheart. The Lord wants us to have it."

The payments on that car were high. Even though I was making $200 a month, I didn't learn my lesson. Two years later I bought a new Buick Riviera, and it was God's will. But, God wasn't within a million miles of it. The passenger side window broke; the bumper fell off. I had to pay somebody to take it. What do you say to your wife when she says, "I thought the Lord told you that you could get that?"

Then I have heard people say, "The Lord told me to marry her or him." You had better make sure it is the Lord. Here is my statement on that: Whatever a person is before you marry him, he will be a bigger one after you are married.

5. Focus

The word focus means to concentrate or direct attention on the "Promisor," not on the promise or the problems. And here is what happened. After Elijah got the promise, everything was thrown at him. Consider what happened! There was a severe famine. Jezebel murdered the prophets. Good people were suffering because of the promise. Further down in I Kings 18, Obadiah came in, and even he argued with Elijah. The people were suffering and there was blood in the streets, because a man had a promise.

If Satan can assail your life, he will. But, you can hold on to this: When Satan vents his hottest rage, something just left heaven headed your way. Satan wants to cheat you out of your promise. That is why when we begin praying and focusing on our children, our marriage, or our jobs, that things go crazy. Your child gets worse; your spouse gets meaner; bills pile higher. You begin to wonder, what is going on. It is Satan trying to steal the promise and the blessing of God. If you get a promise, do not look at the promise—look at the One who gave the promise. Your hope is not in the promise; your hope is in the "Promisor." You're the "promisee"; He is the "Promisor." And that is where your hope comes from.

6. Expect

George Mueller said we often don't receive because we don't expect. Now, the word "expect" has often been used, abused, and misused because it is easy to think the word expect means "It is coming!" Actually, expect is much more complicated, because there are phases to the expectancy. A good illustration of expectancy is in the conception of a child in the womb of a would-be mother.

My wife and I have been blessed to have three children. I have now been through the expecting phases of several people in my life—my sister; my mother who had my sister; a wife with three children; a daughter with one; and another daughter with one; and a daughter-in-law with two. I am not a pro at this, but I have noticed some things about expecting. When God gives you a promise, say, "I am expecting." Somehow, the holy seed of the word of the implanted promise of God has been implanted divinely by the Holy Spirit into your spirit, and you are carrying in you the seed of the fulfillment of the promise of Almighty God. Now when that happens, the expectancy of all that is going to happen is just as real as if it were in the physical realm.

First, there will be this wonderful thing we call conception. It's where you pray, listen, obey, discern, focus, and then you get this wonderful sense if expectancy—for example, "God has indeed given you the salvation of your children." You know that you know, and there is nobody anywhere to steal that from you. And you will hold on to it for 20, 30, or 40 years if you have to. Don't give up. It may have been decades since you got the promise. The promises of God are "Yea and Amen," and not one word of His good promise will fail.

When Peggy was pregnant with our first child, she didn't even weigh a hundred pounds. And oh, was she sick! And I didn't know anything. She would get up every morning and start throwing up. And I went to church and asked everyone to pray for Peggy "because she had been real sick for the past few weeks and couldn't keep a thing on her stomach." Some of the elders took me into a side room to explain the "expectancy situation" to me. We see people on TV who say, "Honey, I am expecting." "Okay, let's have a party." That wasn't the way it was with Peggy. When she was sick, she was SICK!! She would look up at me and say, "Don't you even look at me."

Oh, that scowl! I would say, "Well, pardon me."

After that period of conception comes a period of aggravation. The promise is there, and you are carrying it around, and not everybody else knows it. The aggravation is because of the transformation. God is getting your body, your life, your spirit—all that you are—ready for the miracle when it comes.

Remember, timing is more important than time. Some miracles don't come in a 270-day gestation period; some of them don't come tomorrow or next year. I was preaching one night in a church and a man came to the front. He dropped five bullets on the altar and took out a bottle of whiskey. His face had been scarred. People shuddered. They said he was the meanest man in the county. He knelt on his knees, gave his life to Jesus, and in a moment (and I didn't know any of this), his mother leaped off the chair, ran down and threw her arms around his back and shoulders and said: "Thirty-five years ago God promised He would save this boy, and He has saved him tonight. She carried that promise for 35 years; she was expectant. What God promised He delivered.

Sometimes, the promise of God will outlive you. He can make you a promise and you can be gone on to your reward, but that promise still gets fulfilled. You ask, "How can that be?" Isaiah, Jeremiah, and all the prophets in the Old Testament didn't know what was coming. They just knew they had a promise—a promise of the Messiah who would come as the Son of Righteousness with healing in His wings.

7. Humble

In I Kings 18:41, Elijah went up to the top of the mountain

and bowed down. He also went into the posture of physical labor, as a woman labors to deliver a child. Often, there is labor in bringing forth that promise. God could have done it Himself, but He wants to use us. Elijah bowed down with his head between his knees. Why is it important for God's people to be humble when God is reigning and fulfilling His promises? There are two reasons.

First, our humility is a demonstration to us and to God, and to unseen enemies that we are humbling ourselves before Almighty God. Our humility is a demonstration that there is no bitterness or anger toward God for what we have gone through from the beginning of the promise to the deliverance of the promise into our lives. Some people might ask: Why did You wait this long? Why didn't You do it differently? Why did good people suffer? Why hasn't it worked out the way it ought to work out so that everybody good wins? Why is it that I had to suffer? Why have You waited so long? But when you humble yourself, you begin to understand that we are not God. We don't understand all things. We will never understand. He is higher than the heavens; He is holier than the holies. And we look to Him and say, "Oh God, who am I that I could begin to judge You? You are awesome and sovereign, and I humble myself under Your great wisdom. Second, humility demonstrates that we did not produce the power for the miracle. It is all to God's glory. Whatever part we played was a minimal part.

8. Partner

God is the senior partner. Elijah obeyed God and presented himself to Ahab and said: "I hear the sound of the abundance of rain." God, the senior partner, sent the rain. The devil may say to you, "You are not going to get your promise." But I declare to you as the servant of the Lord, "It is going to rain. It is going to rain in your heart, in your house, in your church. I hear the sound of the abundance of rain."And God is the giver of the rain, so that He can impact the seasons of your lives.

AUTHOR

Dr. Raymond Culpepper

Dr. Raymond Culpepper is a pastor, author, and served as the General Overseer of the Church of God (2008-2012) when this project was launched. The General Overseer is the highest office in the Church of God denomination and has primary responsibility for leading a membership of over 9 million members spanning 180 countries. Dr. Culpepper previously served two terms as First Assistant General Overseer and has been on the Executive "Council of 18" on three occasions. Previously, he served as the Church of God State Youth and Education Director for Northern California, Nevada, Indiana, and Alabama. In 1980, Raymond founded the Riverchase Church of God in Birmingham, Alabama, later renamed Metropolitan Church of God, which grew under his leadership into one of the most well-known churches in the denomination. His books include: *The Leading Man, Lifestyle To His Glory, Power Living, The Great Commission Connection* and *No Church Left Behind.*

Dr. Culpepper holds a Bachelor of Science, Master of Arts degree from the California Graduate School of Theology and a Doctorate of Divinity degree from Lee University where he served for 12 years as Chairman of the Lee University Board of Directors. In 1999, he was selected as Lee University's Distinguished Alumnus of the Year.

Raymond's father, J. Frank Culpepper was an Assistant General Overseer of the Church of God. Raymond has been married to the former Peggy Price since 1970. The couple have three children: Raymond II, Elizabeth and Jessica. Dr. Culpepper currently serves as the Administrative Bishop of the Church of God in Alabama.

CHAPTER TWO

A SOUND PRAYER THEOLOGY

A WINDOW THROUGH TIME

A Tribute to R. P. Johnson

"Did you ever hear a prophet pray?"

"The manner in which he would say, 'Our Father, who art in heaven, hallowed be thy name.' Somehow it would part the cunning veil, and we would slip right into the holy of holies with Him and kneel around the mercy seat. And He would pray.

"We'd pray a little, but it was worth so much more to hear what this man would say. And he would pray for this sin-cursed world that was in trouble. He'd pray for the nation that he loved and the leaders who carried the terrific responsibility. And he would entreat God for the fervent graces on the Church and its leaders, this church for which he had given his life. Then it seems that he always had a whole roster of names. I don't know how he remembered so many people. He would tell God about them, where they were, remember something special, and call their names to God in prayer. And as he would continue with his praying, it seems like the wings of those cherubs over the mercy seat would flutter and the heavenly breezes would fan the fervor of his prayer into a mighty flame. And then – I don't know how other people were impressed by it – but those long arms and big hands you've been hearing and talking about, it seemed like they would just reach out in infinity and for those that were not actually in reality around this place of prayer, he'd bring them in.

"He'd bring Mae's family from next door, then reach all the way out into North Carolina for that one up there, and then way out to Denver, and bring that one in too. And over to Huntsville to bring J. P. and his family around that family altar and he could reach over to our house and bring my whole family with my children around that family altar, up to the north part and bring Mildred and her family, and over to Sue's house. Oh, I can't explain it. I'm just telling you what happened. In that miracle of prayer those big arms would gather us in.

"He'd never forget to pray for those preacher boys in the family and always named his oldest son and his boys who carry the gospel, and the rest."

This tribute was written by David Lemons, son of one of the founders of the Church of God, about R. P. Johnson, his father-in-law.

R. P. Johnson is regarded as one of the greatest preachers in the history of the Church of God. Dr. Charles Conn told me (Doug Small) that R. P. Johnson took Pentecostal preaching in the Church of God to a whole new level – it became "an art-form." And from him came a whole generation of extraordinary pulpiteers influenced by his refined and accomplished style. Among them, arguably, was Dr. Ray H. Hughes.

It is interesting, that the man noted for his powerful and polished preaching, was also a praying man.

Adapted from the work by David Lemons, *Words Fitly Spoken* (Cleveland, TN: Pathway Press, 1988), 138-140.

CHAPTER 2

A SOUND PRAYER THEOLOGY

Dr. French Arrington

Prayer is a vital element of worship. Much of what applies to worship applies to prayer. Worship and prayer are not identical, but it is difficult for us to think of worship apart from prayer. At the heart of our new life in Christ stands the call for us to pray. In fact, it is through prayer that we have come to faith in Christ. One scholar has appropriately described prayer as "faith in action."[1] Our aim here is not to provide practical instructions as to how to pray or the methods we may use in praying, but to reflect the theological significance of prayer as it is found in the Bible.

1. The Character of Prayer

The usual purpose of prayer is to have a conversation with God. At times we talk about "silent prayer" or meditation, which allows us a conversation of the heart without the actual use of words when talking to God. Silent prayer is one way of having a dialogue with God, but God has also given us the capacity to communicate by talking with our Creator. Scripture teaches us that humans are distinct from the rest of God's creatures. The uniqueness of humankind is the result of our being created in the image and likeness of God (Genesis 2:26-27; 2:7), and prayer is a critical aspect of our unique standing

---

1   Emil Brunner, *The Christian Doctrine of the Church, Faith and the Consummation*, vol. 3, (Philadelphia: Westminster Press, 1960), 324.

before God. Due to God's creative hand, we are free persons and have the capacity to talk to and have fellowship with our Creator.

From the biblical view of creation, we are able to address God in prayer and to worship Him. The initiative to pray is from the Creator who from the beginning has instilled in our hearts the desire to have communion with Him. So not only is prayer a form of worship, but it is also a form of communion. Because of that, prayer and worship are rooted in divine grace, indeed giving us the assurance that the Creator of heaven and earth hears and answers prayer.

Many of us who have grown up in the church assume without much thought that we can converse with God. However, there are those who protest this assumption and who argue that it is presumption to believe that God hears and answers prayer. After all, why should we entertain the thought that the Lord of the universe, the King of kings, the Almighty God stoops down to our level to listen to our voices? It is hard, when we seriously think about it, to conceive that the Lord of this world bending His ear to listen to our individual prayers.

ACCENT

Five young college students were spending a Sunday in London, so they went to hear the famed C. H. Spurgeon preach. While waiting for the doors to open, the students were greeted by a man who asked, "Gentlemen, let me show you around. Would you like to see the heating plant of this church?" They were not particularly interested, for it was a hot day in July. But they didn't want to offend the stranger, so they consented.

The young men were taken down a stairway, a door was quietly opened, and their guide whispered, "This is our heating plant." Surprised, the students saw 700 people bowed in prayer, seeking a blessing on the service that was soon to begin in the auditorium above. Softly closing the door, the gentleman then introduced himself. It was none other than Charles Spurgeon.

Behind great preaching is great praying.

In addition to us, He has millions and millions of creatures on the earth. It may appear unreasonable for the Creator to listen to what you and I have to say to Him, but without doubt He hears the cries of the individual and answers our prayers. The everywhere "presentness" of God creates a personal intimacy and an immediacy in which God hears our prayers. The Almighty has endowed us with the capacity and desire for fellowship with Him in prayer and has drawn especially near to us in the person of His Son, Jesus Christ (John 1:9-18; Romans 8:3; Galatians 4:4-6; Philippians 2:6-11). The coming of the Son reminds us that God is at hand to answer prayer and that prayer has an incarnational aspect. Created in the image of the Creator, we have the

Advice to Members in the 13th General Assembly: "Be ready for vocal prayer when called upon or prompted by the Spirit ... Always pray silently for the preacher while he delivers the message ... Spend as much time as you can in secret prayer. Give yourself all you can to intercessory prayer."

freedom to draw near to Him and to seek His face in prayer.

We do well to remember that the pouring out of our hearts to the Lord is both "a gift and a command."[2] Life in prayer conforms to God's demand, but human disobedience and rebellion broke fellowship with the loving Creator. The Heavenly Father took pity on us and sent His Son into the world to remove the wall of sin that divides us from Him and from one another. The outpouring of divine grace in Christ calls us back into fellowship with our Creator and to a life of prayer and communion with Him. Prayer is nothing short of

---

2   Donald G. Bloesch, *Essentials of Evangelical Theology*, vol. 2 (New York: Harper & Row, 1979), 56.

an encounter with the living God whose Spirit so graciously enables us to pray and who prays for us in groans too deep for words when our speech fails to express our needs (Romans 8:23, 26). Because of our plight as the result of present circumstances and a profound sense that only God can help, we may cry out in prayers and laments as Israel did as a nation (Daniel 9: 4, 19; Ezra 9:6-15; Nehemiah 9:9-37). Through the Holy Spirit, God knows our hearts and assists us in prayer, enabling us to cry out to Him from the innermost depths of our beings. Thankfully, our deliverance comes through Jesus Christ (Romans 7:24-25; I Corinthians 15:57). As believers "we are more than conquerors through Him who loved us" (Romans 8:37).[3]

Such Spirit-inspired prayer may not only occur in private worship but also in corporate worship, involving a local body of believers. Corporate prayer tends especially towards set forms, but set forms are not comparable to free, spontaneous prayers of a Spirit-filled church. When inspired by the Spirit, we may cry out to God as children do to their loving fathers on this earth. On those occasions of conversation with God, prayer transcends set forms. The Holy Spirit brings deep prayer—*Abba,* Father—to the hearts and mouths of believers (Romans 8:15; Galatians 4:6). As this occurs, there is a liberating and sanctifying move of the Spirit; and the Spirit illuminates the Word of God (II Corinthians 3:1-18) and builds up the community of faith into Christ (I Corinthians 12:3-14).[4]

Indeed, we have divine resources beyond our own abilities to help us to be a praying people. These resources can be summed in the word we know as *"grace"*—grace through Christ and through the Holy Spirit who conforms us more and more to the image of God's Son as we walk and pray in the Spirit (Romans 8:29; Colossians

---

3   The citations of Scripture aré from the New King James Version.
4   R. P. Mepe, "Spirituality," *Dictionary of Paul and His Letters* (Downers Grove, Illinois: InterVarsity Press, 1993), 911.

3:10). So prayer is vital to spiritual formation, too and is, therefore, an aspect to discipleship.

2. The High Priestly Prayer of John 17

Silence before God has its place in prayer, but God is not an unknown, nameless object of reverence or an unapproachable deity. The Father has revealed Himself in Christ not as a remote god, but as *the* personal God. As the representative of the entire character of God, Jesus said, "I have come in My Father's name" (John 5:43). In John 17, speaking to the Father, Jesus also said, "I have declared to them Your name" (v. 26). Throughout His ministry on the earth, Jesus had made known His Heavenly Father to His followers. Jesus' revealing of the Father provides the foundation for our prayers. He disclosed that God's name is "Holy Father," with an emphasis on *Father* (v. 11). God is holy and distant in a sense, but as the loving heavenly Father He has come near through His Son, and His Son has revealed the Father's name, His loving character. Making known His name enables and permits us to come gladly and boldly to the Father in prayer (Hebrews 4:16). We have a legitimate reason for praying because God's Son has revealed Him as Holy Father.

God has drawn near to us in His Son, and through His Son we can draw to the Father. As we make known our prayers and supplications, God directs us, ministers to our needs and acts

D. L. Moody would say: "Tarry at a promise, and God will meet you there."

Dick Eastman, *A Watchman's Guide to Praying God's Promises* (Jakarta, Indonesia: World Prayer Assembly Edition, 2012; Colorado Springs, CO: Every Home for Christ). See: www.ehc.org; Also: http://www.globaldayofprayer.com/downloads/resources/nations/WatchmansGuide.pdf

on our behalf according to His will. At times our prayers may be desperate and express deep sorrow and grief, but intimacy with the Father in prayer provides us opportunity to embrace His mind and will as our own. Like His Son, we can address the Creator by His name, Holy Father. As we call on that name, He calls us to conform to the character of His Son and enables us to declare His name to others as did His Son (John 17:26).

3. The Divine Will and Prayer

Christ has broken down the wall created by sin between the Creator and humankind (Ephesians 2:14). The preaching of the word of the Cross and trusting in it restores us to fellowship with God. As we talk about God's plan of salvation, we may describe some of God's purposes as ultimate and others as *more immediate*. The ultimate purposes of God for salvation are unchangeable and include the second coming of Christ, the resurrection of the redeemed, deliverance of creation from the curse of Adam's sin, and the final judgment, but His immediate purposes are flexible and open to change through the prayers of His people. God desires to realize many of His purposes by collaborating with us.[5]

Christ gives us access to the Holy Father and makes Him accessible to our call. He has ascended into heaven and is now at the right hand of the Father as our Intercessor (Romans 8:34; Hebrews 7:25). To be sure, Christ knows our needs before we ask, but prayer provides the opportunity to submit to the divine will as well as to petition and to strive and to wrestle with God. When our will does not agree with God's will, prayer should take the form of submission, which does not mean resignation to fate or chance but leaving our desires and requests in the hands of God.[6]

---

5   Bloesch, 57
6   Ibid, 58

The Father does answer prayer, but that does not mean that He always answers every prayer the way we desire. We can pray with confidence that our prayers will be answered. God hears and genuinely answers every prayer. However, just as our Lord did, we must leave the answers with God—"nevertheless not my will, but Yours be done" (Luke 22:42). Many of us have struggled with what has appeared to be unanswered prayer. All prayer is answered, although the answer at times is "No," always meaning "I have something better."

Note on Prayer at the 14th General Assembly: "After singing, the General Overseer asked the congregation to bow their heads in silent prayer, then all prayed the Lord's prayer, after which the congregation sang ... "

4. The Centrality of Prayer

Vital elements of communion with God include supplication, intercession, thanksgiving, petition, praise, dedication and lament. *Supplications* are requests for particular human needs in which the petitioner knows that God can only supply the need. *Intercession* is prayer in behalf of others, and great compassion frequently prompts such prayer in the Christian community. *Thanksgiving* is an expression of sincere gratitude, offered by the congregation in public worship or by the individual believer for the blessings of God. Overlapping with many of the forms of prayer, *petitions* are solemn supplications and requests that recognize the sovereign authority of God. Another type of prayer is *praise*, which is defined as rendering respect and devotion to God for His favor and blessings. A prayer of *dedication* sets apart for sacred use either persons such as priests (Numbers 18:14; Joshua

6: 19) or objects such as the temple or spoils of war (II Chronicles 7: 5; I Chronicles 26: 27). *Lament* is prayer offered often with loud and uncontrolled grief (Genesis 23: 2; II Samuel 1:12; 3: 31-34).

Obviously, petitions have their place in biblical prayers, but should prayer become merely petitionary it has become hopelessly human-centered. The various elements of prayer emphasize the daily importance of this spiritual exercise and lie at the heart of Christian spirituality. Typically, Paul's letters begin and conclude with references to and reports on prayer, and their contents emphasize the great importance of communion with God (Romans 1:8-10; I Corinthians 1:4; Philippians 1:3-12 ; I Thessalonians 1:2-3; 3:9-10). Likewise, Paul requested prayers for himself and for other believers (Romans 15:30; Colossians 4:2-4; I Thessalonians 2:5; II Thessalonians 3:1). Paul also reported that he prayed day and night (I Thessalonians 3:10) and encouraged all Christians to pray without ceasing (Ephesians 6:18; I Thessalonians 5:17) and in every place (I Timothy 2:8).

A variety of terms are used by Paul to describe effective prayer. Among them are: persevering, wrestling, constant, steadfastly, thankfulness and joyfulness (Romans 12:12; Ephesians 6:18; Philippians 4:6). To grow in discipleship, prayer needs to be tireless and anchored and interwoven into the experiences of the hills and valleys of believers' everyday lives. But how does prayer fit into the modern world of science, technology and computers? How can we integrate prayer into the whole range of issues and problems that must be dealt with in our personal lives? What relevance does prayer have to such controversial matters in the church such as the best use of resources to fulfill the Great Commission, the role of women in ministry, or the divorce rate in the church as being about the same as in the world?

Perhaps Paul's words of wisdom apply to these kinds of concerns and problems when he talks about the active presence of the Holy Spirit in the prayer life of believers. Paul confesses human weakness and inability in prayer (Romans 8:26), but the Spirit assists believers in prayer and enables them to practice the presence of God wherever they may be. As Christians are led and directed by the Holy Spirit, genuine prayer can occur at almost any time or place—at a stoplight, standing in line at a bank or at a supermarket, at daily work, while walking at the Y.M.C.A., or with family and friends. Daily communion with God is vital and essential to Christian existence and for meeting the challenges in the world and the church.

5. A Model Prayer

All four Gospels stress Jesus' practice of prayer. He often withdrew by Himself to pray or at times He prayed in the company of some of His disciples. Out of His own experience in prayer, Jesus was able to respond to His disciples' request when they asked Him, "Lord, teach us to pray" (Luke 11:1). What is known to us as "The Lord's Prayer" is better understood as "The Disciples' Prayer." This marvelous prayer stands out as a simple address, indicating that God is at hand here and now and that He hears and understands. All the pronouns in the prayer are plural and remind us that this is really a community or corporate prayer. Even so, there can be no doubt this prayer reflects the content of some of Christ's own prayers that He Himself prayed. In giving this form of prayer, Jesus had no intention of ruling out or minimizing the importance of free, spontaneous prayer. Caution needs to be taken to guard the practice of diversity and flexibility in prayer and worship (John 4:24).

The Lord's Prayer emphasizes Jesus' own teachings on prayer and the priorities of prayer, starting with God and moving to us. The prayer begins with "Father" (Greek: *pater*; Aramaic: *abba*), stressing a God-centered attitude. Generally Jewish prayers put a distance between human beings and the great God, but the Aramaic *abba* was a word used by a child for her earthly father. So Jesus instructs His disciples to speak with the King of the universe as a small child would speak to her father. As Christians—sons and daughters of God—we have the right and privilege of addressing God in prayer as a child would approach the father of her family (Romans 9:15; Galatians 4:6). The prayer underscores the unique relationship Christians have to God and that we can approach our Heavenly Father with childlike trust.

> *The mightiest prayers are often those drenched with the Word of God.*
>
> ~ *Herbert Lockyer*

After the tender address, the prayer consists of five petitions. The last three requests deal with the personal needs of the disciples: bread (all kinds of food), forgiveness of sins on the condition of forgiving others, and the deliverance from circumstances where temptations assail us. But the first two petitions focus on God as the Holy One above all creatures and things, and on the coming of God's kingdom in its future power and glory (Romans 8:18-21; Revelation 20:1-3, 7-10). The kingdom will reach its fulfillment only when Christ returns. Christians are not, therefore, to confine their prayers to narrow interests and reduce them to being only a means of achieving personal satisfaction and success. Nevertheless, we need to continue to pray for our needs. The Scriptures direct us to do that, but according to God's Word, our prayers should include our looking and longing for the magnificent fulfillment of God's ultimate plan and purpose for this world and its people. We live in a world of woes because the kingdom of God has not fully come. This world is a place of danger, suffering, disappointment, heartache, violence and death

Indeed! We are to continue to pray for the lame so that they might walk again and for the blind so that they might see again, for provisions of widows and orphans, for the healing of the sick, for the end of poverty and wars, for liberty of the oppressed, and for the salvation of souls. Our responsibility is to work and pray that these particulars will come to pass, but our prayers need to include more—the coming of Christ in glory and the final coming of God's kingdom, in which the shape of this world will be transformed and sin and death will be no longer.

We cannot force God's hand, but we can pray that God's kingdom come in its fullness to this earth and that His will be done here as it is in heaven (Matthew 6:10). Prayer is our means to bring about mighty results and of influencing the affairs of the world and all concerns of life. No doubt we will not see the ideal state of world affairs until Jesus returns to assume His kingship on the earth, but we are to go on praying for the needs of humankind. At the same time, we are to express our longing for the completion of our Heavenly Father's grand plan for salvation and the full realization of His kingdom.

AUTHOR

French L. Arrington, Ph. D.

Dr. French Arrington is a recognized evangelical theologian, and former chairman of the Department of Bible and Theology at Lee University, a recipient of the Excellence in Teaching Award. He has served as guest lecturer at theological seminaries in Korea, Puerto Rico, Guatemala, Philippines, Indonesia, Ecuador, Virgin Islands, China and Russia. He is now Professor Emeritus at the Church of God Pentecostal Seminary. Dr. Arrington is well-known for his published works on the New Testament, including two scholarly monographs, his work on *The Complete Biblical Library,* and *The New International Dictionary of Pentecostal Charismatic Movements* and numerous other works. He was Greek editor for *A Biblical Theology of the Holy Spirit* and contributor to *Contemporary Issues in Pneumatology.* Hendrickson published *Acts of the Apostles.*

CHAPTER THREE

THE FEAR OF GOD AND PRAYER

A WINDOW THROUGH TIME

In the early part of the summer of 1882, while we were holding a camp meeting … a drunken mob came on the ground, and disturbed the meeting by their profanity and quarreling. They came armed with revolvers, and were determined to break up the meeting. Not having anticipated any such difficulty, no police force had been provided. Our words of expostulation were unheeded, and they went so far as to yell and blaspheme, and shake their fists in the faces of the leaders of the meeting. So great was the disturbance, that for a time the services were entirely suspended, and there was certainly imminent danger that the meeting would be completely broken up.

Realizing that God's help alone could give to His children victory, in the midst of the excitement we went to the woods, and in sobs and tears, fell upon our face. God gave us great help of the Spirit in prayer, and we told Him how we were holding the meeting for His glory and the salvation of souls, and unless He came to our rescue, great reproach would be brought upon His cause.

We obtained evidence that God would deliver, and hastened back to the camp, called for order, and began to exhort the people in the power of the Spirit. A halo of glory came over the meeting. Wicked men turned pale, and acknowledged the wonderful change. Many began to weep, while some of God's children shouted for joy, and many were prostrate under the power of God.

Defeat was changed to almost unthought of

victory, and during all that night the workers were kept busy praying with seekers, and many were saved. Not until the light of the morning dawned could they find time for rest; and the two remaining days of the meeting were days of triumph.

So great was the conviction that some who repeatedly tried to leave were constrained to return, and yield themselves to God. One man said he was determined not to yield, and for the third time started to leave the grounds; but God showed him that this, if rejected, would be his last chance for salvation. So, at about two o'clock in the morning, he came to the altar, and was gloriously saved.

S. B. Shaw, "A Mob Quieted In Answer To Prayer," *Touching Incidents And Remarkable Answers To Prayer* (Grand Rapids, MI: S.B. Shaw, Publisher, 1893), 55.

CHAPTER 3

THE FEAR OF GOD AND PRAYER
P. Douglas Small

Harry Truman became a folk hero in the days prior to the eruption of Mount St. Helens in the state of Washington. He owned the Lodge at south end of Spirit Lake, and he was in the danger zone as the mountain heated up. But he refused to leave. Truman had operated the lodge for 52 years. In the days before the mountain blew its top, reporters featured the gutsy Truman, and he became a bit of a national celebrity. Art Carney would portray the 84-year-old feisty senior in a 1981 docudrama, a year after his death. He had experienced his share of mountain rumbles living at its base. He told one reporter that quakes had been so strong at times that he had been thrown from his bed. But Harry was a fighter and he was unmoved by all the supposed hype. "If the mountain goes, I'm going with it. This area is heavily timbered, Spirit Lake is in between me and the mountain, and the mountain is a mile away, the mountain ain't gonna hurt me ... boy," he dismissively told one reporter. He scoffed at the public's panic and even its concern for him. Reporters checked on him. Children sent him cards. His family worried. But Harry stayed in the shadow of the mountain as most others moved out of the danger zone.

A few, perhaps influenced by Harry's resolve or conceivably as stubborn and unconvinced as him, having lived near the mountain for so long, 56 of them, loggers, campers, reporters and scientists, died along with Harry when the mountain exploded. The pyroclastic flow engulfed the Spirit Lake area and buried Harry and his lodge under one-hundred and fifty feet of volcanic debris. Spirit-lake reformed at a higher elevation. Harry's bravado, no matter how endearing and engaging, his failure to respect the potential for danger, his refusal to act in a reasonable manner, did not prevent the ash and lava from ending his life.

Dave Crockett was a reporter who, on the basis of a hunch, drove into the danger zone and camped out near the mountain the night before it exploded, on May 18, 1980. That morning, debris rolled toward him like a tsunami, collecting trees and creating a wall of mud mixed with lava. He attempted to escape in his vehicle. But suddenly, the road itself disappeared in front of him. At that point, in full panic, he fled uphill for a nearby ridge. But now, the darkness engulfed him. He could only see a few feet in front of him. His life was at clearly at stake. As he fled, he kept his video camera rolling and the record of his narrow harrowing escape is now a classic. In it, he is heard panting, praying, "Dear God …" He confessed at one point in the total darkness, with the burning smell of ash, the cataclysmic sounds, the thunder and volcanic lightning flashing about, that he thought he might already be dead. None of the composure characteristic of a professional and polished reporter was present. He was reduced to a mortal and he was terrorized. The mountain was trembling beneath him, belching, burping, groaning, and heaving. When he realized that he was alive, and he was going to survive, he was overcome with sheer joy.

Crockett epitomizes the cool, calm, collected state of most Americans who have never had a near paralyzing phobic moment that unhinged them. His reaction to the mountain was matched, twenty-one years later, by normally unruffled, self-assured and controlled New Yorkers, who were seen terror-stricken, fleeing from the falling Twin Towers in the streets of New York, on September 11, 2001. They were numb. Panicked. Fearful. Poise and restraint were discarded, as people fled for their lives with panic and fear on their faces, uncertainty about the meaning of it all, and questions that had to be repressed in favor of pure survival. Meetings. Briefs filled with important papers. Expensive cars parked nearby. Everything was discarded. One priority remained – staying alive.

The problem with worldliness is that it is so stealth and subtle. Its' most poisonous bite is not the thing that is obviously naughty or blatantly immodest and shameless, which we know we should avoid. Rather, it is in the unconscious effects, in our careless and heedless assimilation of unbiblical thinking and acting patterns that appear benign rendering us unaware that we are being seduced. Worldliness is like the wall paper in the room, like the music in the background - it is not something upon which we focus. It is in the water and air. It is so pervasive and inescapable, yet simultaneously unavoidable. We live *in* the world; and yet, we are commanded to not be *of* the world. But in subtle ways, small and seemingly insignificant changes come into our lives and are embraced: altered assumptions, caveats to our theology, footnotes and exceptions, a new lens for seeing God, flexible categories for sin, enlightened syncretism in the name of cultural accommodation. The peer pressure to acclimate to social deviations and moral aberrations is huge. There are demands to sign on to new sexual norms, a crusade to modify the definition of marriage, to legalize dangerous drugs, to mandate the provision of abortions, to ban prayer from public space and thus thoroughly secularize society, to allow the most egregious and degrading language. These are treacherous dangers. But our major point of vulnerability is not at the intersection of these major deviances, but at the subtle and seemingly innocent foundations. It is the small incremental shifts that are more dangerous.

The Fear of God – the Beginning of Wisdom

One of the major ideological losses to the theology of the modern Christian and the Church is the complete and utter dismissal of the concept of *the fear of God*. This is no marginal biblical notion. It is mentioned more often than the love of God, some 150 times in the Bible.[1] The exact phrase, "… the fear of the Lord," occurs twenty-seven times, twice as often as the phrase, "… the love of God" (12 times). The age-old expression 'God-fearing' has become archaic and has almost been expunged from popular usage. The change affects our prayer life, our personal and corporate morality along with the quality of our witness, the level of our faithfulness, our language and demeanor, and thus our relationships with one another, not to mention the resultant shallow relationship with God. Moses instructs, "Show your fear of God by not taking advantage of each other. I am the LORD your God" (Leviticus 25:17 NLT).

This distortion of our perspective of God is the essence of idolatry, because it refashions God, and consequently, that reshapes our thinking and behaving. It causes us to exploit grace, cheapen mercy, twist truth, ignore holiness, disbelieve in consequences and judgment, dismiss sin's toxic nature, and argue that God's power is limited to positive enhancements in our behalf.

"The fear of God," we are reminded, "is the beginning of wisdom" (Psalm 111:10; Proverbs 9:10). It is the gateway, the door to proper perception – in prayer, of Scripture, in discerning our world, in hearing the voice of God, in making decisions and more. Without such reverence, we wander into confusion, venture into ignorance unaware, accept unsound insights and become fools. Paul noted when this happens that 'heart lights' go dark. Such people compensate by "professing themselves to be wise," but a mere

1   Sinclair Ferguson, *Grow in Grace* (Colorado Springs: NavPress, 1984), 36.

'profession' does not change reality; any more than Harry Truman's defiance tamed the mountain. The inner darkness comes, though unperceived to those who "changed the glory of the incorruptible God into an image made like to corruptible man" (Romans 1:21-23). Having lost their 'fear' of God, they closed the gate of wisdom, and plunged headlong into folly. When we deny the existence of God or view Him only as an enlargement of ourselves and not as 'utterly other,' we forfeit an appropriate reverence for God. As a result, wisdom, sound thinking, prudent decisions, deep prayer and worship are no longer possible. The problem is summarized in Psalm 50, *"You thought I was altogether like you" (v. 21).*

The Throne Room

God receives prayers in His Throne room – an awesome and fearful place. In the modern era, most westerners were reared in a nation without a king. In the United States, the most comparable throne-like experience for most of us has been an uncomfortable moment before the bench of a judge in a courtroom. Such an experience can be intimidating, especially if you are a defendant, charged by the court or present under the compelling power of a summons. Perhaps in no other setting in our society is respect for office and decorum so forcefully enforced on us. Officers of the court abound and wear firearms on their hips. Being cited for contempt is always a possibility and with it there comes a fine or time behind bars – hats are to be off, weapons (except for officers of the court) are not allowed, cell phones are not permitted, silence is demanded, there is no talking-back, movement is minimized, the bar is to be respected, one stands and sits on command, and speaks only when spoken to and then under oath, and in the confines of strict adherence to rules, then refrains when addressed. All must remain behind the bar, except legal teams, the plaintiff and defendant. Even for them, permission must be given to *approach the bench*; and the command to *stand-back* and *withdraw* is strictly enforced. Those who violate the order and decorum of the court are promptly arrested or forcibly expelled. Still, the comparison of the American Judge and his bench to that of the throne of an ancient unchallenged king, and more so to God, is a woefully inadequate comparison. Notice these glimpses into heaven's throne room.

> *"Woe is me, for I am ruined! Because I am a man of unclean lips ... For my eyes have seen the King, the LORD of hosts" (Isaiah 6:5).*
>
> *"The LORD is in His holy temple, the LORD's throne is in heaven ..."* (Psalm 11:4 NKJV)
>
> *The voice of the LORD twists the oaks and strips the forests bare. And in His temple all cry, "Glory!" (Psalm 29:9 NIV)*
>
> *"Thus says the Lord, The Heaven is My throne and the earth is My footstool ... to this man will I look, even to him that is poor and of a contrite spirit and trembles at My Word"* (Isaiah 66:1; See also Matthew 5:34-35).
>
> *"The Lord is king, and the people tremble. He sits on His throne above the winged creatures, and the earth shakes. The Lord is mighty in Zion; He is supreme over all the nations"* (Psalm 99:1-2 GNT).

Before the throne, in the Revelation, John saw "a sea of glass, like crystal" (Revelation 4:6). The idea conveyed is one of transparency, translucence, a crystal – 'see though' setting with everything reflected and revealed. There is no place to hide before the omniscient (all knowing, all seeing) God. About the throne are beasts "full of eyes – in front and behind" and "within and without." Peals of thunder rumble and flashes of lightning proceed from the throne. Strange and powerful creatures attend God's Presence. This is an awesome scene. Breathtaking. Frightening. Terrifying. It is as rattling as the explosion of Mt. Saint Helens with all its power; or that of the tumbling Twin

Towers. And this is where we meet God!

Oswald Chambers noted,

> "If we have never had the experience of talking our common place shoes off our commonplace feet, and getting rid of all the undue familiarity with which we approach God, it is questionable whether we have ever stood in His presence ... The people who are flippant and familiar are those who have never yet been introduced to Jesus Christ. After the amazing delight and liberty of realizing *what* Jesus Christ *does*, comes the impenetrable darkness of realizing *Who He is*."

In ancient times, in almost any culture, the king or chieftain was the law, thus the principle: *Rex Lex*. The word of the king, whatever his decrees, became law! In the American Revolution, a bold new experiment was attempted. The colonialists would not have a king – they would opt for *Lex Rex*, making the Law itself the king. Thus it is often said, 'We are a nation of laws.' In the nation forged by our Founding Fathers, there would be a President, but not a king. He would be elected from among the common people, yet, he too would submit to the laws of the land. No one, no class, would be above the law. It was a bold idea – that a people could rule themselves. They were the governors. And because of their commitment to be a lawful people, the government itself was limited in powers given to it by the people's constitution. They knew such notion was ludicrous, if the people were not self-governed, and that was possible only if there were some overarching set of shared values that informed the culture, to which all would be submissive; values to which all subscribed, and a God to whom all deferred and were accountable. It was the respect and 'fear' of God which made them safe with and respectful one toward another. Without a reverence for such an invisible God whose hand guided the nation's founding, without a respect for the book of His law – the experiment would fail.

The Unseen Throne behind the U. S. Constitution

A ten-year investigation commissioned by the Supreme Court involved a review of some 500 of our founding documents[2] reaching back to the days of Columbus. This study was designed to discover the prevailing philosophy that informed the American Revolution. The court concluded, "... the case assumes that we are a Christian people, and the morality of the country is deeply engrafted upon Christianity ..." Since the case involved Pennsylvania specifically, it also declared, "... the Christian religion is a part of the common law of Pennsylvania."

As if this ruling were not conclusive enough, the court also observed, "... a view of American life, as expressed by its laws, its business, its customs, and its society, we find everywhere a clear recognition of the same truth." The court cited additional evidence: Oaths on the Bible that invoked God – to lie is to lie against God; political and private assemblies which open with a Christian invocation – gatherings of the people, public and private assume the presence of the invisible God, who is to be honored and respected, and who invisibly presides over all; the standard language of last wills and testaments, "In the name of God, Amen" – even the transfer of property, ownership of the land, finds a reference in the sovereign laws of God; Sabbath laws directed the closure of courts and legislatures,

---

2   This was conducted by the Supreme Court in association with *Holy Trinity Church v. United States*, a case dated February 29, 1892. *Vine & Fig Tree, The Supreme Court of the United States, Holy Trinity Church v. The United States 143 U.S. 457, 12 S.Ct. 511, 36 L.Ed. 226 February 29, 1892, http://members.aol.com/EndTheWall/TrinityHistory.htm, retrieved August 26, 2007.*

offices and businesses on Sunday – thus the old 'blue laws,' those rising from the force of Scripture and thus the Church had equal force with state law; abundant Christians churches and organizations with missionary activity and charitable enterprises under Christian banners – we were founded as a Christian nation, a place where those who had been persecuted as Protestants by the Catholic Church could now be free to worship under new Bible-based reforms. All these are unofficial declarations of the nation's Christian roots. At the time of the research, there were forty-four states and all of their constitutions referenced the Christian Worldview.

"By our form of government the Christian religion is the established religion; and all sects and denominations of Christians are placed upon equal footing, and they are equally entitled to protection in their religious liberty."[3]

"No free government now exists in the world, unless where Christianity is acknowledged, and is the religion of the country."[4]

Dr. Donald S. Lutz[5] is a professor of political philosophy at the University of Houston. He and his research associate, Dr. Charles Hyneman, conducted a groundbreaking 10-year study

---

3   *Bible Law Course*, "Runkel v Winemiller," 4; "Harris & McHenry," 276 (Supreme Court: Maryland; October Term, 1799). http://www.moseshand.com/studies/RvW.htm, retrieved August 26, 2007.

4   *The Founders' Constitution, Vol. 5, Amendment I* (Speech and Press): "*Updegraph v. Commonwealth*," 11; "*Serg. & Rawle*," 394   (The University of Chicago Press, 1824). http://press-pubs.uchicago.edu/founders/print_documents/amendI_speechs30.html, retrieved August 26, 2007.

5   Dr. Donald S. Lutz is professor of political science at the University of Houston. He is author of *The Origins of American Constitutionalism* and *A Preface to American Political Theory;* editor of *Colonial Origins of the American Constitution: A Documentary History*, and co-editor with Charles S. Hyneman of *American Political Writing During the Founding Era: 1760-1805*. For a review of the latter book, see George W. Carey's "*Moral and Political Foundations of Order*".

†ACCENT

Charles baron de Montesquieu was an advocate of the separation of powers in government and one of the foremost political thinkers. Of all the sources that the Founders could have cited, he is next to the Bible, cited the most. He was not a Christian, and yet he believed three things were critical to a republic's survival – and one was morality, the other two, education and surprisingly, a small fixed geographic boundary. While he had no personal faith preference, he held strong views about the compatibility of faith and culture and he believed some religions were best equipped to support healthy government. He observed that Christianity was a "... stranger to mere despotic power" because the "mildness so frequently recommended in the Gospel is incompatible with the despotic rage with which a prince punishes his subjects, and exercises himself in cruelty." He pointed out that this faith that forbade a "plurality of wives" and contributed to

published in *The American Political Science Review.* Some 15,000 documents of the 55 authors of the Constitution were examined, including articles from newspapers and pamphlets, books and monographs. They found that the Bible, specifically the book of Deuteronomy, constituted 34 percent of all the direct quotes of the Founders in the formation of our founding documents.[6] Of 15,000 possible sources to inform the discussion, the one dominant source from which the founders drew their ideas and perspectives, their values and notions about liberty and responsibility, was the Bible. French philosopher Montesquieu† was quoted 8.3 percent of the time, followed by English jurist William Blackstone and his *Commentaries on the Laws of England* 7.9 percent,‡ and then English philosopher John Locke 2.9 percent. In an even

---

6   William J. Federer, *American Minute.* See http://www.amerisearch.net/index.php?date=2004-09-17, retrieved August 27, 2007.

social stability. He was explicit in terms of his view of Islam, noting that Islamic leaders "incessantly give or receive death" whereas Christianity "renders their princes ... less cruel." The Christian religion, he observed, "has hindered despotic power ... and has carried into the heart of Africa the manners and laws of Europe" and of course, behind those laws were biblical principles. Comparing Christianity and Islam, he unequivocally declared, "... we ought, without any further examination, to embrace the one [Christianity] and reject the other [Islam]." His argument was that the proof of the faith was in the social order it created, "... for it is much easier to prove that religion ought to humanize the manners of men than that any particular religion is true." Islam was, he noted, a "religion ... given by a conqueror. The Mahometan religion, which speaks only by the sword, acts still upon men with that destructive spirit with which it was founded." While some might be offended today by the opinion of Montesquieu on Islam, he became even more pointed when he observed differences in Europe. "When the Christian religion, two centuries ago, became unhappily divided into Catholic and Protestant, the people of the north embraced the Protestant, and those of the south adhered still to the Catholic. The reason is plain: the people of the north have, and will forever have, a spirit of liberty and independence, which the people of the south have not; and therefore a religion which has no visible head is more agreeable to the independence of the climate than that which has one." More simply, the model of Catholicism, with its Pope, matched the governments of Monarchs; and Protestantism, the republican governments of the common people. "God who gave us life gave us liberty. And can the liberties of a nation be thought secure when we have removed their only firm basis, a conviction in the minds of the people that these liberties are a gift from God? That they are not to be violated but with His wrath? Indeed I tremble for my country when I reflect that God is just, and that His justice cannot sleep forever."

~Thomas Jefferson, Notes on the State of Virginia, Query XVIII, 1781. There was discussion among the founders, early in the history of the nation, about whether or not, non-Christians could be elected to a public office. Some states had a 'faith' test to insure that only believers were elected. Governor Samuel Johnston, of North Carolina noted, "It is apprehended that Jews, Mahometans (Muslims), pagans, etc., may be elected to high offices under the government of the United States. Those who are Mahometans, or any others who are not professors of the Christian religion, can never be elected to the office of President or other high office, [unless] first the people of America lay aside the Christian religion altogether, it may happen. Should this unfortunately take place, the people will choose such men as think as they do themselves."

~Governor Samuel Johnston, July 30, 1788 at the North Carolina Ratifying Convention.

more astounding discovery, while 34 percent of the quotes were directly from the pages of the Bible, another 60 percent were from men who had used the Bible to inform their conclusions. Thus, 94 percent of the Founding Fathers quotes were based on the Bible, directly or indirectly. This nation was founded with a deep sense of reverence for God, and the moral laws of God.[7] Lutz compiled a list of over 180 sources from which quotes were derived. That one-third came directly from the Scriptures, in the face of such diversity, is a staggering fact, one rarely noted today.[8]

There is another factor, namely, that the U.S. Constitution was the product of a constitution-making tradition that reached back to the charters of the original colonies as well as the states, and from there, the tradition found roots in the biblical covenant. In Jamestown, the first representative government met in the church building, and opened

7   Alliance for Life Ministries, *"America's Christian Heritage, Part II: The Revolution and Beyond"*, http://www.alliance4lifemin.org/categori..../ach_part2.htm, retrieved August 27, 2007.

8   EarsToHear.net, Stephen Voigt, *"How I learned about the root of law... but not in law school"*, December 22, 2005, http://earstohear.net/Separation/rootoflaw.html, retrieved August 27, 2007.

with prayer. The guiding principles are governance were tempered and informed by biblical values. The Pilgrims enacted a 'Bill of Liberties,' a precedent to the Bill of Rights, drafter by a Pastor Nathaniel Ward, informed by Scripture. When Connecticut was founded, it was a governmental structure fashioned largely from a sermon based Dt. 1:13 and Ex. 18:21, and from that sermon sprang the "Fundamental Orders of Connecticut."[9] The colonists came to America with the Bible in their hand. And from the Scripture came their notions of natural law as the basis of the government. Every right articulated in the Declaration of Independence had been discussed openly in the era before the Revolution, and those discussions were led by the clergy and their preaching. David Barton suggests a correlation behind the Declaration of Independence and a listing of sermon topics

> ## ‡ACCENT
>
> William Blackstone wrote Commentaries on the Laws of England. His work was the first comprehensive integration of a system of justice. The multi-year project consolidated English common law into a unified and rational system. The book sold more copies in the colonies than England and had profound impact on the formation of the U. S. Government. Blackstone spoke of the "supreme being [who] formed the universe, and created matter out of nothing, [and] he impressed certain principles upon that matter, from which it can never depart, and without which it would cease to be..." He argued for 'self-government' of individuals as they reminded themselves of their created place of honor as God's noblest creature. "Man, considered as a creature, must necessarily be subject to the laws of his Creator, for he is entirely a dependent being." The failure to observe the laws of the Creator, and remain dependent upon Him, implied consequences. "...

---

9   David Barton, "Building On Firm Foundations," *Ministries Today*, Vol. 30, No. 1 (January/February, 2012: Charisma Media; Lake Mary, FL), 34-35.

as man depends absolutely upon his maker for everything, it is necessary that he should in all points conform to his maker's will." The "will of his maker is called," by Blackstone, "the law of nature." God, Blackstone argued, "endued him [man] with freewill to conduct himself in all parts of life, he laid down certain immutable laws of human nature, whereby that freewill is in some degree regulated and restrained, and gave him also the faculty of reason ..." Behind Blackstone, and the common law of Europe which the jurist codified, was the Bible, and the Creator, the God of the Bible. He called these principles, "... eternal, immutable laws of good and evil, to which the Creator himself in all his dispensations conforms ... as they are necessary for the conduct of human actions." Obedience to the law of God was an idea embraced by Americans until the mid-1880's, when Enlightenment notions gained ground that denied the reality of God and embraced an exalted view of man. Charles Finney, an attorney, found so many b1iblical references in Blackstone's Commentaries that he purchased a Bible, read it, and became a believer, and of course, the great evangelist that impacted America in the Second Great Awakening. He was convicted, and saved – reading Blackstone's Commentaries. Behind it, and English Common Law, was Scripture.

preached in the decades leading up to the revolution, preaching that offered perspectives on public issues, taxes, education, the military, just and unjust wars, governance – these were ideas and in them ideals for nation building. It was the clergy who were behind the revolution. The British called them "The Black Regiment," referring to their clerical robes, and they laid the blame for Colonial unrest on the back of the preachers and the churches. As a result, 10 of the 19 church buildings during the New York occupation were destroyed, and most of those in Virginia met the same fate.[10]

The Bottom Line

They feared God. They reverenced the Scripture. It would

---

10 Ibid.

have been inconceivable to them, that in the future, their children's children, thinking people, would have wrenched the Declaration of Independence and the Constitution along with the Bill of Rights free of their true roots, or attempted to understand it apart from the Scriptures over which they poured as they wrote the founding documents. The people were free only because God was their king! They were free because his law had been written on their hearts and they respected that law.

Simply put, there was a 'fear' of God that allowed such liberty and freedom to exist. Now, in the absence of that fear, the liberty of free but evil men to speak and do as they please has become a threat to all. More to the point, the culture is mentoring the Church in its dismissal of reverence for God. It affects our prayer life. We no longer believe we are 'sinners in the hands of an angry God.' That perception sparked the first Great Awakening and became a shared cultural value in the formation of the nation. No more!

Approaching a Secular Throne

England has perhaps the most prominent remaining Royal Household, a bastion of form, etiquette and regal protocol. There are great pains to insure that ceremony, décor, dress and personal manner are observed when one appears before royalty. Buckingham Palace is a reflection on days past, on the gap that once existed between commoners and kings. The symbols themselves are not as important as the fact that there 'are' symbols, ways and means by which an individual was to demonstrate respect for the king. One feature was white gloves and they are still the norm – representing, supposedly, 'clean hands' or innocence before the King. Criminals dared not present themselves in the court of a king. They were considered to be at war with the crown, by creating disorder in his kingdom, and therefore at war with the king himself. Such insolence might meet with death. The gloves were symbols of clean hands. And they had to be immaculately clean as they touched royal hands.

In ancient times, people were at times 'commanded' to appear before the king. We still speak of a 'command' performance for royalty or some elite audience. As a loyal and dutiful subject you were obligated to attend. Nothing was more important, the king or queen had commanded you. The distinctive invitation came as a *summons* – and it was precisely that, a subpoena that had a potential penalty if one failed to appear. It came complete with the arrival and departure data, protocol and other instructions were also included. Such an invitation could not be resisted outside the most exceptional situation. You would forward a reply, in which you presented your 'compliments' and expressed the fact they they you had 'the honor *to obey* His Majesty's command to attend' the event. The entire company was typically gathered, before the royals arrived and entered the hall. Thus, we 'wait' on the Lord.

At some point, there would be a moment in the evening in which you were invited to stand before the king. The expectation on your part would be that of obeisance. This was a cultural symbol manifesting a deep respect for the throne. Men would bow. Women would curtsey, a unique and difficult maneuver performed as one descends while simultaneously shaking the hand of the Royal. Upon being presented to the king, there were words expected in order to show respect. "Your Majesty" was typically used as the first verbal designation and thereafter the term "Sir" was appropriate. The royal person, king or queen, led the conversation. Only they could change the subject. Only the most polite question was permitted on your part. Insolence, in ancient times, could put you in prison or cost your life. You spoke only when spoken to. And when you disengaged, when you were dismissed, you backed away from the throne, never turning your back on royalty.[11]

Sovereigns would at times 'hold court' and allow petitions to be presented. The medieval king was the guarantor of justice. Today the court is one of few places where one is 'summoned' and a failure to appear has consequences, where one is commanded to stand before authority and where contempt for office or order, for truth and process, can land you in jail. Here is a vestige of the power of the throne.

With this picture of respect and protocol, we gain a better understanding of what it means to appear before the Throne of God. Our world-view affects our understanding of Scripture, and having been stripped of the world-view that prevailed in biblical times, we have arguably lost a piece of what it means to come to God's Throne room. Let's review:

1. Surprisingly, the call in Scripture for our 'reverence' of God is more frequent that the call to 'love God.' It is not therefore, the concern of the Holy Spirit, the author of the text through humans, that we would stop loving God, but that we would stop 'fearing' God; and that would alter in an unspeakable way, the quality of our love for God.

2. The second observation is that the 'fear of God' is irrevocably tied to the 'perception of God,' and beyond that – revelation and insight, the application of knowledge into wisdom. Indeed, the Scripture asserts that the very threshold into the temple of knowledge is the fear of God. Without it, we are blinded by our own shadow, seeing little difference

---

11 A. Morrow, *The Queen* (The Chaucer Press: Bungay, Suffolk, 1983); J. Morgan, *Debrett's New Guide to Etiquette and Modern Manners: the Indispensable Handbook* (Headline; London, 1996).

between mortals and the immortal; deaf by the sound of our own foolish professions. We changed "the glory of the image." Our perception of ourselves; and that of God are interconnected. The more we disdain and dismiss God, the more we distort our perception of humanity and corrupt the race of men; the more we identify with the animal kingdom (evolution).

3. The third observation is that God has not changed. And any significant encounter with the Sovereign, Omniscient God, Holy and Incomparable, Mighty in Power and Splendor – results in a visceral, automated response of 'fear' and 'reverence.'

4. The fourth observation is that God's Law, His immutable essence, and His Sovereignty are bound together. Only in God's kingdom are we safe with Lex Rex, that is with God as King; and the King as Law. Here, God is bound to His Law, it is His very nature. Law is King; and the King, God, is the Law. He is not holy, as a mere corollary, it is His essence. In every other kingdom, we must ask men to be subordinate to divine law and principles, if people are to be safe; and morality is to be honored.

5. The fifth observation is the 'fear of God' and the respect for His law, as recorded in the Bible, specifically the book of Deuteronomy, is behind the Constitution. The Founding Fathers anticipated a self-governing people, governed not by radical free-will and hyper individualism, but by the principles of godliness in Scripture.

6. The sixth observation is that we have lost the idea of any reference point for approaching God in a reverential manner. Only the courtroom remains as a faint connection point to inform our coming to God with respect.

AUTHOR

P. Douglas Small

P. Douglas Small serves the Church of God as Prayer Coordinator. He has been in this role for four years at the writing of this book. Previously, he worked out of the Evangelism Department as a consultant on prayer ministries, and as a national teaching evangelist under the sponsorship of the General Church. He is also President of Alive Ministries: PROJECT PRAY. He serves as a member of America's National Prayer Committee; and a member of the Planning Team of Denominational Prayer Leaders. He has been active in the 'prayer movement' for two decades. He also served as pastor and taught at West Coast and East Bible Colleges. He is author of more than a dozen books and is a conference speaker. He continues to conduct Schools of Prayer. He recently launched a *Prayer Council* movement in connection with the National Prayer Committee. He serves as a consultant on prayer to the *Billion Souls* Campaign. He's the founder of the *Praying Church Movement*.

CHAPTER FOUR

PRAYER - APPROACHING GOD'S THRONE

A WINDOW THROUGH TIME

Visions of Heaven and Hell

In the "Life of William Tennent," that zealous, devoted minister, and friend and fellow-laborer of Whitefield, the author of his memoirs gives an account of Tennent being three days in a trance. He became prostrated with a fever, and by degrees sunk under it, until, to appearances, he died. In laying him out, one felt a slight tremor under the left arm, though the body was cold and stiff. The time for the funeral arrived, and the people were assembled. But a physician, Tennent's friend, plead that the funeral might be delayed.

Tennent's brother remarked: "What! A man not dead who is cold and stiff as a stake?" The doctor, however, prevailed; another day was appointed for the funeral. During the interval, various efforts were made to discover signs of life, but none appeared save the slight tremor. For three days and nights his friend, the physician, never left him. Again the people met to bury him, but could not even then obtain the physician's consent. For one hour more he pled; when that was gone, he craved half an hour more. That being expired, he implored a stay of fifteen minutes, at the expiration of which Tennent opened his eyes.

The following brief account is given in Mr. Tennent's own language, and was related to a brother minister: "As to dying, I found my fever increase, and I became weaker and weaker, until all at once, I found myself in heaven, as I thought. I saw no shape as to the Deity, but glory all unutterable. I can say as Paul did, I heard and saw things unutterable. I saw a great multitude before His glory, apparently in the height of bliss, singing most melodiously. I was transported with my of situation, viewing all my troubles ended, and my rest and glory begun, and was about to join the great and happy multitude, when one came to me looked me full in the face, laid his hand upon my shoulder, and said: "You must go back."

"These words went through me; nothing could have shocked me more. I cried out: "Lord, must I go back?" With this shock, I opened my eyes in this world, I fainted, then came to, and fainted again several times, as one probably would naturally have done in so weak a situation.

"For three years the sense of the Divine things continued so great, and everything else appeared so completely vain, when compared to heaven, that could I have had the world for stooping down for it, I believe I should not have thought of doing it."

To the writer of his memoirs, Mr. Tennent, concerning this experience, once said: "I found myself, in an instant, in another state of existence, under the direction of a superior being, who offered me to follow him. I was accordingly wafted along, I know not how, till I beheld, at a distance, an ineffable glory, the impression of which on my mind, it is impossible to communicate to mortal man.

"Such was the effect on my mind of what I had seen and heard, that if it be possible for a human being to live entirely above the world, and the things of it, for some time afterward I was that person. The ravishing sounds of the songs and hallelujahs that I heard, and the very words that were uttered, were not out of my ears, when awake, for at least three years. All the kingdoms of the earth were in my sight as nothing and vanity. So great were my ideas of heavenly glory, that nothing which did not in some measure relate to it, could command my serious attention.

Mr. Tennent lived a number of years after this event, and died in the triumphs of a living faith, March 8, 1777, aged 71 years; his mortal remains being interred at his chapel, in Freehold, N. J. He was an able, faithful preacher; and the Divine presence with him was frequently manifested in his public and private ministrations. In personal appearance, he was tall, erect, and of spare visage, with bright, piercing eyes, and grave, solemn countenance.

S. B. Shaw, "A Mob Quieted In Answer To Prayer," *Touching Incidents And Remarkable Answers To Prayer* (Grand Rapids, MI: S.B. Shaw, Publisher, 1893), 55.

CHAPTER 4

PRAYER - APPROACHING
GOD'S THRONE

P. Douglas Small

The customary Hebrew term word for "worship" is *chavah* which infers the action of bowing or prostration in deference to God as an act of honor and reverence. The Greek term *proskyneo* is from *pros,* meaning towards, and *kuneo,* to kiss. It is understood as meaning "to prostrate" and is the most common word rendered to worship. It touches the ancient practice of kissing the hand, or even the feet of the king. It is an idea of deep reverence, expressed in some telling manner. In ancient times, approaching a king was a serious matter, one the common man was rarely, if ever, afforded. [1]

The book of Hebrews encourages *'reverence and awe.'*

"Let us be thankful, and so worship God acceptably <u>with reverence and awe,</u> for our 'God is a consuming fire'" (Heb. 12:28, 29).

God told Israel to *"Observe my Sabbaths and have <u>reverence for my sanctuary.</u> I am the LORD"* (Lev. 19:30, 26:2). This is the idea of holy time and space or place. The sanctuary was the gateway to heaven, the portal to another world, the premier place of prayer, and the spot where one demonstrated physically his desire to be near God. The approach demands reverence, a sense of awe, veneration. This

---

1   E. Keith Hassell, "Worship and God's Throne"; *The Vision Newsletter* (August, 2012); www.gracefellowshiprusk.com Grace Fellowship; P.O. Box 260; Rusk, Texas; (903) 683-6550.

was demanded of Israel when their worship center was a tent of meeting and not the gold-plated temple. Approaching God demands the transformation of the common into the exceptional. The most common spot is made sacred by the placement of an altar and the act of prayer.

We quote quite liberally the passage from Hebrews, *"Let us therefore come boldly to the throne of grace, that we may obtain mercy and find grace to help in time of need"* (Hebrews 4:16). Let's examine the passage: *'Come'* – means to come near worshipping, and the tense indicates our continuous action of approaching God. We are to keep on coming. And quite surprisingly, we are to approach the Throne, the ultimate Potentate boldly, implying frankness, bluntness, an outspoken manner, and yet with assurance. We come for the purpose of finding *"help,"* so we are the defendant, the offended, the oppressed – not the plaintiff, not the one with power. It is precisely because we are beaten down, oppressed and lacking in options, that we are urged by God to come so freely and present our case so forcefully. The idea behind the term, *help*, is that of a rope or chain used to rescue a sinking vessel. Whenever we sense our ship sinking, we are to boldly request grace from God!

There is more. Note carefully the attendant conditions that bolster boldness,

> *"Therefore, brethren, having boldness, let us draw near with a true heart in full assurance of faith, having our hearts sprinkled from an evil conscience and our bodies washed with pure water. Let us hold fast the confession of our hope without wavering, for He who promised is faithful. And let us consider one another in order to stir up love and good works"* (Hebrews 10:19).

Closer examination reveals that this is not blind boldness, but calculated confidence. A *'true heart'* is necessary. The idea is one of being real, authentic and one with God's heart; second, one with *faith* that is rich with confidence, *'full' with assurance*, thus a healthy faith is required. Third, the term *'sprinkled'* reaches back to the action of sprinkling blood on the Mercy Seat. The implication is that to approach God, we must have upon our hearts the fresh markings of the blood of Christ. Fourth, it is here, on inner hearts, that God is enthroned by the Spirit. Such a redemptive and regenerative encounter with the cross also alters the state of our deadly inner evil conscience. Fifth, the internal transformation is matched externally by bodies, now consecrated, and *'washed,'* a metaphor for sanctification, for the mortification of the flesh, thus outward purity. And this happens only in the 'pure water' of the laver, what Paul called *"the washing of water with the word"* (Ephesians 5:26; Exodus 40:30). And seventh, we are urged *to hold* – or *lay hold of, unswervingly* (NIV) or *tightly, without wavering* (NLT) to the hope which we then, eighth, are to simultaneously *affirm* (NLT) by professing (NIV), *homologia,* saying the same thing God says, speaking the language of hope and faith, of expectation and anticipation. All of this is in reference to *'He who promised'* and is believed to be faithful. This is not to be done in a self-interested manner. This approach to the throne is to result in our being an example to others – to provoke love and good works.

This is quite a distance from the thoughtless and flippant, *'Come boldly'* often quoted without appropriate appreciation for the context. Boldness without a true heart, in the absence of sincere faith, minus the fresh blood stains of redemption, with fleshly life patterns, while wavering in faith, hopeless and despairing, without the language of confidence in God and a concern for others – is not boldness. It is presumption. Boldness, it turns out, demands intentional preparation for a meeting with God. It is respectful. Prepared. Positive, but fearful in anticipation of the awful - full of the awe of God – encounter.

Moses was told, *"You cannot see my face, for man may not see Me and live"* (Exodus 33:20). In these passages, we encounter a view of God which is rare today. Prayer can never be understood apart from the regal nature of the encounter and the environment it implies, something about which we Americans know very little. That the writer of Hebrews would urge us to *'come boldly'* before God is almost unthinkable. It is like a rash dare – who would do such a thing? It is an invitation possible only by the triumph of mercy over wrath, and therefore only for a people who understand that lightning still flashes around the throne and powerful other-worldly creatures fly about, and the God with whom we meet there has not changed. There is no diminishment of His power or might, His intolerance of sin or His holy nature. Only those who would never dare dishonor the Throne can approach with such unhinged confidence. Isaiah 57:15 (NKJV) declares,

> *"For thus says the High and Lofty One Who inhabits eternity, whose name is Holy: 'I dwell in the high and holy place, with him who has a contrite and humble spirit, to revive the spirit of the humble, and to revive the heart of the contrite ones.'"*

Nehemiah was regularly in the presence of Artaxerxes, the King of Persia. But his repeated exposure to the king did not allow for a familiarity with the king. An appropriate personal distance was demanded. In Nehemiah 2:2, the king confronts Nehemiah, *"Why is thy countenance sad, seeing thou art not sick?"* On first glance, this appears to be a sensitive moment between the king and his cup-bearer, but notice the response of Nehemiah, *"Then I was very sore afraid..."* The reason? Though he appeared frequently, multiple times daily in the court of the king, it was not appropriate to be present with a sad countenance. Personal feelings and the projection of one's own emotions were not allowed in the king's presence. To say it differently, the subjects were not to set the mood of the court; only the king could do that. Here is a reminder, that in ancient cultures, the people, even the loyal servants of kings were nevertheless not in his social class, and one was not to cross the line of familiarity. There was a proper protocol in approaching a king, even by members of his family, princes and courtiers, something about which we know very little today. Nehemiah knew one was never to approach the throne with a sad face or a disposition of depression, in Scripture, called, 'a spirit of heaviness.' Suddenly, he was fearful of the potential consequences.

There is also an example of royal protocol found in the book of Esther. Mordecai, when he heard about the imminent danger to the Jews was said to have 'rent his clothes and put on sackcloth,' but then the Bible notes, *"no one might enter into the king's gate with sackcloth!"* (Esther 4:1-2). Even with a potential death threat looming, he was not allowed to express sorrow openly before the king. Psalm 100:5, notes that one is to *"... come before His presence with singing ... enter into His gates with thanksgiving, and into His courts with praise: be thankful unto Him, and bless His name ..."* The king is to be pleased. The king is to be feared, and revered. We have made prayer and worship about ourselves, God is to adjust to our mood; but in truth, the prescription is exactly the opposite (Psalm 100:1-5). There is a protocol of honor when one comes before the King of kings.

No Fear of God: No Respect for Others

A recent trend has been to eliminate kneelers in liturgical churches. Some see the act as demeaning, but others are in revolt against the movement of church authorities to eliminate this act of reverence. In many Pentecostal churches, the practice of kneeling in prayer has virtually disappeared, as has the practice of coming forward and tarrying at an altar, the congregation gathered before

God on their knees. *"Come, let us bow down in worship, let us kneel before the Lord our Maker; for He is our God" (Psalm 95:6)*. Kneeling is an act of submission and worship, referencing the devotion of a servant and yet offered by the believer freely, not only as an acknowledgement of the dominance of God's power and might, but also of the preeminence of His holiness and majesty. It is a clear indication of our humility and a declaration of God's supremacy.

Our prevailing American culture takes pride in bowing to nothing or before no one. Ego-centricity and virtual self-worship have given rise to a level of self-assertion and rights advocacy which now threaten the stability of the whole society. All humans are equal and are to be valued, that is a biblical tenet. But such level social ground is impossible unless the kindness and deference expected by the one is also given to all others. That demands the personal practice of the rule of love and truth and the awareness that our treatment of the other is a matter of conscience before the God to whom we will have to give an account. In no other context can such abundance of liberty exist. It is our public moments of prayer that remind us, that though we are free, we are not gods. If man is God, and therefore makes his own rules, anarchy results.

Reverence and *respect* are terms which are sometimes used as synonyms. However, *reverence* denotes worship and is particularly appropriate in referencing our relationship with God and the attendant sphere of interaction. Reverence is higher and deeper than respect. It involves veneration and devotion, in a worshipful manner. Respect esteems and admires, but it does not worship. Today, in a culture that reverences little if anything, we have confused the two concepts. As a result, reverence for God has degenerated to mere respect, even among Christians. We are to *respect* parents, for example, and honor them. And we are to respect, honor and obey authorities with more than superficial verbal deference. We are to act and live in a manner that respects or honors all others, that avoids insult and injury, a manner that values others. The absence of the fear of God manifest has a lack of reverence and respect for church sanctuaries and facilities. No longer are children taught to be respectful in 'God's house.' If the tent of meeting in the wilderness was to be revered, then the humblest meeting house should also be honored as a spot that is sacred.

Pentecostal worship is by its character informal and spontaneous, without formal liturgy. Freedom in worship has been a special distinctive of Pentecostals. But informality can sometimes degenerate to inadvertent impertinence, and a lack of reverence for the things of God. We know that even our bodies are 'temples' of the Holy Spirit. As a result we can pray anywhere and anytime. But if there is no space that is sacred in a marked manner, by deliberate corporate agreement, there will soon be no place at all that is regarded as sacred. Sanctuaries remind us that holy spaces are important. Even when the sanctuary is not being formally used, it should be respected. And that respect is meant not for 'the place' so much as it is the 'Person' who is honored there. On this ground, in this space, we have met with God, read and heard His Word, prayed and worshipped, and it is holy ground, sanctified space. It is the place at which we cultivate in ourselves and in our children, a fear and reverence for God.[2] And yet, it is quite a different matter to teach others, or possess ourselves, an awareness that we should '*show*' respect for God; and beyond that to '*feel*' respect for Him. We may show respect for a police officer who approaches our car and demands to see our license after his blue lights flash and signal us to the side of the road; but it is another matter

---

2   The Assemblies of God have produced a guide for their churches on honoring the sanctuary. Some of the ideas in the preceding chapter are drawn from their document on 'Reverence,' which can be at: http://ag.org/top/Beliefs/topics/charctr_20_reverence_.cfm

to feel respect for Him. Generally, we show respect to the office, the badge, the gun, the authority; but we feel respect for the person. And it is at this only at this felt level that fear becomes worshipful awe and reverence in reference to God.[3]

The Error of Daddy God – Affection without Awe

One idea that has eroded the appropriate fear of God in prayer and worship is the promotion of '*abba*' as 'Daddy God.' The phrase has come to dominate current popular thinking and any mention of "fear and trembling" before the Lord is too quickly dismissed, at times discouraged and even disdained. The Hebrew term *yir'ah* is rendered fear or terror. It denotes some awesome or terrifying thing including our perspective of God, promoting respect, reverence and piety. The Greek term *phobos,* from which we get our word *phobia,* also means fear and terror. We dread the thing that provokes terror. Those who are acquainted with phobias know that the reaction is visceral, automatic and instinctive. Perhaps this is the reason Paul amplifies the picture of appropriate fear before God by adding the descriptor, *trembling,* from the Greek word *tromos.* This is not merely cognitive or psychological. This is not a literary device to add intensity to a concept – this is a picture of the whole being, physical and spiritual, before God, trembling.

It was Joachim Jeremias who set forth the idea of '*abba*' as 'daddy' equating it with 'child-babble.' Almost immediately, the proposal was challenged by several scholars. James Barr published an article entitled "*Abba* Isn't 'Daddy'" which appeared in the *Journal of Theological Studies.*[4] Jeremias then retreated from his claim that

---

3   Jerry Bridges, *The Joy of Fearing God* (Colorado Springs, CO: Waterbrook Press, 1997), 15.

4   James Barr, "'*Abba*' Isn't 'Daddy' [*Journal of Theological Studies,* 1988]; See also: Geza Vermes, *Jesus in the World of Judaism* [1983], pp. 41, 2.

"*abba*" connoted "daddy" in the world of etymology, acknowledging that the word, when used by adults, was as a term of respect for seniors and teachers, not by children for their father. But then he continued to assert that infants did make such a sound, and therefore just as we claim the infant's 'dada' as a term of intimacy, he claimed *abba* as an endearing term for God. His claim was then completely disconnected from biblical language or sound language studies.

In the New Testament we have three occurrences of the Arabic *abba,* along with the Greek, *pater,* meaning 'the father' (Mark 14:36; Rom. 8:15; Gal. 4:6). The juxtaposition of the two languages, the Arabic followed by the Greek translation, indicates that what is offered is a literal translation of the two terms offered as equivalents, both meaning - "father." *Abba* is not a diminutive of father in "baby-talk" form. If that were intended, there are Greek diminutives of the term father, but they were not used.[5] There are also distinct terms for 'daddy' in Aramaic – *papi, baba, abbi,* as opposed to *abba.* The Greek term in the New Testament for father is always *pater,* and never a diminutive – such as *papas, pappas,* or *pappias,* any of which could have been used, but were not in the minds of the biblical writers, under the inspiration of the Spirit, considered suitable.

Today, the assertions of Jeremias have been completely discounted by scholars, but the idea persists in popular usage. '*Abba*' is clearly cognate with the Hebrew word '*ab* (pronounced '*ahv*), meaning 'Father.' Specifically, it would appear with the definite article, *ha'ab* - *the* Father. The ending -*a'* on the Aramaic makes it a determined or definite noun. So a translation would be '*the* Father' or '*my* Father' of simply 'Father.' First century folks would not have confused the term with 'daddy.' The use of the term 'daddy God' has served to promote the idea of an approachable God, one with whom we can

5   See - Mary Rose D'Angelo. *Journal of Biblical Literature,* Vol. 111, No. 4 (Winter, 1992), pp. 615-616.

find warmth and intimacy, and though such concepts are, on balance, appropriate, they rise here from the wrong premise and they have failed to be appropriately balanced with a call to retain an awe for God.

Reverential Prayer to God as Father

Why does the Bible call God Father?

First, because He is the Creator. All life comes from Him. Even among the pagans, there is the idea of "the father of the gods," the One from whom all others proceed, the Sovereign among them all. The Scriptures present YHWH as standing alone. What He created He governs. He has no rivals.

Second, the term 'Father' connotes the nature of His relationship to creation. It is ancient covenant and relational language. We are His 'children.' In Exodus 4:22, 23, Israel is identified as God's son in a covenant with God. They were Abraham's seed (covenanted sons). Later, in the days of their kings, God was the 'father' to the king, and the king was his son. Thus, a king would publicly declare by what right and authority he ruled, "The LORD said to me, 'You are my son. Today I have begotten you'" (Ps. 2:7). Peter would say to Jesus, "You are the Son of God." In Romans 8:15, 16, the Spirit prompts us to say, *'Abba', Father,* because we are members of the New Covenant. Jesus taught us to pray, saying, "Our Father ..."

Third, the term father is filial. It was colloquial but respectful, and yet not the equivalent of our child-like expression 'daddy.' It was an affirmation that we are a part of the family of God, the bride-partner of Jesus, and joint-heirs.

> *"Since you call on a Father who judges each man's work impartially, live your lives as strangers here in reverent fear" (I Peter 1:17 NIV).*

The Father is also the Judge – the ultimate Judge! Of every man. And He judges impartially, even though He is our Father, there are no special exemptions for us. Therefore, we are to live as strangers, pilgrims, detached from this world, with a heightened sense of who we are and who He is, with an inside track, not on treatment, but in terms of knowledge, in reverent fear. It is out of reverence for our Father and His character, that we are to avoid conviction in His courtroom. The line between the Law of God, and the character of the Father is a very direct and short line.

The Bible says that we are fearfully and wonderfully made! 'Fear' of God and for God is in our DNA. Only the blind fail to see it. An engineer charged with the task of designing a pump to last for a hundred years, with a 2000 gallon per day capacity, with values that operate up to 5000 times per hour, an output of .25 to one horsepower, and a weight of 300 grams, requiring no maintenance – would wilt at the task! We have just described the heart, only one wonder of the body. A structural designer with the task of building a 'foot' for a soccer player out of twenty-six bones, with dexterity and elasticity, yet strong enough to carry the weight of a man and endure the cumulative force of over one thousand tons in a single game – who would want such a task? The ear is comprised the three compartments, the outer ear that collects data, the middle ear and the inner ear. The design of the outer ears provides stereoscopic capacity, designed to collect data from all directions, slight sounds and explosions. As those sounds, actually vibrations, are collected, they affect the taunt 'drum' at the edge of the middle ear, which beats or vibrates with the frequency and amplitude of the sounds. That disturbs three small bones which then interact in the middle ear amplifying the pressure of the sound vibrations by 22 times and thereby selectively transmitting the frequency to fibers in the inner ear, much in the same way the strings of a harp or piano vibrate in resonance with a particular frequency. That disturbs the fluid of the inner ear, and sends signals to the brain – and you know exactly what is being said! The double helix of the DNA in every cell in our bodies contains the equivalent information found in a thousand six-hundred page encyclopedia volumes. There are 75 trillion of these cells in our bodies. Each is covered with millions of portholes, which open and close on cue, as if opened by an organic key, receiving and sending forth a steady stream of organic materials. Each cell, far from being simple, is "a world of supreme technology and bewildering complexity."[6] The human brain consists of some ten trillion cells, each with ten-thousand, and some as many as one-hundred-thousand fibers all of which are highly organized. If only one-percent were used, the brain would still represent a greater number of connections than the entire sphere of communication networks on the earth, combined.[7]

We were made in such a way – that the fear of God is scripted in us. *"How many are your works, O Lord! In wisdom you made them all; the earth is full of your creatures" (Psalm 104:24).*

---

6   Michael Denton, *Evolution: A Theory in Crisis* (Bethesda, MD: Adler & Adler, 1985), 328-329; See also, Paul Brand and Philip Yancey, *Fearfully and Wonderfully Made* (Grand Rapids: MI; 1980), 70, 45.

7   Denton, 330-331; Bridges, 82.

CHAPTER FIVE

PRAYER - BALANCING INTIMACY AND IMMANENCE

A WINDOW THROUGH TIME

This is the story of a civil war surgeon. At Gettysburg, hundreds were wounded, requiring service at once - legs and arms had to be amputated. A young boy had been in the service for only three months. Too young to be a soldier, he enlisted as a drummer. The assistant surgeon wished to administer chloroform prior to his amputation, but he positively refused it. Told it was the doctor's orders, he said: "Send the doctor to me."

At his bedside, I [the surgeon] asked, "Young man, why do you refuse chloroform? When I found you on the battlefield you were so far gone that I thought it hardly worthwhile to pick you up; but when you opened those large blue eyes I thought you had a mother somewhere who might, at that moment, be thinking of her boy. I did not want you to die on the field, so ordered you to be brought here; but you have now lost so much blood that you are too weak to endure an operation without chloroform ..."

Looking me in the face, he said: "Doctor, one Sunday afternoon, in the Sabbath-school, when I was nine and a half years old, I gave my heart to Christ. I learned to trust Him then ... and I can trust Him now. He is my strength and my stimulant. He will support me while you amputate my arm and leg."

I asked if he would take a little brandy. He refused, "Doctor, when I was about five years old my mother knelt by my side, with her arm around my neck, and said: ' Charlie, I am now praying to

Jesus that you may never know the taste of strong drink your papa died a drunkard ... and I promised God, if it were His will that you should grow up, that you should warn young men against the bitter cup.' I am now seventeen years old, but I have never tasted anything stronger than tea and coffee, and as I am, in all probability, about to go into the presence of my God, would you send me there with brandy on my stomach?"

The look that boy gave me I shall never forget. At that time I hated Jesus, but I respected that boy's loyalty to his Savior; and when I saw how he loved and trusted Him to the last, there was something that touched my heart, and I did for that boy what I had never done for any other soldier. I asked him if he wanted to see his chaplain. "Oh! Yes, sir," was the answer.

The Chaplain knew the boy from having often met him at the tent prayer meetings, "Well, Charlie, I am sorry to see you in this sad condition." "Oh, I am all right, sir," he answered. "The doctor offered me chloroform, but I declined it; then he wished to give me brandy, which I also declined; and now, if my Savior calls me, I can go to Him in my right mind."

"You may not die, Charlie," said the Chaplain but if the Lord should call you away, is there anything I can do for you after you are gone? "

"Chaplain, please ... take my little Bible; in it you will find my mother's address; please send it to her, and write a letter, and tell her that since the day I left home I have never let a day pass without reading a portion of God's word, and daily praying that God would bless my dear mother; no matter whether on the march, on the battle-field, or in the hospital."

"Is there anything else I can do for you, my lad?" asked the Chaplain.

"Yes; please write a letter to the superintendent of the Sands-street Sunday-school, Brooklyn, N.Y., and tell him that the kind words, many prayers, and good advice he gave me I have never forgotten; they have followed me through all the dangers of battle; and now, in my dying hour, I ask my dear Savior to bless my dear old superintendent. That is all."

Turning towards me he said: "Now, doctor, I am ready; and I promise you that I will not even groan while you take off my arm and leg, if you will not offer me chloroform." I promised, but I did not have the courage to take the knife in my hand to perform the operation without first taking a little stimulant myself. Charlie Coulson never groaned ... the lad took the corner of his pillow in his mouth, and all that I could hear him utter was: "O Jesus; blessed Jesus! Stand by me now." He never groaned.

That night I could not sleep. Whichever way I turned, I saw those soft blue eyes, and when I closed mine the words, "Blessed Jesus, stand by me now," kept ringing in my ears. Between twelve and one o'clock, I left my bed and visited the hospital; a thing I had never done before unless specially called, but such was my desire to see that boy. Upon my arrival, I was informed that sixteen of the hopeless cases had died, and been carried down to the dead-house. "How is Charlie Coulson, is he among the dead?"

"No, sir," answered the steward, "he is sleeping as sweetly as a babe." When I came to his bed, one of the nurses informed me that, about nine o' clock, two members of the Y.M.C.A. came to read and sing a hymn. They were accompanied by the Chaplain who knelt by Charlie Coulson's bed, and offered up a fervent and soul-stirring prayer ... and they sang while still upon their knees, "Jesus, lover of my soul," and Charlie joined the singing. I could not understand how that boy, who had undergone such excruciating pain, could sing.

Five days later, he sent for me. "Doctor," he said, "my time has come; I do not expect to see another sun rise; but thank God, I am ready to go; and before I die I desire to thank you with all my heart for your kindness to me. Doctor, you are a Jew, you do not believe in Jesus; will you please stand here and see me die, trusting my Savior to the last moment of my life?" I tried to stay, but I could not; for I had not the courage to stand by and see a Christian boy die rejoicing in the love of a Jesus whom I had been taught to hate, so I hurriedly left the room. About twenty minutes later a steward, who found me sitting in my private office covering my face with my hand, said, "Doctor, Charlie Coulson wishes to see you."

"I have just seen him," I answered, "and I cannot see him again."

"But, doctor, he says he must see you once more before he dies." I now made up my mind to see him, say an endearing word, and let him die; but I was determined that no word of his should influence me in the least so far as his Jesus was concerned.

When I entered the hospital, I saw he was sinking fast, so I sat down by his bed. Asking me to take his hand, he said, " Doctor, I love you because you are a Jew; the best friend I have found in this world was a Jew." I asked him who that was. He answered: "Jesus Christ, to whom I want to introduce you before I die; and will you promise me, doctor, that what I am about to say to you, you will never forget?" I promised; and he said: "Five days ago, while you amputated my arm and leg, I prayed to the Lord Jesus Christ to convert your soul."

These words went deep into my heart. I could not understand how, when I was causing him the most intense pain, he could forget all about himself and think of nothing but his Savior and my unconverted soul. All I could say to him was: "Well, my dear boy, you will soon be all right." With these words I left him, and twelve minutes later he fell asleep, "safe in the arms of Jesus."

Hundreds of soldiers died in my hospital during the war; but I only followed one to the grave, and that one was Charlie Coulson, the drummer boy; and I rode three miles to see him buried. I had him dressed in a new uniform, and placed in an officer's coffin, with a United States flag over it.

That boy's dying words made a deep impression upon me. I was rich at that time so far as money is concerned, but I would have given every penny I possessed if I could have felt towards Christ as Charlie did; but that feeling cannot be bought with money. Alas! I soon forgot all about my Christian soldier's little sermon, but I could not forget the boy himself. I now know that at that time I was under deep conviction of sin; but I fought against Christ with all the hatred of an orthodox Jew for nearly ten years, until, finally, the dear boy's prayer was answered, and God converted my soul.

Eighteen months after my conversion, I attended a prayer meeting in Brooklyn. It was a testimony meeting. After several had spoken, an elderly lady arose, "Dear friends, this may be the last time that it is my privilege to testify ... My physician told me yesterday that my right lung is nearly gone, and my left lung is very much affected; so at the best I have short time ... Oh! it is a great joy to know that I shall meet my boy with Jesus in heaven ..." What the elderly woman said next was sobering. "My son was ... wounded at the battle of Gettysburg, and fell into the hands of a Jewish doctor, who amputated his arm and leg, but he lived five days after the operation. The Chaplain ... wrote me a letter, and sent me my boy's Bible. In that letter I was informed that my Charlie in his dying hour sent for that Jewish doctor, and said to him "Doctor, before I die I wish to tell you that five days ago, while you amputated my arm and leg, I prayed to the Lord Jesus Christ to convert your soul."

When I heard this testimony, I could sit still no longer. I left my seat, crossed the room and taking the hand of Charlie's mother, I said "God bless you, my dear sister; your boy's prayer has been heard and answered. I am the Jewish doctor for whom your Charlie prayed, and his Savior is now my Savior."

S. B. Shaw, "Charlie Coulson, The Christian Drummer Boy," *Touching Incidents And Remarkable Answers To Prayer* (Grand Rapids, MI: S.B. Shaw, Publisher, 1893), 18-19.

CHAPTER 5

PRAYER - BALANCING INTIMACY AND IMMANENCE

P. Douglas Small

We were made for intimacy with God, and that is the essence, the very heart of prayer. But a detached view of intimacy, one without the recognition that we remain mortals prone to sin, relating to a holy God; that we are in a world under wrath, yet we are gifted with a bubble of grace; that the God who is our Father is also Utterly Other and King of the Universe - can lead to a decidedly subjective relationship with God and the loss of biblical objectivity altogether.

First, intimacy and our sense of God's immanence must not eclipse transcendence. Pentecostals and evangelicals speak of the 'felt Presence' of God. *'Experiencing God'* has become a popular term following the release of the wonderful study by Southern Baptists leaders, Henry Blackaby and Claude King. The *transcendence* of God refers to His loftiness, His utter-otherness, His being 'past finding out.' He can be known, but not fully known. He is Father, and yet, the Exalted and Unapproachable One. He is both supreme and incomparable. There is an infinite distance between men and God. We are like Him, created by Him; and yet, there is none like Him (Isaiah 40; 55:8-9; 57:15; 66:1-2; and Acts 7:46-50).

Second, consider the question, "What is the one word that you would use to describe and define God?" Most folks say almost automatically – "Love." They are wrong – indeed, the whole culture seems to be wrong about its view of God. The current cultural drum-roll is for a God who loves all, unconditionally, without standards and without demands. But it is not His love that most clearly defines God, but His *holiness*. We see this aspect of God in reference to moral purity, but it is primarily about His *infinite otherness*. The holiness of God is what makes Him *transcendentally autonomous*. He is utterly holy and wholly entire. His Holiness is not a mere attribute among others – it is the ultimate descriptor of God. Everything else proceeds from His Holiness – His love, truth, His power, grace and wrath, mercy and judgment. The word holy, *qadosh*, actually means 'cut off,' or 'separate.' It is the idea that God is in a class all by Himself, unlike any other creature or created thing. Arthur Pink says He is "solitary in His majesty, unique in His excellency, peerless in His perfections."[1]

Third, intimacy cannot be allowed to degenerate into lightness. The loss of solemnity in worship, at the Lord's table (I Corinthians 11:20-34), "Our God is a consuming fire" (Heb. 12:29), is a neglected notion; eclipsed by a flippant, 'Come boldly into His presence...' (Heb. 4:16). Worship cannot be a matter of mood or affect, nor can prayer. As we are reminded with the earlier example of Nehemiah, our emotional state is to be tempered by the court of the king! The church today prefers intimate terms for God, rather than referring to Him as 'the Almighty,' or the 'Ancient of Days.' Or even yet, "His Holiness!' In a culture that is uncomfortable with God, we dare not dress Him down to make Him 'one of the guys.'

Fourth, the subjective cannot displace the objective. Overwhelmed with the *fruit* of grace, we cannot forget the *work* of grace. Our new life is tied to His death. Our liberation from judgment is not because God has chosen arbitrarily to overlook and casually forgive our sin,

---

1   Arthur Pink, *The Attributes of God* (Grand Rapids: Guardian Press, 1975), 11.

but because Christ took our sin and judgment. Our acceptance in heaven is tied to His rejection and crucifixion. The cross was not merely about God's love, but about the truth of sin – 'Sins wages really are death! And God is no respecter of persons. Sin found on His Son gained no exemption from penalty.' To detach the subjective and emotional experience we have from the redemptive work of the cross is a grave mistake. "Christ lives in me; and the life which I now live in the flesh I live by faith in the Son of God, who loved me, and delivered Himself up for me" (Phil. 2:20). The life of Christ *in* us is rooted in the death of Christ *for* us. Our subjective experiences with God must have their roots in the objective record of biblical history. Moments with God are powerful, but their profound nature is not merely existential, but is found in the explanation in the Scripture itself which explains the basis, the source, and the dynamic profile of their power.

Fifth, the perennial emphasis on love, on the subjective, on relationship feelings and impressions, can drift to detachment from the Scripture as the final interpreter, jurist and the objective guide for such experiences. The Scripture itself is full of examples of men who approached God on their own terms or failed to comply with His requisites or thought themselves exempt – Cain, Nadab and Abihu (Lev. 16:12), the sons of Eli, Uzzah, the Baal worshippers. It can be fatal to approach God on one's own terms.

Sixth, intimacy with God, and 'oneness' or unity with Him must be understood as happening in the context of a monoplueric covenant. God dictates all the terms of the encounter. This is not a partnership between equals, though God treats us as intimates – that is a bequest of His gracious nature, and one about which we must dare not become presumptuous. Ancient mystics and modern day charismatics, though in different ways, often blur the line between the Creator and the creature. We are one with God, by the blood of Christ, upon the forgiveness of sin, joined to His holy nature, sanctified and launched into a process of transformation that we might be 'like Him.' That union, spiritual and moral, is focused on thoughts and behaviors; it is not *metaphysical.* Though we are destined to "become *like* God" and are now agents of His Word and work, we are not destined, in this life or that to come, to "*become* God." Thus, prophetic words, quickened by the Spirit and uttered by us are *potent,* but they are not *omnipotent.* We must not lose sight with the idea that He is God and we are not!

Seventh, familiarity with God due to an aberrant emphasis upon intimacy can lead us to a 'cheap grace' posture. The moment we see privileges as rights, we are in trouble. The loss of humility, and the presumption that God 'owes' us something, the failure to always honor the price paid for us that restored the relationship – these are critical components to our own spiritual health and vitality. Only when we remember that the world in which we live, the house – Adam's house – in which we grew up, is under wrath, and by grace we escaped, only against that backdrop do we have the proper attitude of gratitude so needed to come before God.

The 'Gift' of the Fear of God

One of the unique features of Christianity and Judaism among world religions is the idea that God is to be feared. Aquinas, in the *Summa Theologica*, considered the fear of the Lord to be among seven gifts of the Spirit, the others being – wisdom, understanding, counsel, fortitude, knowledge, piety. The *"Novena to the Holy Spirit for the Seven Gifts"* says the fear of the Lord is:

> The gift of fear fills us with a sovereign respect for God and makes us dread nothing so much as to offend Him by sin. It is a fear that arises, not from the thought of hell, but from

sentiments of reverence and filial submission to our Heavenly Father. It is the fear that is the beginning of wisdom, detaching us from worldly pleasures that could in any way separate us from God. They that fear the Lord will prepare their hearts, and in His sight will sanctify their souls.

The New International Version tends to substitute 'reverence' for 'fear' in its translation in order to indicate that what is meant is more than simple fear. In Scriptural encounters with God, one meets Him at the intersection of adoration and worship, along with holy awe and unspeakable reverence, mesmerizing glory and paralyzing power – and in those is found the idea of the fear of the Lord. One is simultaneously awestruck, speechless, defenseless, exposed, utterly vulnerable and yet magnetically drawn, compelled and simultaneously free.

The fear of the Lord is linked to wonder and awe, an awareness of the glory and majesty of God who is the essence of perfection - perfect knowledge, perfect goodness, perfect power, and perfect love. It is here, on this ground, that humans are separated from God; He, as were ancient kings reflecting an earthly version of His throne, is placed in an altogether different class than others. Aquinas calls this "filial fear," which is differentiated from "servile fear." The first is *filial,* from *filius,* meaning son, and is what a child would experience with reference to offending his father. The second is from the Latin *servus,* meaning slave, and is of a lesser quality, it is a mere fear of retribution. The first is concerned about the relationship; the second is preoccupied in a narrow self-interested way with consequences. The first is disappointed with self in a nobler sense. The valued honor and name of the father as well as the family are at stake, and the regret is profound; the second is not looking at long-term effects of behavior, only this moment, only the avoidance of penalty. The regret here is that one was caught.

The fear of the Lord is said to be the beginning of wisdom (Proverbs 1:7). Proverbs 9:10 adds, "... and the knowledge of the Holy One is understanding." Such reverence positions us to begin the learning process – as finite, dependent creatures. It is foundational. Thomas Aquinas says that wisdom, understanding, knowledge, and counsel are cognitive; while fortitude, piety, and the fear of the Lord are volitional. The fear of the Lord "fills us with a sovereign respect for God, and makes us dread, above all things, to offend Him." This is essential for a healthy prayer life. Psalms 130:3-4 declares,

> *If you, O Lord, kept a record of sins, O Lord, who could stand? But with you there is forgiveness; therefore you are feared.*

The "fear of the Lord" is combined with our disdain of evil (8:13). It is said to prolong life (10:27), and out of it flows confidence and life itself (14:26-27). It motivates us to forsake evil (16:6). It satisfies life (19:23) and is the gateway to honor and wealth (22:4). Absent the appropriate fear of the Lord, human knowledge devolves to foolishness and lives are cut short. We lose our own sense of dignity and devalue ourselves along with life. The quality of our life languishes and with that, satisfaction of life ebbs. We act in less than honorable ways. We make decisions that are costly in measurable ways. We flirt and consort with evil and thereby destruction. We stop growing spiritually. We lose our respect for the laws and God, and moral restraint. Notice, the ethical-practical[2] are bound together. The fear of God has an ethical dimension – it keeps us clean; but that bears practical fruit. Not only is the fear of the Lord the basis of our pleasing Him (Isa. 66:1-2); it is also the basis for sound human relationships. Further, it is the basis of His mercy – only the one who 'trembles at His Word' is promised mercy (Psalm 103:17-18). And

---

2   Jerry Bridges, *The Joy of Fearing God* (Colorado Springs, CO: Waterbrook Press, 1997), 6.

practically, he who shows mercy; receives mercy (Matthew 5:7).

Jeremiah 5:22 (NIV) asks, "'Should you not fear me?' declares the Lord. 'Should you not tremble in my presence?'" In Hebrew the term *yirah* (Jonah 1:16; Psalm 90:11) and *yare* (Malachi 3:16) along with *pachad* (Job 3:25; Psalm 119:120) indicate a reverent fear. The Hebrew terms used for mere respect are *kabad* (Ex 20:12). In Greek, the word for fear is *phobo* (Matthew 28:4; I Pet 2:17). And the idea of reverence or honor is conveyed by *timao* (I Pet. 2:17).

Job links the fear of God to His *sovereignty.*

> *"But He stands alone and who can oppose Him? He does whatever He pleases. He carries out His decree against me and many such plans He still has in store. That is why I am terrified before Him; when I think of all this, I fear Him. God has made my heart faint; the Almighty has terrified me."*

A healthy respect for God motivates us to bear fruit (John 15:2). It keeps us clean morally (II Cor. 7:1). It moves us to hate evil (Prov. 8:13; 16:6). And it leads to repentance (Job 28:28). It moves us to take the high road (Psalm 25:12-14). It is the source of life, a protector from the deadly snares (Proverbs 14:26-27; 19:23). It is a place of provision (Psalm 34:9). It is a place of balance, between the kindness of God and His severe judgment (Romans 11:22).

We have forgotten that it is a "fearful thing to fall into the hands of the living God" (Hebrews 10:31 KJV). The writer of Hebrews observes that the New Testament believers have not had to approach a burning mountain, mid-day blackness, a deafening piercing sound like a trumpet, thunder and lightning. He reminds them that when Israel had such a moment, they begged for it to end. They have not been invited to Sinai. Indeed, God in Christ, has mediated a new covenant (12:18-24). This does not lower the bar, however. Israel, in the wilderness refused to hear, and experienced judgment. Soberly, he notes, if under such grace afforded us, "How shall be escape if we neglect so great a salvation?"

We are living between the times – Christ has come, as a lamb, to receive our due wrath for us; but He will come again as a lion. "Yet once more will I make to tremble, not the earth only, but also the heaven." There is coming a final shaking, and everything that is merely made will fold. Only the unshakable things will endure. And then he urges, "Let us serve God with thankfulness in ways that please Him, and always with reverence and holy fear, for our God is a consuming fire" (12:25-29). The writer of Proverbs reminds us, "Better *a little* [of this world's wealth and comfort] with the fear of the LORD, than great wealth with turmoil. Better a meal of vegetables where there is love than a fattened calf with hatred," (Prov. 15:16-17 NIV). Note the pairings: fear and love; wealth with turmoil and a fattened calf with hatred contrasted with 'little' and 'a meal of vegetables.' The implication is that true wealth is the individual with a healthy fear of God. Where God is feared, others are loved.

Biblical Moments and the Fear of God

The Bible's first implicit mention of the *fear of God* is in Genesis 3, when Adam and Eve hid and covered themselves after partaking of the forbidden fruit. The first explicit reference is in 22:12. There, Abraham is applauded for his faith. And fear, along with reverence and awe is linked to that faith. Worldly fear is always the nemesis of faith. When fear comes, faith flees, as does our awareness of God's presence. "Even though I walk through the valley of the shadow of death, I will not fear, for you are with me" (Psalm 23:4). His Presence keeps fear at bay. Godly fear is the gateway to greater faith. The writer of Hebrews observes,

> *"Abraham, when he was tested, offered up Isaac, and he who had received the promises was in the act of offering up his only son, of*

> *whom it was said, 'Through Isaac shall your offspring be named.' He considered that God was able even to raise him from the dead, from which he did receive him back" (Heb. 11:17-19).*

It is often stated that Abraham's fear of God was an act of trust and the root of his obedience, even in the face of the life of his son. However, the nobler idea is that the fear of God is devotion itself, a necessary discipline in our disposition, rather than a momentary sense of fright. The fear of God in Proverbs 8:13 is connected with "the hatred of evil." The scripture connects it to numerous rewards and its absence to divine retribution.

Abraham's weak moment came in Genesis 20, when Abimelech, a provincial king sent fear through his heart. The king evidently did as he pleased, and had the women of his choice. Abraham felt vulnerable, "Surely there is no fear of God in this place," (10-11). Most of us have had such an uneasy feeling about a place and its people. "They will kill me because of my wife," he believed. In a sad moment in this life, he thought more about himself than Sarah, identifying as his sister (v. 1), to make himself less a target. God warned Abimelech in a dream! For a moment, Abraham feared men more than God; but he was correct in the connection between the absence of the fear of God and a resulting moral disconnect.

In Egypt, as Moses negotiated the release of Israel from bondage, the great obstacle in the parleys with Pharaoh was the absence of his fear of God, "Who is the LORD, that I should obey and let Israel go? I do not know the LORD and I will not let Israel go," (Exodus 5:2). God would give Pharaoh, Egypt and their gods, ten lessons on His superiority! Ten needless episodes of national pain. Every plague was paired with an offering of mercy and grace, and their sad resistance to prophetic pleas compelled the action of YHWH against their gods. Had Pharaoh possessed the appropriate fear of God, and heeded his prophet, no harm would have come to Egypt or his people.

When God brought Israel out of Egypt, He gathered them at the base of Mt. Sinai. The mountain was alive with fire, the evidence of His presence. It was smoking. It shook and trembled, the ground under them vibrating. Lightning danced all around them. It was the Lord's moment of disclosure. They had seen the plagues. They had seen the sea driven back by the wind, and held at bay as they crossed, then mysteriously released to cover the Egyptian army. But now they were beginning to see the forces behind the wild and mysterious wonders, YHWH himself. Here, He would forge a covenant with them. Here He would designate them as His priestly nation, a kingdom of priests to all the nations of the world. Here He would allow them to know Him – but that was possible only if they embraced a fear, a reverence; only if they knew the incomparable nature of His Deity, the unfathomable scope of his power, the immeasurable intensity of His power.

In the days of Eli, the high priest, the absence of fear had produced an immoral and exploitive priesthood, a hatred of sacrifices and a disdain for worship, and the nation found itself in midst of military losses. Eli the high priest dropped dead and his two priestly sons died in a battle that claimed thirty-thousand men of Israel. The wife of Phineas, on hearing of the death of Eli and the capture of the ark, died giving birth, but not before she named the child Ichabod, meaning the glory of the Lord is departed (I Samuel 4:14-22). With Ichabod pronounced over the land, the ark captured, the Most Holy Place empty and the glory of God gone, Samuel would inherit the difficult job of calling the nation back to an appropriate fear of God. He urged renewal in the nation. The Bible said, "Samuel called to the LORD, and the LORD sent thunder and rain that day..." He prayed, and God answered. He prayed, and God sent rain. The connection between prayer and the obvious answer, the elements of nature responding was so convincing that "all the people greatly feared the LORD" and they also feared Samuel (I Samuel 12:18). There could be no national renewal without a national reverence of God, then or now.

The name Jehoshaphat means 'Jehovah has judged.' He was the fourth king of Judah, and he was a godly king. But, he made a covenant with Ahab and the northern kingdom of Israel by marriage (II Chronicles 18:1). And he allowed himself, against the advice of the prophet Micaiah, to go to war against Syria. In that battle, he almost lost his life and Ahab was killed. His army was soundly defeated and scattered, and Jehoshaphat returned home relieved to be alive. Barely back in Jerusalem, he was confronted by Jehu the prophet, "Should you help the wicked and love those who hate the Lord? Because of this, the wrath of the Lord is on you" (II Chronicles 19:1). Jehoshaphat had narrowly escaped the arrows of the Syrians only to find himself in the cross-hairs of God's judgment, a greater dilemma. Without an appropriate fear of God, he would have dismissed the prophet's warning, but the king got the message. He became an evangelist, going throughout the land "from Beersheba to the mountains of Ephraim" with a heart prepared to seek God. He "went out again among the people and brought them back to the Lord God of their fathers." What follows are amazing reforms in the judiciary (vv. 5-8), "city by city." All decisions were to be in reference to the fear of the Lord, without partiality or bribes. He proceeded to reform the priesthood and the Levitical system. He appointed Levites and priests, and chief fathers charging them, "Thus you shall act in the fear of the Lord, faithfully and with a loyal heart" (v. 9). He was calling the entire nation to renew its fear of the Lord.

Notice the movement of the passage. In II Chronicles 18, he was almost killed and his army soundly defeated. In chapter 20, he is again confronted with war – but in the intervening time period, he had instituted reforms that demonstrated his fear of the Lord.

Now, facing another international conflict, "Jehoshaphat feared, and set himself to seek the LORD, and proclaimed a fast throughout all Judah" (II Chronicles 20:3). With a renewed and appropriate fear, the nation joins in prayer – and the battle is won. In fact, they do not fight alone. Angels fight with them. One battle is lost; another is won – the difference, the fear of God with evident action.

Hezekiah too became careless with the Lord. With his life hanging in the balance, he was moved by a holy fear to seek the Lord. And "the Lord relented concerning the doom" (Jeremiah 26:19).

By the time of Malachi, the renewals under Zechariah and Haggai, Nehemiah and Ezra, had waned. Crippled animals were offered at the temple. Tithe was withheld. Marriage was disregarded. Ethics were lacking. They were blind to the favor of God on their lives. They viewed faith only in terms of how it benefited them. Malachi put his finger on the problem, "A son honors his father, And a servant his master. If then I am the Father, Where is My honor? And if I am a Master, Where is My reverence?" Where is your fear of the Lord? (Malachi 1:6). Notice, first he references filial fear – respectful reverence and honor by a son of his father; then, servile fear. In this case, neither is present. The absence of fear produced unthinkable aberrations in their worship, their marriages, the money management, and their ethics. And notice this, Malachi begins with the mention of the father and ends with it.

Whenever the people of God stray and become hard-hearted, the remedy of God is a gracious restoration of reverence.

> *"So will I choose their delusions, And bring their fears on them; Because, when I called, no one answered, When I spoke they did not hear; But they did evil before My eyes, And chose that in which I do not delight" (Isaiah 66:3-5).*

The path to decadence and backsliding is the loss of reverence; and the gate to revival is a restoration of the fear of God. Peter reminds us that when we call upon the Father, we should remember that He judges without partiality. He urges us to live in fear or reverence before such a God (I Peter 1:16-18). The psalmist declared, "My flesh trembles for fear of You, And I am afraid of Your judgments" (Psalm 119:120). Jeremiah, knowing that Judah will soon disappear as a nation, due to their sins, asked them the question of God, "'Do you not fear Me?' says the LORD. 'Will you not tremble at My presence ...'" The root of the sin that drove the abominations, the rebellion, and their lack of repentance was the absence of the fear of God. Jeremiah presents God as the Creator and manager of nature who "placed the sand as the bound of the sea, by a perpetual decree, that it cannot pass ... though its waves toss to and fro, Yet they cannot prevail; Though they roar, yet they cannot pass over it'" (Jeremiah 5:22). The one who controls the force and fury of nature will soon loose wrath on Judah – but they do not tremble at such a prospect.

God would not fully abandon the people, even though they temporarily lost their nation. He looked forward to a time of renewal when the nation would be to Him "a name of joy, a praise and an honor before all nations of the earth," and because of the joy that the renewed nation would bring, He would bless. And these blessings were a kind of global broadcast: the earth "shall hear all the good that I do." And the outcome was that nations "shall fear and tremble for all the goodness and all the prosperity that I provide for it [Judah]" (Jeremiah 33:9). Reverence and fear are God's bottom line.

> *"And now, Israel, what does the LORD your God require of you, but to fear the LORD your God, to walk in all His ways and to love Him, to serve the LORD your God ..." (Deuteronomy 10:12).*

This is not an Old Testament matter. Peter urges, "Fear God" (I Peter 2:17). Jude, the brother of Jesus warned that infiltrators had penetrated the fellowship of the church and virtually were undetected. He called them 'spots' in the love feasts, dangerous apostates. The word is *spilas*, the term used to cause a ship to spill its contents, a hidden ledge of rock, a reef just under the surface of the water over which the sea dashed. The term was used of men who by their conduct damaged others morally, wrecked them. Their most telling mark is that they "feast with you without fear," a reference to the table of the Lord in the context of a larger fellowship meal. The fruit of their lack of reverence is that they "serve only themselves." The absence of the fear of God renders them as impotent, as empty clouds with no hope of rain; as autumn trees void of fruit, twice dead and rootless (Jude 1:12). Jude gives the image of these men as being blown about by the winds, an inference of the spirit world.

John Murray says, "The fear of God is the soul of godliness."[3] Jerry Bridges in his wonderful book, *The Joy of Fearing God,* says "the fear of God is the animating and invigorating principle of a godly life. It is the wellspring of all godly desires and aspirations."[4] Murray calls it "… the reflux in our consciousness of the transcendent majesty and holiness of God."[5]

When the disciples were on the sea with Jesus, He stilled the winds and calmed the storm, and Mark notes, "And they feared exceedingly, and said to one another, 'Who can this be, that even the wind and the sea obey Him!'" (Mark 4:41). This is not a fear of the storm, but a fear of Jesus. Paul urges obedience on the believers at Philippi. They were to work out their salvation with 'fear and trembling' (Philippians 2:12). He urges servants to obey their masters not only when they are looking, as men-pleasers, but in a more genuine manner, from the heart, in the fear of God (Col. 3:22).

---

3   John Murray, *Principles of Conduct* (Grand Rapids: MI; Eerdmans, 1957), 229.

4   Bridges, 25.

5   Murray, 236-237; Bridges, 25.

It is the eyes of God that employees are to remember.

Deuteronomy 13:4 gives us the fruit of an appropriate fear of God. Men who fear Him, "walk after the LORD .... keep His commandments and obey His voice ... [they] serve Him and hold fast to Him." The great failure of King Saul was that he feared the people more than the feared the Lord (I Samuel 15:24). That fear manifest as obedience; whom you fear, you obey. Isaiah 50:10 equates the two – fear and obedience – as conjoined. Such a person, the prophet says, 'has no light.' The renewal under Haggai and Zechariah, prophets; Joshua, the high priest; and Zerubbabel, the civil leader is rooted in a restoration of the fear of the Lord. " ... all the remnant of the people, obeyed the voice of the LORD their God, and the words of Haggai the prophet, as the LORD their God had sent him; and the people feared the presence of the LORD" (Haggai 1:12).

The Fruit of the Fear of the Lord

In the Old Testament, the fear of the Lord is connected to great joy. Proverbs 28:14 declares, "Happy is the one who fears always." Psalm 130:4 notes, "Forgiveness comes from you – therefore you are feared." Grace then, does not dismiss fear, it increases it. In fact, we are to develop, to grow in this fear and reverence of the Lord. Or, to express the concept differently – a signature of spiritual maturity is found in the depth of awe and fear one has before God (II Chronicles 26:5; Psalm 34:11). And yet, this fear does not stand alone. It is accompanied by a delight of God, by a sense of wonder (Psalm 40:3; Isaiah 11:3). If the fear about which we spoke here was servile fear, a mere dread, a self-interested fear, it would have been dismissed by the act of forgiveness. But in Scripture, it increases (cf. Psalm 130).

The fear of the Lord is not merely subjective, that is, it is not about us – but rather, it is a characterization of the awe-filled relationship with the incomparable God. "Is He safe?" the question is asked of Aslan, the Lion figure in the *The Lion, the Witch, and the Wardrobe*, "Course He isn't safe," we are told – He is not safe, "But He's good. He's the king, I tell you."[6] To walk with God is to walk with One by whom we are overwhelmed. It is to be with One before whom we never lose our sense of wonder. It is to understand, increasingly by us that nothing compares to His greatness. It means that we grow in an appreciation for His holiness and awareness of our own depth of sin; and only thereby do we understand His love and mercy. Before such grace one trembles. Such grace constrains us (II Corinthians 5:14). It urges holiness upon us.

Jesus would say,

> *"Be not afraid of them that kill the body, and after that have no more that they can do. But I will forewarn you whom you shall fear: Fear Him, which after He has killed hath power to cast into hell; yea, I say unto you, Fear Him ... the very hairs of your head are all numbered. Fear not therefore: you are of more value than many sparrows. Also I say unto you, Whosoever shall confess me before men, him shall the Son of man also confess before the angels of God: But he that denies me before men shall be denied before the angels of God" (Luke 12:4-9).*

Psalm 19:9 says, "the fear of the Lord is pure, enduring forever." One common translation says, "the fear of the Lord – keeps me clean." The 'fear of the Lord' was a staple phrase, a component of the Old Testament piety. It was expected. And as we noted earlier, Aquinas saw it as an essential for New Testament believers as well.

The idea that 'fear' is associated with Sinai and Law, and is dismissed by grace is flawed theology. Isaiah 11:3 had foretold that the Messiah would "delight in the fear of the Lord." Paul reminds

---

6   C. S. Lewis, *The Lion, the Witch, and the Wardrobe* (Hammondsworth, Middlesex, England: Penguin Books, 1950), 75.

us that the path to depravity begins with the loss of the fear of God, "there is no fear of God before their eyes" (Rom. 3:18, quoting Psalm 36). John Calvin noted:

> All wickedness flows from a disregard of God ... Since the fear of God is the bridle by which our wickedness is held in check, its removal frees us to indulge in every kind of licentious conduct.[7]

On the cross, we can hear the repentant thief rebuking his dying counterpart, "Do you not fear God?" (Luke 23:40). He didn't. He was blind. Jesus characterized injustice as rising from a bench occupied by an irreligious judge, who "neither fears God" and He notes the corollary, "nor cares about men" (Luke 18:2). The two are bound together. Restraint, respect for those created in the image of God is possible only if there is respect for the Creator. Dismiss God, and you lose the race of men.

The New Testament Church walked in the fear of the Lord. Luke says,

> *"Then had the churches rest throughout all Judaea and Galilee and Samaria, and were edified; and walking in the fear of the Lord, and in the comfort of the Holy Ghost, were multiplied." (Ac 9:31).*

These people knew it necessary to "live in the fear of the Lord" (Acts 9:31). Christ had risen from the dead – and they were awestruck. They heard the wind and saw the fire in the Upper Room, and they were not the same. The Spirit poured upon the church is noted by Isaiah's prophecy as the Spirit of Christ, and therefore, the Spirit of the fear of the Lord. John Murray wrote, "The fear of God is the soul of godliness ... If we are thinking of the [marks] of biblical piety, none is more characteristic than the fear of the Lord."[8]

---

7   John Calvin, "The Epistles of Paul to the Romans and Thessalonians," Vol. 8; *New Testament Commentaries* (Grand Rapids: Eerdmans, 1980), 67.

8   Murray, 229.

Mary, the mother of Jesus connected mercy and fear, "His mercy extends to those who fear Him" (Luke 1:50). Paul said that "holiness" was perfected "in the fear of God" (II Cor. 7:1 RSV), and he urged them to "work out your salvation with fear and trembling" (Phil. 2:12), and also to "be subject to one another in the fear of Christ" (Eph. 5:21 NASB). Peter likewise urged, "love the brotherhood of believers, fear God, honor the king" (I Pet. 2:17), and "live your lives as strangers here in reverent fear" (I Pet. 1:17).

Restoring the Lost Fear of God

1. *The Seventh Year National Education Campaign.* In Deuteronomy 31:10-13, Israel was instructed to gather during the seventh year, a Sabbath year, to again read and hear the Word. Israel never celebrated a Sabbath year. Increasingly, they resisted the celebration of the Sabbath day. The purpose of the Sabbath year was for them to leave the routine of life, and give themselves to a season of revisiting the words of the covenant, "...that they may learn to fear the Lord." If they became too detached from Scripture, they would lose their respect for God, they would cease seeing God as unique and exceptional. Consequently, they would drift toward idolatry. The seasons in which they broke from the cycle of normal life and refocused on God could be arguably termed forced 'revival' and renewal moments in their history. Sadly, they never tried God's way, and they became like the nations around them.

   "God is greatly to be feared in the assembly of the saints, and to be had in reverence of all [them that are] about Him" (Psalms 89:7).

2. *The Missed Promises.* The writer of Hebrews warns,

   "Let us therefore fear, lest, a promise being left [us] of entering into His rest, any of you should seem to come short of it. For unto us was the gospel preached, as well as unto

them: but the word preached did not profit them, not being mixed with faith in them that heard [it]." Hebrews 4:1-2.

"Let us labor therefore to enter into that rest, lest any man fall after the same example of unbelief" Hebrews 4:11.

Paul urges,

"Having therefore these promises, dearly beloved, let us cleanse ourselves from all filthiness of the flesh and spirit, perfecting holiness in the fear of God" II Cor. 7:1.

3. *The Necessary Perspective of God.* Healthy fear of the Lord is associated with a reverence and awe of God, *"Let all the earth fear the Lord, and let all the inhabitants of the world be in awe of Him"* (Psalm 33:8). This God is almighty and awesome (Psalm 47:7), a God of power (Joshua 4:23-24) and majesty (Jeremiah 10:7), as well as justice (Revelation 14:7) with holiness (15:4). According to Scripture, His blessings (Psalm 67:7) and goodness (I Sam. 12:24), even His forgiveness (Psa. 130:4), are reasons to 'fear' Him. *"For thus says the High and Exalted One who inhabits eternity, whose name is Holy: I dwell in a high and holy place, and also with the contrite and humble in spirit, to revive the spirit of the humble and to revive the spirit of the contrite"* (Isaiah 57:15).

    Sinclair Ferguson calls filial fear "that indefinable mixture of reverence, fear, pleasure, joy and awe which fills our hearts when we realize who God is and what He has done for us."[9]

4. *The Motivation to Holiness.* A healthy fear of God is associated with a necessary hatred of evil as well. *"The fear of the Lord is to hate evil"* (Proverbs 8:13). Exodus 18:21 equates a fear of God with a disdain for covetousness. Job feared God and turned from evil (Job 1:1, 8; see also Prov. 3:7). If we hate evil, we will avoid it (Proverbs 16:6; Job 28:28).

---

9   Sinclair Ferguson, *Grow in Grace* (Colorado Springs: NavPress, 1984), 35.

5. *The Corollary Respect for Other Humans.* The loss of the fear of God is the root to a loss of respect for everyone and everything else. Isaiah 8:11-13,

    > *The Lord spoke to me with His strong hand upon me, warning me not to follow the way of this people. He said: "Do not call conspiracy everything that these people call conspiracy; do not fear what they fear, and do not dread it. The Lord Almighty is the one you are to regard as holy, He is the one you are to fear, He is the one you are to dread, and He will be a sanctuary."*

6. *The Sagging Credibility of the Church.* The moral descent of the modern church is without a doubt associated with the absence of an appropriate fear of God. It affects our witness as well, since it is difficult to appropriately represent a God who we do not deeply respect. Jerry Bridges observed, "There was a time when committed Christians were known as God-fearing people. This was a badge of honor. But somewhere along the way we lost it. Now the idea of fearing God, if thought of at all, seems like a relic from the past."[10]

    When Isaiah cried out, "Woe is me ... I am undone!" It was not a merely humanity in the presence of God to which he reacted; it was a heightened sense of moral consciousness in the presence of moral purity and excellence.[11] John Calvin urged that his followers be "empty of all opinion of our own virtue, and shorn of all assurance of our righteousness – in fact, broken and crushed by our awareness of our own utter poverty."[12] Jesus called the 'blessed' life one in which we were 'poor in spirit.' This is a recognition of our moral and spiritual poverty before God. The church today attempts to stand on their own merit; the ancient saints were wont to fall humbly before God's excellence.

7. *The Cultural Bias.* Moderns scratch their head at the idea of

---

10 Bridges, 1.
11 H. H. Rowley, *The Faith of Israel* (SCM, 1956), 66.
12 John Calvin, *Institutes of the Christian Religion,* 367.

fearing a loving and compassionate God. The idea is often misunderstood. In Isaiah 2:10, 19 and 21, we find a hopeless dread in the face of God's inflexible justice. It is often rendered as "the terror of the Lord" (RSV). The Hebrew word used is *pachad*, indicating a terror. In the Revelation, there is a parallel passage (6:15-17) where evil men attempt hide from God. This is a repelling fear. Christians are "not appointed to wrath" (I Thessalonians 5:9). The Lord has redeemed, justified and sanctified those who met Him at the Cross. They are not the children of wrath. *"There is therefore now no condemnation to those who are in Christ Jesus"* (Romans 8:1). John 4:17-18 says "In this way love is perfected among us, so that we will have confidence on the Day of Judgment, because in this world we are like Him. There is no fear in love, for perfect love casts out fear, because fear has to do with punishment. The one who fears is not made perfect in love." The "fear of the Lord" is not about such terror. John declares that those who fear God's wrath have a love deficit.

8. *Fear as Reverent Awe.* When the New Testament declares in I John 4:18 that "Perfect love drives out fear," what is in view is the dread of eternal torment. While that 'fear' of punitive action is gone, from those who are saved by grace, reverent awe naturally increases. In the song of Moses and of the Lamb, we hear heaven declare, "Who will not fear you, O Lord, and bring glory to your name? For you alone are holy" (Rev. 15:4). This is not a fear driven by wrath – but by the sense of what He saved us from, and a recognition that to turn back to sin, is sure destruction. Jesus says, *"If you love Me, you will keep my commandments"* (John 14:15). Obedience springs from love.

    Fear and love are bound together.

    > *"Whoever has my commandments and keeps them is one who loves me, and whoever loves me shall be loved by My Father, and I will love him and will disclose Myself to him....If anyone loves Me, he will keep My word; and My*

Father will love him, and We will come to him and make our abode with him." David urges in Psalm 34 to *"Keep your tongue from evil, and your lips from speaking guile. Turn away from evil, and do good, seek peace and pursue it"* (vs. 14-15).

9. *Doing Good as an Expression of Reverence.* Turning from evil is connected here to doing good.

    John 14:21, 23. In this passage, Jesus lists the results of loving obedience. First, the Father determines to love us. In Psalm 103:17, "The loving-kindness of the Lord is from everlasting to everlasting to those who fear Him!" And Psalm 25:14 notes, "The secret of the Lord is for those who fear Him." The Hebrew word 'secret' denotes a confidential, intimate discourse among parties. God promises that we can 'make our abode' or dwell with Him, live in communion with Him. Indeed, God watches over and delivers those who fear Him (Ps 33:18). That affects the length and quality of life (61:5-7). Salvation is near such people (85:9) and they are blessed (112:19) because God satisfies and saves them (145:19). God does not forget them, but He claims them as His own and promises to spare them (Malachi 3:16-17). Upon them, the Sun of Righteousness rises (4:2) and His mercy extends over their families (Luke 1:50; see Proverbs 14:26-27).

    Psalm 97:10 says "Hate evil, you who love the Lord!" Love for God and holy fear are conjoined. To love God is to revere and celebrate His incomparable holiness. To love Him is to hate the evil that is contrary to God. The Holy Spirit is known as the "Spirit of Holy Fear" who gives the gift of the fear of the Lord. We should not test the patience of the Lord, for it still remains a fearful thing to fall into the hands of the living God (Heb. 10:31).

10. *Boldness before the World.* Isa 8:12-13 (NIV), "Do not fear what they [those in the world] fear, and do not dread it. The Lord Almighty is the one you are to regard as holy, He is

the one you are to fear, He is the one you are to *dread."Jesus declares* (Mat 10:28; NIV), "Do not be afraid of those who kill the body but cannot kill the soul. Rather, be afraid of the one who can destroy both soul and body in hell."

He modeled fear of the Lord. Fulfilling Isaiah 11:1-3, He was the 'shoot of the stump of Jesse ... the Branch that bore fruit." And the 'Spirit of the Lord,' of Yahweh, the blessing of God, the Father and Creator was on Him – it 'rested' on Him. It was the 'Spirit of wisdom and understanding ... counsel and power ... the knowledge of the fear of the Lord.' In fact, it was predicted of Jesus that He would "delight in the fear of the Lord."

Those who fear God, obey God. "*That he may learn to fear the Lord his God by carefully observing all the words of this law and these statutes*" (Deuteronomy 17:19). This is what drove Abraham to the mountain with Isaac (Genesis 22:12). Moses exhorted Israel, "*Fear the Lord...to walk in all His ways and love Him*" (Dt. 10:12, 20). Samuel also urged Israelites to "*fear the Lord and serve Him in truth with all your heart*" (I Samuel 12:24). Isaiah (50:10) connects the fear of God with obedience, as does Psalm 86:11; 112:1; 128:1 and Ecclesiastes 12:13. Moses sees the horizontal connection, "Show your fear of God by not taking advantage of each other. I am the LORD your God" (Leviticus 25:17 NLT). People who fear God, respect Him, and see Him looking over our shoulder, are restrained from mistreating others. They too, are made in His image.

Even demons shudder in fear before God (Jas. 2:19). And there is coming a day when "the kings of the earth, the princes, the generals, the rich, the mighty, and every slave and every free man" will hide "in caves and among the rocks of the mountains," and pray to the mountains and rocks, "Fall on us and hide us from the face of Him who sits on the throne and from the wrath of the Lamb! For the great day of their wrath has come, and who can stand?" (Rev. 6:15-17). For covenant breakers and apostates, "no sacrifice for sins is left, but only a fearful expectation of judgment and of raging fire that will consume the enemies of God" (Heb. 10:26-27).

The ultimate moment will be when the earth, and its inhabitants, come face-to-face with their true Creator, the One who has been ignored, displaced, whose existence has been denied, whose Messiah was rejected and crucified – and the reality comes that Yahweh is the true God.

Let all the earth fear the LORD; let all the people of the world revere Him (Psalm 33:8).

This is the Creator, by whom the heavens were made as well as the starry host (v. 6) by His mere word, even His breath (v. 9; 5). This God "foils the plans of the nations, He thwarts the purposes of the peoples ..." while His plans stand firm forever (v. 10-11).

In Psalm 34:11 (NEB), we are told, "Come, my children, listen to me; I will teach you the fear of the Lord." And in Psalm 89:7 (NIV), "In the council of the holy ones God is greatly feared." In Psalm 76:4, 7 (NIV), "You [O God] are resplendent with light ... You alone are to be feared." Paul in II Cor. 5:11 (NIV) says, "Since, then, we know what it is to fear the Lord, we try to persuade men."

The Church needs to become a gloriously dangerous place where nothing is safe in God's presence except us.

CHAPTER SIX

THE WRATH OF GOD AND PRAYER

A WINDOW THROUGH TIME

The 'house' of Adam cast their fate with that of the dark lord, Lucifer. In an act of disobedience, an evidence of their distrust of Yahweh, they tasted the deadly forbidden fruit of the knowledge of good polluted with evil, and Adam and his heirs became a slave of sin, all subject to death. The only alternative was for another Adam to come, one whose blood was not tainted, whose heart was pure and whose resolve had not been compromised; one not of the line of Adam.

Jesus came, born of woman, by the Holy Ghost. Christ came "as a Son over His own house, whose house we are if we hold fast the confidence and the rejoicing of the hope firm to the end" (Hebrews 3:6). This house is to be a house of refuge. It is also to be a house of prayer, "My house shall be called a house of prayer" (Mark 11:17). But, this 'house of prayer' was not established for one nation, but "for all nations?" Jesus was born into the house of Adam, a house under siege. Once he was identified, at his baptism, as the Son of God, Lucifer knew for certain, that He was the one destined to crush his head. Even at His birth, with the angelic choir and the kings of the East, there was a failed attempt to destroy Him by the genocide of the innocents. Now, that it was certain, Satan met Him in the wilderness to tempt Him. But this Adam would not fail as had the first. For three-and-a-half years, they would spare. The Spirit of God had come upon Jesus, and perfect union between God and man had been found, the first one since the Fall. He had, by the miracle of the virgin birth, entered the "strong man's house" to "plunder his goods" (Mark 3:27) – Adam's house, under siege by the strong man, Lucifer.

We know that Lucifer and a significant number of his fallen angelic aides still roam the earth freely. Not until the second advent of Christ will Lucifer be completely and permanently bound and put in the bottom-less pit. And yet, the 'restraint' of Lucifer has already been accomplished. He already suffers from a wound, one that is mortal and final. The atoning work of Christ on the cross was followed by the descent of Christ into the grave and hell, and then by the resurrection from the dead and His ascension into heaven, indeed, by the enthronement of Christ in the heavens; and that has accomplished the legal requirements for the end of Lucifer's illegal siege of the earth. A 'man' has proven the entire race of men worthy of redemption – and that man is Jesus. He, himself, has conquered sin – by His unadulterated obedience to the Father (He came to do the will of the Father), by His perfect commitment to righteous behavior (He was without sin), by His unpopular stance in behalf of truth (He spoke what he heard the Father say; he was the 'Word' incarnate), by His love and care for the outcast, the sick and discarded, the lost sheep of the house of Israel and the world itself (God so loved the world that he gave His only Son). By conquering sin, he overcame death. Crucified, he rose from the dead. And by overcoming death and sin, he triumphed over Lucifer and the grave itself, rescuing those who had died in faith, and were nevertheless, held by death's chains. He emptied Abraham's bosom and moved paradise to better quarters. Jesus declared, "In regard to judgment ... the prince of this world now stands condemned ... the ruler of this world is judged" (John 16:11).

Meanwhile we, the Church, His bride partner, have been left to 'plunder' the house of Adam. We do so by proclaiming the good news of the Kingdom, offering liberation by 'salvation,' baptizing and making disciples. One by one, we transfer men and women from the body (house) of Adam into the (body) of Christ. There is a new king! A new kingdom! Why, if Satan is legally bound, does God not enforce the matter? Judgment on the Satan will result in judgment on the house of Adam. There is coming a day, when God will act in judgment on the world. But now, in the interim, we are involved in a rescue mission. We have the legal right – to offer immunity to those now condemned, to offer eternal life, to proclaim the good news with signs and wonders, the 'Holy Ghost' working with us! He, the Spirit, has come to preach in our preaching, to "convict the world concerning sin and righteousness and judgment" (John 16:8). The great sin now is beyond sins – it is the sin of rejecting God, in Christ. Of crucifying the Savior himself. It is the crime of mutiny against the 'King' of the earth and complicity with the rebel forces of Lucifer's siege. Once aware of the spiritual dynamics and our collusion, we are called to 'switch sides.' We are in a war, and continuing to act in sinful ways, persisting in our own defiant independence, is an act of rebellion and treason against God. Only by surrender and repentance – by renouncing sin and self-rule, do we effectively switch sides, and join the kingdom of God.

At some point, the season of grace and the offer of amnesty will be over. When that comes, the Lord will fully plunder the strongman's house (Mark 3:27). Isaiah declared, "In that day the LORD with His severe sword, great and strong, Will punish Leviathan the fleeing serpent, Leviathan that twisted serpent" (27:1). In this season, Satan has been allowed to retain certain supernatural angelic powers and qualities. For example, he operates 'above' the earth, in the middle heaven, from an invisible throne. At some point, as the calendar of time advances in the midst of the unfolding eschatology of the last days, he will lose that decided advantage. John, from Patmos saw the day, "So the great dragon was cast out, that serpent of old, called the Devil and Satan, who deceives the whole world; he was cast to the earth, and his angels were cast out with him" (Revelation 12:9). In that time, the dragon with beast and the false prophet will come after the righteous with a vengeance. But God will be gracious. "The woman was given two wings of a great eagle, that she might fly into the wilderness to her place, where she is nourished for a time, times and half a time, from the presence of the serpent" (Revelation 12:14). At the end, God will lay "hold of the dragon, that serpent of old, who is the Devil and Satan," and he will be "bound him for a thousand years" (Revelation 20: 2).

When Christ came, we tend to see His coming almost exclusively as being about love. Actually, he came to announce the beginning of the end. He came to start the process of judgment. "For judgment I have come into this world" (John 9:39).. No other human could have done that – all were guilty. A call for judgment by anyone else would have only been a call for self-destruction. Paul argues, "All have sinned ..." By the standards of the law, all were silenced. "Now we know that whatever the things the law says, it speaks to those under the law, that every mouth may be stopped, and all the world be under judgment to God" (Romans 3:19).

There is only 'One' that is righteous. "I have much to say in judgment of you. But he who sent me is reliable, and what I have heard from Him I tell the world" (John 8:26). Notice, the message of judgment is restrained, in favor of another message. "God," the Father "loved the world," and sent the son with a message of grace against the backdrop of impending doom.

Listen to His words, "Now is the time for judgment on this world; now the prince of this world will be driven out. ... Now is the time for the judgment of this world to begin" (John 12:31). In his coming, He sounded a warning about the present and coming judgment. The present judgment is that of light, "And this is the judgment: the light has come into the world, and people loved the darkness rather than the light because their works were evil" (John 3:19). He came to call men and women into the light, "Come unto me ... and I will give you rest". He said to Israel, "How often would I have gathered you together as a hen would gather her chicks," – it was a call to salvation from the coming judgment. Peter declared that we "once were not a people but are now the people of God, who had not obtained mercy but now have obtained mercy" (I Peter 2:10). "In this way, love is made complete among us so that we will have confidence on the day of judgment, because in this world we are like him" (I John 4:17). God has determined that "He will judge the world in righteousness; He will execute judgment for the peoples with equity" – that is with fairness (Psalm 9:8). The Aramaic Bible in Plain English calls it judgment of the "nations in integrity." That judgment is certain, Peter reminds us that God "did not spare the ancient world" after "Noah warned the world of God's righteous judgment." But "God protected Noah when he destroyed the world of ungodly people with a vast flood" (II Peter 2:5). Joel saw the day when God would gather the nations and enter into judgment against them (Joel 3:2).

The final redemption can only be accomplished by an act of judgment Lucifer will not surrender his control of the earth, nor will all of mankind. Defiance will persist, despite the harsh times. Men, rather than bend in honor to their Creator, will scream at heaven in rebellion. As with the children of Israel under Pharaoh, "I am the LORD; I will bring you out from under the burdens of the Egyptians, I will rescue you from their bondage, and I will redeem you with an outstretched arm and with great judgments" (Exodus 6:6).

> *"The LORD is known by the judgment He executes; the wicked is snared in the work of his own hands" (Psalm 9:16).*

Because of the role of Jesus in coming to the earth, and in tasting the bitterness of rejection and crucifixion by men, the Father "has committed all judgment to the Son" (John 5:22). "The Father," we are told, "judges no one." The earth is going to see a strange thing – the wrath of the Lamb. There is good news, "Most assuredly, I say to you, he who hears My word and believes in Him who sent Me has everlasting life, and shall not come into judgment, but has passed from death into life" (John 5:24).

Peter warned, "For the time has come for judgment to begin at the house of God; and if it begins with us first, what will be the end of those who do not obey the gospel of God?" (I Peter 4:17). James offered the standard, "For judgment is without mercy to the one who has shown no mercy. Mercy triumphs over judgment" (James 2:13).

Heaven shouts, "Saying with a loud voice, 'Fear God and give glory to Him, for the hour of His judgment has come; and worship Him who made heaven and earth, the sea and springs of water'" (Revelation 14:7).

CHAPTER 6

THE WRATH OF GOD AND PRAYER
P. Douglas Small

There is a wonderful old story about a small boy in Sunday School who after a series of lessons, some from the Old Testament and then others from the New, wondered aloud, "When did God get saved?" There is a tendency to see the Old Testament through the lens of the law with its punitive edge, and the New Testament through the lens of God's love with its extension of grace. Add to that the plaguing questions about suffering and global calamities, about disease in children and the plight of the world's poor and it is far too easy to indict God: Why, if there is a God, does He allow such suffering? Indeed, we ask, why does He not make life painless? Why is He described as angry? Why is there such a place as hell?

Today, we have a one-dimensional view of the world, grossly oversimplified, and that especially describes our theology. Our sound-bite culture has created shallow thinking and with it a veritable war against multi-layered reason. Television turns a scene every few seconds. Even news service outlets have succumbed to the culture of impatience. We are a bottom line society. We want 'yes' and 'no' answers, and information digests. Footnotes and caveats are not our specialty. We prefer simple rules, favorable to us and our team, and without exceptions. And therein is the problem. In an age of so-called tolerance, everyone wants it, but no one wants to give it!

Love – and Don't Forget to Abhor!

Paul says to the Romans, "Love must be sincere," and then, as if arising from another world, Paul continues, "Hate what is evil" (v. 9). Love and hate – together. The word, *apostugeó*, from *stugeó*, is defined as *to hate*, to find something or someone as detestable or disgusting. The idea is stunning. The opposite is *stygnētós* and is used only in Titus 3:3, describing those who are themselves despicable or detestable because they actively hate good things and good people find them abhorrent. They are enemies of good and godly men, and of God. Christians are predisposed to dislike sin or to be 'horrified' by sinful notions. Sin to them is now loathsome. 'Love the sinner; hate the sin,' has become a highly traded maxim. In principle, it is right; in practice, it is challenging.

In a single-dimensional culture that only wants to embrace 'love,' we have left no room for 'hate' – of anything or anyone. It is clearly accepted and conventional now, to declare that 'hate" – is not to be admitted as a legitimate cultural notion and that would be especially true among Christians. 'Hate' should not find a place in a pure heart, we reason. So severe is our enlightened posture against it, that we now consider 'hate' to be a crime. We are told, by clergy and the culture alike, that as humans, we are to be 'all' love, and beyond that, pure love. Who can argue with such a proposition? It is so entrenched in our thinking, so accepted, and it seems so right!

Yet God's love, though shocking to our sensibilities, implies a hatred; specifically a settled disdain for evil. Even the use of the word out of Scripture is uncomfortable to us; and even if it is applied in an impersonal way, we still long to resist it. And almost all of us do. Worldliness is such an insidious and subtle thing, and we are often swept along in its wave unconsciously. There is a thin line between the cultural accommodation of the faith to achieve relevance, and a cultural capitulation of elements of the faith to assure acceptance.

We are constantly attempting to reduce God to a single word, and the preferred word is – love. But God is far too complex for a one-word definition. In a society where sin is popular, and preachers are increasingly seen as narrow and irrelevant, we often omit the biblical notion of the holiness of God, and that perhaps is a better starting point for understanding God, specifically - "The supreme holiness of God's love, rather than its pity, sympathy, or affection." This is often called "the watershed between the Gospel and the theological liberalism which makes religion no more than the crown of humanity."[1] And thus, "If we spoke less about God's love and more about His holiness, more about His judgment, we should say much more when we did speak of His love."[2] Judgment necessarily proceeds from the essence of God's holy center. The love of God is only fathomless when contrasted with an understanding of both His Holiness and man's sin. Today, we partner God's love with the dignity and nobility of man, ignoring the sin issue; and the sinner blindly sneers, "Why should God not love me? As lovable as I am?" Only when we understand mercy as extraordinary, as the exception, in view of deserved wrath, can we grasp the depth of God's love.

This is not a notion of polar opposites. Hate is not the opposite of love; just as darkness is not the opposite of light, rather it is the absence of it. Evil is present, because men are not driven by love (I Corinthians 13). We are "made perfect in love" (I John 4:18). Hate is not necessary as an opposite to balance love. As strange as it may seem, it is a part of love. Modern Christians are ashamed of the notion of God's wrath. It is rarely spoken of. It is a theological idea that is avoided. It is something about which we feel we must defend God – "He is a nice God," we insist.

---

1   P. T. Forsyth, *The Cruciality of the Cross* (London: Hodder & Stoughton, 1909), 6.

2   Ibid, 73.

Sinners in the Hands of an Angry God

The First Great Awakening was, at least in part, triggered by the sermon by Jonathan Edwards entitled, "Sinners in the Hands of an Angry God." Edwards declared that the bow of God's wrath was bent and the arrow was ready on the string. Edwards believed that justice was the force that drew the string backward and bent the bow. Justice is not a concept we understand in the church today. When have you heard a message about justice, not social justice and the ills of the culture, or a call to make things better in the community or to lighten the burdens of the less fortunate, but rather, a focus on the cosmic scales of moral and spiritual justice that can only be righted by God?[3] This is a focus on due penalty for sin, the triumph of evil, recompense for wrong. The Psalmist (73) was "envious of the boastful" especially when he saw their prosperity coupled with wickedness. They seemed to die easy – "For there are no pangs in their death." And while alive, they seemed strong and vital. Their lives were easier – "They are not in trouble as other men, nor are they plagued like other men." The result was arrogance - they wore pride like an ornament. Their condescension manifest as callousness toward others - they wore violence like a garment. Their language polluted the culture and challenged heaven itself, "They scoff and speak wickedly ... they speak loftily. They set their mouth against the heavens and their tongue walks through the earth..." (73:3-9). They haughtily hold to a personal notion of God as uninformed or absent, "How does God know? And is there knowledge in the Most High?" To even a casual observer, it appears that "the ungodly ... are always at ease; they increase in riches." All of this concludes the psalmist to deduce skeptically, "Surely I have cleansed my heart in vain, and washed my hands in innocence."

3   Jonathan Edwards, *The Select Works of Jonathan Edwards*, vol. 2, Sermon 7 (London: Banner of Truth,1959), 183-99.

ACCENT

The half-way covenant of the early 1700's had filled the churches with people who had not had a transforming encounter with Christ. It led to the conclusion of Jonathan Edwards, that the church was full of "sinners in the hands of angry God." The church then, as now, needs a revival of prayer and holiness. The culture was ripe with "tavern drinking, lewd practices, and frolics among the sexes." Night prowling was common and family restraint had failed. The culture was divided. When the Great Awakening came, in New England alone, an estimated 7 - 14 percent of the population was swept into the Kingdom of God affecting the atmosphere of the whole town.

Henry Blackaby and Claude King, *Fresh Encounters* (Nashville, TN: Broadman, 1996), 8 - 9.

While the life of the wicked seems free of trouble, the believer says, "All day long I have been plagued, and chastened every morning." The system appears to be upside down. The wrong are rewarded; the righteous are punished. The wicked use unchecked violence to increase their wealth; and as a result, the righteous are the oppressed. The psalmist almost despairs. He is caught between what seems to be the prevailing clear reality, and his desire for the next generation not to lose faith, "If I had said, 'I will speak thus,'" – in other words, 'I will capitulate. I will cave in to the prevailing and apparent reality! I will openly admit that justice does not seem to exist and if there is a God, His principles don't seem to be working!' But then, he realizes, "I would have been untrue to the generation of Your children," not 'my' children but 'Your' children. While being true to 'my' children is important; the idea here is bigger – it is the whole of the next generation. This is about God and His generations. Our perspective is too limited and narrow to be the basis of tossing such a precious faith aside. "When I thought how to understand this, it was too painful for me," as it us to us today. But then insight came. "I went into the sanctuary of God; then I understood their end." Judgment is delayed. Wrath is restrained, but not inevitably. There are moments, even in this life, in which selective judgment and unrestrained consequences come to the wicked. "Surely you set them in slippery places; you cast them down to destruction ... in a moment!" He decides to put "trust in the Lord God."

So what prevents the arrow from being released and its finding a target? Only God's mercy. Edward's message was severe. It would be greeted today by disdain, even by arch conservatives. Our view of God is skewed toward His goodness and virtually absent of any place for discipline. We have refashioned God to make Him sweet and nice. And we have so elevated man to make Him noble and good, decent and honorable, worthy only of affirmation and adulation, that the idea of man as a sinner is disallowed. God must love man, because man is so good. Were Edwards in the room, he would be equally shocked by our theology as moderns are by his views.

Ezekiel 8:18 declared that the day had come in God's dealing with Judah, when they had crossed a line, "I also deal in fury; mine eye shall not spare, neither will I have mercy; and though they cry in mine ears with a loud voice, yet will I not hear them." The idea of a God of wrath is thoroughly rejected today. Salvation, in our day, is no longer a matter of repentance; it is rather, an acceptance of the affirmation and the love of God. Such a view produces pseudo conversions and floods the church with the self-interested impious who neither understand the depth of their own sin or the utter-otherness of a holy God; and they have no place for the fear of God in their world.

Rejecting a God of Wrath

In *De ira dei,* by Lactantius, dated around AD 313 or 314, he wrote,

"Many persons hold this opinion, which some philosophers also have maintained, that God is not subject to anger; since the divine nature is either altogether beneficent, and that it is inconsistent with His surpassing and excellent power to do injury to any one; or, at any rate, He takes no notice of us at all, so that no advantage comes to us from His goodness, and no evil from His ill-will."[4]

These ideas had found their roots in the Greek philosophers, not in ancient Hebrew theology. Gnosticism, which vilified the god of the Old Testament, and elevated only Jesus to the status of the true God, the nice and loving God, the one who would allow himself to be crucified as an act of sacrificial grace, the one who would always turn the other cheek – that God, was now placed alone on the pedestal of acceptable gods. For Marcion, a champion of gnostic theology, the bifurcation of the testaments allowed the wrath of the Old Testament to be put away, and the mercy of the new to stand singularly alone. Tertullian would say of Marcion's heresy,

"A better god has been discovered, one who is neither offended nor angry nor inflicts punishment, who has no fire warming up in hell, and no outer darkness wherein there is shuddering and gnashing of teeth: he is merely kind. Of course he forbids you to sin—but only in writing."[5]

The commands of such a God are thus paper thin. They have no force behind them. They are teasers. Is it not clear then – is such a God incapable of judgment? Or does He lack the emotional stamina for severity or reproof? Or was His prohibition against sin and his threat of retribution insincere? Is the flaw in His capacity or His character? Whatever the case, it amounts only to a mere annoyance, and is

---

4   Lactantius, "*A Treatise on the Anger of God," The Ante-Nicene Fathers, Vol. 7* (Grand Rapids: Eerdmans, 1969-73), 259.

5   Tertullian, "*Against Marcion," Tertullian Adversus Marcionem*, Ed. E. Evans, Vol. 1: 1.27 (Oxford: Clarendon, 1972), 77.

therefore easily dismissed. It is only a suggestion without either an intent or capacity for enforcement. His words are thus benign and powerless.

Furthermore, such a God is not offended by sin. He is not genuinely outraged at moral rebellion. He is not moved by acts that injure His own children. Genuine love should move Him to protect His own creation from evil and destruction, but He only smiles and bids us all His good-will. A man who genuinely loves his wife will not smile as torturers have their way with her. A father will fight to protect his children or he is no adequate father. Love at some point, demands aggressive and righteous action. Only the most liberal of theologians naively disallow the idea of force, believing everyone is so good and righteous, that all can eventually be persuaded to play nice in the sandbox and obey the rules. This theology now pervades our foreign policy, particular with regard to Islamic radicals. Proper motivation is needed for change, the argument goes. Diplomacy must be engaged. Rewards must be more equitably distributed. The problem is not men and evil hearts, we are repeatedly assured, but it is environmental and relational.

Modern theology, so uncomfortable with an 'angry' God has suggested, and in part correctly, that the 'wrath' of God should be seen in impersonal ways. The desire is to perceive wrath and retribution as impersonal outcomes of a moral universe, but create a safe distance from them and God. Whereas, the Old Testament narrative would interpret storms and calamities as potential judgments, we are quick to condemn anyone who draws a connecting line between disaster or judgment and God.

There are consequences to sin and these penalties are built into a moral universe, to that idea we can ascribe. The spiritual-moral consequences of disobedience are as real as violations of spatial-physical laws. Break them and there are negative effects. These laws are impartial and incontrovertible. But in an attempt to protect God, liberal voices declare, "The wrath of God is wholly impersonal and does not describe an attitude of God but a condition of men."[6] These are in part 'Enlightenment' era notions which regarded the idea of an angry God as "the crude anthropopathisms of an uncultured age."[7]

Searching for Balance

We persistently wrestle with theological projection. We see God through human eyes. We tend to make Him an enlarged version of ourselves. But is divine anger to be equated with human anger? Certainly, it is not. The basis of our anger is completely removed from the basis of God's anger. The world is not ours – we did not create it. Nor did we have either the purity or power to redeem it. Human anger is seated in our flawed character. God is not capricious and arbitrary. He doesn't have 'bad days.' He is not malicious and petty. His anger is in reference to His righteousness; and surprisingly, for some, rises out of His holiness. But it is ancillary. Luther called God's wrath His alien work, His *opus alienum;* and mercy His proper work, his *opus proprium.*[8] He was probably drawing from Isaiah who spoke of God arising to do "His work, His strange work, and perform His task, His alien task" which was judgment (Isa. 28:21).

God *is* love – that is as aspect of His essence. And yet, that

---

6   A. T. Hanson, *The Wrath of the Lamb,* (Wipf & Stock Pub, 2010), 110.

7   This quote is taken from, and much of the material in this section, adapted from article by Tony Lane, "*The Wrath of God as an Aspect of the Love of God,*" which first appeared in Kevin J. Vanhoozer (Ed.) *Nothing Greater Nothing Better: Theological Essays on the Love of God* (Wm. B. Eerdmans Publishing Company: Grand Rapids, Michigan, 2001). Accessed on-line, September 7, 2012: http://www.theologynetwork. org/christian-beliefs/doctrine-of-god/getting-stuck-in/the-wrath-of-god-as-an-aspect-of-the-love-of-god.htm

8   E.g., A. E. McGrath, *Luther's Theology of the Cross* (Oxford: Blackwell, 1985), 154-56.

authentic and active love necessitates a cure for man's sin. Wrath is unlike God's holiness or His righteousness, which are permanent attributes of God in Israel's view of Yahweh.[9] Wrath is God's response. And while there is no restraint to His love, there is an abiding restraint on His judgments. And yet the two are bound together. Those who deny God the dimension of anger, but allow compassion, embrace a contradiction. God's tender mercy toward a victim of sin is logically connected to His anger against the thing that created the condition. Compassion and indifference can't coexist. He is neither cold and aloof nor dispassionate and disconnected. "He is touched with the feeling of our infirmities" (Hebrews 4:15). He is not merely merciful with regard to our condition; He is merciful with regard to our experience. He does not see us and respond, thus giving us the benefit of His mercy as an indifferent and dispassionate act; rather, He feels our pain. This is the essence of the incarnation. God has walked in our moccasins. He has wept among us and He now weeps with us. He tasted death. And yet, while theologians are ready to admit God's compassion as an "*effectus,* but not an *affectus,*" they persist in a view of that disallows the same for His anger.[10]

In the Old Testament, there are six different terms used for the wrath of God, and together they appear 406 times. Another list includes twenty terms with some 580 occurrences.[11]

---

9   W. Eichrodt, *Theology of the Old Testament*, Vol. 1 (London: S.C.M., 1961), 262.

10 Tony Lane, "The Wrath of God as an Aspect of the Love of God," Kevin J. Vanhoozer (Ed.) *Nothing Greater Nothing Better: Theological Essays on the Love of God* (Wm. B. Eerdmans Publishing Company: Grand Rapids, Michigan, 2001). Accessed on-line, September 7, 2012: http://www.theologynetwork.org/christian-beliefs/doctrine-of-god/getting-stuck-in/the-wrath-of-god-as-an-aspect-of-the-love-of-god.htm

11 Arthur Baird, *The Justice of God in the Teaching of Jesus* (London: S.C.M., 1963), 46; See also, L. Morris, *The Apostolic Preaching of the Cross,* 3rd ed. (London: Tyndale, 1965), 149-50.

"Wherever in the Old Testament one finds a reference to the love of God, His wrath is always in the background, either explicitly or implicitly, and we neglect this element to the impoverishment of the Hebrew concept of love."[12]

"While disaster is regarded as the inevitable result of man's sin, it is so in the view of the Old Testament, not by some inexorable law of an impersonal Nature, but because a holy God wills to pour out the vials of His wrath upon those who commit sin. Indeed, it is largely because wrath is so fully personal in the Old Testament that mercy becomes so fully personal, for mercy is the action of the same God who was angry, allowing His wrath to be turned away."[13]

Theologians argue that wrath and anger are absent from the gentle Jesus. Actually, "The Synoptics record Jesus saying well over twice as much about the wrath of God as He ever did about His love."[14] Paul, in writing to the Romans (3:5), makes the assertion of God's wrath personal. Paul says later in the text, quoting Deuteronomy 32:35, that vengeance *belongs to God,* and he is expected to repay. In I Corinthians 10:22, he references the jealousy of God. And in II Thessalonians 1:7-9, Christ is seen as returning in judgment. The writer of Hebrews (3:10-11; cf. 4:3) describes the disposition of God toward Israel as so angry that He swore against them, pledging His wrath, probably a reference with Psalm 95:10-11 in mind.

There are glimpses in the New Testament, though more rare than the old, where direct judgment is attributed to God (Acts 5:1-11; 12:23; I Cor. 11:30; Rev. 2:22-23). While there appears in the New Testament, a relative 'silence' on the more overt examples of God's wrath, there is never a denial of that aspect of God's nature. Further, it can be argued, that the coming of Christ is in fact, against

---

12 Ibid.

13 Leon Morris, *The Apostolic Preaching of the Cross* (Wm. B. Eerdmans Publishing, 1965) 152.

14 Baird, 59-60, 72.

the backdrop of such wrath, and for the purpose of averting that wrath. This is strange, since the mediating role of Christ is central. The cross is the place and time in history at which God demonstrates judgment on sin and that moment was the destiny of Jesus and the primary purpose of His coming to the earth. The death of Christ makes no sense apart from an understanding of the weighty consequences of Adam's sin that had been held back by the mercy and patience of God. Poured out on sinful mortal man, he would not have endured. The race of man would not have survived. But Jesus, being immune from the toxic, deadly consequences of sin, could dispose of the lethal curse.

> ## ACCENT
>
> In Isaiah 59, the prophet declares that "justice is driven back, and righteousness stands at a distance; truth has stumbled in the streets, honesty cannot enter, Truth is nowhere to be found ... [And] The LORD looked and displeased ... He saw no one, he was appalled that there was no one to intervene" or intercede! Because of that, "... his own arm worked salvation ... He put on righteousness as his breastplate, and the helmet of salvation" – all implements of warfare.
>
> Here is the principle, in the absence of justice and an intervening healthy, praying community, God acts as a warrior. "He will repay wrath to his enemies, and retribution to his foes, he will repay ... he will come like a pent-up flood that the breath of the Lord drive along."†

The idea of God's wrath is unpalatable in our culture. Punishment is a notion with which the modern academic is uncomfortable – whether the idea is applied to children or criminals, rogue nations or terrorists. Reason and education, they argue, is the means to change them. Some occurrence or omission 'made them' the way they are, and they can be transformed! Humanism is endemically deceptive, being circular in nature; man must believe in man. Such thinking

> The parallel to Isaiah 59 is Ephesians 6. The church is to be the intervening agents for change, advocates for the oppressed, with feet shod with the preparation of the gospel of peace – healing the gaps, ending divisions, ministering reconciliation, uniting and not dividing. The confrontation of Jesus at the Temple was not about doves and money, it was about a faith community that had become as corrupt as the sinful city around it. It was an attempt to remove the barriers that obstructed the poor and powerless from coming to God, barriers not in the city, but in the temple itself. The confrontation of Jesus was a fulfillment of God's anger seen in Isaiah 59.
>
> † Ray Bakke, *A Theology As Big As The City* (Downers Grove, IL: InterVarsity Press, 1997), 43.

is pervasive among neoliberals, and it has no room for notions about the depravity of man, the influence of the demonic, the blindness of sin, or the need for outside spiritual redemption and the new birth. It is utterly and completely humanistic reasoning. For such spiritual skeptics, it is not only God's wrath that is intellectually unacceptable, it is the idea of God Himself, particularly a God who meddles in human history and is more than a mere panacea or mere ideological icon. And that is tolerable only among the unenlightened.

Still, evangelicals, in view of the cultural conditioning also equivocate. "God is angry with evil, not with evil people," they argue. "He loves people, He is merely angry at what they do!" In truth, God's wrath has in view not only evil deeds, but the evil men who do them (Luke 21:23; John 3:36; Rom. 2:5, 8; Eph. 5:6; Col. 3:6; I Thess. 2:16). Again, the prevailing tenor of God's disposition toward men is that of love. But He is also equally a God of truth. And sin cannot be seen "as something merely separate from the sinner, which He can lay aside like a suit of clothes. My sin is the wrong direction of my will; and my will is just myself as far as I am active. If God hates the sin, what He hates is not an accretion attached to my real self; it is myself, as that self now exists."[15] As Tony Lane points out, "It is incoherent to say that God is displeased with child molestation but feels no displeasure toward child molesters."[16] While it is true, that the slant of Scripture offers the clearest picture of Yahweh's hatred of evil actions (Deut. 12:31; Prov. 6:16-19; Isa. 61:8; Amos 6:8; Rev. 2:6), that is, in effect, a call to redemption, a plea to abandon such behavior, since it is inconsistent with the nature of God. But there are a number of texts that do reveal specific disdain for individuals. Lane, in his excellent article, "The Wrath of God as an Aspect of the Love of God," offers examples. Yahweh is said to love Jacob, but hate Esau (Mal. 1:2-3; Rom. 9:13). Psalm 5:5; 11:5 and Proverbs 6:16-19, says He hates evildoers. Surprisingly, there are two occasions in which disdain is expressed even regarding Israel (Jer. 12:8; Hos. 9:15).

Wrath Revealed

"For the wrath of God is revealed from heaven against all ungodliness and unrighteousness of men, who hold the truth in unrighteousness" (Romans 1:18). We often miss this huge backdrop of God's wrath which has come into being due to the rebellion of Adam, the continued sin of his offspring, the collusion with Lucifer, and the repeated inaugurations of corrupt and wicked kingdoms, morally disintegrating governments in the sanctified earth. All this occurs with the exaltation of idols, visible or invisible, along with the dismissal of God and His righteous demands by mankind, the rejection of the prophets, the mutiny of the nations against His reign, and most certainly, the revolt of 'the nation' Israel against Him. Sin builds, it becomes the norm. The man, made in His image, now acts in ways completely inconsistent with the character of the Creator,

---

15 William Temple, *Christus Veritas* (Macmillan, 1925) p. 258.
16 Lane.

and therefore, by his actions, he tells lies about God. God's anger, and His just cause for anger, escalates.

So God, in the course of history, comes to the earth Himself. Wrapped in flesh, God in Christ comes, but rather than destroy, He heals the sick and raises men from the dead; He touches the leper and loves the outcast; He cares for the throwaway; He includes the excluded. He reinterprets the law as a means of grace. And then He takes the sin of mankind, and pulls it close to His bosom, and looks into the face of His Father. In that moment, the death penalty that Adam should have tasted, Jesus embraces. He experiences the wrath of God on sin for all humanity. Now at the cross, it should become clear, that because sin is found – not even *in,* but *on,* one such as the son of God, even He is not exempt from wrath; and therefore by example, neither are we. There is no respect of persons with God. There is no exemption from sin's awful consequences, even for God's own son. All are guilty. But by that noble act, all who stand before the cross and acknowledge sin and its horridness may receive mercy.

Until the cross, there was no permanent remedy in time. Now, for a season, grace is extended. Wrath is again postponed. But far from forsaking wrath or vacating the Old Testament disposition against sin, the New Testament, the cross, affirms it – and even more so. In the Old Testament, lambs died; but in the New, 'The Lamb' died. Let's make it clear – God hates sin; and there is a problem between God and the sinner, if he does not repent, if he persists in his sin. So resistant are we to this notion, that we are now hesitant to take a position on morality. We have allowed relativism to erode our convictions. We want to pass no judgment, as if our silence will silence God and restrain Him. In truth, we are in denial. And in such times "morality becomes a matter of taste and choice, and *de gustibus non est disputandum:* there is no point in asking an expert which to prefer."[17]

---

17 J. Sacks, *Faith in the Future* (London: Darton, Longman & Todd, 1995), pp. 37-39.

A Loss of Reverence

Another theological idea that gets little play today is that of the fear of God. If God is all love and no wrath; if there is no recrimination, no consequence, and no penalty for sin; if God is a grand-fatherly type whose warnings are benign – why fear? It is true, that the greater motivator is love, not fear. And yet, to reduce God to niceness and sweetness, to defang Him and recreate Him as less than 'terrible' and awesome makes a very small God, indeed. Augustine noted that in parenting, a free response of love was often conditioned by episodes of coercion. There are things that children need to fear. All places and people are not safe. The problem is not that fear is an invalid motivator, but rather, that it alone is an insufficient stimulus.[18] "The fear of the Lord is the beginning of wisdom" (Prov. 9:10).

When is the last time you heard a sermon on 'hell?' The modern man proudly declares that he has no place for a God who can send a man to hell! As if, that settles the question. The execution of judgment is not the desire of God (Ezek. 33:11; II Pet. 3:9). Man was, after all, created in His image. Christ died 'for all.' And yet, to assert, that God is altogether passive in the role of judgment is a misrepresentation of biblical facts. Lane points out, "The coming final judgment involves God's wrath as well as His sorrow (Romans 2:5, 8; I Thessalonians 1:10)."

The Cross and Wrath

The cross itself is misunderstood as an evidence of God's wrath, interpreted often exclusively, as an indicator of His love. We are often attempting to move away from the notion that Christ on the cross appeased God's wrath. Of course, that idea bifurcates the character of the Trinity, making God the Father, the heavy, the angry

---

18 Lane.

personality; and Christ, the intervening Savior! Nonsense. It is by the Father's love that the Son came, and He came willingly. What was demonstrated on the cross is not the difference in the natures of the Father and the Son, but their synchronous nature, and their simultaneous commitment to love sinful man and destroy sin. It is an act of holiness and love, together; of salvation and destruction, happening simultaneously; of the separation of man from his sin; and the detonation of sin's explosive and deadly consequences; it was the dividing line that sent man's sin to hell, and a man, Jesus, by His perfect obedience, to heaven.

A father, who did not respond to the exploitation of a child with passion, even with righteous anger, would not be a good father. Love involves an investment of energy. It results in an attachment. In the case of children, it involves responsibility and protective care, particularly in the early years. It is reciprocal and dynamic, alive and felt. Such attachment demands emotional energy – positive and negative. The opposite is to be detached and therefore indifferent. Intellectual dissent is inadequate parenting. The absent of legitimate anger against wicked acts perpetrated on our children, deeds that are damaging, if not deadly, would be perceived as "a lack of caring which is a lack of love, [which] is indisputable."[19]

There is no internal struggle in the Trinity between God's love and His holiness, between truth and love, between mercy and wrath. It is not that one member, for example, the Father, is 'wrathful' and another, the Son is 'merciful'. This is not a tension that must be resolved, as if some inner psychosis exists in the nature of God. Mercy and judgment are noted among the ancients as the two feet of God. The monks were warned that neither foot was to be neglected. They were urged to temper their sorrow for sin, with the idea of God's mercy – and avoid despair; and likewise to remember

19 Ibid.

God's judgment – and avoid halfhearted devotion.[20] To see either God's love or discipline as an action arising from an attribute that is separate from Him is a mistake.[21] God is love and mercy; and He is holy and truth; and He is powerful and just.

And further, to see forgiveness as an act of love; and discipline as an act of truth or wrath is equally an error. In mercy, He visits us with wrath. In justice, He forgives. The attributes and actions are bound together. He is not operating on this occasion out of a disposition of grace, and on another occasion from His 'other angry nature.' He is not bi-polar. He is merciful and loving, because He is holy – and whole, and healthy. And He is wrathful, for the same reason. Aquinas argues, "Mercy appears even in the damnation of the reprobate, for though not completely relaxed the penalty is sometimes softened, and is lighter than deserved. And justice appears even in the justification of the sinner, when fault is forgiven because of the love which God himself in mercy bestows."[22]

Paul declares, "While we were yet sinners, Christ died for us" (Romans 5:8). We were, by nature, the children of wrath (Ephesians 2:3), but we encountered the mercy of God, and as result, we were saved from the wrath to come (Romans 5:9; I Thessalonians 1:10). It is not that the wrath does not come. Rather, we are hidden behind the cross. We are in the ark, as the rain falls. Wrath is certain. It is coming. And we, by our sin, by our very humanness, by our being born in sin, and shaped in iniquity, by our lot, born into slavery as sons of Adam – we faced wrath. But God, rich in mercy, has created a shield from wrath. All that is necessary is that we see in Christ, the goodness of God, confess our sinful state, and ask for forgiveness.

---

20   Lane; See also: Bernard, *Song of Songs* I; *Sermon* 6.6-9 (Kalamazoo, MI: Cistercian Publications, 1971), 35-37.

21   P. T. Forsyth, *The Work of Christ* (BiblioBazaar, 2010), 117-18.

22   Thomas Aquinas, *Summa Theologiae, Vol. 5* (Cambridge University Press, 2006), 81-85.

The deadly disease that has ravaged the earth, and destroyed the soul of man, invaded paradise and made of it a hell – that disease, sin, must be destroyed. And such an act, that act of destruction, in behalf of mankind, is an act of love. Thus, as Lane would argue, "God's love necessitates His wrath." And yet, that principle is understood only from God's love for righteousness, and arguable, the conditions that righteousness create. But this is a view toward final judgment. What about moments of wrath in time?

God's dealings with men may at times involve specific and laser-like moments of wrath – to wake a sinful man up to the ultimate consequences of his ways, to enlighten his heart, to turn him to God. This is, in Luther's view, a manifestation of God's love. It is designed to lead to repentance. Paul suggested that one of the ways God's wrath functioned was through genuinely vested authorities who had a responsibility for social law and order (Romans 13:4-5). They executed wrath to accomplish justice and assure a safe society. Peels, quoted by Lane, discusses the modern lack of discernment. Corporal punishment is violence against children, and capital punishment is understood as murder. "If corporal punishment is just 'hitting' and capital punishment is mere 'killing,' then it follows that fining offenders is mere 'theft' and imprisoning them is just 'kidnapping.' The argument concerned is anarchistic in force and undermines all authority of the state to punish."[23]

The cross is foolishness to our world! It makes no sense – even as an act of profound love. Why would a father give his child in death, and declare it an act of love? It is senseless to our culture apart from an understanding of the issue of wrath on sin. "Christ redeemed us from the curse of the law by becoming a curse for us" (Galatians 3:13). Since Christ died, it is doubtful that another era has so profoundly misunderstood the concept of God's judgment on sin at

23 Henrick Peels, *The Vengeance of God* (Brill, 1995), 294.

the cross. The doctrine of the centrality of the cross is so diminished that we can now conceive of a Christianity without the cross. Much cross preaching, aimed at showing the love of Christ for us, attempts to place great emphasis on the physical suffering, as in Mel Gibson's, *The Passion,* placing it in an incomparable category – the nails and the thorns, the cat of nine tails, the physical and grisly torture of crucifixion. To suggest that because the pain of the cross was exceptional, it is therefore redemptive is a groundless argument. Many men and women died as martyrs for a cause in which they believed, many as believers – and while their deaths were inspiring and noble examples of uncompromising dedication, they did not liberate man from sin and death. What was different at Calvary was that a perfect man came under the curse of God against sin. It was not the torture

The power of a handful of righteous people in a city is compelling in the eyes of God. Just ten would have saved Sodom. Jeremiah was told, "Go up and down the streets of Jerusalem, look around and consider, search through her squares. If you can find but one person who deals honestly and seeks the truth, I will forgive this city"

Jeremiah 5:1

or loss of blood, not the lack of ability to breath, common on a cross, not the open wounds that killed Jesus. He was not overwhelmed by nails and thorns, but by the separation, the spiritual darkness that enveloped Him. The cross, for Jesus, was the gate of hell. There He became an orphan of grace and experienced the abandonment of God. No human had known that horror. Even the wicked had known a measure of common grace. Suddenly, the 'blessing' pronounced on mankind in Genesis, in the person of Adam, if only he would observe the boundaries, that blessing was momentarily lost.

R. C. Sproul notes, "Once the sin of man was imputed to Him, He became the virtual incarnation of evil. The load He carried was repugnant to the Father. God is too holy to even look at iniquity. God the Father turned His back upon the Son, cursing Him to the pit of hell while on the cross. Here was the Son's 'descent into hell.' Here the fury of God raged against Him. His scream was the scream of the damned. For us."[24]

At the Old Testament brass altar, God began to teach men that sin demanded death. The sin offering became a staple of Old Testament worship. The altar stood between alienated mankind and God's holy place. It was a barrier, because sin was a barrier. Thus, since the sin of man in the garden and the substitutionary sacrifice, death had stood between man and God. The animal sacrifices only demonstrated the problem and offered a temporary remedy. The permanent solution demanded atonement – the healing of the division, the repairing of the breach between man and God, the putting away of sin, once and for all. Reconciliation had to come and fellowship between man and God restored.

Christ came to end the separation, to put away the awful ritual sacrifices, to deal permanently with sin. At the cross, He made atonement. There, nailed to the cross, the Father placed on Him the sins of humanity and then poured out His wrath on that sin. Christ, in our place, acknowledged before the Father, the just punishment. He carried those sins to hell, to the grave, so that we would not have to go there. Our sins went; but we did not! At Calvary, He became "a curse for us" (Galatians 3:13).[25] Isaiah declared,

---

24 R.C. Sproul, *Tabletalk* magazine, "My God, My God, Why Hast Thou Forsaken Me?" (April 1990), 6.

25 R.C. Sproul, *Essential Truths of The Christian Faith* (Tyndale House Pub, 1992), 137-138

> *Surely He has borne our griefs and carried our sorrows; yet we esteemed Him stricken, smitten by God, and afflicted. But He was wounded for our transgressions; He was crushed for our iniquities; upon Him was the chastisement that brought us peace, and with His stripes we are healed.*
>
> *All we like sheep have gone astray; we have turned—every one—to His own way; and the LORD has laid on Him the iniquity of us all ... by oppression and judgment He was taken away ... He was cut off out of the land of the living, stricken for the transgression of my people? ... although He had done no violence, and there was no deceit in His mouth (Isaiah 53:4-6, 8, 9).*

Of course, it was not merely His death that was a substitute, but also His life. His perfect life is a substitute for our imperfect life. We meet Him at the cross, and we take up His cause, and follow the trajectory of His holy life.

> *Yet it was the will of the LORD to crush Him; He has put Him to grief; when His soul makes an offering for guilt, He shall see His offspring; He shall prolong His days; the will of the LORD shall prosper in His hand. Out of the anguish of His soul He shall see and be satisfied; by His knowledge shall the righteous one, my servant, make many to be accounted righteous, and He shall bear their iniquities. Therefore I will divide Him a portion with the many, and He shall divide the spoil with the strong, because He poured out His soul to death and was numbered with the transgressors; yet He bore the sin of many, and makes intercession for the transgressors (Isaiah 53:10-12).*

God is eager to redeem, and therefore redemption rises from strange places. Ruth, you recall, is in the lineage of Jesus, and is the great-grandmother of David. She is also a Moabite and as such a descendant of Sodom.

Ray Bakke, *A Theology As Big As The City* (Downers Grove, IL: InterVarsity Press, 1997), 55.

At the cross, God demonstrated that He was no respecter of persons. That sin has consequences. The cross was a specific and laser like release of wrath, designed to save all, by sacrificing one. But, if wrath was released on the Son of God, how can anyone, except the humble and the repentant, expect to escape the coming wrath (I Thessalonians 1:10). At the cross, the Father and the Son conspired to snatch mankind from the grip of sin and death, to liberate them from the kingdom of darkness and the coming condemnation on Lucifer, the dark prince. Paul wrote, "God was in Christ, reconciling the world to Himself" (II Corinthians 5:19).[26]

It was not merely a dying Jesus that saved us – it was a praying Jesus who saved us, "Father, forgive them …" Jesus came to the earth to pray. He started His ministry in a prayer retreat. And He ended His ministry by praying into the night in the garden. He came to the earth – to pray. In fact, He came to the earth to pray from the cross, to die praying for our forgiveness. *"Simon, Simon, behold, Satan demanded to have you, that he might sift you like wheat, but I have prayed for you …" (Luke 22:31-32).*

And so it is for all of us!

---

26 Ibid.

CHAPTER SEVEN

THE MERCY OF GOD AND PRAYER

A WINDOW THROUGH TIME

Some placed the miracle of Dunkirk on the same level as that of the Red Sea.

From May 26 until the 9th of June, England held their breath. In those days, the war was largely won. Had the miracle not taken place, England would have not only lost a war. It would have lost a generation. Churchill had warned that the situation was so dire that only a tenth or less of the fighting force trapped at the very edge of France would survive. More than 300,000 were expected to perish. There was no hope.

The whole nation prayed. Churches and mission halls were full. People prayed in the streets. Children prayed. The king and queen prayed. The Archbishop of Canterbury, Churchill and the Cabinet, everyone prayed. Packed along a thin strip of land, with their back to the English Channel, French and English forces held their breath as the Germans closed in. The skies seemed full of planes. Bombs fell in bunches.

It was ghastly, as men marched along the road toward the coast, with no hope that an escape could be mounted from Europe's mainland to England. One report noted, "Ghastly as everything was, there was a strange feeling that something wonderful was happening. As if they were safer than they had any right to feel." A London newspaper reported one incident, "I lay with four hundred men who were marching gunned systematically, up and down, and bombed by sixty enemy aircraft, and in the end, there was not a single casualty." One chaplain was lying on the ground "being machine-gunned and bombed for what seemed like hours to him. I suppose he was praying ... suddenly, he realized that in spite of the deafening noise and the pelting bullets all around, he hadn't been hit at all. So he got up ... the bullets were still pouring down. But when he looked at the ground he saw something he couldn't believe ... his own shape lying on the ground ... a silhouette – a kind of shadow of himself – an outline of his body. Inside the outline, where his body had been, the ground was untouched. But all around the place where he'd lain, the earth looked as if it had been spaded by a gardener."

Suddenly, the weather brought low clouds and visibility making it nearly impossible for the German planes to fly. For some reason, German ground forces stopped their pursuit. And the English Channel, known for its lack of calm became a sea of glass. Small boats, normally unsafe in the open channel, set sail from England to Dunkirk – hundreds of them. Back and forth across the channel they went, transporting handfuls of troops to safety. The fathers went for the sons – in fishing craft, pleasure boats, every sailable vessel available, and they rescued 335,000 men.

Adapted from, "The Private Dunkirk" Margaret Lee Runbeck, *The Great Answer* (Boston: Houghton Mifflin Company, 1944), 61-78, 164.

CHAPTER 7

THE MERCY OF GOD AND PRAYER

P. Douglas Small

The bottom line – prayer is impossible apart from its inexorable link to the mercy of God. We tend to connect it to faith, and purity; to the biblical basis of our appeal, and a humble disposition. All of these are important, but if mercy is not seen as the context, the backdrop, the very heart of the God's invitation to come to Him and ask, as the hope of any answer, the very standing for the right and privilege of our pleas – then we have not understood prayer. Much confusion exists around the effectiveness of prayer, the lack of answers, the seemingly silent heaven, judgment issues and more, because we fail to see the priori of mercy. Pentecostals tend to see faith as the ground on which we approach God, but our faith is often misplaced, focusing on God's ability, rather than His character. And that brings us back to mercy.

Perspective

Cultural bias is bedazzling. We are prejudiced by it unconsciously. For example, though most Christians would resist the idea that they are existentialists, we all tend to pray out of an existential mindset – this moment, this need, this prayer, this fix. And we do so oblivious to the biblical-historical context of our world. The larger issues are lost over the urgency of our narrow slice of pain. We consistently ignore the fact that we are a part of race of men who are in rebellion against God, living on a dying planet – because of sin, whose nature, is groaning under the anxiety of the coming wrath; the Great Commission uncompleted after two thousand years; our very survival, indeed, our blessed state in the West due only to God's mercy.

Man was created in the image of God, an endowment not afforded the angelic community – and then he was allowed to replicate that image. The early verses of Genesis are replete with the phrase, "... it was good." From 1:4 to 1:25, in the six creation days, there are six such pronouncements crowned with the seventh, "Indeed, it was very good" (1:4, 10, 12, 18, 21, 25, and 31). The scope of God's gifts to man is staggering. Man shares God's image. He was given the near divine ability for speech. He named the animals (2:19). He was endowed with 'dominion,' and installed as the veritable king of the earth (1:26, 28). He was 'put' in the garden and charged with the responsibility of 'growing and guarding' it (2:15), though he was not limited to it. Surrounded by the 'good' of God's creation and having been a recipient of the God's blessing, he was presented with only one boundary (1:28; 2:16-17), but he still sinned.

In Genesis 3, Adam and Eve are found contemplating the legitimacy of the imposed restriction (3:1), the serpent having raised doubts. The question asked by the serpent focuses on God's integrity, "Did He say?" –the question comes, creating an uncertainty about God's unqualified goodness. "He did offer everything to you? – the right to fruit from all the trees? Perhaps something," the serpent suggests, "has been withheld. Perhaps God is not as good as He appears. He is possibly," the serpent proposes, "withholding the best." It was an introduction to doubt the character of God; the dangled bait to disbelieve. Eve clarified the matter, noting the one restriction and its consequences, "We may eat," stating the virtually unrestricted rights and liberties, all freely given. But Eve did not then say, 'We may *not* eat ..." in reference to the tree of polluted knowledge in the midst of the garden. She did not affirm unequivocally the prohibition. It was Adam, not Eve, who had heard the command. Sadly, he remained silent as Eve failed declare the door of prohibition securely locked. There she proposed, "*God* said ..." She did not say, "We may eat of all these trees, we have so many wonderful choices ... but we may *not* eat," rather she said, "*We may* eat ... *[but] God says we may not* eat ..." She owned her liberty grant; but she distanced herself from the probative commands of God, and thus she questioned His authority as absolute.

One of the two charges to Adam was *to 'guard'* the garden. The word is translated in later scripture as *watching,* and becomes a metaphor for prayer, for watchman prayer, for intercession, for that role that demands that we step into some middle, between another person and God; a problem or challenge and God; a decision in the hands of another and God. It is to this middle position, one which implies prayer, from which Adam shrinks. He sees, but he does not, in a biblical and prophetic-priestly role, 'watch.' He was passive, rather than active in prayer. He should have engaged God and sounded the warning that an intercessor or watchman is called to sound. Eve's sin was driven by her inquisitiveness about the spiritual. Remember, it was Adam who had spent direct time with God, not Eve. An unsatisfied spiritual hunger was alive within her. The reach for this fruit was not an attempt to feed the body; rather, it was a hunger for something deeper. Adam's sin, on the other hand, was his silence. Her knowledge was indirect, through Adam; his knowledge was direct, from God Himself.

She, by her language, and Adam, by his complicit silence, are now open to doubting words, to contrary language, to alternative thought. The serpent wastes no time. He moves from planting doubt, to promoting complete disbelief. The NLT offers the forceful words of the serpent, "You won't die!" –it's a lie you have been told, "God 'knows differently'" the serpent alleges, than what He is telling. God is duplicitous he was suggesting. The NAS says it more doubtfully, "You *surely* will not *die!*" There is a subtlety in the words. The ASV says, "Ye shall not *surely* die," not certainly and finally or completely die; and the Douay-Rheims, "No, you shall not *die the death.*"

The serpent had now boldly supplanted the command of God. He had erased the restraining boundary. He had presented himself as their better ally, the superior interpreter of actions and consequences. He wastes no time in offering the trophy for their treachery. "You can be as gods," he boldly asserted, as if he himself were one. He offered no evidence. Nothing commended him. Unlike YHWH, he had created nothing. He offered only the abstraction, only what was said to existed in its absence, only potential, only what he wildly proposed. What, in fact, he alleged was being withheld from the Creator God who had imparted life, gave so much freely and required so little. It was only an illusion that the snake offered.

It was God's intention that man and He would walk together, talk and share the earth – this is the essence of prayer, unbroken fellowship with God. Instead mankind responded to an invitation to engage in an alternative dialogue and he admitted a contrary word. This would be forever the struggle – whose 'word' do we believe? And that is basis of healthy prayer. You can never effectively pray to a God you do not trust, one from whom do you not feel love, one with whom you do not feel safe, one that is not truthful and forthright with you. Here is the undermining of prayer. Deceptive ideas. Doubt. Disorientation. Distrust. Disbelief. Disobedience. A deadly transfer of allegiance and trust had now been forged. A breakaway occured and with it, a new bond. There was a realignment. And prayer - the easy conversation between God and man - had been severely damaged.

"You shall be as gods," the serpent whispered. Equality was desired, not subordination. Autonomy would be the new status, instead of gracious dependence. Self-determination, the new right, not divinely prescribed restrictions. Adam and Eve then rebelled against God. Eve took the forbidden fruit and together, the couple ate. Adam had been warned, "In the day you eat thereof, you shall surely die." The act was permanent and corporately consequential. Paul says, "Everyone died - from the time of Adam ... even those who did not disobey an explicit commandment of God" (Romans 5:15 NLT). "Death reigned ... the many died by the trespass of the one man," Adam (5:15, 16). With the deadly action of Adam and Eve, the race of men should have ended – on that day! "In the *day* you eat of it ... *you die*" (2:17). But it did not.

> ### ACCENT
>
> "The 'good' person needs deliverance from the very goodness, that while it brings favor from others, is a stumbling block to the love of God. The issue, finally, is not whether we are 'good' or 'bad' persons in the eyes of society, but whether we are truly experiencing the providential care and saving grace of God."
>
> Charles Ringma, *Seize the Day with Dietrich Bonhoeffer* (Colorado Springs, Colorado: Pinion Press; 2000), See entry for January 28.

An amazing thing occurred. God came searching for the alienated couple. They were not only separated from one another, they were now separated from Him. He came to the garden calling, as if He did not know where the couple could be found or what had happened. In truth, He wanted their free response – as He does ours. The serpent was no protector. He offered no guardianship. He too was powerless. God called out, but Adam evaded Him. Here is the effect of sin on prayer – guilt, covering-up, hypocrisy, and alienation. God desired the encounter with man more than man desired the encounter with God. He confronted their failures and meted out consequences. In Genesis 1, He had pronounced a *blessing*. In Genesis 2, He set *boundaries*. Now, in Genesis 3, there was *banishment* from the garden because of sin, because of the violation of the boundary. There was also a forfeiture of the full blessing. And yet, there was mercy. He covered their nakedness in the skin of an animal, a picture of sacrifice (3:21). He effected the terms of reconciliation – and this too is a prayer concept. In that moment, heaven committed itself to absorb the impact of man's rebellious act. In time – Jesus, the lamb, would take the place of Adam. His robe would cover Adam, has had the skin of the animal. He would die the sacrificial death. It was the only solution. Being without sin, only the last Adam could detonate the bomb of sin with no harm to himself. Only He could take the toxic waste of the sins of mankind to hell, without being himself contaminated and eternally confined. Only He could taste death, but not be overcome by it. And by His death, we would find a new way to interact with the Father. Not over a bloody altar with the blood of an animal; but through the bloodstained cross. In the name of Jesus, prayer, and the full measure of communion with God would be restored.

In Genesis 5:3, the Scripture says, "Adam ... begot a son in his own likeness, after *his* image," as contrasted with the image of God. He is now replicating a fallen-version of what

> *"It is wrong to say that we are being 'legalistic' when we are concerned with the ordering of our Christian life and with our faithfulness in requirements of scripture reading and prayer. Disorder undermines and destroys the faith."*
>
> Bonhoeffer, from "Meditating on the Word," Quoted by Charles Ringma, *Seize the Day with Dietrich Bonhoeffer* (Colorado Springs, Colorado: Pinion Press; 2000), See entry for January 31.

God had intended. The DNA is forever flawed. Man had, with his rebellion, set in motion irreversible consequences. They could be delayed, but not ultimately deferred. The laws in the moral and spiritual universe are as incontrovertible as the laws of nature and science. "The wages of sin *are* death!" (Romans 6:23). However, God intervened – and by a sovereign act of mercy, in Christ – He created time and space for mankind to repent, a period of mercy. At some point, the window of mercy will close. Revelation 14:3 anticipates the moment. A universal declaration comes forth, "Fear God and give Him glory, because the hour of His judgment has come. Worship Him who made the heavens, the earth, the sea and the springs of water" (NIV). The NLT says, "The time has come when He will sit as judge." ESV says, "The hour of His judgment has come," it can no longer be delayed, "the time for Him to judge has arrived" (ISV).

Judgment – the Rule; Mercy – the Exception

It seems that the opposite is true. But judgment, not mercy, is the rule. We are reminded in Romans 8:23 that God "spared not His own son." This is stark, shocking, unbelievable, breathtaking. Paul continues, "… but delivered Him up …" to the cross, to death, in fact, to a criminal's death by crucifixion. No angels were dispatched to save Him or herald His innocence. God Himself, in Christ, was subject to the incontrovertible law of judgment on sin. God's own son, Jesus, when sin was found *not in* Him, but merely *on* Him, was not spared. This moral law of justice emanating from the holiness of God is not arbitrary or artificial. For God to deny righteousness and truth would be self-denial and betrayal. Holiness is His essence. Thus, the sin of Adam was not some slight rule that was broken. It was not a minor mistake. It was an act of war against the nature of God. Death, not life, is the ailment that now prevails because of the irreversible choice that Adam, our flesh-father made. Paul reminds us, "In Adam all die" (I Corinthians 15:22). "Sin entered the world through one man [Adam], and death through sin, and in this way death came to all men ... [and] death reigned from the time of Adam ..." (Romans 5:12-14).

Mercy is the exception not the rule. Because of God's mercy – the line of Adam would survive, though flawed and doomed to mortality. Sin, with all its malevolence, it's horrible and foul effects, would ceaselessly manifest like a deadly virus for which the vaccine had not yet come – guilt and disease, greed and deception, hate and division, anger and revenge, lust and murder, and finally physical death. All of life would be consumed with avoidance of the toxic consequences of sin – and death in some form. The ground that was to yield fruit and sustenance easily, now gave it stubbornly. Weeds and thorns were nature's evidences that a ruinous change had come. The ground, meant to be abundantly fruitful, would now stubbornly yield a food supply (3:17-19), and the race of fallen man would be extended only by painful childbirth (v. 16). The unity that the couple had been meant to enjoy would now be fraught with dissension (v. 16). The curse of sin affected the animal kingdom as well (v. 14). Animals also tasted death (v. 21), and soon human blood would be shed (4:8-12).

Adam was given a 'house,'[1] the earth, in which he was to live and over which he would have ruled. But he became a slave in his own house. John noted, "... the whole world lies in the power of the evil one ... the whole world [house] lies in wickedness" (I John 5:19). The fall of the house of Adam brought it under the power of the Evil One; and it meant that all of Adam's sons would be born into a world under judgment, compounded by the domination of an alien

---

1   By 'house' we do not mean a physical house, a structure, but a house – as the 'house of David' or the 'house of the Burgess.' The term is a reference to a ruling lineage.

king and kingdom. Man had become simultaneously a perpetrator and a victim. Notice, God's response was toward man, mercy and delayed consequences; and toward the serpent, wrath. "God said to the serpent: 'Because you have done this, you are cursed'" (Genesis 3:14). And yet, because of this alliance forged between mankind, Adam and Eve with Lucifer, our fates, though different and that of the earth, have now been intertwined.

For thousands of years, man has lived under the suspended judgment against sin. There was one exception to this suspension of judgment - the 'Flood.' It is the unambiguous prototype of the certain coming judgment, the next time by fire. This is perhaps the reason the biblical Flood has been so assaulted by persistent disbelief and ridicule. Like the assault on creation, it is a fundamental denial of God's sovereignty over man and the earth, and of man's accountability to His standards without impunity. The Flood is a declaration – that when evil ultimately triumphs, God will intervene with catastrophic judgment. It is not a message our culture wants to hear. We live between the judgments – the first by water, an example; and the next by fire, a warning.

God's Remedy – A New Adam and a New House!

Jesus, the Son of God, the Word, was born to Mary, *between* these judgments. And here is the biblical fact we fail to see – Jesus Himself was born *for* judgment, "For judgment I have come into this world" He declared (John 9:39). And His coming was the launch of the first phase of the final judgment, "Now is the time for judgment on this world; now the prince of this world will be driven out ... Now is the time for the judgment of this world to begin" (John 12:31). This is perhaps why both He and John the Baptist began their ministry with a virulent call to repentance.

The judgment that Jesus effected was particular and incisive, like a laser, selective and limited, unique and never-to-be-repeated, and it was carried out like a judicious one-attack-lamb operation. It happened in this way, "And this is the judgment: the light has come into the world ..." (John 3:19) in order "that those who don't see may see; and that those who see may become blind" (John 9:39). And while the earth appears strangely unchanged by this first incarnational coming of God, in Christ, a perforation has taken place "in regard to judgment, because the prince of this world now stands condemned ... the ruler of this world is judged" (John 16:11). The intertwined threads of human sin and angelic rebellion, which seemed irrevocably entangled, and had hopelessly doomed humanity to Satan's judgment, Lucifer having hidden himself behind the skirts of a the woman's vulnerability to deception our of spiritual hunger, and the man's rebellious silence - the threads had now been disentangled.

"The history of mankind will probably show that no people have ever risen above its religion, and man's spiritual history will positively demonstrate that no religion has ever been greater than its idea of God."

Tozer, *The Knowledge of the Holy*, 9.

Adam's house had indeed, fallen – and yet, it remained standing, and still does. Like the twin towers, the terrorists had done their deadly work, and their collapse was inevitable, but even the security staff in the lobby forcefully urged fleeing people back-up the stairs; and engineers calmly sat at their desks, assuring others, that the towers would never fall, but they did. Likewise, the body of Adam, his corporate body, was damned, but now through the coming of Christ a new body is being built, the body of Christ; and a new house has been established in earth, a house of refuge to which men can now flee. A counter-revolution has been launched – a revolution of mercy and grace, a revolution of forgiveness and repentance, a revolution of righteousness and goodness, one of love and kindness, healing and relief from oppression. It is a revolution of prayer, of miracles, signs and wonders; a revolution of care for the broken hearted and rejected, the oppressed and the exploited, those in prison and blind.

Jesus, born of the Spirit by a virgin, did not spring from Adam's line. He was never a slave to sin. Never under the bondage of Lucifer's evil kingdom. "Christ came as a Son over His own house, whose house we are if we hold fast the confidence and the rejoicing of the hope firm to the end." There are two houses, two corporate men, Adam and Christ. "The first man Adam was made a living soul; the last Adam [Jesus] was made a quickening spirit." Adam was "natural" and Christ, "spiritual." Adam, "the first man is of the earth, earthy; the second man [Jesus] is the Lord from heaven." We inherited the sinful, fallen nature of Adam - "We have borne the image of the earthy." And we now may, by adoption, "also bear the image of the heavenly" (I Corinthians 15:45-49).

The Present – Between the Times

Now we are between the times, waiting for the final act of judgment on Satan, and sadly, on Adam's house. Our call is a rescue mission, getting the word out to the nations, pulling men out of the fire, baptizing them into the new body of Christ. Meanwhile, we continue to live under the pall of judgment. "And as we live in God, our love grows more perfect. So we will not be afraid on the day of judgment, but we can face Him with confidence because we live like Jesus here in this world" (I John 4:17 NLT). The NAS says His "love is perfected with us, so that we may have confidence in the day of judgment," or "boldness" as the old King James says. The fuller judgment is coming. The day of the "wrath of the Lamb" will come. What sustains us is prayer. What opens their eyes and makes our message liberating is prayer (Colossians 4:2). What saves others is their prayerful plea of repentance. What advances them in grace is the communion with the Holy Spirit following their justification.

Mercy is the action of God to suspend the rules, to temporarily stay the judgment, to delay the inevitable. And prayer, the very right to pray and appeal to God when man has fallen so short of God's glory and His righteousness, and is morally deficient, that is grounded in mercy! In truth, we should have no right to approach such a holy God. In the garden, we were given so much, so freely, and asked for so little in return – and we trusted the Serpent, over Yahweh, the snake who had created nothing, endowed us with naught, proven to us zilch. In trusting the one, we distrusted the other. In following the one, we forsook God. Our faith was aligned with the words of the Serpent; and not with the Word of God. And now, we should expect an audience with God by prayer? And believe that we should receive a favorable hearing? On what basis should God have any obligation to listen to our pleas, let along respond to us positively? What legal right offers us grounds for such an appeal, or the hope of a sympathetic judgment? Should man have any such expectation of anything but condemnation and punishment? None!

Prayer – Possible Only by Mercy

Our right to approach God and make our prayerful appeals rest on one fact – the mercy of God. Ultimately, it is not primarily the character of man that allows prayer. Not his faith. Not his spiritual vitality. Rather, it is mercy! God's mercy. In spite of sin – God has decided to allow man to approach Him, and He will, given certain dynamics, certain responses from man, hear and answer. What kind of God is this? It is one that the Scripture declares about consistently, "His mercy endures forever!"

We gain an audience with God in prayer and receive grace, not because we are good, but because God is good. Mercy so consistently and repeatedly eclipses the harsh and deadly radiation of judgment, that we now see and expect only mercy. We have made mercy the rule, not judgment. We have made forgiveness the rule, and without repentance. We have disassociated love from truth, and made that rule. The result is a complete misunderstanding of the peril of our world, the mission of Christ, and the coming cosmic judgment – a fact now not allowed in view of the distorted perception of the nature of God's mercy.

> *Our flesh-father sinned, and we are still in a world in which that action has not been adjudicated.*

In actuality, the opposite is the reality, "and that the whole world is under the control of the evil one" or as the KJV declares, "the whole world lies in wickedness" (I John 5:19). Yet, when bad things happen, when storms come, when hurricanes and earthquakes claim property and precious lives, when the doctor's terminal diagnosis brings a cloud over a family and renders an empty chair at our table, when accidents occur and jolt our ordered worlds - we are dazed, dismayed, aghast – why is God doing this? Allowing this? Why does He not answer? Heal? Deliver? We will never understand our world or our God, unless we see that we stand under this dark shadow caused by Adam's rebellion. Our flesh-father sinned, and we are still in a world in which that action has not been adjudicated. We live with the consequences of the rebellion, amidst the spiritual rubble. In this world, the true government has collapsed, and in places, open anarchy reigns. Indeed, everywhere, spiritual anarchy triumphs. No government on the earth is ruled by God! None. There is none that follows His law as the law of the land. And that will not change until Christ returns. We live in a fallen moral economy. Sin continues, unchecked. Death claims its victims. Judgment is the rule; mercy is the exception. But, because of the nature of God; the light dissipates the darkness, the peace of God triumphs over the confusion, the love chases away the fear. As Paul says, "Where sin abounded, grace abounded much more" (Romans 5:20).

"The earth, O Lord, is full of thy mercy" (Psalm 119:64). This is a prayer psalm. "Oh, give thanks to the LORD, FOR *He is* good! For His mercy *endures* forever" (Psalm 136:1), declares. The phrase, "His mercy endures forever" repeats sixteen times in that psalm. Because of His mercy, the psalmist declares, He "does great wonders." Creation flows out of His mercy (vv. 2-9). Redemption rises out of His mercy (vv. 10-13). He overthrows oppressive regimes, because of His mercy (vv. 15-20). He creates space and place for the displaced (vv. 21-22). Because of His mercy, He sees us personally in our humble station, up against enemies, in need of food, and He meets our needs (vv. 23-25). "For His mercy *endures* forever."

In Psalm 107:43, the idea of God's mercy or loving-kindness is bound to the idea of observing, *shomar,* literally, shepherding – tending to, protectively watching, keeping, and guarding. The Lord, we are told, is our shepherd. Sheep are so vulnerable and essentially indefensible. They are not attack animals. The Lord calls us sheep, since as humans, like sheep, we need a shepherd. God, out of mercy is our shepherd. Psalm 121 is another "shepherd" psalm. It is a song, "He that keeps Israel shall not slumber or sleep" (v. 4). 'Keeps' is again *shomar,* conveying the idea of the shepherd. Here is God, the watchman, in an intercessory or intermediary role. The idea appears six times in this psalm. Don't miss the point: He is watchful, because He is merciful. Prayer and mercy are bound together. God, it turns out, keeps 'the watch' with us, as we pray. "Except the Lord watch the city, the watchmen watch in vain" (Psalm 127:1). God watches in our watching; He comes to heaven's wall, as we stand on the wall of intercession. Heaven and earth, are thusly aligned. In prayer, we see the same need; speak about the same concern. The power is not in our watching alone, but in our watching as He watches.

Grace – the Outcome of Prayer

In this world of want and need, deprivation and uncertainty, to God's covenant people He offers promises - God forgives, heals, redeems, gives the grace of kindness, feeds, and perhaps surprisingly, executes righteousness and judgment, reveals himself, all out of mercy (Psalm 103:1-7). These rise out of God's character, "The Lord is merciful and gracious, slow to anger, and plenteous in mercy" (v. 8).

Three Hebrew words are often used together –first, *rahhum* means compassion or it's plural, *rahhamim,* is translated mercies or compassions; second, *hhen,* means gracious; and third, *'hesed,* with a hard 'ch' sound is thus, *chesed* (Kes-sed), and is the premier word for God's covenant love. It is the Old Testament equivalent to the Greek *agape'.* He is a God of compassion, grace and love. These are descriptors for God. But, "He will not always chide; neither will He keep His anger forever" (Psalm 103:9). Remember, judgment is the rule, not the exception. That is, it is inevitable. Mankind and the earth must have their day in the universal court of God over the denials of his rights to the earth by both creation and redemption. God's merciful nature has restrained wrath to this point, but "He will not ... keep His anger forever." But there will come a time when mercy, because it has been repeatedly spurned, because 'chiding' has been ignored, because it has been translated as divine weakness or taken for granted will be withdrawn, and it will no longer restrain wrath.

Apart from this mercy, all that is left for mankind and the earth is wrath. "He has not dealt with us after our sins; nor rewarded us according to our iniquities" (v. 10). Our sinful *actions* cannot be reversed. We are sinners. But God looks for something in the heart of man nevertheless. "For as the heaven is high above the earth so great is His mercy" *(hesed)*, or His covenant love. Notice specifically to whom this mercy is extended - "to them that fear" or reverence Him (v. 11). Reverence for God, the under emphasized 'fear' of God, produces in us deference and respect. It is not our sinful action that disqualifies us, but our reverent attitude that captures God's attention. To receive mercy, and not be respectful, misses the point of the mercy! It is a demonstration of our failure to see how acutely we needed it. And, that we were unworthy of such a priceless gift. And without that dynamic, mercy is not mercy, at least in the narrowness of our own experience. It is convoluted into something else. It is precisely this lack of reverence that is indicative of a hard heart, an arrogant and unthankful nature, of wicked ways and works executed in a cavalier manner. Attitudes and actions are conjoined. To the reverent only, God promises to remove sins, iniquities and transgressions. To those, He is "full of compassion," "plenteous in mercy," relating with "great and large mercy." His "tender mercies are over all His works" (145:9) in our behalf. Seeing the attitude change, He works to liberate and redeem us from sin's enslavement. We often associate God's works with His power, with force, with might. But here, His works in behalf of those with right hearts are associated with tenderness, with mercy.[2]

The first occurrence of *hesed,* the unique word for God's covenant love, surprisingly, is in the chapter dealing with Sodom and Gomorrah (Gen. 19:19). Here the cities of the plain nestled

---

2   Rex Andrews, *What the Bible Teaches About Mercy* (Zion, IL: Zion Faith Homes, 1985), 26.

on the southeastern shores of the Dead Sea are judged, and Lot is rescued. The juxtaposition of judgment and love is a critical key to understanding the tension between a planet under wrath due to its sin and rebellion, and the love of God that moves Him to save, not all, but some. Lot declares, "Behold now, your servant has found grace *(hhen)* in your sight, and you have magnified your mercy *('hesed)*, which you have shown me in saving my life ..." (19:19). The city could have left with him, as could have his own family – but only his unmarried daughters and his reluctant wife chose to leave.

When Jesus recalled this moment, He did not say, in the days of Abraham, the intercessor (Genesis 18), but in the days of Lot. The focus was on Lot who had escaped sudden wrath by "the triumph of mercy."[3] And yet the act of mercy bestowed on Lot is tied to the memory of Abraham's intercession, "God remembered Abraham and sent Lot out of the midst ... when he overthrew the cities" (v. 29). Abraham's intercessory shadow would extend for centuries over Israel, "Thou [God] will perform the truth to Jacob, and the mercy to Abraham, which you have sworn unto our fathers from the days of old" (Micah 7:20). God binds himself to the covenants with individuals, and acts in generations after their deaths, in behalf of those covenants –

As someone has noted, "The gravest question before the Church is always God Himself, and the most portentous fact about any man is not what he at any given time may say or do, but what he in is deep heart conceives God to be like. We tend by a secret law of the soul to move toward our mental image of God."

Tozer, *The Knowledge of the Holy*, 9.

---

3   Ibid, 47.

extraordinary!

When Zacharias was filled with the Spirit, he prophesied of the coming visitation and redemptive action of God as the "mercy promised to our fathers," an act of God designed to "remember His holy covenant; the oath which He swore to our father Abraham …" (Luke 1:65f). Of course, the father of John the Baptist is not speaking merely of the pregnancy of his wife Elizabeth, or the miraculous appearance of the angel that announced that birth – he is speaking of 'The Mercy!" He is foretelling of Jesus, the Merciful One; Christ, the incarnation of God's Mercy. His coming is the beginning of the end.

Proverbs 3:3-4, "Let not mercy (*chesed)* and truth forsake thee: bind them about your neck; write them upon the table of your heart: so shall you find favor *(hhen)* … in the sight of God and man." Rex Andrews says, "To bind mercy about the neck means, significantly, to yield the old stiff neck to the working of the truth of mercy. The stiff neck, and the hard heart, need mercy wrapped around them and written on them …"[4]

Behind the Restraint of Mercy - Wrath

The wrath of the lamb will be seen by the world according to Revelation 6. There will come a time when heaven decides that there has been enough suffering by the innocent. The final round of world oppression will come as the last global conqueror goes forth, one who is decidedly evil. War and famine follow. Pestilence will rage through the earth. The innocent will then cry out and the lamb will reveal His anger. Like a protective husband moving to care for his endangered wife; a father willing to fight to defend his children, the unthinkable happens – God takes sides. His mercy itself will demand His wrath. The two are conjoined; God is not schizophrenic. Someone has said that when a poisonous serpent is in the crib of an innocent infant, its

---

4   Ibid, 56.

violent eviction and destruction is an act of mercy.

No wonder the psalmist declares, "Thy works shall praise thee, O Lord; and thy saints shall bless thee" (145:10). The word *saint* rises from two roots, holy and mercy. Sanctification draws love and holiness together. Saints are holy people of mercy![5] Holiness is too often joined to hardness. And to allow mercy to triumph, holiness is too often compromised. But here they are conjoined. They are bound together holy people who are merciful to others – mercy-saints.[6]

God speaks to Moses and declares that the "Lord God" is "merciful and gracious, longsuffering, and abundant in

> ## ACCENT
>
> The modern Christian conception of God "is so decadent as to be utterly beneath the dignity of the Most High." Doctrinal errors and flawed ethics are always traced back to an imperfect and ignoble concept of God. The modern man, steeped in his skepticism and cynicism, not exclusion of some preachers and liberal theologians have all been remaking God. Sadly, "A god begotten in the shadows of a fallen heart will quite naturally be no true likeness of the true God." At such a moment we fulfill the passage, "You thought I was altogether such a one as yourself."
>
> Tozer, *The Knowledge of the Holy*, 10.

goodness." But it is not only mercy that characterizes God; it is also "truth." But this is not truth that eclipses mercy, which God guards by "forgiving iniquity and transgression and sin," but again, He will "by no means clear the guilty ..." It is this tension between mercy and truth that makes the gospel so unique, and it made Israel the most unique nation on the earth. Their exceptionality was rooted in the law they received from God, their divinely given constitution

---

5   Ibid, 25.
6   Ibid, 26.

– the Torah. In it, law breakers could be forgiven. Sins could be pardoned. Trespasses could be absolved. Reconciliation could be affected. It was a covenant connected to mercy. The extraordinary feature of the Torah was that ultimately it was not about rules and regulations, but a revelation of God, a holy God, a God who they were to love and admire. It made 'the Nation' of Israel unique among 'the nations!'

The Law and Mercy

Ravi Zacharias says that every one of the Ten Commandments can be reduced to one word – 'sacred.' The laws of Israel separated them from the profane. Life and time is sacred, so the Sabbath demanded time for God. The marriage vow is sacred – so adultery is prohibited. The family is sacred – so parents are to be respected. Speech is sacred – so lies and falsehoods were forbidden. The idea of God was so sacred that no image was to be fashioned and called 'god.' Every commandment is a declaration of the sacredness of life.

Not only was the law given to Israel. The tabernacle was also given, and with it, the Ark of the Covenant with its 'mercy seat.' This was Israel's holiest object – the place of mercy. It was also the emblem of its greatest power. Before it was the altar of incense; the place of priestly prayer. Twice daily that altar was lit and its incense symbolized the worshipful prayer and petitions of the nation rising before God. Though the altar was in the holy place, it was ideologically tied to the mercy seat. Inside the ark were placed the tablets, the testimony or the law. The law described the means by which God had forged a 'covenant' with Israel, and thus the golden chest was called the 'Ark of the Covenant' or the law. But notice, with the law *inside* the chest, mercy now covered the law! The law does not go away. It is not dismissed or diminished. But its standards are not achievable; and the redemption of humanity will not be accomplished by perfect compliance. It is the 'schoolmaster' to bring us to God, in Christ. The wings of the cherubim rose over the blood-stained mercy seat, which was viewed as the veritable throne of God. Here, in the Most Holy Place, God was seated on a throne called 'mercy.' Here, mercy covered the law. And yet, the restraint of law, the eclipse of judgment by grace and mercy, the suspension of the penalty of the law was possible only because the mercy seat had been stained with blood. It was prophetic. The law's penalty had been paid from eternity past by "the lamb slain from the foundation of the world" (Revelation 13:1; See also, 5:6, 12). The sin had been put away. The transgression had been commuted. Peace had been effected. The mercy seat is the *kapporet,* it covers. "There," He declares, "I will meet with you, and I will speak with you from above the mercy seat, from between the two cherubim which are on the ark of the Testimony, about everything which I will give you in commandment to the children of Israel" (Exodus 25:22).

The Ark of the Covenant with the Mercy Seat was separated from the tabernacle of Moses for at least a century. The sacrifices went on. The priest did their rituals. But there was no mercy – and no presence. Through the lifetime of Samuel, as the nation recovered from judgment and the prophet-priest interceded for the salvation of the nation, and throughout the fleshly reign of Saul, even into the war years of King David. It was always the desire of David to bring home the ark. And so it is the desire of God, to bring the ark home! To connect the seat of His glory and mercy to His people. So "we see Jesus, who was made a little lower than the angels, for the suffering of death crowned with glory and honor, that He, by the grace of God, might taste death for everyone" (Hebrews 2:9).

Mercy Goes to War

In Exodus 15:11-13, we learn that as a result of God's 'mercy' he led forth Israel out of Egypt. "Who is like You, O Lord, among the gods? Who is like You, glorious in holiness, Fearful in praises, doing wonders? You stretched out Your right hand; The earth swallowed them. *You in Your mercy have led forth the people* whom You have redeemed; You have guided them ..." When God, in behalf of the oppressed sons of Jacob in slavery, went to war in their behalf, the Scripture declares, "You shall know that I am the Lord your God, which brings you out from under the burdens of the Egyptians" – and this was an act of mercy. And "the Egyptians shall know that I am the Lord, when I stretch forth mine hand upon Egypt, and bring out the children of Israel ..." (Exodus 6:7; 7:5). The difference was simple. Israel received His mercy; Egypt resisted it.[7]

When the plagues came, the magicians worked their magic to no avail. When they grew more severe, Pharaoh asked for prayer. "Entreat the Lord for me!" 'Pray for me,' he pleaded. And Moses did; and so should we pray for the world around us. God heard, but then Pharaoh relented. His repentance was superficial, self-serving and insincere. He lacked an adequate 'fear' of the Lord. The plagues persisted. Wrath came in boatloads. There was no need for this. Grace was as available for Egypt as it was for Israel. But, the oppression by Egypt had to stop. So God extended grace to Israel, and He offered by the intercession of Moses, mercy to Egypt. If Pharaoh had been gracious, mercy would have met mercy. After the first series of plagues, Pharaoh seemed to change, "I have sinned this time: and the Lord is righteous, and I and my people are wicked." Moses explained that the events, indeed, the judgments were that "you may know how that the earth is the Lord's." This has been the

7   Ibid, 40.

dispute from the beginning, who does own the earth? Who is in charge? The kings – or the King of kings?

Moses and Aaron came in to Pharaoh and said ...

> *"Thus says the Lord God of the Hebrews: 'How long will you refuse to humble yourself before Me? Let My people go, that they may serve Me. Or else, if you refuse ... tomorrow I will bring locusts into your territory ...'" And he [Moses] turned and went out from Pharaoh.*
>
> *Then Pharaoh's servants said to him, "How long shall this man be a snare to us? Let the men go, that they may serve the Lord their God. Do you not yet know that Egypt is destroyed?"*

Moses and Aaron were brought again to Pharaoh, and he said ... "Go, serve the Lord your God. Who are the ones that are going?" Moses said, "We will go with our young and our old; with our sons and our daughters, with our flocks and our herds." But Pharaoh would only permit the men to go. So the Lord sent the plague of the locusts (10:11-12). And again, after the devastation, Pharaoh called for Moses and Aaron, "I have sinned against the Lord your God and against you. Now therefore, please forgive my sin only this once, and entreat the Lord your God, that He may take away from me this death only." Again, Moses prays for Pharaoh and Egypt, and "the Lord turned a very strong west wind, which took the locusts away and blew them into the Red Sea" (10:18-19). But Pharaoh's heart was not moved by the act of mercy – and that is the key. It remained hard, and he refused to allow the children of Israel to go. He persisted in enslaving them.

In this sense, Pharaoh becomes a metaphor for Lucifer, who will not release the earth or its captives – despite the judgment to come in the era of the Great Tribulation. In the time of Moses, this brought the plague of the darkness. "Moses stretched out his hand toward heaven, and there was thick darkness in all the land of Egypt three days" (10:23). Joel 2:2 predicts "a day of darkness and gloom, a day of clouds and blackness." It is the apocalyptic judgment that is coming. Meanwhile, "The light shines in the darkness, but the darkness has not understood it" but neither can the "darkness ever extinguish it" (John 1:5). The day is coming when darkness will cover the earth, and gross darkness the people, "but the LORD [will] rise upon you and His glory [will] appear over you" (Isaiah 60:2). The darkness is not merely the absence of light. Jude, the brother of Jesus reminds us, "And the angels who did not keep their proper domain, but left their own abode, He has reserved in everlasting chains under darkness for the judgment of the great day" (Jude 1:6). They are "wandering stars for whom is reserved the blackness of darkness forever" (v. 13). Note the coming judgment, "Then the fifth angel poured out his bowl on the throne of the beast, and his kingdom became full of darkness; and they gnawed their tongues because of the pain" (Revelation 16:10). This is painful darkness. It is hollowness in the depth of the soul, a vacuum that creates inner and outer torture.

After all this, "Pharaoh called to Moses and said, 'Go, serve the Lord; only let your flocks and your herds be kept back. Let your little ones also go with you'" (10:24). Moses, not the least intimidated, declared, "Not a hoof shall be left behind" (v. 16). Pharaoh, completely irrational declares, "Get away from me! Take heed to yourself and see my face no more!" Moses responded, "You have spoken well. I will never see your face again" (10:19-20). The blood over the doorways protected Israel from the wrath poured out on the nation. Israel walked out as freed slaves, and headed to the promise land.

And so we are free! By the liberation of another lamb, Christ Jesus. In Christ, mercy again went to war and triumphed over sin and slavery.

Paul said "creation groans" as it lives under the weight of sin and the anticipation of the fullness of redemption. The groaning is a result of a world "in the pains of childbirth." And "we groan" having within "the first fruits of the Spirit," the deposit that promises our full "adoption as sons, the redemption of our bodies." Finally, the Spirit groans (Romans 8:22, 23, 26). It is the groaning of the Spirit that forms the critical link between the now, and the not yet; between the adoption that has occurred, and the one to be fully effected; between the earnest of the Spirit within us, and the full embrace of the welcome home by the Father. In this fog, in the present turmoil, living between the judgments, "We do not know what we ought to pray for, but the Spirit himself intercedes for us with groans that words cannot express" (v. 27). We know that "our present sufferings are not worth comparing with the glory that will be revealed in us" (v. 19). All of creation is waiting for the revelation of "the sons of God to be revealed." What a moment that will be! Lost since Adam's fall, creation has needed a true man, a restored and renewed regent. It too struggles from life under the tyrant empire.

"And the God of peace will crush Satan under your feet shortly. The grace of our Lord Jesus Christ be with you" (Romans 16:20). Meanwhile, we live with the promise, *"My grace is sufficient for you, for my strength is made perfect in weakness" (II Corinthians 12:9).* So, in spite of the suffering and treachery, the difficulties and deficiencies, we join with Paul and "most gladly" boast in infirmities, because in such moments, the power of Christ is seen in a glorious way. *"Therefore, since we are receiving a kingdom which cannot be shaken, let us have grace, by which we may serve God acceptably with reverence and godly fear" (Hebrews 12:28).*

CHAPTER EIGHT

IMPRECATORY PRAYERS

A WINDOW THROUGH TIME

Perhaps there is no greater time to consider 'mercy' and 'grace' in the face of evil, than before considering prayers of judgment – always a last resolve. Here is an incredible story of how one man moved the Gestapo to befriend and protect him.

Konstantine Jaroshevich was a national figure, but also a humble and passionate man, fearless as well. The Gestapo had no idea who he was the day they captured him and threw him into a small holding facility. A man with a slight build, he wore a Colonel's uniform but it was not the military that defined him, it was his faith. He had influenced millions to believe the Bible in Russian and Poland. Someone said he was the only man they ever knew who was completely without self-interest. He preached in the streets and along country roads. His first church was a cattle-shed. When he met people who had no Bible and seemed dedicated, he would tear out a portion of his own – a gospel, an epistle, a handful of the psalms. His Bible grew thinner and thinner as his converts increased in number. Those with pieces of the Bible would sit up nights and share, copying one another's portion.

As tension escalated between Poland and Germany, he ordered his staff, being warned of God, to sell their building and liquidate their assets. Aghast, they obeyed. He instructed them to take the money and buy food, and for a season to hide it. No one saw what he sensed, the havoc that would be created by the invasion of Poland by Germany; no one but Him – by the Spirit. The Prime Minister and President ordered a uniform for Konstantine to wear. He was not a military man, but they knew the national clout he had with the people. And they wanted to empower his leadership. But it was too late. Warsaw would soon fall. The country was crumbling. The military was fleeing. Incredibly, Konstantine and the three highest government officials left in the land met in a coffee shop to consider their alternatives. He had warned them that the attack they had launched on Czechoslovakia the year before was ill advised, but they had not listened. Now, their own nation had collapsed around them. They had to flee for their lives. And they did, to Rumania, essentially leaving him in charge of the country, including the military. A religious man, a pastor, he became the shepherd of the nation for those few remaining days of trouble. Every road was packed with refugees fleeing somewhere. Fourteen hundred people were camped out at Jaroshevich's church – and the food they had purchased from the sale of their headquarters building was now unpacked. With the city under siege, there was nothing to do but wait – and pray. Seeking a quiet place one morning, the clergyman rose to walk out of the city to a hill, only to turn and see fifteen-thousand people following him. Many of them had scorned him only a month before, infidels, they now believed. Having lost everything, for the first time in their lives they were open to God. Bombs fell. Mothers carried wounded and sometimes dead children in the streets with another child frantically following along. It was a horrible scene.

Jaroshevich sought assistance for Poland from Russia. Wearing his military uniform, representing the nation, he arrived and requested an audience with Stalin. There, a high-ranking military officer greeted him, "You may not remember me!" he told Konstantine. He recounted that twenty years earlier, Jaroshevich had been confronted on a train, accused of being a minister. Rather than deny it, he openly admitted his faith. Witty and amiable, he won the soldiers over. At first, they were questioning him intensely, and then they were laughing. The most resistant of them became the most interested, and now he was this high-ranking officer. The two talked till late into the night. Dr. Jaroshevich had told the young communist soldier that he was made in 'the image of God.' Now, twenty years later, he recalled the moment, "I am the boy on the train. You told me I had been created in God's image and likeness – I have tried to live according to that likeness." With his assistance, fruit from a witnessing encounter two decades earlier, Jaroshevich gained an audience with Joseph Stalin.

When he returned, the city was virtually deserted. Only a hundred and fifty people remained of his own congregation. There was nothing left over which to preside. German troops loaded boxcars with people. He himself stood at a train-station and waited three days hoping to get transport that might take him out of the country, but it was all in vain. There were no passenger car accommodations, only rides in freight cars. As the train arrived and the car was opened in which he had hoped to ride, frozen bodies fell out. It had been parked on a railway spur for three days with the people trapped inside. They had all died. He decided to walk.

The weather was cold, frigidly so. Gestapo

brutality reigned. People were whipped for the least offense. Trucks ran people down and ran over them. Walking along the road, he observed a gathered crowd. Investigating, he discovered that a Jewish family was being maltreated, "So you are hungry," the officer said, "then eat with your brothers, the swine." And with that, they were pushed into the pig trough. Jaroshevich would not remain silent, "These are human beings," he protested. The Germans were shocked at his boldness. He turned to walk away, brushing away tears, but not far down the road, he heard the sound of a truck rumbling toward him. It nearly ran over him, and then it quickly stopped. "Your papers. And be quick about it." He handed them his passport, but they never looked at it. Instead, he was heaved into the back of the truck, "So ... You are interested in human beings, are you?"

He was hauled back to the nearest town, and there before him was the community death house. Intellectuals and political prisoners were placed there to die. A mere nine-by-thirteen feet, cold and dark, it was not a hospitable place. Twenty-three men were crowded into the small space. There was barely enough room for the men to stand. No room to lie down or relax. One man died in the afternoon, and two more would die before morning. He knew the type of death house to which he had been committed. It was one in which the prisoners were locked inside, given no provision, and left to die. For some, it took only a few days. Inside were professors, journalist, musicians and artists, those considered dissident. Weak and cold, without the resolve to live, one would slump to the floor.

Those with strength would lift them up, and make them walk in the tight space to stay alive, but only for a few more hours, or at the most days. Temperatures plunged to 25 degrees below zero. Sleep was the gateway to death.

To hasten the final day of a prisoner, the Gestapo entered the small space daily to beat them. Those who had dropped to the floor were kicked. "A man cannot live here more than two weeks," the prisoners confided in Konstantine, "the merciful way is to die the first day." Jaroshevich encouraged them. He recited scripture to them. Some had never heard the gospel; some had never wanted to hear it, until now. "Man of God, pray for us," and he did. Day and night. After a week, food began to mysteriously appear at the door. The villagers had learned that Konstantine, their beloved national spiritual leader was in the death house. The German prisoners ate their fill of the food and then tossed the remains into the death house. Night after night, the food mysteriously came. And night after night, small bits and leftovers were thrown inside. It was not enough to feed one man, but somehow twenty-three got a taste.

Two weeks had now passed. Not a man who had been alive when Konstantine entered the death house now remained alive. All had died and been replaced by others. He was now crippled and bent-over, his body marked by lashes and gashes across his back. His legs had been frozen and his feet were now so swollen that he could no longer keep his military boots on. He crept around, almost doubled over. He prayed and recited Bible verses. He refused to surrender to the seductive cold. "How long can a man live here?" a newcomer asked. "I have lived here thirty days!" he replied, not revealing that most died in two weeks. "Thirty days?" came the hopeful reply, "Perhaps someone will save us. Perhaps the war will be over. Perhaps ..." Men who had never prayed, prayed there, with him. He would recall that there were moments when the dark hole seemed to be full of light, radiance and peace reigned.

Forty days had now gone by. Then fifty. And he was still alive. The guards outside were almost afraid of him now. Some strange force had kept him alive. It was not normal. They were not dealing with a mere mortal. But the head of the Gestapo force was not moved. He was incensed that the preacher continued to live. For him, it was a personal challenge, and one that had gone on too long. Every morning he arrived at the death house, flung open the door, and looked for the man of God, hoping to find him dead. Finding him alive, he delighted in making him the example of an extra-special beating. Three more days passed and there was one more fierce and final beating. When he finished, he announced, "Tomorrow at five, my fine Dokter, you will be shot. I have had enough of you." Every man in the place felt as if the death sentence had been pronounced upon them. "Be of good cheer," the man of God declared, "I have not been shot yet. We shall wait and see. Today we pray, and tomorrow is in God's hand." They prayed and sang an hymn. The night passed slowly.

It was now five o'clock in the morning, but there were no sounds outside. Another thirty minutes passed, and still there were no voices. Hour after hour passed, until it was mid-morning with no boots, no trampling, no loud demands, no warning sounds of the danger that had been threatened. The whole day passed, and it was as if they had been forgotten. It was as if God had interrupted the intended action. It seemed divine. They spoke of spiritual things all through the day. Finally, at ten o'clock in the evening, a key was heard in the lock. The door opened and a strange group of soldiers who had not attended them entered the small space. The young harsh Gestapo Officer who had promised death was mysteriously gone. A senior man had replaced him, old and white-haired. He raised his hand and pointed at Dr. Jaroshevich, "Who is that man?" he asked. The other prisoners separated themselves until Jaroshevich stood alone in the small space. Then a strange thing happened. Sobbing. A clamorous commotion. Not from the prisoners, but from the jailor who had tended them consistently. He had fallen to his knees, weeping and begging for mercy, he threw his arms about the knees of the old German officer. "Please ... that man, sir ... he has been a blessing to all of us ... please let me take him out of here ... let me take care of him ..." It was the Gestapo Jailer who had listened daily through the keyhole, watching with a magnifying glass, strangely drawn to the holiness in the face of the godly leader. He had seen the beatings and belittling. He had witnessed the grace. He had heard the discussions and encouragement, the selflessness.

No one knows how or why, in natural terms, but thirty minutes before death of Jaroshevich was to be administered, new orders had arrived effective immediately for the brutal and eager Gestapo Officer, sending him to a new assignment, and ordering a new detachment to take charge of the death house, leaving only the jailer. By ten-thirty that evening, doctors had been called. Prisoners had their wounds treated – in the death house. Grace had prevailed, at least for a moment. Frost-bite was treated. Food was offered, with tea. The next day, Konstantine was taken out. There was the mockery of a trial, but the old Gestapo Officer had already made up his mind to set the clergyman free. They put him in a cell and allowed him to regain strength. As soon as he was able to travel, his jailers, members of the Gestapo, aided in his escape. They mapped out an itinerary for him. They gave him letters to carry to their own relatives, and he was moved from one to another, without money or passport, down through Italy, and then shipped off to America.

It is the story, in the midst of a national tragedy, of one preacher and one member of the Gestapo who saw in him great grace, and then risked his own life to save him. One moment of life in a death house. One man, carrying on a ministry of hope in the frigid doorway of death itself. One man, trying to save a nation; who may have at least seen one hardened man saved, probably, many more.

There were no imprecatory prayers
- only grace.

Adapted from, "Light in Gestapo Darkness," Margaret Lee Runbeck, *The Great Answer* (Boston: Houghton Mifflin Company, 1944), 211-225.

CHAPTER 8

IMPRECATORY PRAYERS

P. Douglas Small

The "Imprecatory Psalms" are a special class of literary prayer materials in which the disenfranchised and persecuted plea to God, often as a last resort, asking that He intervene in judgment on those who are enemies of the faith and the faithful and therefore of God Himself. None are entirely imprecations. But, the hymn and poetry book of the Old Testament does contain some one-hundred verses, out of 1,134, that match this classification – about 8.8 percent, one in every eleven verses or so.[1] That is significant. They contain prayers for a calamity or a curse to befall an enemy. They plead for God's protection and for His aggressive action against persecutors of the faithful, against those who block justice and whose actions injure the powerless and vulnerable, they ask for God to

---

1 Specifically, they are: 5:10; 6:10; 7:9, 15-16; 9:19-20; 10:15; 17:13; 28:4; 31:17-18; 35:1, 4-6, 8, 19, 24-26; 40:14-15; 52:5; 54:5; 55:9, 15; 56:7; 58:6-10; 59:5, 11-13; 68:1-2, 30; 69:22-25, 27-28; 70:2-3; 71:13; 74:11, 22-23; 79:6, 10, 12; 83:9, 11, 13-18; 94:1-2; 104:35; 109:6-15, 17-20, 29; 129:5-8; 137:7-9; 139:19, 21-22; 140:8-11; 141:10; 143:1. Here are 98 verses scattered throughout thirty-two psalms. Fourteen of these are so ripe with imprecations. The psalm is so characterized as an imprecatory psalm – that is almost one of ten psalms: 7, 35, 52, 55, 58, 59, 69, 79, 83, 94, 109, 129, 137, and 140. This compilation is from the work of John N. Day, "The Imprecatory Psalms and Christian Ethics," *Bibliotheca Sacra* 159 (April – June 2002):166-186. Copyright by Dallas Theological Seminary. www.dts. edu.

defend His own honor. They call out the 'warrior' dimension in God, asking Him to take action in behalf of the righteous and for the sake of kingdom purposes.

The "Imprecatory Psalms" are often stark pleas for dramatic judgment action.[2] And many of us are uncomfortable with such prayer pleas. That they are in the scriptures is troubling. That God appears to hear them is an even greater concern to us, given our cultural bias against a God who judges. But that God answers them is shocking to us. We seem to want a God who is a purer deity, nobler than the imprecations suggests, a 'loving' God who would ever consider a radical use of force, even against His adversaries. But it is not love that most comprehensively defines YHWH, rather, it is holiness. His love is incomparable, *agape,* unparalleled and unequaled, but that is because it issues from His holiness. God's truth is full, complete, balanced, an integrated whole and it is healthy, precisely because it rises out of His holiness. And His judgments are true, because they also arise from His holiness. Yet, because God is holy, there is of necessity, judgment. The holiness of God can be offended and disrespected. It can be scorned and spurned.

We see the psalms as comforting, as sweet devotional reflections, but these imprecations are found primarily in the psalms. They appear in other parts of the Old Testament as well. Even Moses, the "meekest man on the face of the earth," according to Numbers 12:3, prayed imprecatory prayers - *"Rise up, O Lord! And let Thine enemies be scattered, and let those who hate Thee flee before Thee"* (Numbers 10:35). Moses offers a list of potential curses that can be expected to befall Israel, if she rebels. The essence of these curses is repeated a hundred years later by Joshua. Imprecations also occur in prophetic literature - specifically in Hosea, Micah and Jeremiah.

---

2   Here is an alternative list, and as you can see, not all agree on what constitutes an imprecation or an imprecatory psalm. 5, 6, 11, 12, 35, 37, 40, 52, 54, 56, 58, 69, 79, 83, 137, 139, and 143 also fit into this category. Psalm 11, 12 and 37, are not noted in the list above.

In Psalm 69:24, God is asked, *"Pour out Your indignation on them, and let Your burning anger overtake them."* When Babylon invaded Judah and destroyed Jerusalem and the temple, the hatred and prejudice against Babylon and its people among the survivors became acute. Psalm 137:9 is another mournful psalm loaded with angry grief that longs for revenge, even on the young children of Babylon, *"Happy shall he be, that takes and dashes your little ones against the stones."* It is graphic and merciless. It is an example of blind, unfeeling revenge. No Christian is comfortable with such language - or the 'eye for eye' concept of revenge behind it. Elisha had earlier predicted what the army of Syria would do - 'dash' the children of nursing mothers on the rocks and 'rip open' pregnant women. However even Hazael, the Syrian leader, acknowledged the action as a 'gross thing' that only an animal, only 'a dog' would do. It was nevertheless a savage feature known in ancient war. And it may have been how the Babylonian troops treated the women and infants of Judah and Jerusalem in the final siege in BC 586. Migrating a population of tens of thousands of people from the southern sector of the land of Israel to Babylon, a trail of over 900 miles,[3] was not an easy task.[4] There was no time to pacify nursing babies, so they may

---

3   The actual distance is reckoned to be some 500 miles, but the route was not direct.

4   As regards the number of Jews deported by Nebuchadnezzar, there are two divergent reports. According to Jer. 52:28-30, 3,023 Jews were deported in 597 BC, 832 inhabitants of Jerusalem in 586, and 745 Jews in 582, making 4,600 persons in all, only men were counted. Hence 14,000 to 18,000 people must have been deported to Babylon. II Kings 24:14, 16, refer to 597 BC and states that 10,000 men were exiled; but verse 16 says 8,000. These figures are more than twice as high as Jeremiah. As many as 36,000 to 48,000 may have been migrated to Babylon. The total population of Judah was about 120,000, so one-fourth (II Kings 24:16) or, one-eighth (Jer. 52:28-30) was led captive. See: Jewish Encyclopedia – Babylonian Captivity. Online: http://www.bible-history.com/map_babylonian_captivity/map_of_the_deportation_of_judah_jewish_encyclopedia.html

have been brutally killed, dashed on the rocks, perhaps tragically on the stones of the dismantled temple or the walls of city (II Kings 8:12; Hosea 13:16; Luke 19:44; Nahum 3:10; Isaiah 13:16). Here, Israel prays to God for strict retribution – an eye for an eye; an act for an act - that Babylon will taste the same fate in the loss of their children. Still, the rationalization, hardly justifies such a terrible desire for innocents.

Most psalms are positive, in fact, that is the meaning of the word - psalms, which, in Hebrew, *tehilim,* means "praises." But here, in the imprecatory passages, we meet an altogether different genre of literature. The tenor and tone of the New Testament is different, but there are still imprecatory elements there as well as passages that quote imprecations in the Psalms. Jesus quotes them in John 2:17 and 15:25. Paul quotes from Psalm 69, an imprecation, when he writes to the Romans (11:9-10; 15:3). To cherish the likes of Psalm 23 and disdain Psalm 35 – is a double standard. It is true that while we regard the Scriptures as true and reliable, we do not regard every verse and phrase as truth. There is contained in the pages, the whisperings of the serpent, the words of the enemies of God, and the utterances of false prophets. Still, a quick dichotomization of scripture that allows us to dismiss imprecatory prayers as 'the aberrant rants of men' is too glib. Bonhoeffer reminds us that the words of men to God have become, in the scriptures, the Word of God to us.[5] This body of material is too vast to be overlooked. Almost one-in-five

> *Probably in the Day of Judgment, it will be found that nothing is ever done by the truth used ever so zealously, unless there is a spirit of prayer somewhere in connection with the presentation of truth.*
>
> ~ *Charles G. Finney*

---

5   Dietrich Bonhoeffer, *Psalms: The Prayer Book of the Bible* (Minneapolis: MN; Augsburg Publishers, 1970), 13.

psalms have imprecations.

A sister to the imprecatory prayers or imprecations, are prophetic declarations, sometimes in the form of a 'woe oracle.' These are not mere human words. These are Spirit-inspired warnings or declarations of coming doom. They are uttered, not for the redemption of the hard heart that is the subject of the coming woe, but as a warning to others who are listening and the watching the events unfold. Scriptures such as those that follow are only a small sample:

> *May they be like chaff before the wind. Psalm 35:5*
> *Let death take my enemies by surprise; let them go down alive to*
> *the grave. Psalm 55:15*
> *O God, break the teeth in their mouths. Psalm 58:6*
> *May they be blotted out of the book of life and not be listed with*
> *the righteous. Psalm 69:28*
> *May his children be fatherless and his wife a widow. Psalm 109:9*

Such prayerful declarations sound a world-apart from "Turn the other cheek," and "Love your enemies," and "Bless them that curse you!" One of the reasons the psalms are so loved is that we relate to the emotional breadth of the literature. But the outrage of this particular genre of psalm is something we hardly want to legitimately include. It is beyond the lines of acceptability – from our cultural perspective.

Even in the New Testament, there are a number of these 'woe' passages and there are additional warnings about behaviors that appear to trigger the judgment of God. In Matthew 23:13, Jesus pronounces a "woe" on the scribes and Pharisees, calling them "hypocrites!" for shutting the kingdom of God up for themselves, and not being missionaries to the nations; for oppressing widows, and for convoluting with legalism converts to Judaism; for broken promises and oaths based on a system that valued gold higher than the temple itself; for the lack of justice, mercy and faith; for being clean outside and dirty inside; for appearing alive, but being spiritually dead and contaminated; for pretending to honor the slain prophets, but failing to recognize one in their own midst – for all these things, he pronounces 'woe on woe!' He pictures them at the doorway to the Kingdom – a door they themselves have not entered and one they will not allow others to enter. "Therefore ye shall receive the greater damnation" (Matthew 23:14). As Judas conducts his act of betrayal, Jesus pronounces a 'woe!' upon him – "Woe to that man by whom the Son of man is betrayed! It had been good for that man if he had not been born" (Matthew 26:24). It is an imprecation. For Peter, he will pray; but upon Judas he breathes 'woe!' One can be redeemed; the other can't.

Paul offers an imprecatory utterance in I Corinthians 16:22, "If any man love not the Lord Jesus Christ, let him be *Anathema Maranatha*" – let him be detested and despised, accursed and damned. Essentially it means, beyond redemption. In Galatians 1:8-9, "Though we, or an angel from heaven, preach any other gospel unto you than that which we have preached unto you, let him be *accursed.*" It is the same idea. In verse 9, Paul broadens the judgment to "any man." To Timothy, he recalls the harm done to him by Alexander, the coppersmith, and prays, "The Lord reward him according to his works!" (II Timothy 4:14). At Galatia, the church is being torn apart by false teachers who are imposing elements of the law on them. Paul is so disturbed, he pens a prayer, "I would they were even *cut off* which trouble you" (Galatians 5:12).

Digging Deeper

The Legal Covenantal Basis

Deuteronomy 27 and 28 is loaded with God's promises, positive and negative with the whole earth, all of humanity, in rebellion against God and under wrath, God calls the people group to represent

Him in the earth before the nations. He offers them a covenant which provides a shelter of mercy bound to duty. They are promised exemption from earth's curses and blessings - if they will obey. This can never be seen as the beginning point. The whole earth is under wrath. Judgment has been suspended, but it is coming. Meanwhile, a covenant people will carry God's name, with His favor, testify to His moral laws, live under His commands - and be blessed before the watching world. God has created for them a bubble of blessing. But they must live within the parameters of the law to stay in covenant. Even over God's people there looms awesome and awful promises, threats of punishment and violence, if they do not hold dear the sacred trust of the law. "Cursed is the man who carves an image or casts an idol—a thing detestable to the Lord ..." To that concept, the people shouted, "Amen!" This was not a curse upon the nations – but on 'the nation,' on Israel themselves, if they disobeyed. "Cursed is the man who dishonors his father or his mother ... who moves his neighbor's boundary stone ... who leads the blind astray on the road ... who withholds justice from the alien, the fatherless or the widow ... who sleeps with his father's wife ... who has sexual relations with any animal ... who commits incest [in any form] ... who kills ... who accepts a bribe to kill ... who does not uphold the words of this law by carrying them out ..." When all the people said, "Amen!" they were praying, upon themselves, the judgment of God, were they to violate the covenant (27:14-26). Here, the people of God bound themselves, by vow and covenant, to potential judgment. God's own people were not only, not exempted from potential judgment, but they were themselves to be exemplary in the matter of judgment. Should we expect such an exemption?

Jeremiah prayed the judgment of God down on hard hearts as well.

Do give heed to me, O Lord, and listen to what my opponents are saying! Should good be repaid with evil? For they have dug a pit for me. Remember how I stood before Thee to speak good on their behalf, so as to turn away Thy wrath from them. Therefore, give their children over to famine, and deliver them up to the power of the sword; and let their wives become childless and widowed. Let their men also be smitten to death, their young men struck down by the sword in battle. May an outcry be heard from their houses, when Thou suddenly bringest raiders upon them; for they have dug a pit to capture me and hidden snares for my feet. Yet Thou, O Lord, knowest all their deadly designs against me; do not forgive their iniquity or blot out their sin from Thy sight. But may they be overthrown before Thee; deal with them in the time of Thine anger! (Jer. 18:19-23; cf. also 11:18ff.; 15:15ff.; 20:11ff.).

The Courtroom

In Psalm 17, a courtroom psalm, David pleads for a hearing before God in view of the men around him who "have closed up their fat hearts, [and] with their mouths they speak proudly, they have now surrounded us in our steps; they have set their eyes, crouching down to the earth, As a lion is eager to tear his prey, and like a young lion lurking in secret places." Here he asks again, for the intervention of God, "Arise, O Lord. Confront him, cast down; deliver my life from the wicked with Your sword ... from men of the world who have their portion I this life ..." (17:13-14).

But before he asks for such action, he notes, "You have tested my heart; you have visited me in the night; you have tried me and have found nothing; I have purposed that my mouth shall not transgress. By the word of Your lips, I have kept away from the paths of the destroyer" (v. 3-4). In simple language – 'I am clean, innocent.' David is aware that the double-edged sword of justice cuts both ways. That ideally, justice is blind! Yet, in heaven's court, one can ask for the law to be enforced, for the ultimate standard of right to be upheld. But David does so, knowing that he has 'purposed' not to transgress in the matter. His heart and hands are clean. The investigations of God 'have found nothing.' In Psalm 69, the psalmist prays, "Don't let those who seek You be confounded because of me ... for Your sake I have borne reproach; Shame has covered my face ... because zeal for Your house has eaten me up ..." There are times when the negative press, the confusion around us, as in David's case, causes seekers to be 'confounded,' confused, dismayed, and discouraged from seeking God. There are times when God's enemies, earthly and supernatural, attempt to discredit God, by associating His children with some 'shameful or reproaching' matter. David pleads for intervention, not merely for his sake, but for the sake of God's cause. Calvin says that "a holy zeal for the divine glory impelled him to summon the wicked to God's judgment seat."

The requisite for prayers that implore the judgment of God is righteousness. The standard is high, indeed. This is not a type of prayer to be prayed lightly. Rash prayers, like rash vows have consequences. Jephtah, leading the Israelite army, promised God he would offer as sacrifice the first thing that met him when he came back from the battle. It turned out to be his daughter (Judges 11).

A Profile of One Imprecatory Prayer in the Psalms

The Plea for Divine Action: In Psalm 83, there is a plea for God to "not keep silent!" It reads, "Don't be quiet, O God, Do not hold your peace. And do not be still" (83:1). God is being urged to 'speak up' in behalf of His people. He is being pressed to act – 'Don't just sit and watch this happen. Do something!'

The Presenting Problem: The problem is noted in verses 2-8. There is an adversary. In the text, in human form, it is a group of men who "plot together" – first, against God and, second, against

His people. These two factors can never be separated. Judgment is not warranted because someone has merely done *us* wrong – hurt our feelings, inconvenienced us, or made our life more difficult in some way. No. Judgment is warranted only when there are schemes against God or the wicked have placed the righteous in harm's way as a means of subverting the will of God or controverting His Word and holy principles.

The Predicament in Detail: In verses 9-15, we find more specific detail about the predicament of the people, along with pleas for God's intervention, for vengeance against these individuals who are clearly acting as enemies of the Lord and His people – "deal with them ... [like you did] with Midian ... Sisera ... Jabin ... who perished." Here precedents are cited. And on the basis of the pattern, the appeal for judgment is made. The words of the enemies are cited as evidence; and among their words is evidence of their disdain for God. Their words are taken seriously. "Make [the current enemies] ... who said, 'Let us take for ourselves the pastures of God for a possession' ... Make them like the whirling dust ... like chaff ... as the fire burns the woods ... as the flame sets the mountains on fire ... pursue them with your tempest ... frighten them with your storm" (v. 9-15). These intimidating tactics are designed with a purpose in mind. Overwhelmed by the ravages of fire and storm, we tend to recalibrate our own sense of weakness and vulnerability. We see how fragile life can be. We are humbled. All of this is in vain, if there is not a personal and corporate epiphany.

The Overarching Purpose: Note the final section, Psalm 83:16-18,

Cover their faces with shame so that men will seek your name, O Lord. May they ever be ashamed and dismayed; may they perish in disgrace.

The prayer is that these evil men and their wicked deeds will be revealed in order that a measure of revival might take place as others see them shamed. There is little hope that the evil men themselves will change. The prayer is that they "be confounded ... dismayed forever ... put to shame and [that they] perish ... That they (onlookers) may know that You, whose name alone is the Lord, are the Most High ..." As others see the confusion of the once mighty and powerful, observe their dismay, and see their ruin – then the observing population will seek the Lord.[6] There are three groups in view here. First, the evil and arrogant powerful who are the oppressors. The second group is the righteous, who are the oppressed. They are victims and their only hope is the intervention of God in response to prayer. They are praying, asking for divine action in the nation. The third group is those who see the battle between the evil faction and the righteous. But they are not believers. They appear as neutral. But when God's intervention is clearly seen, "They seek your name, O Lord" (83:16). In verses 14-15, there is yet another picture, that of a furious fire that drives the enemy from his own land. This is nature as a tool of God's warfare. How can an enemy fight such a God?

All of the earthly weapons of mass destruction aimed at heaven's pearly gates would do the celestial city no harm. When Christ returns, a thousand fighter pilots with ballistic, laser guided missiles would not affect Him. What affects God is what affects any father – attacks on His young and vulnerable children. It is what affects any man, an attack upon his wife. When the enemies of God are enemies because they engage in war against His people and the purposes for which they stand, God considers action.

"Your enemies make a tumult [an uproar – they are stirred in an adversarial way], those who hate you have lifted up their head [your foes rear their heads, an act of pride, against you, God]. They

---

6   Mitchell Dahood, *The Anchor Bible, Vol. 17, Psalms II* (Garden City, N.Y.: Doubleday, 1968), 277.

have taken crafty counsel against your people [with cunning they conspire] and consult together against your sheltered ones [against those you cherish]. They have said, 'Come let us cut them off from being a nation, that the name of Israel may be remembered no more (83: 2-4).

The Psalmist asserts: "These are 'Your enemies' God. They 'hate You' God, and have lifted up their head, by implication, 'against You, God.'" But how does one wage war against God? What follows is their action against the people of God. The war against God is accomplished by the destruction of His people. And the end result is to attempt to decimate the people of God that they will be no more; no longer a nation – scattered and eliminated as a political and moral force, lost as a visible symbol of God in the earth.

Spiritual assaults come against us simply because we are the followers of Christ. The person that reacts to us so intensely may not confess adversity to our faith. They may not understand their own violent reaction to us. In fact, we may never have seen them before and we may never see them again – but something beyond the norm, beyond mere personality and personal preference triggered a verbal or emotional incident between us. We must not take such attacks personally. The enemy fire around us is not about us, it is about our cause. While we should not personalize such episodes, God does!

> *When God's mercies are coming, their footfalls are our desires to pray.*
>
> *~Spurgeon*

"'Come,' they say, 'let us destroy them as a nation, that the name of Israel be remembered no more.' With one mind they plot together; they form an alliance against you" (vv. 4-5).

This is a description not only of Israel, but of modern America.

There seems to be a plot to destroy Christians and the Church, godly influences and institutions. Godless groups have formed and linked arms to rise against any public display of prayer and faithfulness to American Christian heritage. We are living Israel's history. The psalmist goes on to site God's actions in the past – and urge that He now act, consistent with His pattern of avenging righteousness in yesteryear.

One more note on Psalm 83, and that is a bottom line outcome. "Cover their faces with shame!" he prays, "so that men [not necessarily '*them*' –but other men, men who see God's dealings, who recognize that God is alive and active in history, that there are consequences for evil behavior – *they*] *will* seek your name, O Lord." Some people respond to God's love. Others respond to the message of truth, the gentle Holy Spirit convicting them of sin and calling them to the cross. But still others require a power encounter with God. Perhaps, even among the adversaries, once humbled by the mighty hand of God, some of them will believe. Confronted, as Paul was, in the dust of the Damascus Road, perhaps there is also hope for them. But it is for the larger population that we pray – those who are neither the evil oppressors nor the oppressed. That is the group that must be awakened and moved out of the neutral zone. So why do we pray that God would not withhold judgment? Why, at least at times, is judgment in the present age, an act of grace? It leads to awareness of God, and to conversion. Rom. 2:2-4 indicates that "*God consistently leads men to Himself through judgment.*"

The prayer is that the evil doers will be, one translation says, "like tumbleweed" (83:13). They will become rootless. They will experience the instability of the world without God. Contrary winds will drive them like tumbleweeds tossed about. King Nebuchadnezzar lost his sanity for a season, but when that season was over, something had happened to him.

> At the end of that time, I, Nebuchadnezzar, raised my eyes toward heaven, and my sanity was restored. Then I praised the Most High; I honored and glorified Him who lives forever. His dominion is an eternal dominion; His kingdom endures from generation to generation. All the peoples of the earth are regarded as nothing. He does as He pleases with the powers of heaven and the peoples of the earth. No one can hold back His hand or say to Him: "What have you done?" (Dan. 4:34-35).

David Dickson, a Puritan commentator on the Psalms, had it right when he wrote,

> If any of the enemies of God's people belong to God's election, the Church's prayer against them giveth way to their conversion, and seeketh no more than that the judgment should follow them, only until they acknowledge their sin, turn, and seek God.[7]

Psalm 109 – The Extreme Imprecation

Psalm 109 is one of the more intense imprecations. It is a prayer for the punishment of the wicked,[8] probably with the strongest language of any psalm. C. S. Lewis called it as "unabashed a hymn of hate as was ever written."[9] Many believers find such a passage troubling. Some are shaken by such language. Calvin warned that the psalm was too often misused by so-called believers who in the most cavalier manner prayed for the death of others.[10] Some, who

---

7   David Dickson, *Commentary on the Psalms* (Minneapolis: Klock and Klock, 1980), 2:67.

8   I am indebted to Bob Deffinbaugh for his study, *Psalm 109: A Prayer for the Punishment of the Wicked.*

9   C. S. Lewis, *Christian Reflections* (Wm. B. Eerdmans Publishing, 1994), 118.

10 John Calvin, *Commentary on the Book of Psalms* (Grand Rapids, MI: 1999), 4:276.

wished another dead, but did not have the stomach or desire to acknowledge that they had ever prayed such a prayer, paid others to pray imprecatory prayers for them. The idea was scandalous.

King David is the author of this *dreadful* psalm, so-called, and in these verses he cries out for the destruction of his enemies. There are at least thirty anathemas enunciated in these verses.[11] The plea for punishment reaches not only to the enemies, but to their family members as well. "Let his children be fatherless, and his wife a widow. Let his children wander about and beg; and let them seek sustenance far from their ruined homes" (109:9-10).

> *A graceless man will be a prayerless man.*
>
> The Prayer Meeting and Its History, J. B. Johnston

In Psalm 109, David pleads with God, as in other imprecatory psalms – to not be silent. These cloud-bursts of judgment calls toward heaven seem to follow a season in which the believer or righteous community feels some sense of abandonment by God. Heaven is too silent. Some crisis is unaddressed and now acute. While God remains silent, the enemy has not. With a "wicked and deceitful mouth [he has spoken] against" the righteous "with a lying tongue … with words of hatred" (v. 2). With such toxic rhetoric and negative emotions swirling on every side. There is a sense of things escalating out of control. Words soon move to deeds, they have "fought against me without cause" (v. 3). Despite the 'turning of the other cheek' and other attempts to emolliate the matter, things have intensified. "In return for my love, they act as my accusers" (v. 4). The only recourse now is prayer, "But I am in prayer." It is his only alternative.

In these verses, David makes two assertions. First, he is innocent. The adversary is "without a cause" There is no rational or legal basis

---

11   J. J. Stewart Perowne, *The Book of Psalms* (Grand Rapids: Zondervan [reprint], 1976), I, 305.

for their hatred, their falsifications or the conspiracy of accusation (v. 3). He characterizes them as 'wicked ... deceitful ... liars ... hateful ...unjust and unfounded actors ... accusers ... who reward evil for good, hatred for love' (v. 2-5). All the while these matters have escalated, he has continued his practice of 'praise' (v. 1), love (v. 4, 5), prayer (v. 4), and doing good (v. 5).

Earlier, we noted that imprecations in scripture are usually and ideally related to a defense of God's righteousness, His name, His honor or purposes. But here in Psalm 109, the wrongs are framed almost entirely on a personal basis, and those are injuries against David. This requires some reflection. In the larger context, the wicked deals contemptuously with righteous men and godly leaders, but they do so as an evidence of their disdain for God (See Ps. 37:12; 139:19-20). And here, the attack on David must be considered in reference to his role as king, as divine representative.

Derek Kidner brands men who engage in personal attacks as we have here as character assassins! And it is upon such men that the most severe judgment in all of scripture is called down.[12] It is not upon those who commit the egregious sins – murder and rape, robbery and assault, blasphemy and scandal, idolatry and adultery. It is on the 'character assassins' – the whisperers, the gossip mongers, the dissidents who spread unfounded and damaging rumors at the edges. It is upon those who divide and assault

> *The one thing above all others that bolts and bars the way into the "presence chamber's of prayer is unwillingness to forgive from the heart.*
>
> Samuel Chadwick, *The Path of Prayer,* pg. 31.

---

12 Derek Kidner, *Psalms 73-150* (Downers Grove: Inter-Varsity Press, 1975), 388. See the chapter, "The Character-Assassin."

unity by an attack on leadership. It is upon those who fail to see the sacredness of relationship. These people are the truly wicked. And they are not merely the 'difficult' sheep of David's flock, nor are they 'goats.' They are enemies, wolves in sheep's clothing. And they are God's enemies as well.

David's prays for God's judgment. Often, such evil cannot be dealt with directly. In fact, we fail to see relational sin as even being sin. If someone only 'says' something toxic about another, they are merely exercising their right to 'free speech' – which may be a constitutional right, but not one grounded in Scripture. Attempting to silence an accuser often only serves to explode the division. Dealing directly with the dissident sometimes expands the conflict. It empowers the rebellious and toxic individual. It seems far too much like a personal vendetta or even insecure defensiveness. So, at times, only God can deal with such cancer.

An imprecation, as is found in Psalm 109, is not a 'voodoo-like' pronouncement. It is a sincere plea from the innocent, for the punishment of the wicked. It must be a *just* plea, some righteous standard must have been violated, and some vile action has persisted and is offensive to the very nature of God. Proverbs tells us that a curse without basis has no effect: "Like a sparrow in its flitting, like a swallow in its flying, so a curse without cause does not alight" (Prov. 26:2).

These men have evidently been, at some point, closely associated with David. He has shown them love! He knows them. There have been attempts by scholars to identify the person or persons David has in view here. No one knows for sure. Candidates include Doeg the Edomite (Psalm 52:1; I Samuel 21:7), Shimei (II Samuel 16:5-8), and even Saul, though the latter is doubtful (I Sam. 18–31).[13]

---

13 Perowne, 287-288; See the reference to the article by Joseph Hammond, "An Apology for the Vindictive Psalm," *The Expositor*, Vol. ii., 225-360.

What is fascinating is that David does not name is enemy. He makes his plea to God who knows all things. He will not become a slanderer himself.

David's Imprecation against His Enemies (109:6-20)

In Psalm 109:6-20, David does spell out the possible punishments. We will not delve too deeply into the details, but there are a few interesting points. First, in verses 1-5, the enemies had been noted as plural, as being many. Now, in this section (6-20), David uses the singular. It may be that he sees the group as monolithic whole. It may also mean that the leader for the opposition is the focus of his prayer. By the way, the term adversary here is *satan!* Truly, he is the real enemy. Humans are only His instruments. David prays that "a wicked man be set over his foe and that an adversary accuse him" – in effect, let what he is attempting to do, be turned on his own head. Let his house of cards fall on him. But then David prays also that his life would be shortened. Perhaps, his intention is that the first action of God's intervention might bring a moment for reflection and change. But barring such a heart change, David prays that the "days of his enemy should be few" and that another will "take his office" (v. 8). This would leave his wife a widow and his children as orphans (v. 9). Such a prayer seems unduly harsh, especially in our day of hyper-individualism. No wife or child, we assert today, should suffer due to the actions of a father. And yet, wives and children suffer daily due to the actions or inactions of fathers; and fathers of mothers; and parents of children. We are bound together. We are reminded,

> *He who returns evil for good, evil will not depart from his house (Prov. 17:13).*
> *The curse of the Lord is on the house of the wicked, but He blesses the dwelling of the righteous (Prov. 3:33).*

ACCENT

† Because of the severity of this request, it might be well to consider 'who' the enemy was in this case. One possibility is that this is Doeg, the Edomite. He was the chief herdsman for Saul when he was King (I Samuel 21, 22). It was Doeg who slaughtered the priests. Saul was insanely jealous of David. And when David fled to Nob, he consulted with Ahimelech, the High Priest. Abimelech cared for David and his men on that day, and there David claimed the sword of Goliath. Doeg was present. He observed Ahimelech's reception of David and reported it to Saul (I Sam 22:9). But Doeg told only half the story. In Abimelech's reception of David, he was unaware of the severe rift between Saul and the young warrior. He received David as an emissary of the king, as if he were on a secret mission. Abimelech was not acting in a treacherous way. But Doeg omitted that critical piece of information, distorting the truth, and thereby destroyed the royal support for Ahimelech, who thought, in serving David, he was serving the king.

Doeg not only served Saul in deceit, he betrayed the priesthood, laying the ground work for their slaughter.

Saul was outraged. He ordered the High Priest and his entire company killed. The massacre of holy men was a betrayal of both David and Saul, and an unthinkable blot on Israel's history. Doeg, who set up the king to murder the priests, gladly carried out the executions. Next came the attack on the entire city of Nob, which was also the city of the priests. Abner and Amasa, Saul's lieutenants, had refused to take the matter further. So Doeg himself slaughtered the priests and their families – men, women and children were put to death. Only Abiathar escaped. He fled to David.

As sad as the affair was, it was connected to another great national tragedy. Ahimelech was the great-grandson of Eli whose sons had been so corrupt that they allowed the capture of the ark. The glory of God departed and a curse fell on the House of Eli, declaring that none of his male descendants would live to old age.

David would confess to Abiathar, "I knew that day, when Doeg the Edomite was there, that he would surely tell Saul." And for that reason, David felt personally responsible, "I have occasioned the death of all the persons of your father's

It is not the individual alone who is affected by sin and the consequent judgment. It is the 'house' – the entire family. Actions proceed from attitudes. And the attitudes of the sinning father take root in the family itself. The sins of the fathers are "visited on the children, even to the third and fourth generations *of those who hate God*" (Exodus 20:5; Deuteronomy 5:9). We establish a kind of behavioral trajectory. Our children are like 'arrows' and the direction of their lives are connected to the attitudes and actions they consciously or unconsciously absorb growing up. But, there is a redemptive stream here as well. Moses warned Israel:

> *"You shall not afflict any widow or orphan. If you afflict him at all, and if he does cry out to Me, I will surely hear his cry; and My anger will be kindled, and I will kill you with the sword; and your wives shall become widows and your children fatherless" (Exod. 22:22-24).*

Once a woman is a widow and a child an orphan, they now come under the special protection of God. Redemption is possible. Redirection is plausible. God becomes the Father. A holy seed should now issue forth. But here, David sees no redemptive possibility. He prays for fiscal reversals (vv. 10-11) and for the lineage to not continue (vv. 12-13).†

In Psalm 109:14-20, David, as if arguing in a courtroom, continues his plea for punishment, but on a different basis. He simply requests retribution – that his enemies get their due (Exodus 21:24; Leviticus 24:20; Deuteronomy 19:21), no more and no less. Personal revenge is out. But justice, an act of the court, must proceed, or the nation ends in anarchy. If there is no respect for the rule of law, no enforcement of right, no restraint of evil, and no protection for the innocent – then there is wholesale bloodshed everywhere. Murder is always wrong in scripture; killing, an action of the state, is not. And the failure to distinguish the two leads to injustice. Murder is an act of taking a life by an individual. Killing is an act justified house" (I Sam 22:22). Psalm 52 is written by David after Doeg the Edomite does his evil deed. And he may be the enemy in view in Psalm 109.

Doeg supposedly converted to Judaism. However, his ethics and his willingness to expose, by his own fabrication the priests, and then execute them, hardly makes a case for his being devout. The rabbis have a field day with him. He is the subject of numerous legends. He died at the early age of thirty-four. In Scripture, he appears as a brute. But the rabbinical tradition has cast him as somewhat of a scholar, who was unbeatable in a debate. All who disputed with him were said, in the end, to 'blush.' Or the meaning may refer to his being crude, even in language. Known for brute force and intellect, neither qualified him as godly. He was said to be hateful and jealous with a 'calumnious tongue.' He pretentiously praised David, while he carried a secret grudge. He attempted to disqualify David as a legitimate Israelite on the basis of lineage. As a descendant of Ruth the Moabite, he could not, Doeg argued according to the Law, belong to the congregation of Israel. This placed Doeg in direct contradiction to the prophet Samuel, who had anointed David. To prevent potential ties to the throne, he declared David's marriage with Michal to be invalid, and induced Saul to marry her to another, thus severing the marital connection of David to the royal family. There is also an interesting note in the Midrash that indicates that it was Doeg who tried to preserve the life of Agag, the king of the Amalekites-Edomites, by interpreting Lev. 22:28 as a prohibition against the destruction of both the old and the young in war. Was Doeg scheming to seize the throne of Saul?

The other possibility here in Psalm 109 is Shimei of the house of Saul, though much less likely. The Scripture says, "Now when King David came to Bahurim, there was a man from the family of the house of Saul, whose name was Shimei the son of Gera, coming from there. He came out, cursing continuously as he came. And he threw stones at David and at all the servants of King David. And all the people and all the mighty men were on his right hand and on his left. Also Shimei said thus when he cursed: "Come out! Come out! You bloodthirsty man, you rogue! The Lord has brought upon you all the blood of the house of Saul, in whose place you have reigned; and the Lord has delivered by the court and the law in view of egregious action of the aggressor, and is designed to restore peace and order to the culture.

David will not act in a vengeful manner. He prays that God act in behalf of him and other victims. They are now God's problem. And their sins will continue, if they are not stopped. David has not only the enemy in view, but the generational impetus that drove this evil man. He was acting as his fathers had acted (vv. 14-15). The absence of mercy has been the established pattern in this evil lineage, and so David asked that they not receive mercy (Proverbs 21:13; cf. Matthew 5:7; James 2:13).

David Pleas for Personal Grace (109:21-29)

"God," he appeals, "deal kindly with me for Thy name's sake." He requests deliverance. And he reports that he is both "afflicted and needy," indeed, he has an inner wound, "My heart is wounded within me." He feels like his very life is fading, "I am passing like a shadow ... My knees are weak ... my flesh has grown lean ..." He has been without adequate food. When folks see him, they cannot believe his physical state, "When they see me, they shake their head." Emotionally drained. Spiritually anemic. Physically emaciated. He has rarely been in such a terrible state. "Deal kindly with me!"

"Help me," he pleads. His language is personal. Unvarnished. "Save me according to Thy loving-kindness." He does not base his appeal simply on his need, but on the character of God. Save me – 'for your name's sake!' Help me – 'according to your loving-kindness.' Here is that wonderful word – *hesed*. It is the basis for the covenant. It is the closest Hebrew term to the New Testament, *agape*. 'Do this for me – because of the kind of God you are! Do this – so that your name will be honored.' His appeal is that his life will, one more time, be a showcase for God to reveal himself, "Let them know that this is Your hand; You, LORD, have done it." Again, his confidence is the kingdom into the hand of Absalom your son. So now you are caught in your own evil, because you are a bloodthirsty man!" (II Samuel 16:5-14 KJV)

Shimei was a distant relative of King Saul who harbored resentment against David. "Cursing continuously ..." he attempted to stone David, to incite a riot against him. He characterized him as a "bloodthirsty man ... [a] rogue!" Shimei was not only offensive, he was an agent of personal destruction, set against David and his Kingdom. The personal attack came at a time of vulnerability for David. Spurgeon once said, "Only the coward strikes a man when he is down."

David had actually treated Saul and his family with kindness. While he was a warrior, he was not a bloodthirsty man. It was not David that had brought Saul or his house to ruin, it was Saul himself. David responded to the attack of Shimei with humility. It was Abishai, the son of Zeruiah, his sister, who felt his honor had been assassinated. He said to David, "Why should this dead dog curse my lord the king? Please, let me go over and take off his head!"

David acted with more disgust toward Abishai, than outrage to Shimei. "What have I to do with you, you sons of Zeruiah? So let him curse ..." It was not Shimei who was on David's mind. It was as if the man were only voicing something from some distance away. In fact, David suggested that Shimei was cursing him, "Because the Lord has said to him, 'Curse David.'" No, it was not the words of Shimei, it was the wound of Absalom, "See how my son who came from my own body seeks my life. How much more now may this Benjamite? Let him alone, and let him curse; for so the Lord has ordered him. It may be that the Lord will look on my affliction, and that the Lord will repay me with good for his cursing this day."

David continued along the road, and Shimei walked the hillside above them, continuing to swear and hurl profane language at the King. When words were not enough, Shimei attempted to pelt David with stones. He kicked up the dust, attempting to spray him with dirt. It was too much for the king's company, "All the people who were with him became weary; so they refreshed themselves there." If David had been the man he was accused of being, Shimei would have been dead in a matter of minutes. Blinded by rage, the man could not see the grace being shown him.

rooted in his faith in the character of God, "They curse ... but you bless!" In fact, God had promised Abraham, "The one who curses you, I will curse" (Genesis 12:3).

Paul reminds us, "Behold then the kindness and severity of God" (Rom. 11:22). The two are bound together. They cannot be separated – mercy and penalty, love and truth, forgiveness and consequences. The basis of David's plea for just judgment on the enemies of both He and God, is the same basis for his plea now, for mercy, for intervention, for God's evident hand to be on him so all will know that the Lord has done it.

David's Promises Praise (109:30-31)

He can see light at the end of the tunnel. When it is all over, when he is again recovered from this tragic moment, he can envision his public response,

> *"With my mouth I will give thanks abundantly to the LORD; And in the midst of many I will praise Him. For He stands at the right hand of the needy, To save him from those who judge his soul."* (NASB)

God is the "God of David's praise" (v. 1). In verses 30 and 31, he vows public praise for the coming deliverance. It will not be private. It will be offered in the midst of the congregation (v. 30). David will testify that in the darker moments, he saw God at his right hand as a defender. Then, the accusations will stop. The slanderers will be hushed.

Digging Out

Imprecations: The Prayer Language of Justice

We are New Testament people, and yet, the Old Testament is

David refused to kill Shimei - but at the end of his life, he warned Solomon about the danger that Shimei's opposition continued to present to the throne.

"And, behold, thou hast with thee Shimei the son of Gera, a Benjamite of Bahurim, which cursed me with a grievous curse in the day when I went to Mahanaim: but he came down to meet me at Jordan, and I sware to him by The Lord, saying, I will not put thee to death with the sword. Now therefore hold him not guiltless: for thou art a wise man, and knowest what thou oughtest to do unto him; but his hoar head bring thou down to the grave with blood." (I Kings 2:8-9 KJV)

Solomon wisely took his father's advice. He called for the treacherous Shimei, and instructed him to build a house in Jerusalem - under the King's nose. And then, he placed Shimei under house arrest. "Dwell there, and go not forth ... on the day you got out, and pass over the brook Kidron ... know for certain that you will surely die." He offered Shimei grace, on a short lease. Shimei stayed in Jerusalem for three years, and then fled to the connect with the Achish, the son of Maachah, the king of Gath. Solomon acted swiftly. "You know the wickedness which your heart is privy to that you did to David my father: therefore the Lord shall return your wickedness upon your own head ..." (I Kings 2:36-46 KJV)

rich with truth. Imprecatory Psalms are not admitted in some circles, even with the background provided here. Kittle, a great scholar, calls the Psalm 109 passage "… utterly repulsive … the wildest form of vengeance…" For Kittle, it is "questionable hymn of cursing" loaded with "carnal passion that is utterly inexcusable."[14] There must be a caution raised here. Again, the imprecatory language is not justified as language of personal revenge. It is the language of justice. It is an appeal, beyond the courtrooms of the earth, to the Judge above all judiciaries, to the supreme lawgiver, to the One who is just and merciful – to take note, and intervene, because the balance of power of this earth is bent toward evil, and the righteous are made victims,

---

14   Kittel, as quoted by Leupold, *Psalms*, 763.

and the name of the Lord is disregarded and his purposes thwarted. Moreover, it would become far too easy for us to simply call down fire on this village and that. Our hearts are too corrupt. Great caution must be laid out for us. Uttering imprecatory declarations cannot come from our lips easily. And we must remember that when the rain falls, it falls on the just and unjust (Matthew 5:45). And yet, to suggest, as some do, that these examples are "too lofty ... to imitate" since "such a vehement hatred is a luxury which can be afforded only by the great lovers of God" takes a rather huge swath of prayer options away from the Church.[15]

Angry Praying

Our praying, our angry praying, our frustrated praying, is a kind of therapy. By it, we pour out of pain. Our hurts and dashed hopes are raised before God. "Cold prayers freeze before they reach heaven," Thomas Brooks would say. And Spurgeon added, "Cold prayers ask for a denial!" He also noted, "We always pray best when we pray out of the depths – when the soul gets low enough she gets a leverage; she can then plead with God." The psalms are loaded with complaints – offered as prayer.[16] Pious pretend-praying that denies the true state of the soul when it is disturbed is dishonest praying. It is hypocritical praying. We should pray honestly, forthrightly – our true feelings. And yet always with a heart that longs to align aberrant

---

15 John McKenzie, *The Book of Psalms* (Grand Rapids: Baker Book House, 1982), 96.

16 Hermann Gunkel, *The Psalms: A Form-Critical Introduction* (Fortress Press, 1967; translation of *Die Religion in Geschichte und Gegenwart* [2nd ed; J.C.B. Mohr (Paul Siebeck), 1930]; and Hermann Gunkel (completed by Joachim Begrich), *Introduction to Psalms: The Genres of the Religious Lyric of Israel* (Mercer University Press, 1998; translation of *Einleitung in die Psalmen: die Gattungen der religiösen Lyrik Israels* [Vandenhoeck & Ruprecht, 1985, 1933]).‡

feelings to godly, biblical standards. After making our plea, the pouring out of our honest souls, privately, we then surrender all rights for vengeance to God. That may mean that we embrace the potential for more suffering and rejection. It may mean a need for greater grace to love and forgive. It may require deeper levels of discipline in order to remain meek and gentle while being reviled and persecuted. It is a major trust invested in God.

The Bigger Picture

So often, in such moments when our world seems threatened, acute self-awareness, perhaps self-centeredness is our primary concern. It may shock us to know – that is not the primary concern of God. We are expendable. There are greater concerns than our comfort, even our momentary well-being. There is a cosmic struggle going on, a war over the planet. Adam's house is still

ACCENT

‡ Gunkel classifies certain psalms as 'laments or complaint' literature. Those that are designed for use by the community, are - 44; (58); (60); 74; 79; 80; 83; (106); (125). These call on Yahweh by name, offer a complaint over some misfortune, typically political in nature, thus the corporate form. They petition God to intervene, to act, usually for his own honor or his name. These are often set in the context of some national call to fasting preceding a national calamity – a war, their exile, pestilence, drought, famine, and plagues. There is also a group of individual 'Complaint Psalms.' There are, according to Gunkel, Psalms 3; 5; 6; 7; 13; 17; 22; 25; 26; 27:7-14; 28; 31; 35; 38; 39; 42-43; 54-57; 59; 61; 63; 64; 69; 70; 71; 86; 88; 102; 109; 120; 130; 140; 141; 142; 143. This is a major portion of the prayer material of the psalms – complaints, poured out vertically. They summons YHWH to intervene in much the same way the corporate models do. They are characterized by anger, hurt, pain, betrayal,

and at times a sense of abandonment by God. They rehearse the words of the enemy. And they appeal to God, often as their only source of help. They express confidence that God has heard. At times, they bind themselves by a vow. These psalms are not triggered by the daily chariot rush hour mishaps. They are tied to some life-endangering opponent - sickness, hardship, tyranny, oppression in the face of innocence. And at times, with an admission that they have sinned against God, and the situation may be his way of dealing with them. Psalms 51 and 130 express national penitence as does Psalms 78; 81; 106; cf. also Ezra 9:9-15; Neh 9:9-38; Dan 9:4-19. Here you find the painful awareness of the consequences of sin and the admission that judgment is deserved. Only in that light, against the backdrop of deserved wrath, is there an appeal made to mercy. Some cry out for vengeance against enemies. Others, express hope and trust in God, such as Psalms 4; 11; 16; 23; 27:1-6; 62; 131. Also, Psalm 125 is a national song of trust.

under siege; it has yet to be completely liberated by heaven. A whole planet has been subjugated. Only a minority have been unshackled from sin. Not all have even heard that a redeemer has come. Not all have learned the cause of their suffering. They live and die without understanding the meaning of it all. We are the agents of the kingdom that has come, but not yet fully come. We are whispering the 'good news' at the edge of the darkness. We see flashes of God's glory, but never its full glaring light – that will only come with the Second Advent. We experience moments of the miraculous, confirmations that Jesus is alive. That He, by the power of the Spirit, is working with us. But because we carry reflections of His light and life, we too experience push-back. We experience warfare and come under very real dark fire. In such moments, some of us are delivered from, others are delivered to the Lord, himself

(Hebrews 11:32-39). We pass through flood and fire (Isaiah 43:2). We come under the shadow of death (Psalm 23:4). It is a part of living in a broken world. We have an enemy, one who is very real. And there is a genuine life and death war going on. We have built our houses and malls, our churches and schools on a battlefield. In stretches of seasons, there is no sense of any conflict. At other times, we feel the oppression and we are the casualties of the war. On occasions, we or those who we love are wounded – by enemy fire, or more sadly, by friendly fire. These are the inescapable consequences of living in a fallen world.

Bonheoffer would say, "One is distressed by the failure of reasonable people to perceive either the depths of evil or the depths of the holy."

Bonhoeffer, from "Ethics," Quoted by Charles Ringma, *Seize the Day with Dietrich Bonhoeffer* (Colorado Springs, Colorado: Pinion Press; 2000), See entry for January 20.

There are absolutes - rights and wrongs, despite the contemporary war on law itself, and the attempt to pervert it by the hyper-individualists. There are actions of life and actions of death. There are good deeds and evil deeds. All these actions have consequences, not only here, but in terms of heaven's disposition toward us as individuals and a nation. Grace does not suspend the effects of the law, only the penalty. Sin is still sin. Adultery still pollutes a marriage, even if spouses forgive and reconcile. The painful memory remains. The act of distrust is a fact. Every lie violates truth.

A Prayer Plea for Justice and Righteousness

Each of the Ten Commandments is a call to see some unique aspect of human life as 'sacred.' And it was God's law that stood behind the laws of the land in the founding of America. Prior to America's experiment, for most of history and still in much of the modern world, the rule was and is 'Rex Lex' – the King is the Law. He ruled by decree. But in America, the paradigm was inverted, as it had been in ancient Israel. There, the king was not above the law, but subject to it. The office of the prophet was a balance, as was that of the High Priest. The king, as did all others, which made him a man of the people, had to present himself to the altar and offer his sacrifices for sin. In ancient Israel and among the founders, the rule was changed to 'Lex Rex' – the Law is King. We are often reminded in America that we are a nation of laws. And behind our laws, the most quoted reference among the Founders as they forged the Declaration of Independence and the Constitution, was the Bible; and after that William Blackstone's *Commentary on the Law of England*, which referenced the Bible, as laying at the foundation of all Common Law.

The rejection of God's commands is to desecrate the sacred, to make all of life profane and secular, godless and without any moral boundaries. The ruling of judges in arbitrary ways, contrary to the Bible, is a return to Rex Lex, with the judges functioning in the role of kings, making decrees; and thereby, fostering moral chaos. Standing behind the Law, is God, the Lawgiver. And inscribed into the law are the principles to keep the social order sacred and holy – and therefore 'whole.' The opposite fractures, and desacralizes. Adultery violates the sacredness of marriage. Theft violates the sacredness of property rights, ownership and stewardship. Disregard of the Sabbath is a violation of the sacredness of time, the secularization of all time, leaving no space for God or the holy. The admission of idols conveys the material with divinity. It lessens and cheapens God, and equates Him to the material known world; it makes Him earthbound, knowing Him through the limitation of some earthly medium and image; it degrades His sacred, other-worldliness. The casual use of His name or its use in profanity reveals a marked irreverence, a disdain, a fearless slandering disposition. The one who has no regard for God, will have less regard of others. With such a man, no one is safe. Murder, in whatever form, is a failure to respect and hold dear the sacredness of life itself. Coveting is an admission of the heart that joy and satisfaction is attached to things, not to the intangibles.

The only place to go with complaints that despair of the world as it is, with injustice run amuck, with tyranny unchecked, with little deeds of oppression that threaten life's peace and our poise - is to heaven's court. There we enter a plea, which is answered will of necessity involve God's intervention, perhaps His judgment. At times, there is no other desire but to forthrightly plea for it, even if it requires deadly punitive action by God. Such a matter is not in our hand, we are not to be trusted with such options; but they are safe with a God of love and truth. "Deliver us from evil – nay, from the Evil One, and the evil ones and spare us needless temptations that solicit us to do wrong. Answer our prayer. We do not dictate the terms or details the prescription – we leave that to You. But, we can't live in a world that You, God, do not regulate from time to time. So we invite Your intervention – even if it means the action of Your punitive hand. Need we remind ourselves, that such judgment often begins in your own house – the Church. Nevertheless..."

CHAPTER NINE

IMPRECATIONS IN THE NEW TESTAMENT

A Window Through Time

This story is one of great grace, following a submarine attack on a passenger carrying ship in World War II. While anger would have been the natural reaction, the grace of this missionary, in the midst of unbelievable strain, became a witness to hardened sailors, and to an island.

Ethel Bell was a gentle little missionary. Her husband had died, but she had returned to Africa without him, with their small children. In the summer of 1942, she started home to America on a medium size cargo ship. In Africa, it almost seemed that the rest of the world was at war. Mary Bell, who would be thirteen when they arrived in the states, wanted cream puffs for her birthday. Visas were hard to obtain, but finally, they came through and Ethel with nine total passengers, two missionary families, headed to Trinidad. Two days from shore, on a Sunday, they were struck by a torpedo. It was a dull sound, and then the small ship seemed to 'burp.' Suddenly, things were breaking everywhere at once. The deck tilted. The lifeboats were dispatched and the crew and passengers climbed in. Within minutes, the ship had disappeared under water. Only debris could now be seen – broken chairs, a book, scraps of wood, a cap, a shoe, a picture frame. And the submarine surfaced, shooting at those still scrambling in the water, but only briefly. Then it submerged again. It was eerie.

"God forgive them," Mrs. Bell prayed. The sailors had other things to say! For hours, nothing seemed real. It was like bad dream. The raft was uncomfortable. It had no seats. "We'll only be here a short while," the Captain assured them. Carol Bell was only seven. "Don't be a baby," her brother Richard chided. "It hurts ... my arm ... It's got a bump!" A bump - indeed. It was broken. "God will cover it with His hand," Mrs. Bell declared.

As nightfall came, four rafts held the passengers and crew. The waves were intense and the little rafts crashed into one another. Reluctantly, the Captain ordered the rafts to untie their lines. Nineteen were on the raft with Mrs. Bell, fourteen men and four children. Cramped and soaked. Uncertain and hungry. Fearful and uncomfortable. An eight-by-ten piece of rubber, home for nineteen humans. Water sloshed into the small raft, water with the palm oil that had been in the cargo of the small ship. It was a great sunscreen. There were enough rations on board for four days, plenty of time, the Captain assured them, for rescue planes. They ate lavishly, but they didn't rest. Who could? Monday passed. Then Tuesday. Then came Wednesday, 'Rescue Day!' By night, a strange silence had come to all. Dejection reigned. Men sobbed. The Captain assured all, "Tomorrow!" Two more days passed. Now they were surrounded by sharks. Mrs. Bell worried that a child might carelessly leave a hand or arm overboard, and lose it to a shark. Little Carol said, "It's like Daniel in the Lion's den!" Mrs. Bell agreed. But the sailors didn't know who Daniel was, much less the lions. So Mrs. Bell told them all the story. And every day, she told them another story, one in the morning, and another at night.

The stories created vigorous discussions.

"They just stories, like fairy tales, only these come from the Bible" some of the sailors muttered.

"No," Mrs. Bell insisted, "They are true! If they ever were true, they are still true, became God is true. He hasn't lost any of His power."

"You mean ..." but the sailors couldn't say it. But they didn't need to say anymore, or ask the question.

"Yes," Mrs. Bell declared, "He can save us now, by His Power and Might." She believed. They argued about it. But with the light of dawn, or at the sign of the setting sun, they were ready for another story.

"Tell us one about the sea, tonight!" they'd say. And so she would. There was a Bible verse for the day. The children recited those they remembered from Sunday School. "I will bless the Lord at all times, His praise shall be continually in my mouth." When rainbows appeared, the children shouted with glee, greeting it as sign from God. Even the hardened sailors began to smile when they saw one. The days passed. The Captain died. There was nothing to do, but roll him from the raft into the sea. Mrs. Bell conducted a service for him. Children and men bowed in prayer. The food was gone, so conversations turned to creative imaginations – if you could order anything you wanted, what would it be? Even the children participated. Little Mary still wanted 'cream puffs.'

A dozen times an airplane passed overhead, but always too high to notice them. Still, they screamed and waved. Mrs. Bell would recall, "Those were the loneliest times." With the water gone, she declared, "We'll pray for rain!" It was crazy, the sailors said, to pray for rain with nothing but blue sky overhead. Not for Mrs. Bell. Psalm 68, she said, declares, "Thou, O God, didst send a plentiful rain, whereby thou didst confirm thine inheritance, when it was weary." She quoted it over and over, and on that basis, she prayed for rain. When there was little cloud, she and children pointed it out. But the sailors were not convinced, noticing that the cloud was either against the wind or not the kind of cloud that brought water. That only caused her to pray more, "Father, we need this rain. Please give it to us, Father." Suddenly, the whole sky was dark. Within minutes, big drops of rain began to fall. Plentiful, cool drops of rain. They caught them in the hands. They used the canvas tarp to capture the rain, and filled their kegs with water. Then the rain stopped.

"It could not have been anything but God that did that!" the men declared.

"And if He did that," Mrs. Bell added, "He will save us all the way."

But the days dragged on, and faith again withered. Their clothes were nearly burned away. Feet were puffy and swollen until they looked like cushions. Mrs. Bell was left in her damask slip – they were all in survival mode. That's when the airplane came. It circled. They had been seen. The pilot dipped so low, they could see his face. They were shouting and waving and screaming. He went away, and then came back and dropped a parcel. It burst open, and the sharks quickly devoured the bread. The pilot circled again, and dropped another parcel. This one they retrieved. They broke it open, said grace, and had a feast – chocolate and malted-milk tablets. They sang and prayed; they gave thanks. At dawn, there was a boat on the horizon. It wandered around them all day, never seeing them. It was so far away - miles;

and yet, it seemed so close. Yelling did no good. Nor did standing and waving. Finally, the boat disappeared. The next five days were the most difficult. They had been found, but still they were lost. It was an interesting time for sharing faith. The men had believed, but then they saw their hopes dashed. God had wasted His moment to save them! They were going to be resolute disbelievers. But Mrs. Bell remained steadfast.

Then it happened. A convoy appeared on the horizon. One destroyer pulled away from the line of ships, and seem to be heading their way. They rejoiced, but not for long. Soon, they were under fire. Shells opened the water on both sides of the tiny raft. The children were in dazed silence. The men whimpered and grimaced. They all buried their faces. But there was no place to hide. Now, shells were dropping all around them. They knew that the enemy sometimes disguised his submarines by these small rafts. Mrs. Bell declared, "For I, saith the Lord, will be a wall of fire round about, and the glory in the midst of thee." It was a passage from the prophet Zechariah. "Get up, you men," she shouted. "Look! You're not being hit. God is taking care of you. Get up and wave at them." They lifted their heads with shells falling all around. They all stood, and began to wave. The side of the ship was lined with sailors looking on. In a matter of minutes, it seemed, they were being lifted off the tiny raft. Their feet were so swollen and tender, that they could not support their weight. Medical attention was given, as were new clothes, food and water. Everyone marveled that they had survived the ordeal in such good shape. The ship dropped them off in Barbados and the island celebrated them like heroes. When they learned that it was little Mary's birthday, and all she wanted was 'cream puffs,' they came from all over the island – dozens of them, along with presents and dolls, and bows and ribbons.

It was miraculous. Forty-two had boarded four life-boats. Only one other raft was recovered, with only one survivor. Those with Mrs. Bell, save the Captain, had been saved.

Louie, one of the seaman, never a strong believer in God, became a believer in Mrs. Bell, "She save'a my life ... She made'a the rain come; she made'a the rain stop."

Louie at least gained a friend who knows the Friend.

Adapted from, "A Friend of a Friend of His -," Margaret Lee Runbeck, *The Great Answer* (Boston: Houghton Mifflin Company, 1944), 79-98.

CHAPTER 9

IMPRECATIONS IN THE NEW TESTAMENT
P. Douglas Small

In the New Testament, we are confronted with calls for judgment by Jesus himself. After His preaching and ministry tours, the unbelieving cities of Capernaum, Chorazin and Bethsaida, He declared, were under the threat of greater judgment than Tyre, Sidon or even Sodom, because they had heard the message and seen the miracles. How could they not believe? (Matthew 11:20-24) Peter told Simon the Sorcerer, "Your silver perish with you!" (Acts 8:20). The imprecation was conditional, only to take effect if Simon did not repent and if he persisted in his twisted values that he apparently and ignorantly sought to import to Christianity. "Repent of this wickedness of yours, and pray the Lord that, if possible, the intention of your heart may be forgiven you" (v. 22). The bold line was meant to protect the purity of the faith, not only of Simon, but of the newly established community in which Simon, due to his notoriety, was likely to have significant influence. The risk is high; so Peter's leadership is bold and assertive; and the potential for judgment stark.

Paul boldly told the Corinthians believers, "If anyone does not love the Lord, let him be accursed" or damned – *anathema* (I Corinthians 16:22). This is not a warning issued here to the world – but to the church. There are some compromises that are so severe, some potentially damaging to the whole, that a line of repentance must be laid for the few to save the integrity of the church itself.

This is the same word used in Galatians 1:8-9 regarding the warning against preaching a different gospel. A man preaching such a deceitful message is to be 'eternally condemned!'

The three most severe imprecatory movements in the Old Testament, found in Psalms 35, 69, and 109, are the most often quoted in the New Testament. Peter quotes both Psalms 69 and 109, noting that they "had to be fulfilled, which the Holy Spirit foretold by the mouth of David concern Judas" (Acts 1:6). David's enemy was both historic and prophetic. The imprecation he uttered related both to his own time and to that of his son, who was destined for his throne – Jesus. Thus, the imprecatory psalms are both historic and prophetic. The same dynamics are expected to repeat at different times with different faces and names and with the same results.

Jesus – And the Fig Tree

One of the most striking imprecation moments in the New Testament is in Mark 11:14. Jesus, in the last days of His earthly life, was on His way to the temple. He passed a fig tree. It had foliage, which He pulled back, searching for fruit. Finding none, He cursed the tree, which in the narrative, serves as an allegory for Israel (11-13). There is in the tree, as in Israel, as at the temple, the appearance of life – it is loaded with foliage, but has no fruit. It has been suggested by some that this is an unreasonable analogy since it was a bit early in the year for fruit, "… it was not the season for figs" (v. 13). Others have suggested that a certain species of fig trees had 'pre-figs,' the gardener's sign that figs were certainly coming. On this tree, there was neither fruit, nor was there the promise of fruit. "May no one ever eat fruit from you again" (11:14; Matthew 21:19) and so the curse was pronounced, both on the tree and Israel. God would find another vehicle to feed the nations.

From the fig tree, Jesus and the disciple band journeyed to the temple courts. There He found greed and exploitation. Exorbitant rates were imposed by the money-changers on sincere worshippers who had brought out of town currency and wished to give to God at the temple. The price of sacrificial lambs, even doves, was inflated. Those who brought their own animals often found them disapproved as acceptable for the altar. As a convenience, they were purchased by the establishment, and then resold a short time later for a profit, strangely and magically acceptable. It was all a racket. Jesus surveyed it all. At every turn there seemed to be some obstacle erected by the temple authorities between the common seeker and the altar, some method to exploit them for profit in their sincere attempt to access grace.

Suddenly, Jesus seemed to fly into a rage. He upended the tables of the money-changers. Coins flew everywhere. He released animals. The scene was mad. His disciples must have thought He had lost His mind. In fact, in this moment, He may have sealed His fate – "... the scribes and chief priests heard it, and sought how they might destroy Him" (v.18). In truth, He was acting out what His Father would do in Jerusalem within one generation if there was no repentance. He was also fulfilling prophetically, the imprecatory movement in Psalm 69:9, "Don't let those who seek You be confounded because of me ... for Your sake I have borne reproach; Shame has covered my face ... because zeal for Your house has eaten me up ..." Within a generation, in some forty years, the Romans would do the same thing – and take down the house. God would allow the destruction of the temple and entire religious enterprise. "My house shall be called a house of prayer for all nations, but you have made it a den of thieves" (11:17). On the journey back from the temple, the disciples noted how quickly the fig tree had withered. Indeed, within forty years, the Roman troops would sack the city, the temple would be destroyed, and God's fig tree, Israel, would be cursed.

The Martyrs Final Plea for Judgment

In the Revelation, the martyred saints, under the altar prayerfully plea, "How long, O Lord, holy and true, until you judge the inhabitants of the earth and avenge our blood?" (Revelation 6:10) This is a prayer. It is a plea for God to act in a judicious way against global tyrants. The victims of the brutality of a cruel and evil world, these godly martyrs died untimely deaths, in an unjust way. They did not retaliate. They did not return blow for blow. Their blood was shed as innocent victims. Their only crime was that they believed that the earth belonged to the Lord, and that Jesus, the Christ, was God Himself. For their faith, because of their witness, they died. Now, their blood cried out. Now, they plead. "How long," they ask, "will such injustice continue?" The roots of this moment in Revelation 6 reach all the way back to the blood of Abel. And to Deuteronomy 32:43 (See also II Kings 9:7; Psalm 79:10), to the Song of Moses where God promises to "avenge the blood of His servants." The theme resurfaces in Psalms 58:10-11; 79:5, 10; 94:1, 3. In Revelation 6, the age-old cycle is once more and for the final time set into motion – one goes forth to conquer, war and famine follow as does disease with the oppression of the innocent. "How long?" – the martyrs plead, will this ungodly tyranny triumph in the earth? Following that prayer are the cosmic signs of disorder: an eclipse of the sun and a blood-red moon, comets and shooting stars, and then what is described as a global earthquake with an attendant tsunami. Panic sweeps the earth as men and women run to find safety. Everything secure seems shaken. Suicidal attempts escalate. The sense of utter frailty in the face of nature's fury has humbled the whole earth. Suddenly, God the Father is revealed to the people of the earth, as is the Lamb.

This revelation of Christ is a shock. He is not dead, but vitally alive. The earth did not, as had been postulated by skeptics and unbelievers, rid itself of Him. The crucifixion did not put Him away. He was not a mere man. The very lamb the earth rejected, the 'Jesus' who has been ridiculed and whose followers have been persecuted, the one offered willingly by the military and political powers, religious men and rulers, as a sacrifice – now this lamb is back, and He is angry. It is an unthinkable notion – an angry lamb. The picture hardly seems congruent. Jesus – the suffering Messiah, the 'turn the other cheek' prophet, is full of fury. "The great day of His wrath has come, and who is able to stand?" (Revelation 6:17). The answer to that query? No one will be able to stand either physically, by their own power or force, or judicially, by their own merits or holiness. Kings will cower and cringe. The mighty will tremble and be humbled. The arrogant oppressors will recoil and be rendered powerless. All will collapse and be silenced.

Bonheoffer would note, "The first moments of the new day are not the time for our own plans and worries, not even for our zeal to accomplish our own work, but for God's liberating grace, God's sanctify presence."

Bonhoeffer, from "Meditating on the Word," Quoted by Charles Ringma, *Seize the Day with Dietrich Bonhoeffer* (Colorado Springs, Colorado: Pinion Press; 2000), See entry for January 22.

What follows this scene is silence, a moment perhaps of anticipation in heaven. Prayers are then offered on the altar in heaven (8:3), prayers that have been held in abeyance, not denied, but not yet answered – the implication is that earth's prayers will now join heaven's prayers. God will finally act. Fire is to be flung into the earth, from the altar in heaven (8:5). Here is a profound profile of prayer

– mysteriously motivating heaven's action. The result is clamor and quaking, thunder and lightning. Suddenly, trumpets sound – the vegetation of the earth suffers, the sea is polluted, fresh water turns bitter, earth's light patterns are altered, and arguably photosynthesis processes with it. Three 'woe' declarations follow (8:7-13). And then, from the bottomless pit emerge scorpion-like 'locusts.' Some suggest that this an invasion of supernatural creatures from hell itself, a demon-like army loosed with destructive energy on man-kind (9:1-12). If that is true, then we have another snapshot of the earth, caught in the conflict between heaven and earth. Here is prayer that motivates heaven to act; and hell to react. God's measures are enacted followed by Lucifer's counter-measures which, though destined to fail, still afflict more pain on the earth and its residents. Here is Lucifer's refusal to surrender, his recalcitrance against repentance, like a madman now cornered, he refuses to release his hostages – they will die with him, but not without one final round of the most brutal torture. Sadly, though God could rescue men from such torture, it is not their desire to be a part of his kingdom. On Mount Zion, the Lamb stands with those who have the Father's name written in their foreheads (14:1). Others, have refused such identification with the Lamb and the Father. Instead, they have chosen to "worship the beast and his image, and receive his mark in his forehead or in his hand ..." (14:9) and now they are victims of cruelty at the hands of the very god they chose to worship and serve.

Through the pages of the Revelation, the plagues and pandemics roll over the earth – loathsome skin disorders, a deadly sea-plague, erratic solar-flare activity, great human pain (16:2-11). But still there is no repentance. The cursing and blasphemy against God only intensifies. There is no hope now of the redemption *of the ungodly* here, it is only the redemption of the earth itself that is now in view, *for the godly.* Prayer has made its final plea. God has acted. The Lamb, abused for His people, will no longer be abused nor will He allow His people to be abused. Redemption will now be finished. Suddenly, heaven breaks out singing not one song, but two – the song of Moses and the song of the Lamb (15:3-4). There is no incongruence between the covenants. They are welded together. "Behold I am coming as a thief. Blessed is he who watches and keeps his garments …" (16:15).

Mercy – the Tender Call to Change

"Jehoshaphat," the King of Judah, the Bible declares, "had riches and honor in abundance, and joined affinity with Ahab" (II Chronicles 18:1), the king of Israel. Ahab, arguably Israel most wicked and notorious king had convinced him to join in Israel's war with Syria. In that battle, Ahab died and Jehoshaphat barely escaped. At one point, the archer's had him in their sites. He was dead man, but grace spared him. They were after Ahab, so mysteriously they allowed him, the king of Judah to live. The armies were routed in a decisive Syrian victory. "Jehoshaphat the king of Judah returned to his house in peace to Jerusalem," (19:1). But the peace was to be short-lived. Grateful to be alive, the king was barely home when he was greeted by "Jehu the son of Hanani, the seer" – a prophet. He confronted the king with this question, "Should you *help* the ungodly, and love them that *hate* the Lord?" The word *help, azar,* is not the idea of showing mercy as we would commonly know it. Rather, it is the notion of providing comfort, of furthering the cause of the wicked, of protecting and supporting, of even comforting or succoring. The word *hate, sane,* we have seen before. It is the idea of detesting, of recognizing another as an enemy – in this case, of God and righteousness. Jehoshaphat failed to discern the depth of evil represented by Ahab and his administration, and it almost cost him his life. The prophet declared "… therefore is wrath upon thee

ACCENT

A Muslim who is also a leader in a secret society considered a team of church planters in his community a threat. He and others plotted to kidnap one of the church planters and take him to a sacred spot where they could kill him. That would surely frighten the others away. Before he could finalize this plan, the Muslim leader's son became deathly ill. Muslim clerics could not help. The leader's wife begged him to let the church planters pray for the boy. Reluctantly he agreed, and his son recovered. The leader eventually repented and told the church planters what his intention was. Today all the members of the family are Christ followers and are active in sharing this testimony publicly.

~ Joel News Report

from before the Lord" (19:1). He had escaped from the battle, only to return and find that God was at war with him. His action and association with an evil man, his complicity, had cost more than casualties in a significant military defeat. It had brought him and the whole nation under the wrath of God. There can never be peace, and at the same time complicity with evil. The prophet declared of him, "Nevertheless there are good things found in thee ..." (19:2). He had purged the land of idolatrous groves. He had sought God. So a measure of mercy had been granted him.

Sobered by his narrow escape, followed by the confrontation of the prophet, "Jehoshaphat dwelt at Jerusalem: and he went out again through the people from Beersheba to mount Ephraim, and brought them back unto the Lord God of their fathers" (19:3). The King became an evangelist. Throughout Judah and Israel, he conducted campaigns calling the people back to the God of their fathers. What a national moment. "And he set judges in the land throughout all the fenced cities of Judah, city by city, and said to the judges, 'Take heed what ye do: for ye judge not for man, but for the Lord, who is with you in the judgment. Wherefore now let the fear of the Lord be upon you; take heed and do it: for there is no iniquity with the Lord our God, nor respect of persons, nor taking of gifts'" (19:5-7). Righteous judges would rule by the law of God, in the fear of God, without partiality or the influence of bribes. A revival of righteousness and justice was taking place in Judah. Next, he instituted reforms among the Levites and priests (19:8-9), "he charged them, saying, 'Thus shall ye do in the fear of the Lord, faithfully, and with a perfect heart.'"

Notice the scope of this revival – it touches the people, the masses; it is out of the transformation of the life of the king; it reforms the judiciary and the priestly sectors. All three offices, all three dimensions of the government are reformed, along with the people – the executive, the judicial and the representative branches (king, prophet-judges, priest-Levites). This is the effect, the profile of an awakening. This averts the judgment of God. This turns wrath into mercy. In the next chapter we find one of the most amazing stories in the Bible. Moab and Ammon engage in war against Judah. Jehoshaphat prays and decides to send a choir ahead of his army. Angels join the warfare and the enemy is routed (20:21-22). In the chapter prior to the revival, the army is defeated; and in the chapter following the revival, the army does not fight alone – heaven fights with them and they prevail. The difference? Righteousness.

Alexander McClaren noted, "Perhaps, it would do modern tenderheartedness no harm to have a little more iron infused into its gentleness, and to lay to heart that the King of Peace must first be King of Righteousness."[1] William Holladay noted, "The call to love one's enemies must be exercised within the context of the claims of justice: if an injustice has been done, then it needs to be made right."[2]

---

1   Alexander McClaren. *The Psalms,* Volume 3 (New York, NY: George Doran Company, 1892), 375.

2   William Holladay, *The Psalms Through Three Thousand Years* (Minneapolis, MN: Fortress Press, 1993),311-312.

Love cannot be allowed to muzzle truth. The noblest Greek word that the Scripture uses for love, even when enemies are in view, is *agape*. It is not a matter of emotion. It is not a reaction –but a matter of will. It is a disposition toward others. "While we were yet enemies, Christ died for us" (Romans 5:8). This love is stunning, breathtaking, but it does not exempt us or others from the consequences of sinful actions. Nor does it assume the impossibility of discipline, even judgment, and further, of eternal separation from God. His love is informed by His holiness and it demands justice.

Love and Hard Hearts

We are to forever and relentlessly take the disposition of love. It is our attempt to overcome evil with good. We are to pray – for our enemies. Look for ways to be reconciled. Do them good. Feed them. Forgive them. Bless them. And this is all to the end that *love* overtakes them and invites them to know the *truth* of God (Matthew 5:13-16, 25, 44; Luke 6:27; Romans 12:20; I Peter 2:12). And it is to the end, that we not be overcome by the spirit that works in the world. Indeed, it is to the end that we prove the enduring quality of God's love in a hateful world. We are to be salt – halting decay. And light, pushing back and intruding into the darkness. We are to be kindness, in the face of cruelty and ruthlessness. We are to be gentle in the face of brutality (II Timothy 2:24), as a "servant of the Lord" we must not strive, "but be gentle unto all men," indeed, "showing all meekness" (Titus 3:2), "peaceable ... easy to be intreated, full of mercy ... without partiality and without hypocrisy" (James 3:15). This is our disposition not only to those who are good to us, but also to the brute and insensitive (I Peter 2:18).

If however, we have worked our good works and loved through rejection, and there is still a resolute determination, not only to reject the gospel, but also to destroy it and its followers, the individuals revealing themselves as an "enemy of the cross" (Philippians 3:18) and perhaps, launching a veritable crusade against the righteous, then all we can do is commit them to God for just action, in view of His holiness, and His love for the larger mass of people and for the earth itself. Such incorrigible people will ultimately experience "the revelation of our Lord Jesus from heaven with the angels of His power in flaming fire, rendering vengeance to them" (II Thessalonians 1:7-9). They do not know God, nor do they want to know Him. And of course, they do not obey the gospel, even though some of them have heard it, and perhaps have known it at some point. But they have now crossed a line of no return. All that awaits them is the coming judgment. Some will taste it in eternity. Others may experience it here and now, for the cause of righteousness and God's immediate purposes. That is in the hands of God.

As believers, we look to the end, toward the consummation of redemption, but that glance forward may fail to provide the necessary and immediate comfort for us when we are under fire. And yet, it is in no small way reassuring to know that in the end, truth and right will prevail and the incorrigible will be appropriately rewarded. A. F. Kirkpatrick offers a warning so needed today, "Men have a need to beware, lest in pity for the sinner they condone the sin, or relax the struggle against evil."[3] Meanwhile, we are dealing daily with the fallout from toxic values, increasing persecution, the thwarting of the forward movement of kingdom purposes by legal restraints and very real violence. At times, there is no other solution but to pray. To pray the uncomfortable and unthinkable imprecatory prayer – the prayer that must forever be a last resort, the prayer for God's intervention, the prayer for space and grace to finish the great commission, the

---

3   A. F. Kirkpatrick, *The Book of Psalms* (Cambridge, England: University Press, 1906), xciii.

pray for the hand of evil and evil men to be restrained, even if that means judgment.

Still, many today are reluctant to suggest that we, as New Testament believers, should pray imprecatory prayers. It is, on balance, the more noble position. However, such a position may assume that we have found a higher means of dealing with our own anger and hurt; our frustration of being denied justice, our sense of powerlessness in a world that plunges headway into hell. In truth, many tend to live in denial. At the personal level, exasperation along with feelings of revulsion and disgust over both national and world events, as well as personal incidents, are inescapable. And when they are denied, they simply manifest in another way – depression, anger turned inward and upside down – suicide, guilt, manipulation, passive revenge and resistance, avoidance and more. Further, we take the toxic feelings that come from disappointments, from injustice, from betrayal, from assaults by some enemy, known or unknown, and we must then deal with the reality of the experience. So we talk – to others, about others. We experience correspondence between our pain and another person, one who may have had nothing to do with our previous, but unforgettable lingering negative experience. And we tragically transfer the toxic emotions to the new situation and the unsuspecting victim of our unfinished anger. In the process, our poison, our anger, our toxins spread to others. The matter is no longer about the justice of God. It is personal.

The one place we can go with all our pain and irrational reactions to it, is to God. With Him, we can pour out our souls. With Him, we can express our deepest and rawest feelings. With Him, we can be unfiltered. We are not in danger of corrupting Him or of polluting Him. And He alone is the one who can bear such toxic talk. Denial only pushes the poison deeper within us. It only delays the time bomb. But by pouring out our pain, verbalizing our hurt, examining our wound before God's love and light – that alone brings a measure of healing. And being able then, to leave the matter with Him, and trust His righteousness, His timing, and ask for grace not to rejoice if and when the judgment comes – that is Christian grace and evidence of growth.

Martin Luther believed, that even in the recitation of the Lord's Prayer, we were daily clearing our heart of malice by committing to the reigning, ruling action to God, and inviting His regular, daily intervention into our time-space world. "Hallowed be thy name" – May your name continue to be regarded as sacred and held in honor. "Thy kingdom come, thy will be done" – May you assert your Lordship, use your authority, enforce your will, subdue your enemies, move aside the offenders, clear the way for your word! It is one thing to pray, "Thy kingdom come …" in a benign manner as if such an action had no consequences. Indeed, it means the pulling down of all opposing evil kingdoms. It is revolutionary not in relational, but super-natural sense; not by our hands, but by His devine hand, it is wonderfully subversive. It is the call for disorder, in order that a new order might emerge.

Such ideas are too bold for us. They are too daring, too audacious. This is far beyond the personal, this is cosmic, and global; this is about kings and kingdoms, about a mega-power shift, about renewal in social networks. And yet, it is precisely the prayer that each person is to pray. Our hurts and hopes must be bigger than us. Imprecatory prayers, moments when we plead for God's just intervention, must not be about our narrow slice of pain. Something bigger is happening, not only in the earth, but in our very lives. The pain of living in a broken world issues forth from us as the sound of labor, a new kingdom is being birthed. But the advance of the light always demands the end of the night. The two cannot exist together. Every conversion is a power shift as men and women are 'pulled from the fire' (Jude). In ancient Israel, where justice was trampled, vengeance was required. When laws had been broken, retribution was necessary. This was the law of the altar. It is, Walter Brueggemann argues, the other side of God's compassion, the 'dark side' of His mercy.[4]

In II Thessalonians, Paul warns:

> *God is just: He will pay back trouble to those who trouble you and give relief to you who are troubled, and to us as well. This will happen when the Lord Jesus is revealed from heaven in blazing fire with His powerful angels. He will punish those who do not know God and do not obey the gospel of our Lord Jesus. They will be punished with everlasting destruction and shut out from the presence of the Lord and from the majesty of His power on the day He comes to be glorified in His holy people and to be marveled at among all those who have believed. This includes you, because you believed our testimony to you (1:6-10).*

Luther, the great reformer, commented on John 17:9:

> Thus the saintly martyr Anastasia, a wealthy, noble Roman matron, prayed against her husband, an idolatrous and terrible ravager of Christians, who had flung her into a horrible prison, in which she had to stay and die. There she lay and wrote to the saintly Chrysogonus diligently to pray for her husband that, if possible, he be converted and believe; but if not, that he be unable to carry out his plans and that he soon make an end of his ravaging. Thus _she prayed him to death, for he went to war and did not return home_. So we, too, pray for our angry enemies, not that God protect and strengthen them in their ways, as we pray for Christians, or that He help them, but that they be converted, if they can be; or, if they refuse, that God oppose them, stop them and end the game to their harm and misfortune.[5]

Habakkuk prayed, "Lord ... in wrath remember mercy" (Hab. 3:2;

---

4   Walter Brueggemann, *Praying the Psalms,* (Wipf & Stock Pub, 2007), 62.

5   Martin Luther, *What Luther Says* (St. Louis: Concordia, 1959), 1100.

see Ps. 11:6; Prov. 25:22; Rom. 12:20). He declared that he had "heard of ... [the Lord's] fame" and that, as a result, he stood "in awe of ... [the Lord's] deeds ..." but he had not witnessed them. So, understanding the potential power that could be unleashed, the consequences, he pleaded that the deeds of the past, the direct intervention of God into history might take place again on his watch. "O Lord. Renew them [the deeds of the past, your intervention] in our day, in our time make them known ..." He recognized that such a request placed him at the intersection of 'wrath and mercy.'

SOLUTION – What Do We Do With Imprecatory Prayer

In an age that is all 'love' and no truth; all forgiveness and no judgment, we hardly know what to make of the 'imprecatory' passages we have reviewed or of the whole matter. To some, they offer ethical challenges to our theology, to say the least. Some well-meaning scholars attempt to rescue God from the harsh image of this language. But the purpose of such language is to sound an alarm, to convince all that there are lines that when crossed bring impunity, and actions that foster consequences – consequences that are at times irreversible and deadly. The Bible and one's relationship with God is not mere religious talk or noble ideas and ideals – these are life-and-death matters. And the fences flow with high voltage electric energy.

To suggest that the imprecations of Scripture are merely cathartic, merely for effect, is to offer a tame and toothless God. He is blind and does not see evil; maimed, his arm is short and He cannot respond. There is no real power there. No threat exists in reality. No consequences will be forthcoming. In contemporary thought, heaven may or may not exist, but certainly, hell has been put on ice! It is an antiquated notion. And therefore, the assumption follows, these imprecations are for mere literary effect. They were effective in an unsophisticated age when people were superstitious and more easily intimidated than they are in our modern scientific era. We know better. We have, we smugly declare, dismissed such archaic notions and put away such an ancient god, replacing him with a powerless, but nevertheless, kind and benevolent, gender-free parent and friend.

Some scholars have even suggested that given Israel's diminutive size and strength, with Assyrian to the north, Egypt to the south, and Babylon to the east, that such a bold, fire-breathing God was designed to bolster confidence to Israel. Thus, it was a psychological tactic to embolden the faith of the small nation. God was there or at least His conjured image was present – and He was angry with His foes. Israel could not repay their enemies, they were no match for them, but Yahweh certainly would, the theory went. However, the idea that such language is merely figurative, metaphorical, only serves in the end to be another means of demythologizing God. Of reducing Him to a nice, but benign deity, devoid of real power or the ability to defend His holiness, to enforce His will or to judge enemies.

It is true that imprecatory movements appear in the context of hope for a new day, mercy for the victims or the faithful, and a blessing for those who are on the Lord's side. And they also may be instrumental in informing Israel of the kind of behavior that is regarded by God as unacceptable and worthy of judgment. Thus, the promise of God's aggressive action against an opposing and transgressing nation is simultaneously a call for repentance in Israel. This is a critically important theological parallel. But it should not be considered a lame spiritual threat, a mere literary and prophetic ploy, not for one committed to take Scripture seriously.

For years, the Catholic Church carried forth the language of imprecatory psalms in its liturgy. But the Second Vatican Council led to reforms that removed them, in favor of securing a more positive image of God and a more peaceful and conciliatory mood among God's people. That leaves us with the question, what do we do with these passages? In the last few decades, the evangelical church has followed the cultural trend, de-emphasizing the judgment of God, and highlighting grace. Now, hell is off-limits; and a God who judges others is deemed far too intolerant. The Church has allowed culture to redefine our perception of God. Paul reminds us that "many though there be that are called gods … there is but one God, the Father, of whom are all things, and we in Him; and one Lord Jesus Christ …" (I Cor. 8:5-6). Elijah reminds us, "the God that answers by fire," we must "let Him be God" (I Kings 18:24). In that day, they fashioned their own gods as well.

To 'imprecate' means to call for a divine curse upon another, in the biblical context, due to their hard hearts and their persistent godless acts. It is a plea to God for their accountability to Him, for judgment, for justice for some evil or harm to come upon those who have sown evil.[6] These imprecations have caused scholars to declare David's theology as flawed and other psalmists who advance this form of prayer as ethically wrong, as acting and speaking out of anger – and therefore out of harmony with the nature of God himself. This is the lesser light – the Old Testament, not the New, they argue. It is the inferior ethics of the old, not the higher standard of the new. Of course, there is some truth in that position. There is a higher standard in the New Testament, but not a radically different standard. It rises out of the same legal and justice system, one Jesus said He came not to destroy, but to fulfill – even to enforce. And yes, there is also a stark contrast between the Church – a *spiritual* entity in a political world; and the nation of Israel, with a *political* structure

---

6　Psalms 7, 35, 55, 58, 59, 69, 79, 109, 137 and 139 all call for God's judgment.

in the context of nations themselves.

However, the dismissal of these Psalms merely on the basis of old-new testament variance in tone is not an adequate argument. Some have suggested that in the Old Testament, we were to love our *neighbors,* but in the new, we are to love our *enemies.* That higher standard should be noted and embraced. But these are principles, and principles, are dynamic. Further, they are not single-dimensional. And finally, they are not merely a New Testament phenomenon. David attempted to meet the New Testament standard. He pleaded, "In return for my love they [my enemies] act as my accusers, but I am in prayer. Thus they have repaid me evil for good and hatred for my love" (Psalm 109:4-5). David adhered to the nobler standard – love your enemies. And this was not the only example of such action on his part. While David showed kindness to King Saul; Saul, in contrast, was attempting relentlessly to murder him (I Samuel 24; 26). The Old Testament has multiple examples of love, which is to be displayed, not merely for one's neighbor, but for one's enemy. Exodus 23:4-5 urges, "If you come across your enemy's ox or donkey wandering away, you shall surely return it to him. If you see the donkey of someone who hates you fallen down under its load, do not leave it there; you shall surely help him with it." Proverbs 24:17 warns, "Do not gloat when your enemy falls; when he stumbles, do not let your heart rejoice." And the New Testament treatment of enemies is built on the old (Romans 12:19-20 on Proverbs 25:21, 22).

It was in the period between the testaments where hatred of enemy rose to be an acceptable notion. Neither the idea nor phrase is found in the Old Testament. In the Rule of the Qumran Community (IQS), there is the note "to love all the Sons of Light" and "to hate all the Sons of Darkness" [IQS 1:9-11]. The 'hatred' demanded the withholding of compassion.[7] There is also a note in Sirach 1:27, an apocryphal book, "Give to the good man, but do not help the sinner." Jesus may be addressing these entrenched ideas when He asserted, "Love your enemies!" Even those who hate believers.

It might also be easy to brush the imprecatory psalms aside as examples of great men and women who lost their temper and afterwards returned to a state of serenity. But such psalms, literature that amounted to nothing more than a personal vendetta, would not have been admitted to the circle of sacred writings. They would not have made it into the biblical narrative. They would have brushed aside as something to be hushed and about which one, having now regained poise, was ashamed. Instead, these are not only admitted; they are lyric poems, set to music. They are not merely steam rising from a hot head, but they are studied and deliberate compositions, which the nation sings. They are litanies and lyrics found in the Old Testament hymnal.

Still uncomfortable with such language and vehemence, we might rationalize then that this is not the dominate portion of the psalms. And further, the psalms only contain imprecations in the context of some larger concern. They don't alter the overall character of the book of psalms. True again. Still, imprecatory moments decorate a far too significant number of the psalms to ignore. Another suggestion is that since much of the wisdom literature contains hyperbole, these might be exaggerations, purposeful literary excesses meant to drive home a point. David says in Psalm 6:6 that he cries so much at night that he 'makes his bed swim,' indeed, that he 'dissolves his couch

---

7   James Charlesworth, Ed. "*Rule of the Community and Related Documents*," Vol. 1; *The Dead Sea Scrolls: Hebrew, Aaramaic, and Greek Texts with English Translations* (Louisville: Westminster John Knox, 1994), 6-7, 46-47.

with tears.' The language is meant to be overstated and colorful. The imprecatory language that calls for the 'breaking of teeth' of the enemy sounds cruel, but that enemy is also pictured as a pride of ruthless lions on the hunt. The image is exaggerated on both sides. Thus, the prayer amounts to a plea for a toothless enemy – at least if he acts like vicious lion. Still, the plea for the death, even of a villain may seem excessive. Indeed, we should insist that imprecatory prayers related to people who merely disagree – are not only wrong-spirited, they are groundless. Christians who hold their doctrines tightly have been known to pray judgment prayers on the church across the street for preaching heresy, according their doctrinal creed. Such actions go beyond bigotry – they demonstrate a failure to grasp the essence of the gospel itself. Nor should the church engage in a 'holy war' of words with non-Christian faiths.

The Cultural Lens that Blinds

There are few things in our modern culture that bring such a resounding public rebuke as 'hate' speech. And imprecatory movements in scripture, in the context of contemporary thought, is perceived by some to be completely inappropriate, off-limits, even damaging to the kingdom. Indeed, we may also find such biblical language offensive, especially against the background of our cheap grace culture. It is talk that is too tough. It bifurcates. The preferred language today, even in the Church, is that '*all men* are the children of God,' and *none* are to be identified as the children of the devil or darkness. We now refrain from using language that suggests that men are 'lost' or 'unsaved.' With naiveté and blind sincerity, we have come to believe that all can be won by love. We are in danger, having assumed such ostensibly high ground, of indicting God Himself, who, were He to exhibit enough love, the right quality and quantity, all enemies would become honorable and principled friends. We are self-deceived.

Underneath the imprecatory psalms is the belief that only the direct and severe intervention of God can assure, at certain moments, justice in the earth. War is necessary; and by that we mean, war from heaven. "YHWH is a warrior" (Ex. 15:3), we are reminded. There are certain moments in history when there is an evil dynamic in the earth or a nation, or some other entity that can only be addressed, only curbed by the intrusive action of God. This dark force manifests itself through humans and often goes beyond the brutal to an inconceivable infliction of injuries. In such moments, God intervenes. These imprecatory utterances are the prayerful longing for the righteousness of God, for justice, for due punishment upon such unrestrained evil. We may quarrel with certain phrases, the blunt tough language; and we may wish to translate the concepts into own cultural terminology. But in the end, even with new language which is more culturally palatable – we face the candid fact, that the very idea of imprecations is offensive in our day.

God is certainly loving and gracious. But it is not of His love or yet His grace that heaven cries out in triplicate. The three-fold repetition "holy, holy, holy" is called a *trihagion,* found in both testaments. The holiness of God is the most challenging theological concept to explain. It is the primary aspect of His essential attributes, and it is unshared. Others include omnipresence, omniscience, and omnipotence. But it is God's holiness that elevates Him as segregated and dissimilar, as wholly other. His faultlessness or flawlessness is certainly in view; His excellence and incomparability are components; but it is His "utter-otherness," His transcendence, the mystery and awe of His mesmerizing majesty that causes even heaven to gaze and reverently fall down in worship that marks God in the most unique manner. He is also loving and righteous and powerful, gracious, and yet committed to irrefutable truth and holy standards, with the power to enforce those standards. These are immutable characteristics of God. They are not things that merely describe Him, they represent His essence. God *is* holy. He *is* true. Evil acts are therefore not independent from God; they are not neutral and impartial. They are attacks against His very nature. They are poisonous to Him – and to us, since we are made in His image. And of course, they are damaging to our world and contrary to the laws upon which it was created to operate.

C. S. Lewis found the imprecatory psalms offensive, devilish. He did observe, however, that the fiery and "ferocious parts of the Psalms serve as a reminder that there is in the world such a thing as wickedness and that . . . is hateful to God."[8] At times such a world can only be dealt with by God, and there are times, when it may be appropriate to ask God to intervene – and do so now. So the imprecatory psalms are our calls for God to demonstrate His avarice for sin, to defend righteousness and holiness. To stop the spread of the toxic tide of sin and the uncompensated acts of sinful men. He alone can rightfully deal with sin in judgment, since He alone is absolutely holy. "The transgressors must be destroyed; the posterity of the wicked cut off" (Psalm 37:38). And it is "God that will bring them down to the pit of destruction and not allow the bloodthirsty and deceitful to live out their days" (Psalm 55:23).

PURPOSE: The Point of Imprecations
A Plea for Justice

It is critical, at this point, to note again, that imprecations are not connected to personal revenge. This is not tit for tat. In this

---

8   C. S. Lewis, *Reflections on the Psalms* (New York, NY: Harcourt, Brace, and Co., 1958), 33.

sense, the turning of the cheek as a personal matter, as a private response to the evil aggression of another, is always the behavior urged on us. The context of a passage determines interpretation; and the context of these imprecations is not that of personal revenge or even pride. These pleas are a matter of God's own righteous standards that have been ignored or obliterated. They are a plea for justice, for the bridling and restraint on evil and evil men. They are a plea for God to uphold His own righteous standards – and thus the ethical and moral values tied to absolute truth, which are weakening in the current culture, and as a result, the people of truth are also suffering. And God's purposes and causes are at stake. Only God can prevent these egregious actions. Walter Kaiser has observed:

> "They [these hard sayings] are not statements of personal vendetta, but they are utterances of zeal for the kingdom of God and His glory. To be sure, the attacks which provoked these prayers were not from personal enemies; rather, they were rightfully seen as attacks against God and especially His representatives in the promised line of the Messiah."[9]

Psalm 58 declares, "The righteous will rejoice when he sees the vengeance; he will wash His feet in the blood of the wicked. And men will say, 'Surely there is a reward for the righteous; surely there is a God who judges on earth!'" Such language – 'vengeance,' the mention of 'the blood of the wicked' in such a personal and almost light manner - is a bit much for us today. The focus of David's frustration here is the court, specifically, rulers or 'judges' in the community, men of standing and position, whose role it was to insure justice and equity. Thus he says, 'you judge' (v. 1), and offers the contrast with another 'who judges' (v. 11), God Himself. The problem is incongruence between the throne of God and the earthly

---

9   Walter Kaiser, *Hard Sayings of the Old Testament*, (Downers Grove, IL: InterVarsity Press, 1988), 172.

judge's bench – and the people, who are caught in the middle with no recourse, but an appeal in prayer to heaven's Court. The contrast is deepened with the notion of these men, these earthly judges who sit as 'gods' (v. 1), presumptuously and independently ruling, as if they had no accountability to anyone or anything above or beyond them; disconnected from, acting disrespectfully toward the true 'God' (v. 11). For them, the law is not the king; they have become kings, writing their own laws, ignoring 'the law.' Their arrogance is now idolatrous. There is a lack of justice 'on earth' (v. 2) which is due to silence on issues where the voices characterized by 'righteousness' ought to be sounding out, but they are not (v. 1). These men are themselves dishonest (v. 3), and violent as well (vv .2, 6). To their stubborn godless nature is added the poisonous bite of cobra (v. 5), deadly and deaf, the venomous snake cannot, does not hear – he can't be reckoned with, no charmer can any longer manage him. He must be destroyed. The association is drawn from Deuteronomy 32:33, where Moses likens the persecutors of God's people to serpents. So the hope now is for action by God in behalf of an oppressed and unrepresented 'righteous' people (v. 11). There is no other solution. The judges pass perverted laws, because they themselves are 'wicked' and their rulings weigh out violence' (vv. 1-2), they are the cause of a culture now disintegrating. Further, there is little hope of change, since they are fostering another generation that will 'go astray as soon as they are born' (v. 3). With the truth so lost, wickedness so pervasive – the only hope is that surely there is a "God who judges in the earth" (v. 11).

Even the contextual explanation above, does not take away the shocking language in the text, of feet washed in blood. It is no comfort to observe middle-eastern zealots even of our own times, who make use of similar stark and aggressive language. The larger point, however, should not be missed. "The righteous will rejoice when he sees ... there is a God who judges on earth!" The point is that those acting and ruling on God's behalf are traitors, not only to the people, but to God, and His law. And this happens, as God seems powerless and inactive. The wicked perpetually triumph over the weak. They shed innocent blood and collect their fees under the protection of the law. What do the righteous do? Who defends them? Here, when intervention, which could have only come from heaven, against a wicked aggressor accomplished, there is a sense of relief. When evil men and empires are suddenly and certainly gone, there is cause for joy.

Divine Restraint of Evil

Similarly in Psalm 109, one of the most forceful imprecatory moments in all of Scripture, the *reason* for the call for judgment is seen in verses 16-18,

> "*Because* he did not remember to show kindness, but persecuted the afflicted and the needy and the brokenhearted, to put them to death. He also loved cursing, so it came to him; and he did not delight in blessing, so it was far from him. He wore cursing as his garment; it entered into his body like water, and into his bones like oil."

Such over-the-top actions by evil men on the already afflicted, the powerless, the needy, those whose hearts had already been broken, only to face more grief – such action by men with foul language, who delight in inflicting pain and seem to have an anointing (oil) for evil – such men deserve the attention and direct intervention of God, so argues the palmist.

Dislodging Evil

Likewise, in Psalm 55, *the reason* judgment is requested from heaven, is that "*evil* finds lodging" (v. 15) among such men. It lives 'in the midst, or middle of them." It is as if, evil is here personified, as in the Evil One, Satan himself. They have become 'lively stones' not for God, but for this unholy presence and malevolent anointing which moves them along, empowering them, furthering the injuries they might inflict as mere humans. Evil, and by implication, the 'Evil One' inhabits their company. The connection between them and the dark energy can only be broken by a direct judgmental intervention of God. So the verb tense here is imperative – God must act. "Destroy, O Lord!" (55:9).

Survival of the Righteous

The current situation makes the righteous feel "overwhelmed by troubles" (v. 2) with "enemies [who intimidate and] shout ... making loud and wicked threats" indeed, bring actual troubles on the godly who "angrily hunted down" (v. 3). "My heart pounds in my chest. The terror of death assaults me. Fear and trembling overwhelm me, and I can't stop shaking" (v. 4-5). These are graphic images . And on the mind of the righteous is one idea – escape. "Oh, that I had wings like a dove; then I would fly away and rest! I would fly far away to the quiet of the wilderness" (v. 6-7). The environment is described as a "wild storm of hatred" (v. 8). There is nowhere else to God, but to God in prayer.

So the imprecations follow – "Confuse them, Lord, and frustrate their plans, for I see violence and conflict ... the real danger is wickedness within the city. Everything is falling apart; threats and cheating are rampant in the streets" (v. 10-11). Now the Psalm becomes quite interesting. The enemy here is not a foreigner (v. 12), nor a foe in a classical sense. It is a "companion and close friend" who has turned traitor. It is someone with whom there had been "good fellowship" and with whom we had "walked together to the house of God" (v. 14-15). No more. Abandoning God, they now live with evil. They are comfortable with it – or him. And only the Lord can intervene against such a visible and invisible foe.

The plea is against the incorrigible, "For my enemies refuse to change their ways; they do not fear God" (v. 19). And yet, this enemy is not seen so clearly by others as an enemy, "His words are as smooth as butter, but in his heart is war. His words are as soothing as lotion, but underneath are daggers! (v. 20-21). Deception is at an epic level here. "I am trusting you [Lord] to save me."

That the Name of the Lord Be Honored

Another component of these psalms is that God has His own name to defend. Evil men curse, swear, and demean His name – His sacred name. They violate His law. Asaph, in Psalm 79, pleads that God would "pay back into the laps of our neighbors seven times the reproach they have hurled at you, O Lord" (Psalm 79:12). Do it, for *the sake of Your Name.* Do it, to make clear *your sacred honor.* At times, the evil men are not primarily and foremost the enemy of the *psalmist,* whose reflections contain reactive pleas to God to take sides with t*hem* and *defend them* against these wicked adversaries. Rather, they are foremost the enemies of God, and secondarily therefore, the enemies of the psalmist.

> "Do I not hate those who hate You, O Lord, and abhor those who rise up against You? I have nothing but hatred for them; I count them my enemies" (Psalm 139:21-22).

There is something bigger at risk here than personal safety and comfort. God's name and honor in a nation which was supposed to revere Him are now imperiled. The moral lines in such moments are so blurred that nothing is any longer wrong or right. The Yahwehist and the idolaters seem to stand on equal ground. There is no longer a distinction between covenant keepers and law breakers. The name of God is everywhere used in vain – and no one objects. The sacred is now profane. So, this is a time to distinguish between those who genuinely love the Lord, and those whose values have so warped national morals and standards Israel's godly heritage is threatened. A line must be drawn in the sand. In times past, there has been a failure to distinguish evil men and see their influence as a threat to the nation, but no more. They are enemies of God and Israel. They are enemies of a secure and godly future. The national security issue is no longer beyond the borders, it is inside; no longer with an alien enemy, but with the neighbor, even the family member, who is an enemy to God.

If we use the Revelation as a model, it is not until the righteous themselves are willing to pray for the liberation of the earth – even if that means judgment, that God acts, and the final consummation ensues (Revelation 6). Perhaps this is a paradigm. When all else has failed, when there appears no hope, when we are willing to pray the unthinkable prayer, one never prayed casually – perhaps that is the time to invoke the imprecatory prayer option. It seems clear, that such a prayer is not motivated by core malice. It is a merciful plea. It is 'the bomb' that brings some battle and in the end, the war itself to a close. It is the incisive action, focused on a few, for the good of a larger group.

For a moment, let's pull back from the eschatological picture, and attempt to apply the concept to a contemporary situation. Our prayers for God's intervention, even for His judgment, are pleas to Him, for His action – not ours. However, they require the capacity of parallel action. This is very important. "If your enemy is hungry, feed him; If he is thirsty, give him a drink" (Romans 12:20). This command is set in the context of one of the most sobering challenges in Scripture, regarding the behavioral standards of a believer – "love ... hate evil ... be kindly affectioned ... honor others ... be diligent ... fervent ... serve ... bless those that persecute you, do not curse ... repay no evil for evil ... live peaceably." What a standard. And then there is the reminder, "Do not avenge." But notice what strangely follows, "... give place to wrath... Vengeance is Mine, I will repay" (Romans 12:9-19). The message is simply – the witness of the Christian, even before a hostile world, is to be pristine – in terms of the way we relate one to another, and also to the hostility of the world. But this is the twist: our restraint, our refusal to 'repay evil for evil' then *gives place to wrath* – to God's wrath. The giving of food and water, to an enemy, is the final plea for change. It is the creation of space and time for his repentance. His ability to continue to abuse and injure, and his inability to respond to acts of kindness – reveal him as an enemy of God. What follows is judgment, "In doing so, you will heap coals of fire on his head. Do not be overcome by evil, but overcome evil with good" (Romans 12:20-21).

Luther noted, "We should pray that our enemies be converted and become our friends, and if not, that their doing and designing be bound to fail and have no success and that their persons perish rather than the Gospel and the kingdom of Christ." [10]   David Dikinson, from the Reformed perspective argued,

> "If any of the enemies of God's people belong to God's election, the Church's prayer against them giveth way to their conversion, and seeketh no more than the judgment should follow them, only until they acknowledge their sin, turn, and seek God." [11] Calvin as well noted that believers should "anxiously desire the conversion of their enemies, and evince much patience under injury, with a view to reclaim them to the way of salvation: but when willful obstinacy has at last brought round the hour of retribution, it is only natural that they should rejoice to see it inflicted, as proving the interest which God feels in their personal safety." [12]

10   Luther, Ibid.

11   David Dickson, *Commentary on the Psalms* (Minneapolis: Klock and Klock, 1980), 2:67.

12   John Calvin, *Commentary of the Book of Psalms*, James Anderson, Translator (Grand Rapids, MI: Baker, 1979), 2:378.

This prayer dynamic – a plea for God's incisive judgment, an imprecatory prayer; in the context of and out of a life of evidentiary godliness and healthy, Christ-like relationships; offered simultaneously with a desire that the enemy become a friend, that the aggressor become peaceful, that the conflict and oppression cease, that the hostile agent of the darkness will come into the light and be saved; coupled with deliberate overtures of kindness, grace-based acts, offered sincerely, not under the cloak of a double-standard that secretly longs for the enemy to remain incorrigible; but nevertheless, prayed, because there appears to be little hope of change, no indication that the situation will improve, and thus no alternative for the righteous but an appeal to God – is a position that the persecuted church, around the world, now must consider embracing. Indeed, it is one that the entire church must consider. It is not one that we arrive at easily. It is one that we reluctantly embrace. It is one that must be handled with great grace. To pray such prays easily reveals the heart. They earn the rebuke of heaven, "You do not know what manner of spirit you are of" (Luke 9:55).

Again, this is a back-against-the-wall, no-place-to-run, out-of-other-options prayer. The situation is untenable. The remedy is not earthly. Attempts at conciliation have failed. God's name is being dishonored. His honor is offended. His values are disregarded. His laws are broken. His very purposes are at risk. His people are threatened. The nation itself is at risk. The imprecatory plea is one that God judge 'some' to show mercy on the 'many'. It is a prayer prayed at the 'warning track' – a line has been crossed, we are nearing the cliff, the point of no return has been reached. The feeding of the enemy, the gracious actions, the deeds of love and kindness, are the last offers, the final appeal. They evidence a window of grace. And they reveal the hearts of both the oppressed and the oppressor. Met with disdain, seen as a joke, greeted with a cheap laugh, the righteous shamed by their attempt to even the approach the wicked – their heart is thereby revealed as incorrigible. That sets up the judgment of God.

We are in a war, but the "weapons of our warfare not carnal," not earthly, not physical, not of this sphere. And yet, they "are mighty" but only "through God" who is engaged, and invited into this war, by our acts of dependent prayer. He "pulls down strongholds" (II Corinthians 10:4). Paul urged the Ephesians who lived under the shadow of Diana and goddess worship, a church whose very existence had been threatened by the demonic cult to "Take ... the sword of the Spirit, which is the word of God. And pray in the Spirit ... with all kinds of prayers ..." (Ephesians 6:1-18). The passage, rooted in the context of warfare and conflict, is a prayer passage. The Christian is seen as in a battle, and his only viable means of survival is prayer, spirit-fed prayer, rising out of the authority of Scripture. Appeals to God, out of Scripture, inspired by the Spirit – are acts of warfare. He is not merely "beating the air" (I Corinthians 9:26). Nor is he to offer superficial, sweet and benign prayer-talk. This is war. It may be rooted in Psalm 74:10-12, "How long will the adversary reproach? Will the enemy blaspheme Your name forever? Why do You withdraw You hand?" – Why are You not fighting? Why is Your hand removed from the scene of this conflict? And then there comes the plea, "Take it out of Your bosom and destroy them. For God is my King from of old, working salvation in the midst of the earth." Likewise, Psalm 35 urges God, prayerfully, to "fight against those who fight against me. Take hold of shield and buckler, and stand up for my help. Draw out your spear ... against those who persecute me. Say to my soul, "I am your salvation!"" (Psalm 35:1-3). Here, God is pictured as adorned in the garb of a warrior. Indeed, the implied parallel is this – when we pray, God is somehow moved to protect, to take action, to engage both our and His enemies. The parallelism is fraught with mystery.

Who moves who? Are we moved by a warrior God, ready to act? Or do our prayers engage Him, obviously in manner to which He is disposed – to help us, to further His own purposes, to consummate the work of His son? Jeremiah, the praying, weeping, intercessory prophet of Judah who virtually stood alone, was told, "Thou art my battle axe and weapons of war: for with thee will I break in pieces the nations, and with thee I will destroy kingdoms …" (Jeremiah 51:20f).

The vertical plea – full of raw feelings, angst and honest ill feelings, cannot be dismissed. But such feelings are legitimately expressed only to God, not to the individual in focus. To that individual is shown an act of love. The vertical and the horizontal are by discipline separated. And this is not hypocritical. One might argue that either the act of kindness or the diatribe offered to God – only one is authentic. But duplicity is a fact of life. The war between the spirit and the flesh are not merely theoretical. We pour out our pain to God, but were we to act on such feelings, the entire earth would be a bloody battlefield. We can only manage such negative emotions by the therapy of prayer, and we can only overcome them by acting toward others the way God acted toward us when we were His enemies in sin – in love. That moment changed us. We were won, overcome, drawn, and changed by His love. Will it now do the same for these men and women who appear as His enemies now and have injured us and others? For their salvation we should pray. We must pray for that, and for them. In fact, if we do not, we ourselves have been overcome by evil and our own hearts have revealed us.

In the final analysis, the act that destroys evil and evil men belongs to the Lamb. He is alone is perfect and sinless. He has suffered more than we have endured. And the earth, twice His, first by creation and then redemption, He has a right to claim. We, his bride partner, left to serve as His witness, injured and affected, rejected and treated as a slave, abused and disregarded – appeal to Him, our bridegroom, for protection. However, and whenever he effects this redemption, necessitating judgment, based on the cross – we believe will be just. If indeed, it is His right – to judge, then it is our right, and perhaps, our responsibility to pray, "Even so, come Lord Jesus."

ACCENT

In his book, Successful Praying, F. J. Huegel offers ten rules for prayer:

1. The Law of the Atonement – We enter the holiest place by the blood of the atonement, by the work of Christ in our behalf (Hebrews 10:19).
2. The Law of Position – We are seated with Christ in the heavenly realm (Ephesians 2:6).
3. The Law of Faith – Ours is 'the Faith of the Son of God' and we stand united with Him in the power of His resurrection (Phil. 3:10).
4. The Law of Right Relations – We must be in right relationship with God and others (Psa. 66:18).
5. The Law of God's Will – He will hear us if we ask according to his will (I John 5:14).
6. The Law of the Spirit's Inspiration – He makes intercession for us (Rom. 8:27).
7. The Law of Praise – Praise leads us through to victory (Psa. 34:1; 22:3).
8. The Law of the Right Motive – We must seek God's glory (Rom. 8:7-8).
9. The Law of Right Diagnosis – Listen to God. Learn his viewpoint (Hab. 2:1).
10. The Law of Warfare – We need to be aggressive against Satan (Col. 2:15).

F. J. Huegel, *Successful Praying* (Minneapolis, MN: Bethany, 1967), 68, 74.

Final Observations:

1. Living in a land of such relative peace and safety, we hardly have a reference point for David's imprecations or the intensity and the cruelty of his adversaries. Perhaps we should trust the Holy Spirit, who chose to preserve these snapshots and this slice of uncomfortable prayer theology. Walter Brueggemann argues, "... the voice of a woman who is victimized by rape, who surely knows the kind of rage and indignation and does not need 'due process' to know the proper outcome... For such as these, the rage must be carried to heaven, because there is no other court of appeal. 'Love of neighbor' surely means to go to court with the neighbor who is grieved."[13]

2. Without the attempt to thoroughly bifurcate the testaments, there is in the Old Testament a greater emphasis on the law and justice. There is also the economy, not of the church, but of the state – and therefore a different judiciary. Further, there is the 'now' without the clear view of eternity, the teaching on future judgments (II Cor. 5:10) or the unsaved (Rev. 20:12-15). There is therefore a more compelling need to see justice here and now, in this life, within a certain time.

3. The imprecatory psalms cannot be dismissed on the simplistic basis of the old and the new, of grace verses the law, the tension between justice and mercy. The scripture is more holistic than that. There is an overarching truth in both testaments. These are not 'different' gods. The New Testaments is loaded with notes about judgment, justice and even condemnation. Frankly, Jesus speaks of hell more than anyone, and has sharp words of condemnation. Love of our neighbor is found in the Old Testament, as is the teaching on restraint. The prohibition against vengeance. Paul reinforces that idea, telling the Romans, to not act in vengeful ways (Romans 12:17-21), and he does so quoting

---

13 Walter Brueggemann, *The Message of the Psalms* (Fortress Press, 1984), 87.

Deuteronomy (Rom. 12:19; Deut. 32:35) and Proverbs 25:21ff. (Rom. 12:20). Jesus did not set aside the law, or the justice for which it appealed. He reinterpreted the law, arguably raising the bar.

4. The imprecatory psalms cannot be dismissed as an emotionally charged moment in the life of the psalmist – a bad day that he got over. The style of writing is lyric poetry, prose, with deliberation in meter and language. We have less of "a quick, volatile explosion" and more "of a smoldering fire." (Exodus 34:6; Numbers 14:18; Psalm 86:15).

5. The petitions are logical and legal, based on justice, pleas for divine intervention. They appeal beyond the tribunals of the earth, to heaven's courtroom. They ask God to act on the basis of His own character, as a just and righteous Judge. They appeal to His covenant promises (e.g. Deut. 28). They consider His past actions (Numbers 16) and anticipate His contemporary behavior.

6. The imprecatory passages are deeply relational. The person claims a special relationship with God, on the basis of covenant, for example. In our culture, we tend to say that God loves all people – the same! That He has no favorite, "He is no respecter of persons." However, it is far too easy to substitute constitutional thinking, "All men are created equal and endowed by their Creator with inalienable rights" – and biblical ideas. There is, for example, a difference between 'common grace and love' and the distinct love that God has for His twice-born children, who have entered into a new covenant with Him by the work of His Son on the cross. Here, there are now covenant obligations – on both sides, on our side, in terms of faithfulness to God; and on His side, in terms of protection and direction, blessings and benefits. Paul exhorts, "Husbands, love your wives" and he draws close the analogy, "as Christ loved the Church" (Ephesians 5:25). Husbands may love their sisters, their daughters, their mothers, but there is now a new and distinctive covenantal

obligation on them – the unique manner in which they love their wives. And that cannot be in the same way in which they love other women, such actions are Biblically inexcusable. Imprecatory prayers are privileged prayers – for the individual in covenant with God; who appeals to Christ, the Husband, for advantaged protection. Love of enemies is a common grace; but love of disciples, and love of God, is in a different class. Respect for all men, human dignity, is a common grace; but honor to one's spouse, and attention to one's children is particular and special.

7. Once the prayer is prayed, the outcome is up to God. Men and women, wounded and treated unjustly, have had their day in court. They have stated their claims. Paraded their hurts and showcased their damages. God has seen. He has heard. He is just. He is fair. Now, on the basis of His character, and His covenant, He must be trusted to act.

8. The prayers demonstrate a capacity to be, on the one hand, brutally honest about the treatment and the feelings that linger toward the enemy, and on the other hand, to demonstrate a personal grace to the same enemy, while in his presence. David could have killed Saul. Instead, he cut off the corner of his tallit. He showed mercy and restraint. The event humbled Saul. "You are a better man than I," he confessed (I Samuel 24:1-8).

9. There are imprecatory moments in the New Testament that are quite striking. Elymas is cursed by Paul for his resistance to the gospel (Acts 13:6-11). Further, Paul prayed for judgment on any who perverted the grace of the gospel (Galatians 1:8-9). Peter presided over the deadly judgment on Ananias and Sapphira, who dropped dead (Acts 5:1-11). Paul prayerfully and prophetically delivered Hymenaeus and Alexander to the Devil (I Timothy 1:20). He did the same thing to the Corinthian who was committing sexually involved with his father's wife (I Corinthians 5:5).

10. As much as we may want to claim some high ground,

imprecations are in both testaments. And they are a part of the prayer language of a people dealing with forces – that have no resolution, except by the direct intervention of God.

The imprecatory psalms represent a blunt, straightforward, no-nonsense view of sin. They call for judgment – here and now. They respect, more acutely, both the holiness of God and His concern for present justice. And they insist that God intervene; that God interrupt certain patterns, that He stops – in their tracks, certain people – whose incorrigibility indicates that they will never be saved. Sin is taken seriously here. Consequences are insisted on. And it is also understood that the intervention of God; will be an occasion for others to repent.

SECTION TWO

HISTORICAL PERSPECTIVES

CHAPTER TEN

CHRISTIAN PRAYER - AN OVERVIEW

A Window Through Time

On January 9, 1912, at 10 AM, at the Church of God General Assembly, the General Overseer read a Scripture lesson from I Peter 1, and offered prayer. Following this, he delivered his annual address. He spoke about the great need of more pastors and how the wolves were destroying the flocks on account of the absence and shortage of shepherds.

The burden became so great that he had to discontinue the discourse for an interval of several minutes, while the hearers prostrated themselves before God in tears, weeping and intercessory prayers with groanings of the Spirit.

Later, the Assembly while standing began singing, "Old time religion," and shaking hands. Tears were in almost all eyes, and under the white heat of God's love, all present were melted into one solid mass of love and fellowship. All then kneeled down and were led in prayer by Jonah L. Shelton. "Behold how good and how pleasant it is for brethren to dwell together in unity" (Psalm 133:1).

Minutes of the Seventh Annual Assembly of the Churches of God. Held at Cleveland, Tenn., January 9-14, 1912.

CHAPTER 10

CHRISTIAN PRAYER - AN OVERVIEW

P. Douglas Small

[1] It is a difficult and even formidable thing to write on prayer, and one fears to touch the Ark.[2]

John Bunyan defined prayer as "a sincere, sensible, affectionate pouring out of the heart or soul to God, through Christ, in the strength and assistance of the Holy Spirit, for such things as God has promised, or according to His Word, for the good of the church, with submission in faith to the will of God."[3] The great fundamentalist, John R. Rice, would agree. He believed prayer was merely asking. And yet most certainly, it is more. However, the failure to ask is clearly a failure to obey God. Further, we forfeit the opportunity to demonstrate to a watching world that our source is divine, that we trust God, and that we believe that He both listens to our pleas and responds by answering prayers. It is functional atheism. It is arrogant self-sufficiency. Yet, a prayer life that is all asking, and no communion is unbalanced; and one that is superficially spiritual,

---

1   This Chapter and Section are difficult to title. As I started to include a brief 'chapter' as an overview on prayer in the Bible, the volume of materials seemed to explode. While this is meant to be a serious synopsis, it is not comprehensive, by any means. It is not a 'history of prayer' per se, in that it excludes non-Christian views on prayer. It is primarily concerned with prayer – in the Old and New Testaments.

2   P. T. Forsyth, *The Soul of Prayer* (Regent College Publishing, 1916)

3   John Bunyan, *Prayer* (London: Banner of Truth Trust, 1965), 13.

Great Biblical Prayers

- Abraham - Genesis 18:23-33 (intercession)
- Jacob – Genesis 32:23-32.
- Moses - Exodus 15:1-18 (praise); 32:11-14 and 33:12-17 (intercession); Numbers 11:10-15 (complaint); 14:11-19 (pleading)
- Gideon – Judges 6
- Hannah - I Samuel 2:1-10 (praise)
- David - II Samuel 7:18-29 (thanksgiving); I Chronicles 29:11-20 (praise)
- Solomon - I Kings 3:6-9 (for wisdom); 8:22-53; 54-61 (praise); II Chronicles 6:14-42 (praise and petition)
- Elijah – I Kings 18
- Hezekiah - II Kings 19:14-19 (intercession)
- Isaiah 6; 63:7 – 64:12.
- Jehoshaphat – II Chronicles 20
- Jeremiah - Jeremiah 32:16-25 (praise and questioning); 10:23-35; 15:15-18; 18:19-23; 20:7-18.
- Ezra - Ezra 9:5-15 (confession)
- Nehemiah - Nehemiah 9:5-27 (praise and petition)
- Daniel - Daniel 9:1-19 (confession and petition)
- Jonah 2:1-9
- Habakkuk - Habakkuk 1:12-17 (questioning)
- Job

This inset offers 18 prominent examples of prayer in the Old Testament. Seven of the listed prayers are for the salvation of cities – almost half the examples. And two are for the most wicked cities in history – Sodom and Ninevah, one that is destroyed; and the other spared, at least initially. The third prominent city is Jerusalem, which is found to be in the condition of Sodom, and is destroyed, but restored. These are prayers by kings, priests and prophets – and arguably, by common men. Some are personal in nature. Some are missional. They include prayers of repentance and confession, the need for personal and national renewal, intercessions and praise. The list could be expanded – it is only a sampling.

New Testament
- Mary - Luke 1:46-55 (praise)
- Zacharias - Luke 1:68-79 (praise)
- Simeon - Luke 2:29-32 (praise)
- Early Church - Acts 4:24-30 (praise and petition)
- Paul - Colossians 1:9-12; Ephesians 1:1-23; Philippians 1:9-11 (praise and petition)
- Church Triumphant - Revelation 4:8-5:14 (praise)

above asking, misses the heart of humble dependence on God.

Bunyan's definition needs closer examination. He calls for sincerity – the word means without pretentiousness. The prayer and the pray-er should be pure. Second, he says prayers should be sensible, reasonable, and in a sense practical. 'Snow in August' is a plea for mere magic – unless you live at one of the poles. Third, it is to be affectionate, with heart, with passion. Fourth, you pray with the enabling of the Holy Spirit. He prays with us and through us. Prayers need supernatural power. Fifth, you pray the promises. Your plea must be pleadable, based on covenant promises – that is, based on the Scripture. The promise may be general, simply something in the Bible God promises to those who trust Him; or it may be a 'word' He gave you by the Spirit. Sixth, it should not be narrow, only for you, but for the good of the Church itself, connected to God's larger purposes. Finally, it must have a faith connection. You pray out of your position in Christ.

In recent years, we have seen an exploding 'harp and bowl' movement - prayer as worship mixed with intercession. Bunyan's classic definition omits, or perhaps assumes the central place of communion with God, which is the very heart of prayer – the essence of which is worship itself, and that, the experience of God's love in the context of holiness. In similar fashion, he omits the primary role of thanksgiving with which all petitions are to be wrapped, a reminder that prayer is fundamentally tied to the nature of God. Thanksgiving is a discipline that reminds us of our history with God, the memories of His timely provision and intervention. Such a perspective simultaneously views both the ability of God and His character in action in our behalf. It emboldens faith. Indeed, movements through the years have tended to emphasize components of prayer, slices and not the whole.

Ronald Clements notes, "If we had done nothing more than

lift our hearts to God in praise, we should have achieved the greatest goal possible for any prayer."[4] And yet, it is Christ Himself, who bids us to invite His Kingdom, to seek His will, to petition for daily bread, to obtain forgiveness, to request deliverance from evil. Slices.

What is prayer? Heiler says, "Primitive prayer is real communion of man with God."[5] Brueggemann adds, "It is intensely relational and assumes a partner who hears and responds ... that there is something commensurate between the partners, namely, a capacity to communicate in dialogical fashion."[6] Cullman calls prayer "a conversation with God. The experience of God's presence." And he

> **ACCENT**
>
> Let methods be changed, therefore, if necessary, that prayer may be given its true place. Let there be days set apart for intercession; let the original purpose of the monthly concert of prayer for missions be given a larger place; let missionary prayer- cycles be used by families and by individual Christians; let the best literature on prayer be circulated among the members of the Church; let special sermons on the Subject of intercession be preached. By these and by all other practical means a larger, deeper, wider spirit of prayer should be cultivated in the churches (John R. Mott).
>
> Spurgeon in his autobiography described his gratefulness for being blessed with a praying church. "I always give all

warns, "As soon as purposes creep in which distract from this goal, prayer is profaned, and if it is then supposed to be talk with God, it becomes blasphemous hypocrisy." Cullman observes, "The Pharisee

---

4   Ronald E. Clements, *In Spirit and in Truth* (Atlanta: John Knox Press, 1985), 1.

5   Friedrich Heiler, *Prayer: A Study in the History and Psychology of Religion* (London: Oxford University Press, 1932), 96.

6   Walter Brueggemann, *Great Prayers of the Old Testament* (Louisville/London: Westminster John Knox Press, 2008), xvi.

the glory to God, but I do not forget that He gave me the privilege of ministering from the first to a praying people. We had prayer meetings that moved our very souls, each one appeared determined to storm the Celestial City by the might of intercession." Spurgeon regarded the prayer meeting as the spiritual thermometer of a church. His church's Monday night prayer meeting had a worldwide testimony for many years. Every Monday night a large portion of Spurgeon's sanctuary was filled with earnest and fervent intercessors.

In Spurgeon's eyes, the prayer meeting was the most important meeting of the week. He taught his people to pray. And throughout his ministry, those who knew him and were moved by his preaching were more affected by his praying.

is pretending to himself and others that he is thanking God. In reality, in his prayer, he only has himself and other human beings in view ... whereas the publican with his petition for pardon, in awareness of his sin, is seeking to make contact with God."[7]

The Bible – A Book About Prayer

There is no single and conclusive definition of prayer in the Bible, but the concept is pervasive. The Bible uses the word *prayer* or expresses a prayer in 61 of its 66 books, with close to 1,100 distinct references to and about prayer.[8] Prayer, in explicit reference and form is absent only from Esther, the Song of Solomon, Obadiah, Haggai, and Second John. An argument can be made that the book of Haggai implies prayer, since it records the meeting of God's people at the temple site (Haggai 1:1-4, 6-9, 11), and a prophetic plea to rebuild the temple, certainly implying the essence of prayer,

---

7   Oscar Cullman, *Prayer in the New Testament* (Minneapolis, MN: Fortress Press, 1994), 17.

8   James E. Rosscup, *An Exposition on Prayer in the Bible* (5 vols.), Bibliacom.

the restoration of the altar for the nation, for personal and family relationships with God. Also, the Song of Solomon many interpret as encoded symbolism of our intimacy with God - thus prayer. That would reduce the number of books where prayer was absent to only four.

Books that are laden with prayer content include – Genesis, Numbers, Judges, Matthew, Luke, Acts, II Corinthians, Ephesians, Colossians, I and II Thessalonians, James, and I Peter. Of course, the Psalms stand in a class all by themselves. In the Revelation, we are given a glimpse into heaven's worship in chapters four and five and prayer moments throughout. Arguably, the book itself is an answer to the prayer in chapter six.

Actual prayers are recorded in fifty-seven of the sixty-six books. In the Pentateuch, there are fifty-eight prayers. In the historical books, there are seventy prayers. In the wisdom literature, there are fifty prayers (apart from the Psalms). And in the prophets, there are fifty-six prayers. A total of 242 prayers are found in the Old Testament. The exceptions are: Leviticus - which is loaded with prayer material. The essence of prayer is throughout the book, detailing how to approach the altar, the offering of sacrifices (Leviticus 1-5), the priesthood, the feast day descriptions (Leviticus 23), the falling of fire at the first sacrifice, the act of blessing by Aaron after he and Moses had gone before God (Leviticus 9:22-24). Proverbs - here you have the pleas of Wisdom, crying in the streets, a form of prayer (1:20-33). Ecclesiastes - deals with prayer and fatalism as a topic (1:12-18). Ruth – does have a benediction (2:10). And the concept of prayer - Ruth pleaded with Naomi, "Entreat me not to leave you!" (Ruth 1:16). To entreat is to persuade. Here it is the idea that the 'power' or final decision lies in the hand of the other – they must grant the request. Esther - implies dependence on God and obedience for the salvation of the Jewish people (4:13-17; 9:18). Haggai - prayer is assumed and the people gather at the former temple site, the prophetic comes forth to urge them to rebuild the temple (1:1-4). Zephaniah - prayer is absent, but implied (1:7-8; 2:1-3; 3:8-9, 14-17f). Zechariah – has prayer aspects (3:1-5; 2:10, 13; 1:12-13; 10:1). For example, Joshua, the high priest is seen standing at the altar before the Lord (3:1f). There is the prophetic formula: 'Not by might, nor by power' (4:6) in answer to the concern that the task of rebuilding is too great. The Song of Solomon is about passion. And though prayer is not mentioned, per se, the essence of the book is about the love of the bridegroom and the bride (1:2, 4; 2:4, 8, 10, 14; 3:1; 5:2). This is the heart of prayer. In Obadiah, Micah and Nahum we can say that prayer is noticeable absent.

> *"God's word is a record of prayer – of praying men and their achievements ... "*
>
> E. M. Bounds, *The Best of E. M. Bounds on Prayer* (Grand Rapids: Baker; 1981), 11.

In the New Testament, recorded prayers are found in twenty of the twenty-seven books. There are fifteen recorded prayers prayed by Jesus. The gospels contain fifty-five prayers. The Luke-Acts tandem has thirty-one prayers. There are twenty-three recorded prayers in the letters of Paul. In the General Epistles, we find sixteen. And in the Revelation, there are nine.[9]

The New Testament books that do not have *recorded prayers* include: I Corinthians - though the subject of worship, indeed, the operation of the gifts of the Spirit are found there, with great detail. Galatians - includes prayer facets, but not a formally recorded prayer (1:3-8). I Timothy – has references to prayer, but not a prayer (1:12, 16-17; 2:1-8; 4:16; 6:12-16). Titus - no prayer, but there is

---

9   All these figures are extrapolated from Herbert Lockyer, *All the Prayers of the Bible*. See the chart in the index for a complete list. The figures vary, depending upon the researcher, but only slightly.

a benediction (1:4). Philemon contains a glimpse at the effectiveness of prayer, but no prayer (1:4-7, 22). I John – it is implied, but there is no formal prayer recorded (1:9; 3:22; 4:15-16). II John – there is no mention of prayer apart from an illusion in verse three.

You cannot read the Bible without stepping into prayers – not merely the topic of prayer, but actual recorded prayers. The statistics above only reference points at which the *content of the prayers themselves* is preserved in scripture. The topic is pervasive as is the record of what was prayed.

> ### ACCENT
>
> God shapes the world by prayer. Prayers are deathless. The lips that uttered them may be closed in death, the heart that felt them may have ceased to beat, but the prayers live before God, and God's heart is set on them and prayers outlive the lives of those who uttered them; outlive a generation, outlive an age, outlive a world.
>
> E. M. Bounds, *The Best of E. M. Bounds on Prayer* (Grand Rapids: Baker; 1981), 75.

Prayer – God's Idea

That people in different cultures pray is not the issue. Brueggemann argues that the difference in prayer "is determined by the particularity of the God to whom they pray." It is the nature of God that dictates the nature of prayer. Israel prayed "to the God of the exodus who is the Creator of heaven and earth," and that perception, and those twin themes - creation and redemption, influenced the character of their prayers.[10]

The Israelites "groaned under their slavery, and cried out" (Exodus 2:23 NSRV). Remarkably, the prayer is not addressed to God, specifically. And yet, it does not end up in the dead letter file. Do

---

10   Walter Brueggemann, xii.

such groans and cries really constitute prayer? Brueggemann claims that they are "the most elemental prayer ... the raw articulation of the most desperate bodily need, an out-loud utterance of unbearable suffering and misery that must be voiced." In the desperate cry, is nevertheless, the kernel of faith, for the cry itself is "an act of hope ... addressed to 'an open sky.'"[11] It is a reach to the beyond – "whomever may be 'beyond' who is capable of hearing."[12]

People in desperation – pray! Their prayers are raw, not formal. They are stripped of theological language and form. This stripped-down class of prayers represents a kind of desperate faith that God rewards. This is perhaps the concept that Jesus pictures when, in teaching on prayer, He unwraps the story of the widow (Luke 18). Driven by her adversary, she plowed through the courtroom doors and demanded a hearing, one to which she was not legally entitled. Thrown out, her case dismissed, she continued to barrage the court for relief. She had nowhere else to go; no one she confidently believed could effectively intervene. It is precisely out of the exclusive and exalted position that she held of God, in the image of the judge, that she was motivated to pray. Her perception of God as powerful and just are not ideas about which she has necessarily deeply contemplated. This is a thought that rises more from the heart, than the head; more out of something deep within, something perhaps forgotten, something painted over by modernism, something repressed in an affluent culture – but now primitive instincts of the noblest kind come to her aid. She presses herself on the court pleading for intervention.

If history be true, God's great men were all men of prayer.

Prayer is inevitably linked to the character of God. We pray –

11 Ibid, xiii.
12 Ibid, xiv.

because He is good, and He invites us to pray. He welcomes our fellowship and petition. We pray – because He is able to act in our behalf. It is not word therapy. It is not self-talk. We engage a Deity who is not removed from life and from our life in particular. He sees. He hears. He loves. He acts – because we prayed.

In the remarkable case of Israel, they prayed, not knowing if they would be heard. But, they prayed anyway. This is evidence of the deep faith, the profound and subterranean knowing in the psyche of every human. "Their cry rose up to God!" – though 'God' is not addressed by any name. A generic term appears here. And God hears. The God who answers is merciful (*rachum*), a term specifically used for God alone, never of humans.[13] It is His job – mercy and compassion are His DNA. And therefore, He hears formless prayers, when they are only cries.

Prayer and theology both deal with God, but from different perspectives. Theology, like a telescope, views the distant stars of His qualities. Prayer, like a space vehicle, that moves us among His qualities. Theology studies God -prayer engages Him.

~ Ben Jennings, The Arena of Prayer

What does prayer say about God? It was His idea! It is of course, primarily a clue about God's relatedness.[14] He is trinity. Jesus 'prays to the Father.' While it is not appropriate to think of *God* as praying – in the sense of the worship or dependence on another, yet there is within the Trinitarian family a dynamic relatedness. The Father loves the Son.

---

13 Ibid.
14 Samuel Balentine, *Prayer in the Hebrew Bible: The Drama of Divine-Human Dialogue* (Overtures to Biblical Theology; Minneapolis, MN; Minneapolis Fortress Press, 1993), 34.

And the Son, in His incarnate form, prayed to the Father, with the enabling of the Spirit. The Father, by prayer, in turn, and specifically through Christ, the intercessor, relates to mankind and the world.

The God of Scripture is incomparable. And yet anthropomorphic language is used to intensify His relatedness to us. He has a face, eyes and ears, hands and feet. He sees and smells. He feels and acts. He is capable of both love and anger. He remembers and He forgets. The representation is theological accommodation. God wants to be known by man. How can we know one who is past finding out? How would one without eyes and ears see and hear? The metaphorical language is for the purpose of our relating to the utterly other God. And these are in the face of multiple warnings against idolatry (Isa. 40:18-20; 41:7; 44:9-20; 46:5-7). While He offers a means by which we can conceptualize Him, He warns that idols are made (Isa. 44:13-18). They are deaf and dumb, blind and dead. Cut down and hammered into shape. Accommodation for the purpose of relatedness is not the same as idolatry. This God will not be fashioned. He dictates His own form.

In Scripture, we meet two things prayer transcends – time and space. There are two special areas about which the Bible is concerned: heaven and earth. "The heavens are the Lord's heavens, but the earth He has given to human beings" (Psa. 115:16). The means of interchange between these two spheres is prayer. "The prayers of the people are heard in heaven" (I Kings 8). God hears. And He answers. And He speaks into the earthly sphere as well. The separateness of heaven and earth does not equate with inaccessibility.[15]

Prayer also transcends time. We travel through time from the past into the present, and look toward a future. God knows the beginning, from the end. In a sense, He was present at creation to launch the boat. And He will be present at the end of the age, to welcome it. He

15   Ibid, 38-39.

moves from the end, backward in time, sitting outside the realm of time, in a condition the Bible calls the 'eternal.' There are things God announces as having determined to do. But He does not make that announcement

> *We have a church that operates on the continuum of maintenance and not empowerment.*

from the inside of time, but rather, outside of time, and therefore the announcement comes 'into' time. For us, there is only the pulsating moment. There is the provocation – a moment in time, which for us is quickly past and undoable. For God, there is also the anticipated – a warning or even a potential consequence, something that is planned or promised, imminent perhaps, announced by the prophets and anticipated. And then there is an in between, a time for reversal or withdrawal. It is in this season, the 'now,' that God often calls for a divine-human consultation. And in such a moment, with the human's response to God's planned or announced intention, history may be altered.[16] This exchange is called prayer. Prayer, it turns out, by the design of God, alters the course of things on earth. God intervenes by prayer in our time-space world.

Humans Pray – It's a Simple Fact

According to the Pew Forum and the US Religious Landscape Survey, nearly six-in-ten (58 percent), of North Americans claim to pray every day. Jehovah's Witnesses (89 percent) and Mormons (82 percent) top the list, with members of historically black (80 percent) and evangelical churches close behind (78 percent). The survey provided no breakout of statistics for Pentecostals. Catholics and mainline Protestant church members (58 and 53 percent) also say they pray daily. The numbers for Buddhists (45 percent), and Jews (26 percent) were lower. But six-in-ten Hindus (62 percent) say they

16 Ibid..

pray at a shrine or home altar weekly, as do one-third of Buddhists.

A significant minority of Americans say they get answers to prayers at least once a week (19 percent). Another 31 percent, thus half, say they get answers to prayer at least monthly.[17] In an even more transparent fact, 21 percent of so-called atheist, when probed, admitted that they actually believe in God, and twelve percent of them believe there is a heaven. Further, ten-percent acknowledged that they pray at least once a week.

The Princeton Religious Research Center asked 688 adults their views on prayer.[18] Some 90 percent indicated that they *most often* prayed in some other place than a house of worship, essentially, other than church. They reported that they heard voices when they prayed, and saw visions (23 percent). They claimed to feel better after prayer (86 percent). Ninety-five per cent claimed that prayers had been answered. Prayer provided a feeling of increased peace and hope.

While these are *personal* results of prayer, and may seem narrowly self-interested, still yet, this data is not to be so easily discounted. It is true that the scope of biblical prayer is much larger. The point, however, must be made that despite over a century of modernism's assault on faith and the Bible, the seeming triumph of science and skepticism, prayer persists. And its practice is amplified more so apart from the church than in or at the church itself. Humans pray!

Prayer and the Christian life are inseparable.

"As soon as a Christian has been justified by faith and thus becomes God's child, he begins to commune, with God. The personal conversing of the Christian with God is called prayer. It is altogether Scriptural to define prayer as 'the conversation

---

17 The Pew Forum on Religion & Public Life / U.S. Religious Landscape Survey. See: "The U.S. Religious Landscape Survey." On-line at http://religions.pewforum.org/pdf/report2religious-landscape-study-key-findings.pdf.

18 "Prayer, *The Reporter*, "*The Importance of Prayer to Nearly Everyone,*" (May, 1994), 12.

of the heart with God' (Psalm 27:8), whether the heart alone communes with God without clothing the prayers in words of the mouth or whether the mouth utters the prayer of the heart."[19]

And yet, while *instinctive* prayer is admitted and embraced, the systematic discipline of prayer is resisted. Excuses include - "Prayer is too complicated – too many forms and types of prayer ... I don't pray, because I am not good at it ... Deep down, I doubt that prayer really works ... I don't feel good enough to deserve an answer ... I feel that I can't reach God, He is too distant ... I understand that I am to pray in line with God's will, and I don't know what that is ... It requires too much time to be effective."

Richard Foster reminds us:

> Prayer catapults us onto the frontier of spiritual life. Of all the Spiritual Disciplines, prayer is the most central because it ushers us into perpetual communion with the Father.[20]

In the unredeemed state of sin, under wrath, men avoid God. An unsaved man naturally, if his conscience is still alive, fears God and evades Him (Heb. 2:15; Gen. 3:6). But when, by faith, he has been justified and reconciled, he immediately enters into joyful communion with God (Rom. 8:15). He prays. He revels in the peace of God. He walks in the love and light of God. He wants to talk to God, to pray. There can be no genuine Christian life without it. Luther called prayer, "the pulse-beat of inner life."[21] Leonard Allen said, "The Church is a school of prayer." If it is not teaching on and

---

19 Francis Pieper, *Christian Dogmatics* (St. Louis: Concordia Publishing House, 1955), III, 76-77.

20 Richard Foster, from *Celebration of Discipline*. Quoted by, Leonard Allen, *The Contemporaries Meet the Classics on Prayer* (West Monroe, LA: Howard Publishing Company, 2003), 1.

21 E.W. Plass, *What Luther Says* (St. Louis: Concordia Publishing House, 1959), II, 1024-1101. See also: Martin Reu, *Lutheran Dogmatics* (Decorah, Iowa: Wartburg Theological Seminary, 1951), 376.

moving people into prayer, it is failing in its task.[22] Further, he says, "Prayer is the central avenue God uses to change us. If we are unwilling to change, we will abandon prayer as a noticeable characteristic of our lives. The closer we come to the heartbeat of God, the more we see our need and the more we desire to be conformed to Christ."[23]

As William Carey reminded us, "Prayer – secret, fervent, believing prayer – lies at the root of all personal godliness."[24]

Bennie Triplet noted in his book, *Praying Effectively:*

The Bible speaks of multiple places of prayer such as the altar of sacrifice in Genesis 12:7, 8; 13:4; walking in an open field in Genesis 18:23-33; and standing by a well in Genesis 24:12-14. Some places of prayer even seem a bit peculiar, such as Jacob praying while wrestling in Genesis 32:24-30; Balaam praying while riding on a talking ass in Numbers 22:34; Samson praying while bound in chains to a mill in Judges 16:21-31; Jonah praying from the belly of a great fish in Jonah 2:1. The rich man prayed in hell and so did Jonah (Luke 16:19-31; Jonah 2:2). Jesus prayed while being baptized in the river Jordan (Luke 3:21, 22), in the wilderness (Luke 5:16), at the tomb of Lazarus (John 11:41, 42) and while hanging on the cross dying for our sins (Luke 23:34). Paul and Silas prayed in the Philippian jail (Acts 16:25) and during a shipwreck (Acts 27:23-25). The final place I will mention refers to the souls under the altar crying, 'How long, O Lord, how long?' (Revelation 6:9-11).[25]

---

22 Leonard Allen, *The Contemporaries Meet the Classics on Prayer* (West Monroe: LA; Howard Publishing Company, 2003), 2.
23 Ibid, 16-17.
24 Quoted by Leonard Allen, 16.
25 Bennie Triplett, *Praying Effectively* (Pathway Press: Cleveland, TN; 1990), 43.

CHAPTER ELEVEN

GENESIS AND THE EARLY PERIOD

A WINDOW THROUGH TIME

The story of Eliezer, commissioned by Abraham Genesis 24:1-9 to find a bride for Isaac is one of the great prayer stories in the Bible. Abraham is some 150 years of age. Sarah is dead. And Isaac, the son of promise is still unmarried (22:15-18). His bride must not be from among the pagan Canaanites – so the choices are narrow. Abraham calls on his trusted servant Eliezer to find a bride, and yet, this is a tale that does not leave out hearts – a story full of metaphor and type. Abraham serves as a type of the Father, Isaac of the Son, Eliezer the Spirit, and Rebekkah the Bride, the Church. The name Eliezer is from *El,* the common abbreviation of Elohim, a reference to God; and from the verb *azar* which means to help or support. Thus, it means God, our helper or supporter; God, our comforter. What a perfect word picture of the Holy Spirit. The word is used of Eve in reference to Adam, 'I will make him a helper,' referring to Eve (Genesis 2:18).

Eliezer is Abraham's long-standing and most trusted servant, and he is now charged with the greatest task of his life, that of finding a bride in the city of Nahor where Abraham's extended family lives. Eliezer is not alone in the mission. Incredibly, Abraham assures him that "the LORD, the God of heaven . . . will send His angel before you," (v. 7). This is no doubt, the Angel of Yahweh, a pre-incarnate manifestation of the one we know as Jesus, the same angel that appeared to Abraham and Sarah (Genesis 18) before the birth of Isaac and at other times as well. It is a Theophany (16:7; 21:17; 22:11;

Exod. 23:20, 23).

Before Eliezer prays, provision has already been made. Before he begins his journey, heaven has assigned an angelic companion. The prayer is simple. It begins with a qualifier to the specific petition. "O LORD God of my master Abraham, please give me success this day ..." Not a bad prayer! And then, he adds the purpose of that success, namely, to serve another, to "show kindness to my master Abraham." The prayer is for a blessing, in order to be a blessing; and further, to accomplish the larger purposes of God. Then he offers the specific petition. "Now let it be that the young woman to whom I say, 'Please let down your pitcher that I may drink,' and she says, 'Drink, and I will also give your camels a drink'—let her be the one You have appointed for Your servant Isaac. And by this I will know that You have shown kindness to my master." The prayer anticipates the common, a specific player and a prop – a young woman with a pitcher, having come to the well to draw water. But, then it also anticipates a kind act in response to a personal request, "Give me a drink of water!" It anticipates the attitude of a servant, and specific language. It anticipates a more than gracious response, "I will also take care of your camels!" – anticipated, and yet offered freely and spontaneously on the part of Rebekkah. It is as if Eliezer has seen and heard the future, and is watching it played out before him, he himself, being one of the players. He prays, and then lives God's will.

Still breathing his prayer, still constructing the scenario, Rebekah appears immediately, before the prayer is even complete. Suddenly, every detail of the prayer request is fulfilled, leaving Eliezer 'wondering' or marveling at the quick work of God. Pray does tap into the future. It is a gateway, a doorway, a portal through which we enter God's will.

After the deeds are done, more confirmations come. He discovers the pedigree of Rebekah. She is the daughter of Bethuel, a member of Abraham's clan. The prayer has truly been answered. Eliezer's immediate response is worship, and that should be our reaction to answered prayer, He "bowed down his head and worshiped the LORD." He 'blessed' the Lord who showed "mercy and truth" toward Abraham, an act that caught him in the middle. After Bethuel hears the story, he concludes the thing is from God, and Eliezer again bows in worshipful prayer. (24:28). He repeats the act of prayer in verse 52, when permission is given for Rebekkah to return and marry Isaac. Here is prayer on top of prayer! Godly missions are fulfilled only in a spirit of prayer.

Now headed home, as Eliezer approaches the camp of Abraham, Isaac has gone into the field to pray at the close of the day (24:61-67). He sees the caravan approaching, and Rebekkah sees him. It is love at first site.

Here is a wonderful story of a father's concern for his son. Of a son, who has a hole in his heart following the loss of his mother. Of a faithful servant faced with an extraordinary task, being a matchmaker. Of circumstances and coincidences that bear the finger prints of God. Of God's concern for the happiness of two people – Isaac and Rebekkah. Miles apart, they belong together. It is so ordinary an issue. Who will I marry? Does God have someone for me? For my son, my daughter? How do I find them? Connect them? How do I protect them from making a wrong choice in marriage? Prayer factors in. So does the Holy Spirit. Here, an angel plays a role; actually, 'Jesus' in angelic form. Incredible.

And yet, the story is also one filled with prophetic metaphor. It is a story of God, longing for a relationship with man. It is a story of the Holy Spirit's search in this far country, the earth, for you and me to be eternal companions of Jesus, the Christ, the Messiah, the One loaded with promise. It is the story as well of little things – kindness, a servant heart, a willingness to greet a stranger with grace not knowing that it may change the destiny of our very life. It is a story of God's direction. Of His involvement in our daily doings. It is a story of prayerful dependence. Of the simple promptings of the heart. Of a prayer being answered before it is completely prayed. Thus God's willingness to answer prayer. Indeed, God's guidance even in the prayer that we pray. It is the tender story of God's interaction, not simply with the great Abraham, but with his servant Eliezer. It heightens the status before God of the common man, that of the servant. It is a reminder when that when we are given a task, no matter our status, God is willing to be involved in the faithful fulfillment of that task.

CHAPTER 11

GENESIS AND THE EARLY PERIOD
P. Douglas Small

The Earliest Period

In Genesis, there is considerable attention given to prayer, to altars and sacrifice. Adam *walks* with God. Cain and Abel worship God, each bringing an offering. A point in history is noted, when men begin to "call upon *the name* of the Lord" (Genesis 4:26). Enoch walked with God and God took him (Genesis 5:24). Hebrews tells us that "before his translation he had this testimony, that he pleased God" (Heb. 11: 5). Noah heard from God, built the ark and saved humanity, and when the waters subsided, he built an altar in gratitude (Genesis 8:20-22).

The Patriarchs and the Building of Altars

Abraham, Isaac and Jacob all built altars which are implicit of prayer. There are ten altars in all, beginning with Abel's in Genesis 4:3-5 and continuing through to Jacob's second altar at Bethel found in Genesis 35:6-14. Abraham built four altars. Bethel is the link between him and his grandson, Jacob. Abraham's fourth altar, on Mount Moriah cast a shadow forward to John 19 and Hebrews 11.

An altar indicates man's desire to meet with God and be heard of Him, and God's demands that man recognize the wages of sin as death. Here man dies to self and sin, and is reborn to the God and

His purposes. The altar is a portal, a place where heaven and earth connect, a place for communion and sacrifice. Life and death are both bound up here, and honest, sacrificial prayer is the difference between the two. The first altar of Abram/Abraham is in reference to both the seed, his desire for an heir and the promised land. *"Unto thy seed will I give this land"* (Genesis 12:7). At that point, he built his first altar. Prayer affects place/space as well as time/generations. At Bethel, the Patriarch built another altar and *"called upon the Name of the Lord"* (Gen. 12: 8). Notice how prayer comes to be aligned with the *Name*, and that *'Name'* is to be attached to both the land and a particular people.

A famine temporarily sends Abraham to Egypt, but he built no altar there. Nor had he built an altar in the Ur of Chaldees before responding to the call to come to the land he and his seed would be given. His altars are only on the holy and promised land. There is an attachment to these places of prayer and the altars - *"... unto the place of the altar, which he had made there at the first: and there Abraham called on the Name of the Lord"* (Genesis 13: 4). At Mamre, near Hebron, he would build yet another altar (13:18). Isaac, at Beersheba (Gen. 26: 24) built his altar and called on the Name of the Lord.

Abraham and the Angel of Yahweh

Genesis 18 is a watershed moment in prayer. In this chapter, Abraham entertains three men, actually angels, and in doing so – the Angel of YHWH. His gracious hosting of heaven's visitors represents the point in his life when the twenty-four years of waiting for the promised child is ended. For the first time, Sarah has had a direct encounter with God – in fact, the two have stood together in the tent door. And they are adamantly informed, "Sarah will have a child!" In verse 18, Abraham is assured that through him "all nations of the earth shall be blessed." Though Abraham has responded to the angels by hosting them, the initiative in coming was with God – He has chosen to 'know' Abraham, a term of intimacy (18:19).

Brueggemann offers a startling insight on Genesis 18:22-32. Abraham is pictured there as "standing before YHWH." This is the occasion of solemn intercession on the part of Abraham for Sodom and Gomorrah. But Brueggemann calls our attention to a "scribal correction" in verse 22 noted in the NRSV as "another ancient tradition." In the earlier version, it is YHWH that "stands before Abraham." Brueggemann suggest that the roles here are reversed. YHWH appears in the position of the supplicant. The text has implications regarding our posture in prayer. This is not

> ## ACCENT
>
> J. C. Ryle, in his Practical Religion and the chapter titled "Prayer," asserts that "prayer is the most important subject in practical religion." He provides seven reasons for this proposal which are listed as follows:
>
> 1. Prayer is absolutely needful to a man's salvation.
> 2. A habit of prayer is one of the surest marks of a true Christian.
> 3. There is no duty in religion so neglected as private prayer.
> 4. Prayer is that act of religion to which there is the greatest encouragement.
> 5. Diligence in prayer is the secret of eminent holiness.
> 6. Neglect of prayer is one great cause of backsliding.
> 7. Prayer is one of the best recipes for happiness and contentment.
>
> J. C. Ryle, *Practical Religion*, pp. 46-59.

a textual variation, but one of the few places where the ancient scribe changed the text – "a deliberate theological-interpretive 'correction.'" The scribe apparently felt it inappropriate for YHWH to stand before God, so he reversed the role, retaining the superior position in reverence for God.[1] But the idea did not need to be interpreted as a matter of reversed inequality. God stopped by Abraham's tent to wake up in him the action of intercession. He now waits to see what Abraham will do. This is significant – that God's actions are somehow tied to our interactions with Him in prayer. Human agency can 'tip the scales.' Likewise our passiveness may be paired to His inaction. This does not turn the sovereignty of God on its head, it rather, emphasizes the limited sovereignty, respected by God, in His gift of dominion to Adam, authority lost in the fall, but slowly and incrementally restored by prayer, in the context of the covenant, and finally, completely, in Christ.

Abraham confidently confronts God, inquiring, though simultaneously anticipating the worst, about His intentions regarding Sodom and Gomorrah. The ability of YHWH to wipe out the city is not in question. Abraham appeals to the "ethical-covenantal-legal categories of the 'righteous wicked.'"[2] YHWH, Abraham believes, is moving quickly toward the act of judgment. And prayer, in this moment, is designed as a reminder, that our power of appeal is vested in the character of God Himself. "Far be it from you," is better translated, "It would be defiling of you … It would make you polluted."[3]

Abraham insists that YHWH must treat the righteous (Lot) different than the wicked (Sodom). The argument is an appeal to the holiness of God. And indeed, that the presence of the righteous among the wicked, is a basis for the salvation of the whole city. This is an expression, not only of confidence in the character of God, but

---

1   Walter Brueggemann, *Great Prayers of the Old Testament* (Louisville/London: Westminster John Knox Press, 2008), 4.
2   Ibid, 4-5.
3   Ibid, 5.

also in His profound respect of the righteous.

Our assumption is that it is the job of God to remember, and draw distinctions that guarantee that the righteous will always be protected – and that is an automatic function of heaven. It may be the opposite. Namely, heaven's disposition toward the earth and mankind is that of judgment, due to the excess of rebellion and wickedness, and only in prayer, only in a judicial moment in which a righteous advocate intercedes is mercy necessarily invoked. That being the case, the rampant atrocities in our world that are the natural consequences of a world gone mad, are not to be laid at the feet of God, nor yet at the feet of the blind sinners under the spell of the darkness and in bondage to their own fleshly impulses, but at the feet of inactive intercessors. Sin deserves judgment. It has wages, and the check must be made out to someone – and justice demands that the wages not be

---

ACCENT

When James Cross, former General Overseer, was President of Lee College, one Sunday evening he shared a prayer moment he had experienced. While pastoring in Lakeland, his son was on military assignment in the Far East. In the middle of the night, Brother Cross was awakened. He rolled out of bed – and began to fervently pray, not for a member or a friend nearby, but specifically for his son on the other side of the world – or so he thought. He didn't know the nature of the problem as is often the case in intercession. He simply cried out to God and for some season. Actually, his son was not in the Far East. He had caught a hop to the West Coast, and was hitchhiking across the nation to get home to Lakeland, FL. He had made it into the barrenness of West Texas and had been given a ride by a group of young guys – who quickly made both driving and riding treacherous. They were drinking heavily. He persuaded them to let him drive and to his surprise and relief, they did. But soon, they were all dead

---

asleep, and he was so drowsy that his driving was as threatening to his life and theirs as their drunk driving had been. He knew if he stopped, one of them would insist on driving again – and this was no place to stop. This was West Texas. He would be abandoned on a highway in the middle of the night – he had to keep driving. Soon he was virtually careening from one side of the road to the other. His passengers were sound asleep and that is when he heard it – his name. Screamed. Shouted. With such an urgency that it jolted him awake just as he might have wrecked the car and possibly killed himself and everyone in it. He turned and surveyed the sleepers. All were sound asleep – but he was now wide awake. Hundreds of miles away, his Dad was on his knees, passionately calling out his name to God. When he reached Florida, his father, surprised, but glad to see him, would tell him, "I was just praying for you!" And he in turn would disclose to his father, "That was just about the time I was in West Texas in danger of a terrible accident ..."

withheld. Mercy and grace are not the rule in such a situation, they are the exceptions. And it is up to intercessors to plead with the court for such exceptions to be made.

While the scribe may have attempted to tilt the text to protect the superiority of YHWH, Abraham, after his bold confrontation is himself, self-effacing, showing proper reverence for God. "I am but dust and ashes and I have taken it upon myself to speak to the Almighty," (Genesis 18:27); and then "do not be angry" (v. 30), a declaration of deference followed by yet another assertive moment, "Let me speak again" (v. 31), followed by another note of apologetic reverence - "do not be angry" (v. 32). [4]

Intercession, *pagha*, means – to make intercession. Originally, it meant "to strike upon" or "against." It also meant "to assail another with petitions," or "to urge." And of course, it has the representative

---

4   Ibid, 7.

idea, to do so for another (Ruth 1:16; Jeremiah 7:16; 27:18; Job 21:15; Genesis 23:8; Isaiah 53:12; Jer. 36:25). The English word intercession is derived from the Latin, intercede, meaning to come between. The term can mean either to obstruct or to interpose as an advocate.

Abraham and Isaac – Foreshadowing Jesus

On Mt. Moriah, Jerusalem, Abraham would build a singularly significant and prophetic altar,

> *"Take now your son, your only son Isaac, whom you love, and go into the land of Moriah; and offer him there for a burnt offering upon one of the mountains which I will show you" (Gen. 22: 2).*

The obedience of Abraham is noted in Hebrews. His action revealed his faith *"that God was able to raise him [Isaac] up, even from the dead; from whence also he received him in a figure"* (Heb. 11: 19). Here the Lord intervened and the place was forever called, *Jehovah-jireh*, meaning, 'the Lord will provide.'

Eliezer's prayer is recorded in the Bible, as he goes to find a wife for Isaac (Gen. 24:12-18, 22-24, 45). Jacob wrestles with God (32:25-30) prayerfully pleading for a blessing, and experiencing an unexpected name change. He would have a life-altering moment with God at Bethel and build an altar there (35:1).

Summary Observations

Prayer in this period is simple, direct and unencumbered by a complex system of beliefs and ceremonies (Gen. 15:2; 17:18; 18:23; 24:12). Sacrifice is already connected to worship (Gen. 12:8; 13:4; 26:25). Certainly, the blood covenant is known, in some measure. And perhaps the threshold covenant is already known since it is in the doorway of his tent that Abraham sits as he is approached by the angelic party (Gen. 18:1f).[5]

In this period, it is incumbent on the head of the family to offer mediation and therefore sacrifice. He is the priest, the one who bears the responsibility of keeping his family connected to their God. Noah fulfilled this role (Gen. 8:20), as did Abraham (Gen. 12:7, 8; 15:9-11), Isaac (Gen. 26:24f), and Jacob (Gen. 31:54; 33:20). Job, whose book sits among the poetic literature, but historically belongs to this period, offered sacrifices in behalf of his children (Job 1:5). The term mediator, middleman, is not found in the Old Testament. The Greek term, *mesites*, occurs in the Septuagint as a translation of Job 9:33, *"Neither is there any 'daysman' between us."* That word, 'daysman' is a translation of the Hebrew *mokhiach* which means arbitrator or umpire.

In this season of the patriarchs, prayer is primarily, but not exclusively a personal matter. Israel's role as a representative corporate entity has not yet been constituted. From the early pages of Genesis, we hear the prayerful plea of innocent blood. To Cain, "The LORD said, 'What have you done? Listen! Your brother's blood cries out to me from the ground'" (Genesis 4:10). In Genesis 18, the collective cry of the oppressed rises from the city of Sodom and the unceremonious plea is heard by God. He sends angels to investigate and answer. And Abraham is raised up as an intercessor in the path of the potential judgment. In Exodus 3:7, the collective cries of the Hebrews under the harsh task-masters is also heard by God and that begins the movement that will result in their liberation. Job 31:38 tendered the idea that the land for which he was responsible also prayed, *"If my land cries out against me, And its furrows weep together; If I have eaten its fruit without money, Or have caused its owners to lose their lives, Let briars grow instead of wheat, And stinkweed instead*

---

5   P. Douglas Small, *Entertaining God* (Kannapolis, NC: Alive Publications, 2008).

of barley." The prophet Jeremiah reported that the Lord heard "cries of fear," of "terror, not peace" (30:5). James, in the New Testament, says that the cries from harvesters who have labored only to be defrauded of their just wages are heard by God as a prayer (James 5:4).

There are numerous examples of intercession in this period. Adam is to 'guard' the garden (Genesis 2:15), a task at which he fails. The term is later related to 'watching,' a form of intercession and prayer. Noah blessed Japheth and cursed Canaan (Gen. 9:25-27). Abram interceded for Ishmael (Gen. 17:20), for Sodom (Gen. 18:23-33), and Abimelech

> ### ACCENT
>
> In the time of the godly lineage of Seth, the successor of Abel (4:25-26), "men began to call upon the name of the LORD." Matthew Henry says, "Now began the distinction between professors and profane, which has been kept up ever since, and will be while the world stands" – the godly pray; and the ungodly do not.† The grandson of Adam was Enosh, and his name means "mortal or frail." Now the effects of the Fall are becoming evident. There is marked difference that only Adam could know, between what he was before the Fall, and what he sees in his seed. Man is in descent. Sadly judgment is inevitable (Genesis 6-8). The righteous begin the practice, the only

(Gen. 20:17). Isaac prayed for Rebekah (Gen. 25:21). Melchizedek blessed Abram (Gen. 14:19), and Jacob blessed his sons (Gen. 48:15, 20; 49:28).

One notable prayer principle is that the clarity of God's guidance was proportionate to the importance of the crisis. Thus, the direction to Adam and Eve regarding the tree was clear (Gen. 1:28-30; 2:16-17). His instructions to Noah were unmistakable. All of humanity hinged on Noah's obedience (Gen. 6:13-21; 7:1-4). His call to Abraham was also clear (Gen. 12:1-3, 7; 15). The directions regarding a bride for Isaac were clear – since through Isaac, the promises given act that can sustain them in a broken world – prayer. John Bunyan observed, "All true religion beginneth with fervent prayer: Or thus, That when men begin to be servants to God, they begin it with calling upon Him. Thus did Saul [who became Paul, for Ananias was to "inquire at the house of Judas for a man from Tarsus named Saul, at which he observed], "Behold he prayeth" (Acts 9:11). When we acknowledge our creatureliness, only clearly seen in view of His Glory, we are moved to cry out dependently upon God for grace. Limitations and weakness motivate prayer. Pride, self-sufficiency and blindness do not.

† Matthew Henry, *Commentary on the Bible*, I, p. 46.

to Abraham would be fulfilled.

In this period, prayer is seen as a means of generational extension in the prayer for an heir (Genesis 15; 18). It is associated with revelation (Genesis 17). It is revealed as having the potential power to spare a wicked city (Genesis 18; 19). It can be associated with a vow (Genesis 28), and with reconciliation (32). It has the power of generational blessing (48; 49; see also Numbers 6:24-27). Even as a vague groan, it is heard by God as a plea for relief (Exodus 1; 2). It is expressed in the season of the Exodus as a partnership with the Omnipotent One (Exodus 8-10). It is an appeal in a time of peril (17) or need (22:22-24; Numbers 10:35, 36). It is employed as a means of mercy, to delay deserved judgment (32; Numbers 11:1-2).

As noted, Job belongs to the period of the Patriarchs. The entire book is a treatise on prayer, specifically, the problem of a silent heaven – the problem of unanswered prayer. Here Job's effective intercession for his children (Job 1:5) is challenged in heaven. His consistent acts of altar building and consecration of his children have created such an invincible hedge that they are inaccessible to Satan. Heaven is challenged. Job is charged with serving God, allegedly, only for the benefits. Were the hedge removed, were the effectiveness of his prayer abated, were heaven to not respond to him – he would abandon God and faith. Suddenly, and unknowingly, he is the victim of a spiritual war. While heaven and hell know what is happening. Job, along with his friends, is oblivious. All he has is lost. His story is one of faithfulness in the face of unanswered prayers. Still faith survives. At one point, he declares, "Even now my witness is in heaven. My advocate is there on high" (16:19 – NLT). All he can do is weep, but he perceives his tears are a kind of

---

ACCENT

A Sample of PRAYER IN THE LIFE OF JACOB

1. Jacob's birth (Gen. 25:19-26).
2. Jacob's desire for the birthright (Gen. 25:27-34).
3. Jacob's deceit in laying hold of the blessing rightly belonging to Esau (Gen. 27:1-45).
4. Jacob at Bethel (Gen. 28:10-22).
5. Jacob at Haran - the acquisition of Rachel (Gen. 29:1-30).
6. The expansion of his family - polygamy (Gen. 29:31-30:24).
7. His gains from Laban (Gen. 30:25-43).

---

prayer. Then he laments the need for a more articulate spokesman, "I need someone to mediate between God and me, as a person mediates between friends" (16:21 NLT), someone to "argue the case of a man with God" (ESV). At the end of the book, the Lord commands Job to pray, but not for himself. Rather, he is instructed to pray for his so-called friends (Job 42:8). These men were no comfort to Job during his severe trial. They became accusers, adding emotional pain to all his losses and to his physical issues – and he is is to intercede for them. This may been his greatest challenge. It implies forgiveness and a heart bent toward reconciliation. In the intercessory prayer for them, the Lord turns his fortunes and blesses the latter end of Job more than the former.

8. Jacob's exodus from Haran with Laban in pursuit (Gen. 31:1-24).
9. The conflict between Laban and Jacob (Gen. 31:25-42).
10. The covenant offered by Laban (Gen. 31:43-55).
11. Jacob's desired reconciliation with Esau - fearful of revenge (Gen. 32:1-8).
12. His anxiety in prayer (Gen. 32:9-12).
13. His prayer for his family (Gen. 32:13-23).
14. Blessing by prayer (Gen. 32:24-32).
15. Jacob's prayer of desperation, (Gen. 32:9-12).

In this season, prior to the Exodus, corporate worship was family worship. Noah offered sacrifices at the conclusion of the flood. Abraham's altars are family altars. Jacob would take his entire family back to Bethel. Rachel would die on the journey, but for the grandson of Abraham, connecting his children with his own spiritual roots was critical. As Genesis closes, there is the corporate, yet personal, blessing of the sons of Jacob, who would be foundational to the tribes. The lesson is critical. The first order is family prayer – before prayer in the congregation or the nation.

After the Exodus, we are introduced to the Aaronic priesthood. Prior to that, in the time of Abraham, we had been introduced to the priesthood of Melchizedek. There is forever a tension between these two. Aaronic priesthood is linear and inherited, a given. The priesthood of Melchizedek is free, not inherited, mysterious, non-linear. It is dynamic and relational, the other prescribed and positional. One is out of the heart, the other is an issue of rote and function. One is linked to the tabernacle below, the other, to the tabernacle above. One reaches back to Aaron, the other forward to Christ. Melchizedek was a priest forever. He offered no sacrifices at the tabernacle or the temple. He is timeless. It is after the order of Melchizedek that Jesus comes. It is his priestly rank that is highest.

Aaron's priesthood is prescribed, defined by garments and rituals, place and ceremony, sight and smell. It is the more inferior of the two.

One of the remarkable things about prayer in the history of Israel is how it gets hooked to someone or something in the past. For example, Israel, in Egypt's slave service had forgotten YHWH. When they prayed – cried out – God heard them and "remembered His covenant with Abraham, Isaac, and Jacob. God looked upon the Israelites, And God took notice of them" (Exodus 2:24-25). It is significant, that God does not respond to the 'cry' alone, but to the cry in reference to the covenantal relationship. He knows them – through their godly fathers. And He responds, not merely on the basis of their current crisis, but on the basis of the relationship. YHWH also 'remembered Noah' (Genesis 8:1), and He 'remembered Rachel' (30:22). The prayers and alms of Cornelius were remembered as well, "Cornelius, your prayer is heard and your charity is a memorial before God" – a memorial (Acts 10:31 Aramaic Bible).

> Samuel Balentine calls prayer "divine-human communion or partnership where radical dialogue is both normative and productive ... The partnership is clearly between persons of unequal power and authority. God is the Creator, and God is the covenant maker. But in the Hebraic notion of covenant, god is not the only one with power, not the only one having a voice in what is to take place. The human partner also has a say ... on those occasions when the hurt and pain of life do not permit a simple 'Yes' or a manufactured 'Hallelujah,' Israel does not retreat into passive silence. On these occasions the dialogue calls for lament and the covenant relationship permits it – indeed, even requires it."

> "The point here is that covenant relationship, like human relationships, requires communication. The better the communication, the better the relationship, that is, the healthier

it is and the more possibilities it has for growth and development. In the same way, restricted communication, or worse, silence reduces the possibilities within the relationship."[6]

Broader Observations

1. Prayer is not a practice reserved to a select and elite circle.

2. We will discover that it transcends the barriers of race and class. The cries of the both the Hebrews in slavery and the exploited in Sodom are heard. Sarah is cared for, as is her handmaiden.

3. Prayer is not restricted by time or place.

4. Posture is important only as a reflection of the heart – it is the heart that matters.

5. Prayer is not an escapist mechanism.

6. Prayer demands faith, but not blind faith, not faith that lacks integrity and authenticity.

7. Prayer is connected, even in the Old Testament, with fasting and giving – the three principle disciplines noted by Jesus (Matthew 6).

8. Prayer is related to 'the Name' and then 'the Names' of God.

9. Answered prayer should be memorialized – by the stories we tell our children; and the monuments we raise up in the land.

10. Prayer demands persistence – you must prevail in prayer.[7]

There are a wide variety of the types of prayer we meet in the Old Testament.

---

6   Samuel Balentine, *Prayer in the Hebrew Bible: The Drama of Divine-Human Dialogue* (Overtures to Biblical Theology; Minneapolis, MN; Minneapolis Fortress Press, 1993), 288.

7   Howard Peskett, "Prayer in the Old Testament Outside the Psalms," See: D. A. Carson, *Teach Us To Pray* (Grand Rapids: MI; Baker Book House, 1990), 22-29.

1. Thanksgiving and Praise, including prayer as song (psalms).
2. Adoration and Worship.
3. Confession and Repentance.
4. Petition and Supplication.
5. Intercession – prophetic and priestly.
6. The Watch – and Mediation.
7. The Lament.
8. Prayer as a Vow.
9. Consecration and Sanctification.
10. Invocation.
11. Benediction, Blessing Prayers.
12. Imprecatory/Judgment/Curse Prayers.[8]

Prayer References

Genesis

1. Abraham for an heir (40 words; Gen 15:2-3). Answered because God had promised (Gen 21:1-8).

2. Abraham for Ishmael to be his heir (seven words; Gen 17:18). Unanswered because it was not in harmony with God's word and plan.

3. Abraham for Sodom to be spared if ten persons were righteous (176 words; Gen 18:23-32). Unanswered because 10 righteous persons weren't found (Gen 19:24).

4. Eliezer, steward of Abraham, for a bride for Isaac (110 words; Gen 24:12-14). Answered because it was according to God's word (Gen 12:1-3,7; 13:15; 15:18; 17:7,19; 21:12).

5. Jacob for a blessing (Gen 28:20-22). Answered because of God's plan for him (Gen 32:1-33:17).

6. Jacob for deliverance from Esau (130 words; Gen 32:9-12). Answered because of God's word and plan for him (Gen

8   Ibid, 29-33.

25:19-23; 26:3; 27:28-29; 28:3-4,13-15; 32:9).

References to prayer as entreating the Lord, calling on the name of the Lord, groaning or being afflicted (Gen 12:7-8; 13:4; 16:11; 20:17-18; 25:21-23).

Job

1. Job-prayer of thanksgiving and resignation (30 words; Job 1:20-22).

2. Job in complaint and for relief and forgiveness (114 words; Job 7:17-21). Answered (Job 42:10).

3. Job in complaint and for relief (571 words; Job 9:25-10:22). Answered (Job 42:10).

4. Job in complaint and for life and forgiveness (198 words; Job 14:13-22). Answered (Job 42:10).

5. Job for a fair trial (48 words; Job 23:3-5). Answered (Job 38-42).

6. Job, prayer of confession (34 words; Job 40:3-5).

7. Job, prayer of repentance (87 words; Job 42:1-6). Answered (Job 42:10).

Finis Jennings Dake, *Dake's Annotated Reference Bible* (Lawrenceville, GA: Dake Bible Sales, 1963, 1991).

CHAPTER TWELVE

THE EXODUS TO SAMUEL

A WINDOW THROUGH TIME

The prayer of Hannah is one of the great prayer moments in all of Scripture. It is a prophetic declaration, a vivid description of God, offered by a woman who had known the pain of barrenness, the rejection of her husband, the rivalry of a bitter adversary, the inner rumblings of doubt and self-despair. In I Samuel 1, she progresses along a continuum of despair. She is in a decidedly adversarial relationship, and she is unprotected. "Her rival provoked her," and "severely" so, making her experience more than unpleasant. The word used in Hebrew means 'to roar' indicating that she was the victim of rage. It was a deliberate attempt to make her angry – consistent, repetitive, purposeful, manipulative agitation. It became painful to endure, day after day, year after year. She was experiencing an assault on her very soul, and damage was being done to her psyche daily. She was "miserable," literally 'vexed' or angry, but she turned her anger inward. The KJV version uses the term 'sore,' indicating pain or sensitivity associated with pain. All of this was aggravated by her barrenness, something attributed to the sovereignty of God. Even at the tabernacle, the senseless provocations and belittling continued. Hannah wept; a sign of her inwardly turned anger, her depression. And she did not eat. This was more than a voluntary fast; it was also a sign of deprivation. She had stopped feeding herself. She reached a point of desperation. Her fast was partially spiritual, and partially psychological. Her husband noticed her behavior, "Why are you grieved?" Grief is a love word. It is also a sign that something has died. And something was dying in Hannah, slowly and surely. Note the progression: first, there was an adversary; second, there was inner discomfort as well as interpersonal inflammation (sore); third, it was exacerbated by the provocation, the roaring, the yelling, the intimidation, the inhuman treatment of her rival; fourth, she was vexed. Her very real anger couldn't be expressed outwardly. Her social situation was so precarious that her standing in the home was threatened. An outburst could result in her being homeless. She suppressed, she turned her anger inward. Fifth, she was in depression. Sixth, she stopped feeding herself. Self-care diminished. This was combined with a religious fast, no doubt, but that was a partner to inner and personal desperation. Seventh, she was grieving – what might have been, what should have been, the unfairness of life, the unfairness of barrenness, the plight of her own marriage, the desire for a child of her own, the loss of her sense of worth [she considered herself a daughter of Belial, meaning, worthless]. She was grieving over her own sad life! The word also means to 'tremble.' Perhaps she had just experienced one more encounter with Penninah, her adversary and rival one more shouting match, one more tirade of which she was the victim, and now left alone. She was shaken and shaking, physically reacting in fear to the episode, on the edge of a break. Suddenly, she was at the warning track. The word 'bitterness' occurs in the text, "She was in bitterness of soul." When Paul uses the term bitterness in the New Testament (Eph.

4:31), he uses the term *pitkria,* which can be translated 'venom.' Once you allow the venom, the toxic nectar of the serpent's injection to flow through your being, your end is near. You may join the walking dead, but you also become a force for the poison inside. This was the warning track, and Hannah knew it. So she poured her soul out to God. She prayed. She wept as she prayed. This was more tears than talk. Charles E. Cowman said, "The devil is not put to flight by a courteous request. He meets us at every turn, contends for every inch, and our progress has to be registered in heart's blood and tears." She wrapped her prayer in a vow. If God gave her a child, she determined to give the child back to Him. She knew her answer was not an answer – it was God himself, hearing her! She prayed, and then she persisted in praying. She ran out of words, but her lips continued to move. It was her heart praying. This is the best prayer. While prayer demands words, the best praying is on the other side of words! Eli assumed that she was drunk. Indeed, she was intoxicated – lost in the presence of God. Rebuked by the high priest for a lack of restraint, she was immediately sober, "No, my lord, I am a woman of sorrowful spirit: I have drunk neither wine nor strong drink, but have poured out my soul before the Lord." Eli assured her that God had answered, and she went on her way in peace.

In I Samuel 2, we find one of most profound descriptive declarations of God in all of Scripture. And it comes out of the prayer of Hannah.

1. She claims joy from the Lord (v. 1).
2. He has exalted her.
3. She now smiles at her intimidating enemy! No more trembling.

4. God is a God of salvation, a Deliverer.

5. He is incomparable, solitary, without equal, unique (v. 2).

6. He is Holy.

7. He is immutable, unchanging; He may be relied upon, even as a rock (Ps. 62:2, 6-7).

8. He is omniscient, all knowing, and therefore not ignorant of problems such as Hannah's, or ours - the God of knowledge weighs our actions (v. 3).

9. He is a warrior God, all-powerful, especially against enemies, (vs. 4-5). "The bows of the mighty men are broken ..."

10. He is not detached from life. He is benevolent, bountiful in His supply to the needy (v. 5). "Those who were full have hired themselves out for bread, And the hungry have ceased to hunger."

11. He is the God of Life – "Even the barren has borne seven ..."

12. He is Sovereign, and therefore in total, unflustered control of mankind, and what He orders is according to the good pleasure of His just and perfect will (Eph. 1:11). "The LORD kills and makes alive; He brings down to the grave and brings up. The LORD makes poor and makes rich; He brings low and lifts up."

13. He is sensitive and gracious, that is, He upholds those who acknowledge their impotence and need of His sustaining power (v. 9). "He raises the poor from the dust; And lifts the beggar from the ash heap, to set them among princes

and make them inherit the throne of glory."

14. He is Creator, "For the pillars of the earth are the LORD's, and He has set the world upon them."

15. He is a Protector, "He will guard the feet of His saints, but the wicked shall be silent in darkness. For by strength no man shall prevail."

16. He is Judge, " The adversaries of the LORD shall be broken in pieces; From heaven He will thunder against them. The LORD will judge the ends of the earth."

17. He is King behind kings, "He will give strength to His king, and exalt the horn of His anointed." At a time when Israel had not King, Hannah prophetically declares that Israel will have a king! An anointed king, a reference to the Messiah.

Hannah gave birth to Samuel, and he reset the spiritual and moral compass of the nation. He gathered twelve disconnected tribes and forged them into a nation. He anointed a young shepherd to be their king, and that man, David, became a prototype of the Messiah. He subdued the kingdoms around him. He stretched the boundaries of Israel to include parts of modern nations like Jordan, Lebanon, Syria, Babylon – perhaps more. He gave the equivalent of 21 billion dollars to build the temple. And his Son, Solomon prayed at the dedication of the house his father so wanted to build, and the glory of God fell. Israel was at its zenith! Its peak. In those few short years, it had no enemy, no rival. Arguably, it was the dominant empire of the Middle East, which unlike its predecessors or his successors, did not seek to extend its boundaries and dominate the world.

If there had been no Solomon, there would have been no temple, no glory, no great crowning moment. And if there had been no David, Solomon would not have existed and could not have accomplished what he did. And if there had been no Samuel, David would not have been anointed as king, mentored as he was hunted by Saul's jealous treachery. And if there had been no Hannah, no barren lonely housewife, no passionate intercessor, who God touched with life, there would have been no Samuel.

History turns on the back of the insignificant. "History," Walter Wink has declared, "belongs to the intercessors." David gave us a huge hunk of prayer theology in the psalms. Did he get it from his father, who did not even call him to be present at the visit of Samuel, a father who had written him off? Unlikely! Samuel was his mentor! And from where does Samuel get his theology, his view of God and the world? – from his mother. And I Samuel 2 is a sample of that theology. It came out of the pain of Hannah's daily life, and a profound encounter with God that shaped her new world-view.

CHAPTER 12

THE EXODUS TO SAMUEL

P. Douglas Small

Prayer in the Exodus and the Season of the Conquest

Even into the Exodus and subsequent periods of history, there is still this very simple and direct connection between a human and God (Ex. 3:4; Num. 11:11-15; Judges 6:13f; I Samuel 1:11; II Sam. 15:8; Psa. 66:13f). Eventually, as the covenant broadened from the family to the nation, prayer shifted to become a formal priestly matter, although the abandonment of personal-family prayer was certainly never the will of God. It was the desire of God for all men to know Him, recognize His voice, and introduce others to Him. Israel was invited to the base of Mt. Sinai to meet God. The whole nation was to be a 'kingdom of priests,' in essence the priestly nation among the nations (Exodus 19:6). But Israel declined the offer (Exodus 20:18-21). So, the sons of Levi would serve as a priestly class acting as a mediator, seeking to sustain the relationship between God and Israel by ceremony and sacrifice (Dt. 21:5; 26:3; Leviticus 1-5).

This period opens with the "cries" of Israel (Exodus 3:7) coming before God as pleas for relief. And God responds with the call of Moses as deliverer. Again, we are faced with the dilemma – do prayers move God? Or are our cries, the intensification of prayer, the chief earthly indication that God is Himself on the move? Certainly, He has anticipated the moment. He has prepared Moses for this *kairos* season. And in the relationship between Moses and YHWH, a unique form of prayer emerges, a genuine dialogue between Moses and Yahweh. Only in Abraham have we seen such extensive interchange. It is, however, the opposite of our notion of prayer. We usually ask, and perceive God to be resistant. Here, God makes the request, and Moses is the resistant one. In truth, this is a more accurate portrayal of prayer. God seeks to engage us in His purposes, and we resist. He persists. If we are to be blessed, we surrender!

With Moses, the national spirit of Israel is born. Suddenly, prayer is no longer a vague plea for relief from heavy bricks and blistered backs. It is interpreted by heaven as a corporate cry for liberation. The Hebrews would have been content with some alleviation of their burdens - some concession to their enslavement. But through Moses, God gives birth to a vision for the nation, for their own homeland and constitution – freedom, liberty, national purpose, and sovereign destiny. This is ultimately prayer's purpose. Not to accommodate narrow and self-interested petitions, but to use painful moments as windows to see what can be, what must be, and to transition to greater destiny.

Moses – the Intercessor

Moses has no prior equal in prayer. Only Jesus and David are mentioned more often in biblical literature. The name of Moses appears 740 times. He is the national representative of Israel for God and before God. He was allowed to come near Yahweh, to speak *face-to-face* as man speaks to his friend (Ex. 33:11). Abram had been a friend of God, but Moses was a confidant in a manner that exceeded mere friendship. He climbed the mountain and "reported the words of the people" to God as an ambassador might do in the secret quarters of the king who commissioned him. Such matters are of the highest secrecy. Such meetings demand the highest security clearances and credentials. They speak of the accreditation of Moses (Ex. 19:8). He was God's man, His representative. God trusted him and invested authority in him, allowing Himself to be persuaded by the very compassion He sought to cultivate in the heart of Moses (Ex. 32:12-14, 30-32).

Exodus contains numerous encounters with God and Moses, interventions that demonstrate the superiority of Yahweh over the gods of Egypt. Upon exiting Egypt, God gives Moses the model for the tabernacle, a veritable road-map for prayer and worship. And Israel is invited to Mt. Sinai. The whole nation will become a kingdom of priests. All will know God. Each man will be a personal representative of God. And Israel will be the representative nation of God among the nations.

In the wilderness, the intercessory ministry of Moses

ACCENT

Psalm 90 is one of the great prayers of the Bible. There, Moses intercedes for Israel. There are three movements in the psalm: The 'glory' of God; the 'guilt' of man; the plea for 'grace!'

First, he focuses on God. And he appeals to God, first, as Adonai, the abode of the people of God (v. 1). And then as El[ohim], the eternal ground of the whole creation (v. 2). He is Lord and Creator!

Second, he acknowledges God's power over man; and his persistent call to repentance in men, "You turn man to destruction," and for God, our days are like a millennium to him, "A thousand years in Your sight are like yesterday when it is past; And like a watch in the night." Man's life passes so swiftly, "In the morning they are like grass ... it flourishes and grows ... in the evening it is cut down and withers."

Second, there is the call to repentance. God is aware of our sins, "You have set our iniquities before You, Our secret sins in the light of Your countenance." The result, he knows, is wrath - "For we have been consumed by Your anger, And by Your wrath we are terrified." Sin and its consequences are the reason for our fleeting days, our fragile and shortened life, "all our days have passed away in Your wrath; we finish our years like a sigh ...

[our] boast is only labor and sorrow ... soon cut off, and we fly away."

Finally, there is the plea for compassion and mercy. "Return, O LORD!" Renew the relationship. Only you can fix our earthly and mortal dilemma. "How long?" will it be that the earth, that man suffers under the burden of sin and death. The plea: "Have compassion ... satisfy us early with Your mercy, That we may rejoice and be glad all our days!" The next line is freighted with contradiction. "Make us glad according to the days in which You have afflicted us," in other words, this life is a kind of affliction. We live under wrath. We know this world is full of trouble, but the Psalmist also knows a secret. Even in the worst of times, there is a 'gladness.' Even in the debris field of sin, "the beauty of the Lord our God [can] be upon us!" Even with the principle of death and waste, he can "establish the work of our hands."

The plea is for his presence (v. 13); the satisfaction of his covenant love and grace (v. 14). The gift of joy in the midst of a sad world (v. 15). And a dose of majesty manifest among the fallen race of Adam (v. 16). And for the favor to be fruitful, not barren, the grace to be productive, a measure of blessing and bounty in a world under the curse (v. 17).

will continue. He is praying at every point. In Egypt, he was the representative between Pharaoh, Yahweh and his people. There, he had interceded regarding the elimination of the plagues (Ex. 15:25), and for Israel's release from captivity. He becomes the intercessor in a complex scenario – between Israel and God; between Israel and Pharaoh; and ultimately between God and Pharaoh. At first, the Egyptian Royal was resistant. As the plagues created a near pandemic, Pharaoh pleaded with Moses, "entreat" the Lord for me (Ex. 8:8). His own gods were no longer adequate. His own priests could not approach YHWH. To entreat is to be persuaded, or to be successful in the negotiation. To entreat is to make a request. But it can also mean to plead, even to beg. It also means 'to deal with' as a negotiator. It is the action of mediating the details of a treaty or covenant.

Moses prays for water at Rephidim (Ex. 17:4), and for

triumph over the Amalekites (Ex. 17:8-16). He prays for Israel after the idolatrous episode with the golden calf (Ex 32:11-14, 21-34; 33:12f); and again, after the covenant renewal and the receipt of the tables (Ex 34:9). In the journey, as the ark sets forth and stops, he intercedes (Nu 10:35 f). After the fire at Taberah (Num. 11:2), he prays. And after the rebellion of Aaron and Miriam, he intercedes for the healing of Miriam's leprosy (Num. 12:13). When the spies return, he prays (Num. 14:13-19). At the episode of the fiery serpents, when death is in the camp, he intercedes (Num. 21:7). When the daughters of Zelophehad present a puzzling dilemma to him, asking for an inheritance, as a new cultural and legal norm, he seeks direction of the Lord (Num. 27:5). When it is apparent, his successor must emerge, he prays again (Num. 27:15). There is a recital of his prayer for the people for their entrance into Canaan (Deuteronomy 3:23f). There is also a recital of his prayer for the people after the worship of the golden calf (Deuteronomy 9:18f). Another recital of prayer is for the rebellious people (Deuteronomy 9:25-29). He institutes a prayer command in behalf of the man who pays his third-year tithes (Deuteronomy 26:15). And there is his final blessing of the tribes (Deuteronomy 33).

The character of these prayers is often passionate. They are not perfunctory. They rise from the heart of a man full of life. They are fraught with reality, with authentic emotions, with life-and-death urgency. They have a depth and warmth, a critical and significant edge to them. And yet, in this same period, prescribed prayer is also introduced. It is found in the Mosaic code (Numbers 10:35-36; Psalm 68:1). These prayers constitute corporate language to be used by the people in the setting forth of the Ark of the Covenant. In Deuteronomy 21:7-8, there is a prayer recorded for community atonement. And in Deuteronomy 28:5-10, Israel is given prayer language to be used when they offer their first fruits to the Lord in the third-year tithe offering.

The Priest and the Men – A Class of Intercessors

After the gift of the tabernacle and the creation of a special 'class' of priests in Aaron and his sons, worship takes on a formal and corporate form not known previously. Priests and rituals are prescribed (Exodus 28). The covenant of God with Israel is encoded in a detailed manner by Moses. In this season, God ties His name to a people and binds His glory to Israel as the nation before the nations. The annual feasts not only decorate their calendar, but they also encrypt their destiny.

It had been the desire of God for all men to be priests. *"You shall be a special treasure to Me above all people; for all the earth is Mine. And you shall be to Me a kingdom of priests and a holy nation"* (19:5-6). He had brought them out of Egypt, and Exodus 19-20 was to be the moment when He forged a covenant with the whole nation, every man a priestly representative. But Israel refused. They backed down the mountain (20:19-21). They did not want to fellowship with the fire. And in that moment, God chose Aaron and allowed a layer of priestly men to serve as intercessors between Him and Israel. It was His second choice.

Prayer was still to be a national function, and Israel was to be a nation of pray-ers, specifically the men. Moses instructed,

> *Speak to the people of Israel, and tell them to make tassels on the corners of their garments throughout their generations, and to put a cord of blue on the tassel of each corner. And it shall be a tassel for you to look at and remember all the commandments of the LORD, to do them, not to follow after your own heart and your own eyes, which you are inclined to whore after. So you shall remember and do all my commandments, and be holy to your God. I am the LORD your God, who brought you out of the land of Egypt to be your God: I am the LORD your God. (Numbers 15:37-41).*

This is a reference to the *tallit*, more commonly known as 'a prayer shawl,' a four-cornered garment used as covering for Jewish males. It is viewed by the Jews as a symbol of the scriptures themselves, and as a kind of mini-tabernacle, as a mobile prayer closet. The idea is powerful – prayer meant wrapping oneself in scripture, and talking with God. To enter the 'prayer closet' was to enter into the Holy Scripture – and pray from its covenant.

A *tallit* was precious, so it passed from generation to generation, from father to son. A Jewish man was often presented one at his wedding, a reminder of the connection between his role as husband and father, and that of prayer. And it became a symbol of the transfer of authority and anointing. It is often associated with the Old Testament term, 'mantle.' The colors were a reflection of those in the tabernacle – blue, purple and scarlet woven or dyed into linen cloth. The dominate colors of the high priestly *tallit* were crimson, purple and royal blue. For the Levites, the colors were red (blood red, crimson), with black and white stripes. Those colors were also reflected in the banners of the tribes.

The wearing of the *tallit* was a visible symbol of the commandments, of the constraint of obedience, of the call to be a special people. It was to be an objective reminder, a guide, and a tether to their identity. Neither their heart nor their eyes were reliable. But the commandments, the law, the clear 'do's and don'ts' were objective and measurable. It was precisely the blue thread in the corner tassel that represented their covenant relationship with God through the mediated law at Sinai. They were to be a people apart. The Lord was their God – none other. He was their liberator. He had redeemed them. He had settled them into the good and promised-land. He had given them victory. The *tallit* was a reminder of all that He had done, of what was promised as well. They had destiny on their lives.

The *tallit* also told the family connection. Different families developed distinctive ways of tying the knots which became a kind of signature. The 'status' of the family could also be known by the style of the *tallit*, the number of expensive blue threads, the enlarged and elaborate markings and tassels. Sadly, the simple symbol became a corrupt icon, a tribute to pride. The Pharisees delighted themselves in wearing a long flowing *tallit* (Luke 20:45-47). Since the blue dye for the tassel threads was so rare, the number

> *Don't let a prayer group become an excuse for not taking sacrificial action. Pray – and give. Pray – and go. Pray – and do – what God has given you the ability to do.*
>
> *- Lucille Walker*

of blue threads became an indicator of wealth. Sadly, with the acquisition of more 'blue' one could buy a higher spiritual status.

When David said that he desired to "dwell" in the Lord's tent forever, it might have been his own *tallit* about which he spoke (Psa. 61:4). There, in the Lord's tent, under the *tallit*, is "the shelter of your wings." Indeed, the spreading out of the *tallit* appears to give men wings. Remember, it was not the structure, not the boards and silver foundation pieces that comprised the tabernacle. Rather, it was the simple ten-curtain covering visible only from the holy and most holy place, made of blue, purple and scarlet colors, with the faces of cherubim woven into the fabric – that was the tabernacle.[1] When David cut off the corner of Saul's garment, proving that he was close enough to kill, and held it up for him to see, it was probably a corner tassel from Saul's *tallit*, essentially defiling the garment and sending Saul home. The spiritual covering for Saul had been violated- it was a bad omen, how could he continue to fight?

The Greek word for closet is *tameion*, meaning 'inner chamber'

---

1   P. Douglas Small, *Principles of Worship and the Tabernacle of Moses* (Kannapolis, NC: Alive Publications, 1990, 2012).

or secret room. Away from home, anywhere, the *tallit* allowed a man to create a closet (Mat. 6:6). He wrapped himself in the colors of redemption – blue: reminding him of the God of heaven; purple: the King of Israel, and for us, Christ Jesus, our King; crimson – the color of blood, the sacrifice, the blood of the lamb; and linen: the symbol of purity, righteousness. These are the colors that tell the story of God's love for man, and the basis of a new relationship with Him. Wrapped in a *tallit*, man was insulating himself from this world, having been redeemed by God; and consecrating himself to another.

In this sense, the *tallit* is the ultimate symbol of prayer for the Jewish man. And prayer rises out of the covenant. It is possible only on the back of the *covenant*. We too are a people of destiny. We too are to live by the constraint of Word and Spirit. We are to be led by the Spirit, indeed, directed and even driven by the Spirit. Prayer, as the commandments, the objective reality to which the *tallit* pointed, should also tether our lives. Purify us. Remind us that we are a representative people. We have upon us destiny. We have been redeemed, liberated, and given new living places – the abundant life. And the best is yet to come. Such is the 'tent' in which we are to pray, and live (Psalm 36:7).

Jesus probably wore a *tallit*. In Matthew 14, Jesus passed through the land of Gennesaret. The news spread quickly, and they "implored Him that they might only touch the fringe of His garment. And as many as touched it were made well" (Matthew 14:35-36). It is not unreasonable to assume that there may have developed a belief that virtue flowed from Jesus through the sacred *tallit*. The woman with the issue of blood only desired to touch the 'hem of His garment,' probably a corner tassel of His *tallit* (Mat. 9:20), believing she would be healed. There is no power, however, either in a *tallit* or a handkerchief (Acts 19:12 – 'prayer cloth'). The power is in God. Many believe the seamless garment for which the soldiers gambled at the cross was the *tallit* of Jesus.

ACCENT

"God has of his own motion placed himself under the law of prayer, and has obligated himself to answer the prayers of men. He has ordained prayer as a means whereby he will do things through men as they pray, which he would not otherwise do. If prayer puts God to work on earth, then, by the same token, prayerlessness rules God out of the world's affairs, and prevents him from working. The driving power, the conquering force in God's cause is God himself. 'Call on me and I will answer thee and who thee great and mighty things which though knowest not,' is God's challenge to prayer. Prayer puts God in full force into God's work."

E.M. Bounds, *The Weapon of Prayer*, Ch. 2

The Corporate Aspect of Prayer

In previous seasons, the integrity of the human-divine relationship was largely personal. Leaving Egypt, the Passover had been celebrated home-by-home, but when Israel left Egypt, they did so as a nation. While the personal-family dimension continues, in the concept of the tribes there emerges a decidedly corporate aspect. This is especially true on festival days, but specifically in the Day of Atonement on which the High Priest prays a representative prayer for all the people and makes a representative appearance in their behalf before God in the Most Holy Place with blood (Lev. 23). Now, sin is clearly perceived not only as an individual matter, but as a corporate matter. People repent (the sin and trespass offerings: Leviticus 4, 5) – and so must families and nations. The preparation for meeting God became more of a solemn matter. The Psalms of Ascent (120-134) are designed for use by the people in coming to the house of the Lord.

In time, the prophet would also act in an intercessory role, seeking to correct, to point out the necessary conditions for reconciliation to be achieved effectively and for lost blessings to be restored (Ex.

32:11-13; I Sam. 7:5-13; 12:23). God never desired, despite the gulf created by sin, such an estrangement from humans, or for that matter, from the people He chose to use as an intercessory-priestly nation. Israel was redeemed and liberated from Egypt 'to know Him!' He wanted them to be a 'kingdom of priests' serving as a representative nation to the nations. Their rejection of His offer became the root of their apostasy.

Leviticus offers a blueprint for approaching God in sacrificial worship. In it are the feast-days that will decorate Israel's calendar. Here, worship is outlined. The pattern for both personal and corporate worship, the essence of prayer, is prescribed.

Deuteronomy is a prescription for behavior. More precisely, behavior is to be altered after the encounter and covenantal connection of Israel with the holy Yahweh. This is the outgrowth of prayer. Meeting with God *should* change us. Walking in a representative covenant relationship with Him *demands* change.

From the Conquest to the Judges

From **Joshua**, we only have his prayer for the people after the sin of Achan (Josh 7:6-9). On the other hand, while the record of Joshua's prayer is scant, the record of God's words to Joshua is frequent. The connection between the personal and corporate are painfully demonstrated in the sin of Achan (Joshua 7:6-9). Personal sin results in a deadly defeat for the entire nation in the early stages of their conquest, following the Exodus and the subsequent entrance into Canaan. In a parallel manner, the private sin of Ananias and Sapphira is revealed early in the history of the New Testament Church (Acts 5:1-5). The placement of these austere examples of judgment early in the corporate history of Israel and the Church seem to carry a message – that private sin is not private. The personal and the corporate are bound together.

Judges records the period from Joshua to the era of Samuel. It profiles seven cycles of apostasy and moral decline, followed by subjugation, then supplication, and then another season of liberty. In bondage, Israel 'cries out' to God, who then raises up a deliverer and restores national moral and spiritual vitality (Judges 3:9 15; 4:3; 6:6-7). Sadly, again, they apostatize. The key words in the book are - evil and judgment. They are inseparably bound. It is the bloodiest book in the Bible, decorated with ethnic and civil war. At the root of the conflict is the absence of corporately shared values. Instead, *"... every man did that which was right in his own eyes"* (21:25). God had promised Israel that obedience would bring blessings, but disobedience would result in God's discipline. A note of grace also promised that if the people returned to the Lord, if they cried out to Him and repented, He would deliver them. There is a hint of intercession in Deborah's song (Judges 5:31), though it is stern and warlike. Gideon's life is alive with prayer, echoing the same reluctance to deliver seen at first in Moses (Judges 6:13). He emerges from the uncertainty to revive the national and religious life of his people (see Judges 6:24). Still, he is no Moses (Judges 8:27), and after his death, there is again abundant apostasy, even in his own family (Judges 8:33f). Manoah's prayers are also found in Judges (13).

The book of Judges climaxes with a story of self-styled faith. Micah, deeply religious and hungry for the spiritual, secures a priest for his own house. The idea sounds noble. But it is a microcosm of the day (21:25) in which each person chooses their own values and fashions their own worship. The book climaxes with two tragic stories. The first, in chapters 17-18, is the story of Micah's development of a paganized place of worship. The end result is the corruption of the entire tribe of Dan who abandon their allotted territory while adopting Micah's corrupted religion. The second story, in chapters 19–21, is the sad experience of sexual assault (19:22-30) resulting the disciplinary removal of the tribe of Benjamin. Here is idolatry and sexual sin, juxtaposed against one another. The climax of the evil seems to shock the nation, "Nothing like this has ever happened or been seen from the day when the sons of Israel came up from the land of Egypt to this day. Consider it, take counsel and speak up!" (19:30).

These low spiritual-moral episodes provide an occasion for prayer in the face of imminent civil war (Judges 20:27f), and the people's mourning and prayer following the defeat of the tribe of Benjamin (Judges 21:2f). Despite the sieges of crisis praying, what sadly characterizes the book is the

ACCENT

Margy and Roy Stricklin were involved for years in Ministry to Military. Margy relates the story of Su Pasek, who learned of the ministry's needs. Su lived blocks away from three military installations. She never saw herself as a solution to the need, but she agreed to pray – asking God to give someone a burden to come to her church and fulfill this need. As she prayed about the need, one day she found herself singing the song, "Send a revival ... let it begin in me!" She had never even been on the nearby base. Suddenly, newspaper and magazine notices about the base and various issues began to catch her attention. She 'accidentally' met the base chaplain's wife, and learned that they planned to retire and a ladies group led by

absence of healthy and consistent prayer throughout, and it is this lack of genuine communion with God that is devastating to the nation. Two tribes are essentially gone. The national security and spiritual identity of the nation is consistently threatened by self-styled faith. Ties of blood are placed above loyalty to the Lord. In the end, the resultant gross morality and idolatry cannot be defended. And 'crisis prayer' is not enough to feed the soul of the nation.

the chaplain's wife did not have a leader – ladies who lived around Su. Suddenly, the burden that she had been carrying for someone else became her burden. She and another lady started a women's Bible study focused on military wives. Su became the leader of the new effort. They met – and studied together, and prayed. One lady, from a financially stressed family about to lose their home saw the miracle of a job provision; another the healing of an infant; another the healing of a marriage; another lady with a ten-year back problem was healed. Su prayed – and God provided. He provided her! And he provided for others through her.

Lucille Walker, *What To Do When You Pray* (Cleveland, TN: Pathway Press, 1998), 15-16.

Both the tribes of Benjamin and Dan appear earlier in Judges. From the tribe of Benjamin, the Lord had raised up the deliverer Ehud (3:15). From the tribe of Dan, who abandoned their assigned inheritance and adopted pagan prayer practices, the Lord had raised up Samson (13:2, 5). Not all in these tribes were corrupt. But the slight godly influence is inadequate to save the corrupt tribes. The two stories provide a transition from the fractured and individualistic faith-quests that characterize the book, and they point to the need for a national and unifying faith tradition, for standards that prevent the syncretism of idolatry and true faith or at least mitigate against it. In this sense, the story of Micah belongs to the bridge that connects the bloody and unstable season of the Judges to the rise of a national identity, a unifying faith and moral code under Samuel.

The whole design of the book portrays an age without consistent righteous leadership and as a result self-styled faith. Unfaithfulness is normal. The allurements of idolatry and paganism pollute Israel. Only by the grace of God was Israel not overwhelmed and completely absorbed by the pagan nations around them. Sadly, God's purposes for the nation come to halt. They are only marking time.

From Anarchy to Order – Samuel the Man of Prayer

In the early chapters of **Samuel**, a further description is offered of the age. The priests are corrupt and greedy (I Samuel 2:12-14). They treat the people as objects for personal gain. They exploit the faith of the people for a prize, ignoring the rules of the altar (2:15 - 17). They hated worship. They "despised the offering of the LORD" (2:17), seeing the gifts men gave to God as an act of prayer and worship as despicable. They wanted the 'offering' for themselves. They exploited the women at the tabernacle (2:22). The lampstand was not cared for, so the light in the holy place went out (3:3). This was a dark spiritual time.

In this generation, Samuel emerges as a kind of national intercessor for Israel in the transition from the era of the judges to the monarchy (I Samuel 8; 12:10-11, 19, 22-23). In Samuel, we transition from the free-lance seer or soothsayer to a new prophetic order. Samuel gives prophets a new standing, an elevated status in Israel, one unknown before. The literary prophets will follow him. The prophetic will be more securely linked to God's revelation, the law. The casting of lots will give way to direct revelation from God, "Thus saith the Lord!" In Samuel, we also have the disappearance of the priestly line of Eli, whose sons were not worthy of the holy office to which they had been called (I Samuel 3:14). In this period, prayer and worship are tethered to holiness. Integrity among leaders becomes an important feature. The nation is being given exemplary leaders. Not only does God reject a line of priest, but He also cuts off Saul's kingly line from the throne. A new standard is now imposed on both priests and kings.

Here, we have one of the most powerful examples of prayer in Scripture in Hannah's plea (I Samuel 1:10-18; 2:1-10). Hannah's song is one of the most profound prayerful declarations in all of Scripture. The downcast and barren woman has triumphed in prayer. She rejoices in the triumph of the Lord (2:1), in His incomparable and holy nature (2:2). He is omniscient (2:3), a warrior God (2:4), sovereign and sensitive (2:6-8). He is the Creator (2:8b) and also the protector of the saints (2:9). Only in His strength do we prevail. He is the ultimate Judge (2:10). What a prayer! The insights here appear not only to be an expression *in* prayer, but they have come *by* prayer. Gratitude is laced with a prophetic intercessory spirit (I Sam 2:1-11). In the midst of her passionate prayer, barrenness is broken, and Samuel is born. He emerges as the real successor of Moses in terms of prayer.

From their lives and literature, comes our Old Testament. Abraham, Moses, Samuel and David stand like mountain peaks in an Old Testament parade of prayer giants. They remind us, that ultimately prayer is about God and His gracious desire to interact with man! And prayer is about a man, and men, who desire to know God, and whose relationship with Him become prototypes for us. It is about men, who obediently and faithfully respond to God's call - and set off chain reactions of God's glory that echo through time. In Samuel, intercession is again distinctive and effectual. Jeremiah classifies Samuel with Moses in intercessory mediation (Jer. 15:1; I Sam. 7:5-12; Ex. 32:30-32).

There is his prayer at Mizpeh (I Sam 7:5). And the recognition by the people, that they acknowledge and understand Samuel's national role (I Sam 7:8 f; see also 8:6,21; 10:17-25; 12:19). At this point in history, the role of prophets, true and false, have earned a unique cultural niche. And men, wanting some kind of divine word, have adopted the custom of inquiring of the Lord through a seer, the ancient word for prophet (I Sam 9:6-10). Samuel is acknowledged to be the ultimate 'seer' in Israel in his generation. His perception of God, his moral and spiritual clarity become legendary. Samuel prays for Saul, the king of Israel (I Sam 15:11). He is the intercessor, between God and the King. Samuel prays for him, even when he fails to inquire of the Lord through intercession (I Samuel 28:6). In Saul's final appeal for guidance through the witch of Endor (I Sam 28:7-20), it is Samuel who appears, shocking the witch. Such things are too mysterious for us to understand.

Prayer References

Exodus

1. Moses for Aaron to go with him (16 words; Ex 4:13). Answered because God wanted to please Moses (Ex 4:14-17).

2. Moses in complaint to God for not delivering Israel (42 words; Ex 5:22-23). Answered because of God's word (Ex 3:8,12, 17-22).

3. Moses for forgiveness for Israel (39 words; Ex 32:31-32). Answered because of atonement and intercession (Ex 32:11-14,30-35) and because of God's word (Ex 33:1-6,12-14).

4. Moses for God's presence to go with Israel to Canaan (138 words; Ex 33:12-13,15-16). Answered because of God's word (Ex 33:12-14) and His grace (Ex 33:17).

References to groaning, sighing, crying, and entreating the Lord (Ex 2:11,23-25; 3:7,9; 10:16).

Numbers

1. Aaron for the blessing of God upon the people (32 words in the form of benediction; Num 6:24-26). Answered because of God's promise (Num 6:27).

2. Moses for God to bless on the journey (27 words; Num

10:35-36). Answered when Israel lived free from sin, but unanswered when they sinned, which was according to God's word (Ex 32:32-33).

3. Moses in complaining to God because the burden was too heavy (136 words; Num 11:10-15). Answered because of God's words (Num 11:16-20,25-30).

4. Moses for God to show him what to do to give the people flesh (56 words; Num 11:21-22). Answered because of God's word (Num 11:21) and to show His power (Num 11:23).

5. Moses for the healing of Miriam (8 words; Num 12:13). Answered because of God's love for Moses (Num 12:14-16).

6. Moses for God to spare Israel and uphold His own honor (208 words; Num 14:13-19). Answered because of Moses' prayer (Num 14:20).

7. Moses for judgment on sin (20 words; Num 16:15). Answered because of sin (Num 16:23-34).

8. Israel for forgiveness of sin (25 words; Num 21:7). Answered because of Moses' prayer and by type of Christ on the cross (Num 21:7-9; 3:14-16).

9. Moses for a new leader of Israel (56 words; Num 27:16-17). Answered because of God's plan for Israel (Num 27:18-23).

References to prayer (Num 11:2; 21:7).

Deuteronomy

1. Moses asking to go over into Canaan (59 words; Deut 3:24-25). Unanswered because of sin (Deut 3:26; Num 20:12).

2. Moses for Israel to be spared (114 words; Deut 9:26-29). Answered because of intercession of Moses (Ex 32:11-14).

References to prayer (Deut 9:20,26), also what to pray for elders at murder trials (Deut 21:6-9) and what all Israel should pray after obedience to the law (Deut 26:5-15).

Joshua

1. Joshua in complaint because God had not given victory (90 words; Josh 7:7-9). Answered so sin could be put away (Josh 7:10-15).

2. Joshua in the form of a command for the sun and moon to stand still (14 words; Josh 10:12). Answered because of necessity for time to finish God's work (Josh 10:13).

Judges

1. Israel for guidance (14 words; Judg 1:1). Answered because it was in harmony with the will of God for the nation (Judg 1:2).

2. Gideon for revelation and guidance (135 words; Judg 6:13,15,17-18,22). Answered because of God's word and will for Israel (Judg 6:12,14,16,20-21,23).

3. Israel for deliverance and forgiveness of sins (36 words; Judg 10:10,15). Answered because of God's plan for Israel (Judg 11:1-33).

4. Jephthah for victory (55 words; Judg 11:30-31). Answered because of God's plan for Israel (Judg 11:32).

5. Manoah for an angel to appear and give him directions (91 words; Judg 13:8,11-12,15,17). Answered because of God's plan for Israel (Judg 13:9,11,13,16,18).

6. Samson for one last victory (33 words; Judg 16:28). Answered because of his reconsecration to the Nazarite vows (Judg 13:4-5; 16:22).

7. Israel for guidance (14 words; Judg 20:23). Answered because of judgment on sin.

8. Israel for guidance (19 words; Judg 20:28). Answered because of judgment on sin.

9. Israel for revelation (24 words; Judg 21:3). No answer recorded.

I Samuel

1. Hannah for a son (55 words; I Sam 1:11). Answered because of God's plan for Israel (I Sam 1:20-23) and promises to bless with children upon obedience (Lev 26:3-13; Deut 28:1-14).

2. Hannah to express gratitude for answered prayer (264 words; I Sam 2:1-10). No request to answer.

3. Saul for guidance (16 words; I Sam 14:37). Unanswered because of sin (I Sam 13:1-14; 14:37).

4. David for guidance (7 words; I Sam 23:2). Answered because of God's plan (I Sam 23:2).

5. David for revelation (72 words; I Sam 23:10-12). Answered because of God's plan.

6. David for revelation (10 words; I Sam 30:8). Answered because of God's plan.

References to prayer (I Sam 7:9; 8:6; 12:18; 15:11; 28:6).

Finis Jennings Dake, *Dake's Annotated Reference Bible* (Lawrenceville, GA: Dake Bible Sales, 1963, 1991).

CHAPTER THIRTEEN

KING DAVID TO THE POST-EXILIC RESTORATION

A WINDOW THROUGH TIME

By 1884, a growing spiritual restlessness characterized the region on Western North Carolina and Eastern Tennessee, near the Georgia border.

R. G. Spurling and Richard Spurling, along with John Plemmons entered a prayer covenant. They prayed and studied for two years. They "expounded to the church the need for a genuine awakening and reformation. Guided by the Word of God and example of the post-apostolic church, these men delineated the course that should be followed. With 'praying and weeping and pleading' an analogy was drawn between the pre-Reformation church and the present complacency and departure from the faith. But their pleas fell on deaf ears and dumb hearts; revival did not come."[1]

On August 19, 1886, they formed the Christian Union, devoted to prayer – until God sent revival. Among other stated goals was the ultimate objective – "to restore primitive Christianity and bring about the union of all denominations."[2]

Ten years later, a group of Baptists fourteen miles away were also stirred. In Cherokee County, North Carolina, they sponsored a revival meeting that set the country-side on edge. They arranged to use the Shearer Schoolhouse and three evangelists – not necessarily great preachers, but "good talkers" came to the area. "The meetings were begun with singing, without musical accompaniment, unless some person handy with a guitar happened to bring his instrument along." The hymns of the day were sung. Testimonies were given. "When the time of prayer came, no one person prayed for the group while others were silent, but the entire congregation prayed aloud in unison..." Dr. Charles Conn quotes Philip Schaff, "They prayed freely from the heart, as they were moved by the Spirit, according to special needs and circumstances."[3] Then came the preaching.

Conn notes that almost from the beginning the Schoolhouse was too small. Crowds came from as far away as thirty-miles – a far distance in that day, given the conditions of the roads and the terrain. "The people were hungry for the pure and simple Christianity propounded by these untutored men who knew no complex theology and whose logic began and ended with 'Thus saith the Lord.' As more and more people filled the altars, praying until their burdens and doubts were relieved, the expectation of each service became steadily higher."[4]

Conn quotes Howard Juillerat, an earlier history:

> The people earnestly sought God, and the interest increased until unexpectedly, like a cloud from a clear sky, the Holy Ghost began to fall on the honest, humble, sincere seekers after God. While the meetings were in progress, one after another fell under the power of God, and soon quite a number were speaking in tongues as the Spirit gave them utterance.[5]

1 Charles W. Conn, *Like a Mighty Army* (Cleveland, TN: Pathway Press, 1977), 5.
2 Ibid, 11.
3 Ibid, 19. Confer with Philip Schaff, *History of the Christian Church* (New York: Charles Scribner's Sons, 1910), Vol. 1, 462.
4 Ibid, 20.
5 Conn, 25; Quoting Juillerat, *Church of God Minutes* (Cleveland, TN: Church of God Publishing House, 1922), 7-8.

CHAPTER 13

KING DAVID TO THE POST-EXILIC RESTORATION
P. Douglas Small

The Monarchy – David, a Man after God's Heart

D avid, as we noted, inherited Samuel's prayer mantle (II Samuel 7:18). And with it comes Hannah's theology. She is arguably the spiritual grandmother of David, as Samuel is his spiritual father. We have an early glimpse of David and Saul, worshipping together (I Samuel 16:23). What a powerful picture.

During the time of David, the place of corporate prayer and worship find a new zenith. Under David, there is a breath-taking alteration to the worship code and style given by Moses. Radical changes are implemented with access by both Levites and priests before the ark. The revisions to the prayer and worship codes given by Moses are huge. But David is reminded, as he attempts to move the ark 'the wrong way' that he can't do just anything. The death of Uzziah is a solemn warning by God, that He still makes the rules, that revisions have limits, that access to His presence is not without reverence. And that protocol must be reserved. In this season, the majority of the psalms are collected and written. There is the arrangement of two tabernacles – the tabernacle of Moses and the tabernacle of David. David expanded the priestly craft, providing for priests at both tabernacles. The priests were charged to carry out specialized duties, worship and prayer, serving the people and ministering to the Lord (I Chron. 16:4; 25:1-3; II Chron. 7:6-7; 29:28-30). One tabernacle related to Moses, is rooted in rituals and washings, sacrifices and ceremony, Old Testament prayer and worship. The other, David's tabernacle, looks forward to a new era, a new covenant, free access to God's presence and by implication, New Testament worship. With the creation of the tabernacle of David, the ark is brought to Jerusalem and not returned to the tabernacle of Moses. Perpetual prayer, praise and worship are instituted in Jerusalem. Under David, for a short season, corporate prayer and worship undergo a major shift. Priests may now enter before the ark – for prayer and praise. More than seventy of the 150 psalms are conservatively attributed to David.

Kyu Nam Jung categorizes the prayer content in the psalms into five categories:

1. Psalms of Petition. In this category he also places the 'lament' psalms, as is found in Psalm 13, "How long O Lord?"

2. Psalms of Penitence. Here he lists seven psalms – 6, 32, 38, 52, 102, 130, 143. While all are psalms of repentance, only 32, 38 and 51 actually involve confession of sin.

3. Psalms of Intercession. Among these he includes the 'Royal' psalms, usually constructed to provide language for prayer in behalf of the king. Psalm 72 is an example, as is Psalm 10, 20 and 21.

4. Psalms of Thanksgiving. These are 'confident' prayers. He cites as examples Psalms 9 and 40.

5. Hymnic Prayer. These are prayers of praise set to music. These richly demonstrated in Psalms 8, 33, and 65. Components are found in 41:13; 66:1-7; 72:18-19; 89:52; 106:48 and 150.[1]

Of course, some psalms are not so easily categorized. Psalm 40 is classified as a psalm of thanksgiving, but it also contains a lament

---

1 Kyu Nam Jung, "Prayer in the Psalms," D. A. Carson, Editor, *Teach Us To Pray* (Grand Rapids: MI; Baker, 1990), 36-47.

(v. 12), and a petition (v. 13-17).[2] Psalm 27 is similarly diverse, the second part being that of petition. Laments were also hymnic. And there is a noticable genre of judgment or imprecatory psalms.

The most common word for prayer in the psalms is *tepillah*. It occurs some thirty-two times.

The temple built by Solomon was dedicated as a 'house of prayer' (I Kings 8; Isa. 56:7). With it, both tabernacles were folded and the ark was placed in the temple. Under Hezekiah, the priests along with the Levites were further organized for worship (II Chron. 31:2; 23:30; II Chron. 2:4-6; Ps. 5; 55:17). But it is David, above all others, who emerges as a man after God's heart. He is the most prolific recorder of written prayers – the Psalms. No one but Jesus is mentioned more in the Bible.

David prayed for his house (I Chronicles 17:16-27). But his greatest failure was as a father - not as a warrior (I Samuel 17:32,

2   Ibid, 44.

45); Not as the adopted son of Saul (I Samuel 24:9-11); Not as a King (II Samuel 8:15; 19:9-110. David failed as a father. Amnon may have taken a cue from his own father in the violation of his sister – whatever his motive, David, perhaps still dealing with the personal guilt over Bathsheba, failed to act in reinforcing moral boundaries in his own home. He was busy with the kingdom (I Samuel 13). The action of Amnon created a bitter rivalry between him and Absalom, and David failed to either see it or address it (13:24, 25). Somewhere in his late teens or early twenties, Absalom disconnected from his father emotionally – and the result of the division in the family, was subsequently a rebellion in the nation.

David prayed for deliverance from a national plague, one brought on by his own disobedience (I Chronicles 21:17). He stood at the threshing floor of Onan and there, where the temple would eventually stand, built an altar and saved the city of Jerusalem from judgment. David, though absent at the dedication of the temple, was nevertheless present, by prayer. He prayed, before his death, for the people and for Solomon at the offering of gifts for the temple (I Chronicles 29:10-19).

Solomon's high prayer moment was at the consecration of the temple his father had longed to build (II Chronicles 6:1-42; I Ki 8:12-61). This is a spiritual zenith in Israel's history. The manifest glory of God comes. King Asa also offered prayer (II Chronicles 14:11). As did Jehoshaphat (II Chronicles 20:5-13). Solomon's personal request in prayer was for wisdom to govern the people (I Kings 3:5-15).

The Divided Kingdom

With the death of Solomon, the nation was divided. Jeroboam, who had been a leader under Solomon's leadership, and had been exiled, returned to attend the coronation of Rehoboam – and split the kingdom. To disassociate the northern tribes from the temple, and by association, Judah, he changed the nature of prayer and worship – in both form and place. Following the division, the ten northern tribes would quickly become apostate, polluting worship with pagan and idolatrous notions and emblems in their attempt to sever both their obligation and loyalty to Jerusalem's temple and festivals. The motive of Jeroboam, the King, was to cut ties to Jerusalem's temple, to taxes and tithe (I Kings 12:4). Israel disassociated itself with the throne of David (12:16). They altered 'prayer' and worship, mixing pagan elements designed to redirect the nation (12:25-32) away from the temple, the festivals and the history they represented, and from an exclusive tie to YHWH. The experiment worked. Israel disconnected, first to apostasy and then to exile.

Jeroboam would taste judgment from God early in the process. In the inauguration of the new, national altar, acting as both king and high priest, God would paralyze his hand as a result of a verbal altercation with a holy man of God. Frightened by the withered limb, he immediately appealed not to his false priests and prophets for prayer for the healing of his hand, but to the holy man (I Kings 13:6). It was graciously restored, but sadly, the experience did not result in his true conversion or that of Israel returning to the Lord. A series of evil leaders followed Jeroboam, furthering apostasy, and climaxing in the reign of Ahab and Jezebel, who made paganism the official state religion. Their most formidable apparent obstacle to their perversion of prayer and worship was the prophet Elijah.

In Elijah, the nation again, mercifully, had a man of prayer. He prayed for the widow's son (I Ki 17:20), and for rain (I Ki 18:42). The confrontation of Elijah and the prophets of Baal (I Kings 18:36-37) on Mt. Carmel is one of the Bible's most memorable stories. Still, it is a brief, but futile, moment of revival in Israel, that only endured

ACCENT

King Hezekiah was a godly king (II Kings 18:4-6; 31:20-21) and in time of national crisis, he turned to God in prayer (II Kings 19; II Chronicles 37; Isaiah 37; possibility Psalm 46). His name means "God is my strength" (cf. II Kings 18:4-6). He reigned for 29 years over Judah, 715-690 BC, following the wicked Ahaz whose idolatry desecrated the land. Ahaz closed the Temple, introduced child sacrifices, and became allied with Assyria (II Chron. 28:19, 23-25; Isa. 29:13). Sadly, Hezekiah's son, Manasseh, followed the example of his grandfather becoming the most, wicked king Judah would know! But under Hezekiah, there is a brief revival (II Chron. 29:3- 31:21). In it, the Temple was cleansed and true worship reinstated (29:3-31:21). The Passover was practiced again (30:21-22). The brazen serpent (Num. 21:4-9), by then an idol, was destroyed (II Kings 18:4). The great engineering feat, a 1,777' tunnel excavated through solid rock, captured water from the Gihon spring (32:4).

When Sennacherib, the king of Assyria, assaulted Israel, he also routed Judah's 46 walled cities and deported 200,000 captives. He rendered Egypt defenseless, and extracted tribute from Jerusalem (II Kings 18:14-16), causing Hezekiah to strip the Temple of gold. He would have captured Jerusalem and destroyed Judah with Israel, but Hezekiah prayed (II Kings 18:17-19:13).

With the Assyrian army on his doorstep offering an ultimatum (18:17-37), Hezekiah appointed his palace governor as negotiator (18:18) and he went to prayer. The Assyrian General wanted surrender. Egypt, Judah's military ally was a "crushed reed" (18:21). The General scorned Hezekiah's army (18:23) and treated Hezekiah's diplomacy with contempt. He spoke in Hebrew and stuck fear into the general population (18:26, 28), belittling the King and Yahweh (18:29, 31). Irreligious and disrespectful, he insulted the gods of the nations (18:33-35), placing YHWH in the same category.

Hezekiah consulted with Isaiah (19:1-7; cf. Isa. 37:33-35). Divine assurances came. Assyria would be turned back (II Kings 19:1-7). They would not prevail (Isa. 37:33). And this victory was for God's sake and honor in reference to the promise made to David (Isa. 37:35). As Isaiah had prophesied, Assyrian forces did withdraw (II Kings 19:8-13). As Hezekiah waited for Isaiah's response, he went to prayer. The extraordinary prayer appeals to the character of God, vs. 14-15. He spreads his problem before the Lord (Phil. 4:6-7). He makes his appeal in the freshly cleansed temple - the house of God. His faith and plea are child-like. He asserts that his problem is really God's problem. He surveys the attributes of God, v. 15, an important thing to do when faced by something overwhelming. Remember to 'Behold your God!' He is a God of covenant; the holy God who tabernacles between the cherubim (cf. Exod. 25:18-22). He is not a territorial or national god. Jehovah is God of all the nations, including Assyria. And his sovereignty extends to all heaven and the earth. Hezekiah appeals to God act, vs. 16-18. His scope of God is inspiring: God is both immanent and transcendent; both holy and merciful. And yet the language of the prayer is anthropomorphic, 'God, bend your ear from your great and holy height ... attentively listen to my urgent plea. Focus your omniscience and omnipotence on the challenge of this crude barbarian,' v. 16a. God's honor has been assaulted. The pagan ruler has not merely challenged Judah; he has challenged YHWH, v. 16b. If other nations and their gods have fallen, YHWH has permitted it, cf. v. 15; vs. 17-18. Thus, it is not Assyria that is powerful, but God. However, Judah cannot likewise fall. They, unlike Israel, have repented. Hezekiah requests vindication through deliverance, v. 19; national and personal salvation, and he acknowledges, only Jehovah can save, v. 19a.

Suddenly, Hezekiah seems to assert, the whole world has its eyes on Judah and Jerusalem, and the outcome of their contest with Assyria. A defeat for Assyria will send an international message, one of God's glory, justification, his power and character, and this will resound though the earth. This is the King praying!

God hears, and 185,000 Assyrians are slain by the Angel of YHWH (II Kings 19:20, 28, 32, 34-37).

Hezekiah becomes a model for kings and Presidents, a man of prayer who would not trust the "arm of flesh" (II Chron. 32:7-8). He appeals to the character of God as the basis for intervention. The answer will call attention to God and give Him glory in a world that ignores and disdains Him.

for a span of some thirteen years. Elisha received his mentor's mantle and ministered for twenty-five years. He too continued as a praying prophet, a symbol of extended grace to the corrupt and dying nation. He too prayed for a widow's son (II Kings 4:33). Surrounded by an enemy army, he prayed for the opening of the eyes of his servant to see the unseen army of angels (II Kings 6:17). The two praying prophets represent God's grace to Israel. But still, the nation would fall. Here is prayer, and praying men, graciously placed by God as intercessory representatives in the midst of apostasy. In the period of Elijah and Elisha there is a season of irregular miracles, twenty-four in all, which seem designed to wake up an idolatrous nation.

In the season between Elijah and Elisah, we meet another prophet - Micaiah. His name means 'who is like Yah?' (Yahweh). It is Micaiah who Ahab summons to a national prayer gathering reguarding the advisability of winning a war with Syria. Micaiah, like Elijah, stands along against 400 false prophets and declares Israel's defeat and Ahab's death. As the scene unfolds, Israel is in a national prayer gathering – but one designed to manipulate and pressure the prophet into complicity with the majority decision. Above the earth tribunal, Micaiah sees and another courtly session being conducted in heaven.

Ahab will die, and Jehoshaphat will barely escape the battle alive. He will return home, only to meet the Prophet Jehu, who will inform him that he has fallen into the hand of God. Jehoshaphat, sobored, heads a national spiritual revival – among the people, the Judges, and the priests and Levites (II Corinthians 20).

The Ten Northern Tribes - Lost

The Assyrian captives began in approximately 740 BC, though some argue for a later date, 733/2 BC. The tribes of Reuben, Gad, and the eastern half-tribe of Manasseh were carried away first (I Chronicles 5:26). And deportation affected the tribe of Naphtali (II Kings 15:29). Then, in 722/21 BC, nearly twenty years after the initial incursions, Samaria fell after a three year siege. Unlike Judah, a portion of which returned from its captivity the ten tribes of the Northern Kingdom were never granted permission to return and rebuild their homeland.

As God dealt with Israel in the last few decades of Israel's life as a nation, a stunning thing happened. Nineveh turned to God. And there, judgment upon that wicked city was averted. Jonah had been sent to preach and was certain that God's wrath was both deserved and guaranteed. "Forty days and Nineveh shall be destroyed," he cried out in the streets. But Nineveh repented.

> *So the people of Nineveh believed God, proclaimed a fast, and put on sackcloth, from the greatest to the least of them. Then word came to the king of Nineveh; and he arose from his throne and laid aside his robe, covered himself with sackcloth and sat in ashes. And he caused it to be proclaimed and published throughout Nineveh by the decree of the king and his nobles, saying, Let neither man nor beast, herd nor flock, taste anything; do not let them eat, or drink water. But let man and beast be covered with sackcloth, and cry mightily to God; yes, let everyone turn from his evil way and from the violence that is in his hands. Who can tell if God will turn and relent, and turn away from His fierce anger, so that we may not perish? (Jonah 3:5-9).*

The repentance of Nineveh came as a shock to Jonah. And it might have been intended by God as a lesson to Israel. If a pagan nation could be judged by YHWH for wickedness – then Israel, on God's laws and standards, were even more culpable. And further, if a pagan nation could be spared, then they too had hope, if only they would repent.

One-hundred and fifty years later, as God dealt with Judah and the southern kingdom, He was again dealing with Nineveh, this time through the ministry of Nahum, the prophet. But Nineveh would not repent, and they would fall. And that too, would serve as a warning, this time to Judah.

The Persistence of Idolatry

From the time of the golden calf to the exile of Judah, idolatry and paganism were constant enemies. In whatever form it manifested itself, it eroded pure faith. It reshaped notions about God. And it altered behavior and relating patterns, especially in the family. It created a rationale for the normalization of prostitution and child sacrifice (II Kings 23:10), homosexuality and goddess worship. It altered the image of God himself in the minds of the people. It polluted the whole of culture. By the time of Jeremiah, Asherah poles were set up in the temple introducing goddess worship. The prophet was taking a singular and decided position against the Queen of Heaven (Jeremiah 44:15-19). It should come as no shock that Jezebel was the daughter of the high priest of Baal in Tyre, and the patroness of goddess worship in the northern kingdom – a movement that Elijah fiercely opposed. The priestesses of the movement were ritual prostitutes. Homosexual prostitution was also practiced with the pagan rites.[3]

The pollution and compromise of prayer and worship eventually brought a complete loss of the nation. A people were now gone forever. O how important is the purity of prayer. The apostasy detailed in Judges had resulted in two lost tribes, now ten are gone. Subsequently, Judah would also be invaded by Babylon. Returning from Babylon, the invitation would be extended again (Isaiah 61:6).

---

3   Charles Pfieffer, *Ras Shamra and the Bible* (Baker Book House, 1962), 30-32.

But again, Judah said, 'No!'

In the south, Hezekiah launched a national moral renewal. He sought to eliminate pagan worship (II Kings 18:4). "He trusted in the Lord God of Israel, so that after him was none like him among the kings of Judah" (18:5). He prayed for the people who had not prepared themselves to eat the Passover (II Chronicles 30:18). When the city was threatened, King Hezekiah conferred with the prophet Isaiah (II Kings 19:4) and the king personally prayed, going up to the house of the Lord (II Kings 19:14-19). Hezekiah prayed,

> *"O Lord, God of Israel, enthroned between the cherubim, you alone are God over all the kingdoms of the earth. You have made heaven and earth" (II Kings 19:15). "Give ear, O Lord, and hear; open your eyes, O Lord, and see; listen to the words Sennacherib has sent to insult the living God ... Now, O Lord our God, deliver us from his hand, so that all kingdoms on earth may know that you alone, O Lord, are God" (v. 16, 19).*

And God turned back the armies of Assyria and extended the life of the nation of Judah.

Josiah led the final attempt to renew the nation. It was in his reign that the "book that was found" (II Kings 22:13; II Chronicles 34:21). How could "the book" be lost in the house of the Lord? Sadly, the renewal was short-lived.

Only brief moments of corporate renewal occur in either the north or the south until all of Israel and Judah are carried into captivity.

The Exile and Post-Exilic Period

Disobedience has jeopardized the dialogue (Isa. 1:15; Jer. 7:16; 11:11, 14; 14:11-12; Ezek. 8:18; Mic. 3:4). Men may mouth nearness with their lips, but if their behavior is not marked by holiness, then God is "far from their hearts" (Jer. 12:2) – and such people will find that God will not give them a hearing until the sin is removed.

Israel "followed the practices of the pagan nations ... practices the kings of Israel had introduced" (II Kings 17:8). Their secret practices did not please the Lord. Pagan shrines appeared everywhere – "in all their towns, from the smallest outpost to the largest walled city ... sacred pillars and Asherah poles at the top of every hill and under every green tree ... sacrifices on all the hilltops ..." (II Kings 17:9-11).

> *Again and again the Lord had sent His prophets and seers to warn both Israel and Judah: "Turn from all your evil ways" ... But Israel would not listen ... [they] refused to believe in the Lord ... They rejected His decrees and covenant ... they despised all His warnings.*
>
> *They even sacrificed their own sons and daughters ... They consulted fortune-tellers and practiced sorcery ... (II Kings 17:13-17).*

The result was the exile of the ten northern tribes. The Lord "swept them away from His presence" (II Kings 17:18). Shalmaneser, after a siege of three years, took Samaria in BC 721, deporting the survivors into Assyria, ending the northern kingdom. The southern kingdom, the tribe of Judah remained in their land, but they too "refused to obey the commands of the Lord" and "followed the evil practices that Israel had introduced" (17:19). It was only a matter of time before judgment came to them as well. In BC 605, Babylon invaded, deposed the king and took young potential leaders along with vessels from the temple. In B. C. 586, the third invasion came. This time, they destroyed both the city and the temple. Jerusalem was an ash heap. Among the exiles, Ezekiel is an intercessory prophet. To both the kings of Babylon and Persia, Daniel is also an intercessory prophet. In Jerusalem, it is Jeremiah who carries the message of God.

With the monarchy gone, Jerusalem in ruins and the temple demolished, the faith of Israel along with prayer, was necessarily adapted. Israel reached back, beyond the monarchy, and the temple with its ceremonies to the covenant behind it. That covenant, related more to the throne of God rather than the earthly regent supposedly representing Him, began a sustaining factor. With the temple gone, the fire of the altar quenched, prayer – the altar's essence – came to the fore. Again, this was not so much a move away from, an evolution of faith on this side of the tabernacle/temple tradition, as it was a recovery of the very roots of tabernacle/temple essence.

Since the days of Solomon, in particular, the connection with God had been at the temple. In II Chronicles 7:12, for the second time, "The LORD appeared to Solomon by night, and said ... 'I have heard your prayer, and have chosen this place for Myself as a house of sacrifice." In II Chronicles 6:40, Solomon prays that God's "eyes be open" and His "ears be attentive to the prayer made in this place" – notice the phrase, *"in this place."* And then, the people are advised in II Chronicles 6:20 that God is also attentive to the prayers prayed, not only *in*, but also *toward the place* associated with His name.

In II Chronicles 6:26, God promises through the prophet, "When the heavens are shut up and there is no rain" and sin is the issue, "when they [Israel] pray *toward this place* and confess Your name, and turn from their sin" then the prayer prayed toward this place will be heard "in heaven," and forgiveness will come, and with it rain. There is a similar promise in the well-known text of II Chronicles 7:13-16.

The Jerusalem temple was the official connection point between God – and the earth, God and His people, who were in turn to be a 'kingdom of priests.' Distance was eliminated with this *directional* prayer. Even in the absence of the temple today, Jews still turn toward Jerusalem when they pray. For them, their holiest site is what remains of the temple, the 'western wall' of the temple compound.

ACCENT

In II Chronicles 20:1-30, we have the prayer of King Jehoshophat for Judah. His name means "Jehovah has judged." Like his predecessor Asa (I Kings 15:9-24), he was a godly king (II Chron. 17:3-6; 19:3-4), who purged the land of sodomites (I Kings 22:46; cf. 15:12), as well as idolatry resulting from the worship of Baal and Ashtoreth. One of the unique features of his reign was a discipleship effort. He conducted regional Torah events (II Chron. 17:7-9), inculcating biblical principles in the people. These were led by princes and priests, with positive results (II Chron. 17:10-11). He reformed the courts, appointed priestly as well as civil judges with high certification requirements. (II Chron. 19:6-11). He fortified cities (II Chron. 17:2, 12), built a strong military (II Chron. 17:13, 19), accumulated both wealth and honor (II Chron. 17:5), and at the same time, won the respect of heathen (II Chron. 17:11).

He was not perfect. He allied himself with Israel, during the time of the wicked king Ahab (II Chron. 18:1-34). His son married the daughter of Ahab (II Chron. 18:1), and during a state visit, he agreed to fight with Ahab against Assyria, even though the prophet Micaiah warned against it (II Chron.18:2-3, 29). Defeat came. Ahab died, and Jehoshophat barely averted death (II Chron. 18:30-34). Returning home, he was met by the prophet Jehu, and informed that the wrath of God was against him. Consequently, he launched measures against idolatry, but without completely eliminating it (II Chron. 20:33). After his experience with Ahab, he allied with Ahaziah, and suffered another military defeat, losing a fleet of ships (II Chron. 20:35-37). Then he faced his own war, the threat of enemy invasion against Judah (II Chron. 20:1-4) by the Moabites, Ammonites, and Edomites, whose combined forces were less than a day away (II Chron. 20:1-2).

In fear, he turned to seek God (cf. II Chron. 19:3); and the nation joined him in prayer (II Chron. 20:3-4). In prayer, he appealed to the character of God, vs. 5-9, in the temple, v. 5. An assembly of people gathered with him. The king and the people were praying together in the court of the Lord. What a site! He pleaded God's covenant name following the promise of Jehovah, recorded by Solomon, to be used in a time of national crisis (I Kings 8:33, 35); vs. 4, 5-6. YHWH was their God, the God of their 'fathers, Abraham, Isaac, and Jacob, as well as the God of the covenant. He is God of glory who resides "in the heavens," the One, absolute in authority, unequaled in dominion. He is the God who rules the nations, yes, even the Moabites, Ammonites, and Edomites! And he is the God who in times past had been faithful. His record was one of aid and assistance to Judah. Therefore, he can now be relied upon as in the past, v. 7.

The land, now under dispute, was given as a promise to Abraham (Gen. 12:7, 8). He reaches back to Solomon's prayer at the dedication of the Temple (I Kings 8:22-53), vs. 8-9. Standing in the court of the Lord, where the glory had descended, he suggests that an attack against Jerusalem and the temple was an attack against God, v. 8. He repeated Solomon's prayer (cf. I Kings 8:33-34, 37-40, 44-45), v. 9. Though they had been merciful to the neighbor nations, those nations were not ready to extend mercy. When Israel had moved into the land of promise, they passed along the borders of these nation-states and left them unmolested. They had not sought to drive them from their lands (Num. 20:17-21; Deut. 2:1-29, 37), but now they were being challenged.

Jehoshophat frames their challenge as an attempt to dispossess them of YHWH's land, a home he gave them, v. 11. He prayed that God would manifest His justice by His delivering might, v. 12a. He confessed his weakness and that of Judah, their having nowhere to which they can escape, v. 12b.

Only God could save them (II Chron. 14:11). The crowd gathered involved not only men, but families - wives, children and infants, vs. 12c-13.

God answerd Jehosophat's prayer, II Chronicles 20:14-30. He promised victory, vs. 14-17. Jahaziel, a Levite prophesied that "the battle is the Lord's" (I Sam. 17:47). Such a notion should bring peace of mind, vs. 14- 15. God will be glorious. He will save (cf. Exod. 14:13). The event would be a work of his hand, and allay fears (cf. Isa. 41:8-11), vs. 16-17. The people believed the prophet. They fell on their faces and praised God, they sang praise, vs. 18-21.

This did not prevent the actual battle. That still had to be endured. But the Ammonites, Moabites, and Edomites were ambushed by an unknown adversary. The suddenness and nature of the attack created such confusion, that they turned on one another, vs. 22-24. The spoils of the battle then belonged to Judah, v. 25. Victory follows, vs. 26-30.

Here the long tradition of prayer that appeals to the character of God continues. It is prayer with the covenantal relationship in view (Dan. 11:32; cf. Heb. 11:1-40). A godly, praying king saves the nation. The people gather as a grand family and appeal to God under the open heaven. The prayer is recorded in seven verses, four of which devote themselves to the greatness of God and his faithfulness. The pressing national crisis is met, not by diplomacy or military tactics, but by a nation in prayer.

There had, of course, been other places. When Israel came into the land, the tabernacle was set up at various locations, and finally at Shiloh. There, Israel was to meet with God. There, they prayed. But at Shiloh, under Eli, corruption reigned, and God withdrew His glory. Eli, the High Priest died, his line was cut off, the ark was captured and never returned to the tabernacle of Moses. Jeremiah reminds Israel of those difficult days, "Therefore I will do to the house which is called by My name [the temple], in which you trust, and to *this place* which I gave to you and your fathers, as I have done to Shiloh" (Jeremiah 7:14). Huldah the prophetess, in days of Josiah, had warned, "Thus says the LORD:

> *'Behold, I will bring calamity on this place and on its inhabitants, all the curses that are written in the book which they have read before the king of Judah because they have forsaken Me and burned incense to other gods ... Therefore My wrath will be poured out on this place, and not be quenched'"" (II Chronicles 34:24-25).*

Josiah's tender heart and his reforms pushed back that judgment.

But now in the season of the exile, the monarchy is gone – but the covenant remains. And so the law becomes paramount. Now, though the temple and sacrifice are gone, prayer is not, so prayer replaces the temple, the sacrifice, and the altar.[4] In this period of exile, God's deliverance is selective. He delivers Daniel and the three young Hebrew rulers – when, in the case of Daniel, he defies the edict prohibiting prayer; and in the case of the three Hebrews, they refuse to comply with the command to bow before an idol. Pure prayer, to Yahweh alone, and avoidance of idolatry are in view. If Israel will remain faithful, and pray, despite pagan edicts against it, God will deliver. If they will refuse to adopt or bend and bow before

---

4   Samuel Balentine, *Prayer in the Hebrew Bible: The Drama of Divine-Human Dialogue* (Overtures to Biblical Theology; Minneapolis, MN; Minneapolis Fortress Press, 1993), 47.

an idol, He will send divine protection.

But selective deliverance is all that can be expected. Jeremiah and Ezekiel are told that the weightiest intercessors in Old Testament history, Moses and Samuel, could not persuade Him to hear the prayer of Israel. Moses is mentioned because he had prayed that God would forgive Israel when they sinned, and his intercession had spared them (Ex. 32:32; Psalm 196:23). Samuel had also pleaded in behalf of the sinful nation and had been heard by God (I Samuel 7:8, 12, 19). Amos, in the eighth century, had a similar success in intercession (Amos 7:2, 5). But not now (Jeremiah 15:1), a century later, Jeremiah is warned, prayer for salvation is futile. The people have hopelessly apostatized (Jer. 16:11, 14; 14:11). Deliverance will not come this time. Heaven will be silent.

Ezekiel is also told that the nation will not be spared, in fact, that the greatest saint - and three are mentioned: Noah, Daniel and Job – could not, by righteousness, prevent the exile. All they could expect would be their own deliverance, but not that of others (Ezekiel 14:14-26).

> 'Son of man, if a country sins against Me by committing unfaithfulness, and I stretch out My hand against it, destroy its supply of bread, send famine against it and cut off from it both man and beast, even though these three men, Noah, Daniel and Job were in its midst, by their own righteousness they could only deliver themselves,' declares the Lord GOD. (Ez. 14:13-14).

Fellowship with God carried the promise of answers to prayer. However, when fellowship was disrupted by sin or idolatry, for which the people would not repent, the privilege of answered prayer dried up (Dt. 1:45). Even Moses was denied the right to enter Canaan because of his sin (Dt. 3:25). At Gilboa, Saul's rebellion had grown so great, that when he prayed, God refused to respond, directly, or even by the aid of a priest or prophet (I Sam. 28:6). So Saul found a substitute – witchcraft. There, one finds no moral threshold necessary for interaction. Even David, after the sin with Bathsheba, could not persuade God to allow the child to live (II Sam. 12:16-18). Proverbs declares, *"The sacrifice of the wicked is an abomination to the LORD, But the prayer of the upright is His delight" (Prov. 15:8 - NAS).* Isaiah would boldly point out this moral connection with prayer as well, *"So when you spread out your hands in prayer, I will hide My eyes from you; Yes, even though you multiply prayers, I will not listen. Your hands are covered with blood"* (Isa. 1:15 – NAS). Even the multiplication of prayers, the increase in intensity, will not overcome sin. The only antidote is repentance.

> *Free those who are wrongly imprisoned; lighten the burden of those who work for you.*
> *Let the oppressed go free, and remove the chains that bind people. Share your food with the hungry, and give shelter to the homeless. Give clothes to those who need them, and do not hide from relatives who need your help.*
> *Then your salvation will come like the dawn, and your wounds will quickly heal.*
> *Your godliness will lead you forward, and the glory of the Lord will protect you from behind. Then when you call, the Lord will answer. 'Yes, I am here,' He will quickly reply (Isa. 58:6-9 - NLT).*

Isaiah's prescription is repentant *action*. Not merely words. Repentance is behavioral, with relational and social implications for the whole of culture. The treatment of others in significantly moral ways, opens the heavens for answers to prayer. In fact, Isaiah declares, *"Before they call, I will answer. While they are yet speaking, I will hear" (Isa. 64:24).* Nothing happens faster than the prayer connection between God and a moral people.

In the season of the returning exiles, Haggai and Zechariah will confront the crowds gathered at the ruins of the temple for prayer, and move them to rebuild the temple seventy years after its destruction (Hag. 1-2; Zech. 1-4). Seventy years later, Ezra and Nehemiah will lead a corporate renewal that will result in the rebuilding of the walls of the city. Their ministries are decorated with corporate prayer events (Ezra 8:21-23; 9:1-15). An extraordinary example of corporate prayer, specifically of repentance, is found in Ezra 10 (See also Neh. 9:1-38; 12). Ezra's involvement in the restoration effort came out of his times of prayer (Ezra 7:10), as did those of Nehemiah (Nehemiah 1:5-11). One in Babylon, the other in Persia, both moved to return to Jerusalem, but used of God to rebuild the city and lead spiritual renewal.

Prayer References

II Samuel

1. David for revelation (16 words; II Sam 2:1). Answered because of God's plan.

2. David for revelation (14 words; II Sam 5:19). Answered because of God's plan (II Sam 5:19).

3. David for fulfillment of Davidic covenant (364 words; II Sam 7:18-29). Answered partially, and will be fulfilled in all eternity when Christ comes to reign (Isa 9:6-7; Luke 1:32-33; Acts 15:13-18; Rev 11:15; 20:1-10).

4. David for forgiveness of sin (29 words; II Sam 24:10). Answered, but judgments fell (II Sam 24:11-25).

References to prayer (II Sam 5:23; 12:16; 15:7-8; 21:1).

I Kings

1. Solomon for wisdom (146 words; I Kings 3:6-9). Answered because it pleased God (I Kings 3:10-14).

2. Solomon, prayer of dedication (1,050 words; I Kings 8:23-

53). Answered according to obedience of Israel.

3. Elijah for resurrection of boy (35 words; I Kings 17:20-21). Answered because of faith in God (I Kings 17:22-24; Heb 11:35).

4. Elijah for fire from heaven (63 words; I Kings 18:36-37). Answered because of faith (I Kings 18:38).

5. Elijah for death (18 words; I Kings 19:4). Unanswered because it was contrary to God's plan which was to translate him and permit him to live bodily in heaven until time to come back to earth as one of the two witnesses (II Kings 2:9; Zech 4:11-14; Mal 4:5-6; Rev 11:3-11).

References to prayer (I Kings 13:6; 18:42-43).

II Kings

1. Elisha for his servant's eyes to be opened (11 words; II Kings 6:17). Answered by faith.

2. Hezekiah for deliverance (133 words; II Kings 19:15-19). Answered by faith (II Kings 19:35).

3. Hezekiah for a longer life (30 words); he received 15 years more (II Kings 20:3). Answered by faith (II Kings 20:5-6).

I Chronicles

1. Jabez for enlarged coast (33 words; I Chron 4:10). Answered because of God's word to give Israel all the land (I Chron 4:10; Gen 15:18-21).

2. David for Solomon and Israel (326 words; I Chron 29:10-19). Answered partially, in the temporary obedience to God of Solomon and Israel.

References to prayer (I Chron 5:20; 21:26; 23:30).

II Chronicles

1. Asa for victory (50 words; II Chron 14:11). Answered by faith (II Chron 14:12-14).

2. Jehoshaphat for victory (224 words; II Chron 20:6-12). Answered by faith (II Chron 20:20-25).

Psalms

1. David. In 50 prayer-psalms he made requests for various blessings, most of them being answered because of faith in God's promises (Ps 3-7; 9; 12:1-13:6; 16:1-17:15; 19:1-20:9; 22; 25:1-31:24; 35:1-36:12; 38:1-41:13; 51; 54:1-61:8; 64; 69:1-70:5; 86; 108:1-109:31; 119; 124; 132; 139:1-144:15). The ones unanswered will be answered in due time for David even prayed about future events.

2. An unknown psalmist (perhaps David) prayed for many kinds of blessings, which were granted or will be granted (Ps 10; 33; 43:1-44:26; 71; 85; 88; 102; 106; 118; 120; 123; 125; 129; 137).

3. Asaph made many requests to God (in 5 prayers) for various kinds of blessing which were granted or will yet be granted (Ps 74; 79:1-80:19; 82:1-83:18).

4. Moses makes requests to God (Ps 90).

5. Ethan made requests for God to remember the reproach of His servants (Ps 89).

Thus, in 72 of the 150 psalms there are personal requests to God, making them definitely prayer-psalms. A few of the other 78 may also be considered such because of the general nature of the subject matter. Even in the listed prayer-psalms many subjects are more outstanding than the prayers. See notes on these psalms in Dake's Bible.

Isaiah

1. Isaiah for cleansing (38 words; Isa 6:5). Answered (Isa 6:6-7).

2. Hezekiah for deliverance (133 words; Isa 37:16-20). Answered (Isa 37:36).

3. Hezekiah for healing and length of days (30 words; Isa

38:3). Answered (Isa 38:5).

References to prayer (Isa 1:15; 7:11; 16:12; 26:16; 55:6-7). There are also prayers that Israel will make in the time of their restoration as a nation (Isa 12; 64).

Jeremiah

1. Jeremiah, confession of inability to obey God (12 words; Jer 1:6).
2. Jeremiah, accusing God (24 words; Jer 4:10).
3. Jeremiah for judgment (80 words; Jer 10:23-25). Answered (Dan 5).
4. Jeremiah, questioning God (133 words; Jer 12:1-4).
5. Jeremiah for help for Judah (95 words; Jer 14:7-9).
6. Jeremiah for help for Judah (81 words; Jer 14:20-22).
7. Jeremiah, judgment (118 words; Jer 15:15-18).
8. Jeremiah for judgment (158 words; Jer 17:13-18).
9. Jeremiah for judgment (174 words; Jer 18:19-23).
10. Jeremiah for judgment (214 words; Jer 20:7-12).
11. Jeremiah, concerning captivity of Judah (209 words; Jer 32:17-25).

References to prayer (Jer 7:16; 11:14; 14:11; 21:2; 29:7,12; 37:3; 42:2,4,20).

Lamentations:

1. Jeremiah for judgment (108 words; Lam 1:20-22).
2. Jeremiah for consideration (113 words; Lam 2:20-22).
3. Jeremiah for judgment (158 words; Lam 3:55-66).
4. Jeremiah for the oppressed people of Judah (300 words; Lam 5).

Jeremiah could be called the praying prophet as well as the weeping prophet. He has 15 recorded prayers.

Ezekiel

1. Ezekiel protesting what God wanted him to do (41 words; Ez. 4:14).
2. Ezekiel for the remnant (20 words; Ez. 9:8).
3. Ezekiel for the remnant (14 words; Ezek 11:13).

Daniel

1. Daniel for forgiveness of sins and fulfillment of prophecy (550 words; Dan 9:1-19).
2. Daniel for revelation (11 words; Dan 12:8).

References to prayer (Dan 2:17-18; 6:10).

Amos

1. Amos for forgiveness s (16 words; Amos 7:2).
2. Amos for help (16 words; Amos 7:5).

Jonah

1. Sailors for mercy (33 words; Jonah 1:14).
2. Jonah for deliverance from hell (198 words; Jonah 2:1-9).
3. Jonah for death (70 words; Jonah 4:2-3).

Habakkuk

1. Habakkuk for God to act (75 words; Hab 1:1-5).
2. Habakkuk for judgment (156 words; Hab 1:12-17).
3. Habakkuk for revival (474 words; Hab 3:2-19).

Ezra

1. Ezra-prayer of thanksgiving (50 words; Ezra 7:27-28).
2. Ezra for forgiveness and help (419 words; Ezra 9:5-15). Answered (Ezra 10:1-19).

References to prayer (Ezra 8:21-23).

Nehemiah

1. Nehemiah for confession of sins and help (256 words; Neh 1:5-11).
2. Nehemiah for judgment (53 words; Neh 4:1-6).
3. Nehemiah for help (7 words; Neh 6:9).
4. Nehemiah for help (31 words; Neh 6:14).
5. Israel-confession of sins (1,205 words-the longest prayer; Neh 9:5-38).
6. Nehemiah for blessing (29 words; Neh 13:14).
7. Nehemiah for blessing (18 words; Neh 13:22).
8. Nehemiah for judgment (21 words; Neh 13:29).
9. Nehemiah for blessing (7 words).

Finis Jennings Dake, *Dake's Annotated Reference Bible* (Lawrenceville, GA: Dake Bible Sales, 1963, 1991).

CHAPTER FOURTEEN

THE GOSPELS AND PRAYER: AN OVERVIEW

A WINDOW THROUGH TIME

S. D. Gordon offers a composite picture of the prayer life of Jesus.

1. TIME - He had regular times of prayer; a habit seems plainly to have been to devote the early morning hour to communion with His Father, and to depend upon that for constant guidance and instruction. This is suggested especially by Mark 1:35; John 7:16; 8:28; 12:49.

   He sought opportunities for secret prayer as special needs arose; late at night after others had retired; three times He remained in prayer all the night; and at irregular intervals between times. Note that it was usually a quiet time when the noises of earth were hushed. He spent special time in prayer before important events and also afterwards.

2. PLACE - He had favorite places of prayer: He suggested, "Enter your inner chamber and when you have shut the door, pray to your Father in secret." But He had no fixed chamber, no house or home during His public ministry. Homeless for the three-and-a-half years of ceaseless traveling, His place of prayer was a desert place, "the deserts," "the mountains," "a solitary place." He loved nature. The hilltop above the Nazareth village, the slopes of Olivet, and hillsides overlooking the Galilean lake were favorite places. It was always a quiet place, shut away from the discordant sounds of earth.

3. WITHOUT CEASING - He lived in a constant prayer, never out of the spirit of prayer. He could be alone in a dense crowd. There are all sorts of solitude, namely, of time, as early morning or late at night; solitude of place, as a hilltop, or forest, or a secluded room; and solitude of spirit, as when one surrounded by a crowd may watch them unmoved, or to be lost to all around in his own inner thought. Jesus used all three sorts of solitude for talking with His Father.

4. *KAIROS* MOMENTS - He prayed in the midst of the great crises of His life: Five are mentioned: Before the awful battle royal with Satan in the Quarantanian wilderness at the outset; before choosing the twelve leaders of the new movement; at the time of the Galilean uprising; before the final departure from Galilee for Judea and Jerusalem; and in Gethsemane, the greatest crisis of all.

5. PERSONAL INTERCESSION - He prayed for others by name, and still does.

6. JOINT INTERCESSION - He prayed with others: A habit that might well be more widely copied. A few minutes spent in quiet prayer by friends or fellow-workers before parting wonderfully sweetens the spirit and cements friendships, and makes difficulties less difficult, and hard problems easier of solution.

7. BREAKTHROUGH PRAYER - The greatest blessings of His life came during prayer. Six incidents are noted: 1. While praying, the Holy Spirit came upon Him; 2. He was transfigured; 3-5. Three times a heavenly

voice of approval came; 6. In His hour of sorest distress in the garden a heavenly messenger came to strengthen Him.

Prayer meant much to Jesus! It was not only His regular habit, but His resort in every emergency, however slight or serious. When perplexed He prayed. When hard-pressed by work He prayed. When hungry for fellowship, He found it in prayer. He chose His associates and received His messages upon His knees. If tempted, He prayed. If criticized, He prayed. If fatigued in body or wearied in spirit, He had recourse to His one unfailing habit of prayer. Prayer brought Him unmeasured power at the beginning, and kept the flow unbroken and undiminished. There was no emergency, no difficulty, no necessity, no temptation that would not yield to prayer, as He practiced it. Shall not we, who have been tracing these steps in His prayer life, go back over them again and again until we breathe in His very spirit of prayer? And shall we not, too, ask Him daily to teach us how to pray, and then plan to get alone with Him regularly that He may have opportunity to teach us, and we the opportunity to practice His teaching?

S. D. Gordon, Taken from the Chapter: "Jesus' Habits of Prayer," *Quiet Talks On Prayer*, 1904.

CHAPTER 14

THE GOSPELS AND PRAYER: AN OVERVIEW

P. Douglas Small

Joachim Jeremias observed,

> At no other point does the inner corruption and the decay of the Hellenistic world ... in New Testament times become so apparent as in the sphere of prayer. Measured by biblical standards, Greek prayer was lacking in seriousness and reverence even in the pre-Hellenistic period. This is evident, for example, in the fact that from ancient comedy onwards, parodies of prayer had become a stock convention for comedians ... Foolish, immoral, ridiculous, and even obscene prayer are woven into the action of the play and provoke the audience to uproarious laughter.[1]

We are witnessing a similar cultural parallel in the satire and irreverent comedy of late-night cable television. It is utterly disrespectful of biblical values, and of Jesus himself, not to mention the vilification of Christians. Prayer, in this historic era, as well as our times, is dismissed, treated as a crude culturally backward act by the ignorant.

The New Testament and Prayer

It is fitting then, as we turn the pages of the Bible and enter the New Testament, to discover God, (John 1:1-3) having come to

---

1   Joachim Jeremias, *The Prayers of Jesus* (Philadelphia: Fortress Press, 1978), 66.

the earth Himself, to pray (Isaiah 59:16)! Here, prayer goes to an altogether different stratum. Here, God on earth agrees with God in heaven (John 10:30), regarding the future of man and the earth (John 17). He has come to mediate a new covenant (Matthew 26:28; Hebrews 9:15). It is not merely men He seeks to infuse with prayer, but He comes to call a people to prayer – just as God had attempted to call Israel to be a people of prayer, a 'kingdom of priests,' an invitation they declined (Isaiah 61:1-6; Luke 4:18-19). Now, Jesus comes to call men and women, to know God, to walk with Him as Adam had done in the garden, and to invite the heavenly kingdom to the earth. *"Thy kingdom come; thy will be done!"* Fractured humanity is now united, *"Our father ..."* we are to pray. It is not prayer split away from the corporate, not prayer for one's narrow slice of pain, but prayer that is prayed as a representative of others - "Give *us ...* deliver *us ...* lead *us ...*"

David Bosch observes:

> To offer that prayer implies believing Christians make a difference to this world, that things are not to remain the way they are. It implies having a vision of a new society and working for it as though it is attainable. It means in other words, getting involved in God's mission in the world ...[2]

Despite the tirade by the liberals, that petition for personal needs, even one's daily bread is ignoble, it runs against the evidence of Scripture itself and centuries of Christian tradition. Paul, writing to the Philippians (4:6), encourages us to pray about everything. The Lord's model for prayer touches the physical – bread, daily needs; the psycho-social and relational – forgiveness, reconciliation; the spiritual – the Evil One, temptation, deliverance. It covers the whole sphere of existence. Everything is taken to God in prayer. We are to ask for bread, for a fish, for an egg – and the coded language

2   David Bosch, Quoted in *A Clarified Vision for Urban Mission*, 85.

is suggestive of the three spheres in which we exist: the *land* from which the bread comes; the *water* from which the fish comes; and the *air* in which the bird will fly. Prayer engages all of life – land, sea and air. Further, there is the implication that in committing the needs to God, He will not give us – a stone, a serpent, or a scorpion; all of which are spurious substitutes.[3]

Prayer is also anchored to faith in the goodness of God. He will give us bread – and not a stone. He is our Father, who gives good gifts. "Every good and perfect gift cometh down from the father of lights, in whom there is no variableness or turning." (James 1:17) His character is fixed. He is not a chameleon whose disposition constantly shifts, making Him unpredictable and capricious. That was the profile of the Greek gods.

Jesus and Prayer

In the New Testament, by means of the life of Christ, we are elevated to a new altitude in prayer. Here, in terms of the habit and example of personal prayer, is the most active person we have met

---

3   There may be some inference to the Zeus legend. But that aside, the stones bore a similar shape to the round oval loaves of bread. Satan suggested that Jesus turn the stones into bread. The mountainside was plenteous with them. After 40-days of fasting, he must have supposed Jesus susceptible to a mirage. At the very least, there is a logical connection between the stones and the loaves of bread. In the same way, the Sea of Galilee was at times infested with water-snakes, a nuisance to net fisherman. A haul of fish might also introduce a serpent into the boat. Every fisherman had to be prepared to be 'snake-handler.' Finally, scorpions were known to curl into a ball the size of a bird egg, and might be unnoticeable to an undiscerning egg-gatherer. All of these are potential substitutes. And Jesus promises – if you commit your need for bread, i.e., to God, He will not give you a substitute. Thus, we pray about everything. We commit all needs to the oversight of God. We do not arrogantly assume that God's sphere does not reach to the material, that He is too holy and noble to be concerned about such things. Those ideas are more gnostic than incarnational.

ACCENT

The dominate words for prayer in the New Testament are:

- *Eucharistia* – a prayer of thanksgiving, frequent in the writings of Paul. Occurs 15 times and is variously translated - giving of thanks 3, gratefully 1, gratitude 2, thankfulness 1, thanks 2, thanksgiving 4, thanksgivings 2. In Acts – 1; I Corinthians – 1; II Corinthians – 3; Ephesians – 1; Philippians – 1; Colossians – 2; I Thessalonians – 1; I Timothy – 3; Revelation -2.

- *Deomai, deesis* – intercession due to want, lack or desire, to long for, to ask, even to beg the thing asked for, to pray, make supplications. It is used some 22 times as follows: ask 1, beg 6, begged 1, begging 2, beseech 2, implored 1, making request 1, please 1, pray 2, prayed 3, praying 2. In Matthew – 1; Luke – 8; Acts – 7; Romans – 1; II Corinthians – 3; Galatians – 1; I Thessalonians – 1. The usage is almost exclusive in Luke-Acts (15 times) and in Paul (6 times). In Paul, this term is indicative of his apostolic calling (Romans 1:10; I Thessalonians 3:10).

- *Aitema* – a petition or request, used only three times, twice in connection with prayer (Philippians 4:6; I John 5:15; and then of the 'demand' of the Jews - Luke 23:24).

- *Proseuchesthai, proseuche, proseuchomai*: to pray – prayer in general, often in the sense of worship. *Proseúxomai* is a compound which derives from *prós*, meaning "towards or exchange"; and *euxomai*, indicating a prayer or a desire, a wish. The resultant meaning is - to exchange wishes. Literally, to interact with the Lord by switching our human wishes or ideas for His wishes as He imparts faith and understanding. Praying is closely related to *pístis* ("faith") in the New Testament. See: Acts 6:5, 6; 14:22, 23; Ephesians 6:16-18; Col 1:3; 4; II Thessalonians 3:1, 2; James 5:13-15; Jude 20.

- *Latreuein, latreia* (see also *eulogein*) – meaning 'I serve, worship' especially God, perhaps simply: 'I worship.' *Latreúo*, from *latris*, is "someone hired to accomplish a technical task because they are qualified." It means properly, to render technical, acceptable service because of being specifically trained, skilled and in all the pages of Scripture, without exception. David is only the character whose prayer life, evidenced by the psalms, comes close. Jesus lives in and out of prayer (Mt. 26:36-39; 27:46; Mk. 1:35; Luke 3:21; 5:16; 6:12; 9:16, 29; 22:32, 39-46; 23:34-46; John 11:41, 42; 17:1-26). He is God – in the flesh, incarnate (John 1; Matthew 16:16). And yet, He prays. His prayer is not unrelated to the everyday life of the common man. For example, Jesus prays as He breaks bread (Luke 9:16; 22: 17, 19; 24:30). He evidences a dependence on the Father not seen in the same manner prior to Him. This should settle the debate regarding the efficacy, the importance of prayer. Sadly, it does not. What arrogance, to determine that though Jesus seemed to acknowledge by His need for prayer dependence on and fellowship with the Father, we can live with it or without it.

Not only does He practice prayer, but He teaches its importance (Luke 11:5-9; 18:1-14; see also Mt. 5:44; 6:5-8; 7:7-11; 9:38; 17:21; 18:19; 21:22; 24:20; 26:41). He encourages the use of a personal closet for private daily at-home prayer. The word for room used in Matthew 6 is a reference to the 'storeroom, a pantry, a storage area' where no guest would ever come, and in that sense, the most private place in the house. It may be significant that Jesus suggested the use of the 'storage room,' the family treasury as a place of prayer. God is said to be *in* the secret place. Here is the hiddenness of God – present, but not visible.

He also models such solitary prayer (Mk. 1:35, 45; John 6:15). For Him, prayer was a relationship, like that of a child with His father (Mt. 6:8; 7:11). And yet, here was the wiser dependence on the Father's wisdom, not typical of a mere child. Whatever was requested, needed to be consistent with the will of the Father (Mt. 7:11; 6:10; 26:39, 42; I John 5:14). This is a level of intimacy in prayer not known in the Old Testament. Abraham called God father, but never 'my father!'

equipped. It occurs 21 times in the New Testament and is more common in Luke. It reaches back to the tradition of the priests and Levites introduced by Moses (Deuteronomy 6:13; 10:12; Joshua 24:15; Matthew 4:10; Luke 4:8 out of Deuteronomy 6:13; Acts 7:7; 24:14; 27:23; Hebrews 9:14; Revelation 7:15; 22:3. It is used in relation to the worship of idols in Acts 7:42; Romans 1:25 (see also Exodus 20:5; 23:24; Ezekiel 20:32). In the strict sense of "performing sacred services, to offer gifts, to worship God in the observance of the rites instituted for his worship" – see Hebrews 9:9; 10:2; specifically, of the priests who officiate, and discharge the sacred office and also of the sacred thing to which the service is rendered - Hebrews 8:5; 13:10; Romans 1:9 (the spiritual worship Paul offers out of his apostolic office. The term is applied to the Christian life in Philippians 3:3 and II Timothy 1:3.

- *Kauchasthai, kauchema, kauchaomai (kow-khah'-om-ahee):* to boast or glory, i.e. - I glory (exult) proudly. To live with the "head up high," i.e. boasting from a particular vantage point by having the right base of operation to deal successfully with a matter (see II Corinthians 5:12). Likely comes from the root, *auxen,* (neck), the thing that holds the head high or upright. It infers living with God-given confidence. It occurs 38 times – in Romans 2:17, 23, 28; 5:3, 11; I Corinthians 1:19; 3:21; 4:7; used by Paul 35 times; and by James twice; to glory I Corinthians 1:31; 4:7; 5:12; 10:15; 11:12; 13:3; II Corinthians 7:14; 9:2; 10:8, 16, 17; 11:30; 12:5; Philippians 3:3; Ephesians 2:9; Galatians 6:13; II Thessalonians 1:4; James 1:9; 4:16.

- *Krazein* – from *krazó (krad'-zo):* to scream, cry out. It is the equivalent of the Septuagint *qara,* used in Romans 8:15; Galatians 4. "I cry aloud, shriek." It is an onomatopoetic term for a raven's piercing cry ("caw"). Its derivative meaning is to cry out loudly with an urgent scream or shriek, using "inarticulate shouts that express deep emotion." You can almost hear our English word – 'crazy' here. In variant forms it is used 55 times in the New Testament, not usually of prayer. See Matthew 14:26, 30; 8:29; 9:27; 15:23; 27:50; Mark 1:26; 3:11; 5:5, 7; 9:24, 26; 10:48; 11:19; 15:14, 39; Luke 9:39; 18:39; Acts 7:57, 60; 14:14; 19:32; 21:28, 36; 24:21; James 5:4; Revelation 10:3; 12:2; 14:15; 18:18; 19:17.

In Matthew 6:7, Jesus warns against 'babbling' or vain repetitions. Luther suggested that this meant the multiplication of words. Prayer, he said, should not be 'many words.' The suggestion misses the point – Jesus is not encouraging either short prayer sessions or brevity. Rather, he is primarily condemning the practice of the pagans in which mere sounds were perceived as prayers – babblings that were both headless and heartless. And second, he is suggesting that though prayer involves words, its center is found beyond well-formed phrases. God is not impressed with a theological vocabulary. Humility and integrity, authenticity and simplicity seem to get His attention.

Jesus probably drew from the rich Jewish tradition of prayer and praise. Many of the psalms would have been committed to memory, and spoken prayerfully, just as we speak the 'Lord's Prayer.' The language of Old Testament praise, borrowed from both the psalmists and synagogue traditions would have had a liturgical character.[4] We would propose that His prayer life was at times fixed and memorized prayers, the psalms, and other times extemperaneous and directly from His heart.

In John 17, in the closing hours of His life, He radically alters the character of personal prayer. He instructs His disciples that hence forth, prayer was to be addressed to the Father, in the name of the Son – that is, in His Name! Such prayer was promised an answer (John 16:23, 24, 26). Never before, had the covenantal people been invited to approach God in the name of another human. No one had prayed in the name of Abraham or Moses, Samuel or David – never! This is a new channel of access (John 17:19; see also Heb. 4:14-16; 10:19-22). Of course, prayers offered in 'the name of' Jesus were also to be 'in harmony with' the will of the Father (John 15:7; see also I

---

4   Oscar Cullman, *Prayer in the New Testament* (Minneapolis, MN: Fortress Press, 1994), 29.

John 3:22f; 5:13f).

Jesus prayed in His greatest moment of distress. And He prayed about the trial and the cross He faced. His prayer was not plastic. It was sweaty and bloody praying. And it was quite human, "If it is possible, let this cup pass" (Mark 14:35). The writer of Hebrews gives us a graphic glimpse into the moment saying that Jesus prayed "with loud cries and tears." Mark says "He threw himself on the ground," and Matthew, "He fell on His face," while Luke is milder, "He knelt." Why would the disciples give us such images of Jesus were they not true? What motive would they have for painting such holy desperation into the character or their leader, if it were not

> **ACCENT**
>
> In his book, *Successful Praying*, F. J. Huegel offers ten rules for prayer:
>
> 1. The Law of the Atonement – We enter the holiest place by the blood of the atonement, by the work of Christ in our behalf (Hebrews 10:19).
> 2. The Law of Position – We are seated with Christ in the heavenly realm (Ephesians 2:6).
> 3. The Law of Faith – Ours is 'the Faith of the Son of God' and we stand united with Him in the power of His resurrection (Phil. 3:10).
> 4. The Law of Right Relations – We must be in right relationship with God and others (Psa. 66:18).

true? "They would neither have invented nor handed down a prayer which shows Jesus in such a human state had it not existed."[5]

In the New Testament, and the teachings of Jesus, faith is a prerequisite for effective prayer. And yet, who can argue that Jesus ever prayed a prayer without faith. Still, His prayer for the cup to pass in Gethsemane was not granted the answer He requested (Mark 14:35). The potential denial is aborted with the resolution, "Not

5   Ibid, 24.

> 5. The Law of God's Will - He will hear us if we ask according to his will (I John 5:14).
> 6. The Law of the Spirit's Inspiration - He makes intercession for us (Rom. 8:27).
> 7. The Law of Praise - Praise leads us through to victory (Psa. 34:1; 22:3).
> 8. The Law of the Right Motive - We must seek God's glory (Rom. 8:7-8).
> 9. The Law of Right Diagnosis - Listen to God. Learn his viewpoint (Hab. 2:1).
> 10. The Law of Warfare - We need to be aggressive against Satan (Col. 2:15).
>
> F. J. Huegel, *Successful Praying* (Minneapolis, MN: Bethany, 1967), p. 68, 74.

my will but Thine be done!" So faith, we learn here, must always have a partner in the waiting, "the unconditional readiness to submit to the will of God." [6] Faith cannot be seen as our forcing our will on God or otherwise sovereignty would be turned on its head. The goal of faith is to believe God for His will, that His will would be revealed and be done. Our alignment with God's will is often an evolution of discovery, "if it is possible" (Mark 14:35), "if it is your will" (Luke 22:42), "however ... but ... I will but what you will" (Mark 14:36; Luke 22:42).[7] Nothing on this earth meant more to Jesus than the deep mysterious unity He and the Father enjoyed – nothing. If the cross was necessary to that unity – so be it. If His journey to retain that unity led through hell and the grave – let that come as well.

The use the Lord's name implies the bridal motif – and with that comes a change of name, the adoption of the name of the bridegroom by the bride. This not only signals a relational and identity shift, but a new legal status as well. It implies inheritance, new authority and

---

6   Ibid, 32.
7   Ibid, 33-34.

rights, indeed a partnership. We may now use the name of our Lord as His bride partner, committed to finish His work in the earth.

Women and Prayer

The most striking thing about the role of women in the life and teaching of Jesus is the simple fact that they are there. Although the gospel texts contain no special sayings repudiating the view of the day about women, their uniform testimony to the presence of women among the followers of Jesus and to His serious teaching of them constitutes a break with tradition which has been described as being 'without precedent in [then] contemporary Judaism.'[8]

Jesus gave no explicit teaching on the role of women in the church. In fact, He left no teaching at all concerning women as a class of people.... He treated every woman He met as a person in her own right.[9]

And yet, there are striking observations. For example, Jesus raised two persons from the dead. In both cases, the resurrections involve restorations of the dead to women — the only son of the widow from Nain (Luke 7:11-17); and Lazarus, the brother of Mary and Martha (John 11:1-44). New Testament scholars point out a relatively high number of references to women when contrasted with literary works of the same period. In the biblical record, Jesus treats women with incredible respect. He elevates them. He lifts them out of their stereotyped roles. While His teaching is not explicit, His manner is instructive and implicit. Of all the founders of other religions, Jesus towers in His treatment of women.

Twenty-four times in Luke, Jesus either met a woman,

8   James Hurley, pp. 82-83, citing W. Forster, *Palestinian Judaism in New Testament Times.* (London, 1964), 124.

9   Grenz, Stanley, *Women in the Church: A Biblical Theology of Women in Ministry.* (InterVarsity Press, 1995), 71.

talked about a woman, or mentioned a woman in a parable. All of these 24 times are instructive and positive. The words 'accepting, sensitive, and affirming' sum up what Luke and the example of Jesus Christ teach us about Jesus and women.[10]

Matthew and Luke place at the front of their gospel accounts a focus on women – Matthew on Mary, the mother of Jesus (Matthew 1:18-25); and Luke on Mary and Elizabeth. Mary is featured as hearing from God through an angel (Luke 1:28-38), and Elizabeth as receiving the Holy Spirit on hearing the voice of Mary, and then uttering a prophetic word (1:39-45), followed by Mary's *Magnificat*! And it is Luke who gives us a glimpse of Anna, the prophetess, who "served the Lord with fastings and prayers night and day," a widow of 84 years who did not depart from the Temple, on seeing Jesus "in that instant ... gave thanks" (Luke 2:36-38).

It was Luther who first pointed out that all four of the women in the genealogy of Jesus are foreign. Tamar and Rahab were Canaanites. Ruth was a Moabite. Bathsheba was probably a Hittite. Not only is Jesus missional and inclusive, He himself is a product of God, the Holy Spirit, by nations. In this way, Matthew begins with missions and ends with the Great Commission. Jesus, on His mother's side, was a product of the international family tree. He belongs to the nationas.

The first miracle of Jesus is at the request of His mother in Cana of Galilee, at a wedding, where He turns the water into wine (John 2:1-12). He heals the mother of the wife of Peter (Matthew 8:14-15). He healed the daughter of Jarius, a synagogue ruler, who was reported dead due to His delay in arrival (Mark 5:22-24, 35-43), a delay created by His encounter with the prayerful and desperate woman with the issue of blood (Mark 5:25-34). He heals the Gentile

---

10 Doug Clark, "Jesus and Women," See: http://enrichmentjournal. ag.org/200102/024_jesus_and_women.cfm

woman's daughter and extols her faith as great – a rebuke to His Jewish kinsmen (Matthew 15:21-28).

It is Luke who shows us pure worship by the contrast of a sinner woman who brings an alabaster box and anoints Jesus in the home of the righteous Pharisee, Simon (Luke 7:36-50). Luke reports Jesus as saying, because 'she loved much' her sins were forgiven – a radical idea. And following that, Luke reports many women who ministered to Jesus (8:1-3). In a similar vein, Mary and Martha welcome Jesus into their home, and Mary is seen 'sitting at His feet' – a picture of worship (Luke 38-42). This invitation to women to worship in such a personal way is as radical as His affirmation of a sinner woman over a Pharisee.

In Luke 13:10-17, He ministered to a bent-over woman, in a synagogue on the Sabbath, preferring care and healing for her over the legalistic encumbrances of the Pharisees. There, He gives priority to the woman – over the ruler of the synagogue. Shocking!

In Luke 18, He turns convention on its head, and uses the story of a widow to teach on prayer. Without legal standing, she dares to go to court and press for relief from an adversary. Her example is set forth by Jesus as an ultimate principle in persistent prayer.

In John 5, in a similar vein, we have a contrast between the spiritual hunger exhibited by the woman at the well in Samaria, who realizes early that Jesus is the Messiah, and that of the more spiritually dull disciples. They return from the nearby town with the temporal – food for the hour; she returns with the townsfolk themselves following – looking for water that will allow them to never thirst again. The entire encounter is a kind of prayer – a search for meaning in life, contrasted with the spiritual dullness of the disciples.

It is the women who are prominent at the cross and first at the tomb – evangelists of the resurrection (Matthew 22:1-10). This is by no means exhaustive, but it is clear, that women are allowed to be close to Jesus, treated with respect, used by Him as teachers, by their hunger and example, to teach others. They are allowed to pray and to worship. They receive angels, hear from God and prophesy.

Prayer References

Matthew

1. The prayer Jesus taught His disciples (66 words; Matt 6:9-13).

2. Leper's prayer for healing (9 words; Matt 8:2). Answered (Matt 8:3).

3. Centurion's prayer for his servant (73 words; Matt 8:6-9). Answered (Matt 8:13).

4. Disciples' prayer for help from drowning (5 words; Matt 8:25). Answered (Matt 8:26).

5. Demon's plea for temporary liberty (37 words; Matt 8:29-31). Answered (Matt 8:32).

6. A ruler's prayer for healing (18 words; Matt 9:18). Answered (Matt 9:25).

7. A woman's request for healing (11 words; Matt 9:21). Answered (Matt 9:22).

8. Two blind men pray for healing (8 words; Matt 9:27). Answered (Matt 9:29-30).

9. Jesus gives thanks to God, the Father (38 words; Matt 11:25).

10. Peter's request to walk on water (13 words; Matt 14:28). Answered (Matt 14:29).

11. Peter's plea for help from drowning (3 words; Matt 14:30). Answered (Matt 14:31).

12. A woman asks for the healing of her daughter (36 words; Matt 15:22-27). Answered (Matt 15:28).

13. A man desires the healing of his son (39 words; Matt 17:15-

16). Answered (Matt 17:18).

14. A mother wants exaltation for her sons, James and John (23 words; Matt 20:21). Unanswered because of wrong motive and not in harmony with God's plan (Matt 20:23).

15. Two blind men desire healing (27 words; Matt 20:30-33). Answered (Matt 20:34).

16. Jesus prays to be saved from death in the garden before He could die on the cross (62 words; Matt 26:39-44). Answered (Heb 5:7).

17. Jesus prays on the cross (9 words; Matt 27:46).

References to prayer (Matt 6:5-13; 7:7-11; Matt 14:23; 18:19-20; 21:22; 23:14).

Mark

1. A demon pleas for temporary freedom (31 words; Mark 1:23-24).

2. Jesus prays in healing a deaf mute (2 words-the shortest prayer; Mark 7:34). Answered (Mark 7:35).

References to prayer (Mark 1:35; 6:41,46; 9:23; 11:22-24).

John

1. Nobleman prays for the healing of child (7 words; John 4:49). Answered (John 4:50).

2. People pray for living bread (6 words; John 6:34).

3. Jesus prays at the resurrection of Lazarus (40 words; John 11:41-43). Answered (John 11:44).

4. Jesus prays for glorification (19 words; John 12:27-28). Answered (John 12:28).

5. Jesus prays for His disciples (638 words; John 17).

References to prayer (John 7:37-39; 14:12-15; 15:7,16; 16:23-26).

Finis Jennings Dake, *Dake's Annotated Reference Bible* (Lawrenceville, GA: Dake Bible Sales, 1963, 1991).

CHAPTER FIFTEEN

LUKE'S THEOLOGY OF PRAYER

A WINDOW THROUGH TIME

S. D. Gordon says of Jesus, "No man seems to have understood prayer, and to have prayed as did He ... A habit is an act repeated so often as to be done involuntarily; that is, without a new decision of the mind each time it is done. Jesus prayed. He loved to pray. Sometimes praying was His way of resting. He prayed so much and so often that it became a part of His life. It became to Him like breathing — involuntary."

There is no thing we need so much as to learn how to pray. There are two ways of receiving instruction; one, by being told; the other, by watching someone else. The latter is the simpler and the surer way. How better can we learn how to pray than by watching how Jesus prayed, and then trying to imitate Him? Not, just now, studying what He said about prayer, invaluable as that is, and so closely interwoven with the other; nor yet how He received the requests of men when on earth, full of inspiring suggestion as that is of His present attitude towards our prayers; but how He Himself prayed when down here surrounded by our same circumstances and temptations.

Gordon finds eleven significant prayer moments in the gospel of Luke, Paul's traveling companion. He suggests, that this a clue, not only to the prayer life of Jesus, but that of Paul.

In Luke 3, at the double baptism of Jesus, it is Luke that adds the not about Jesus "praying." It was while waiting in prayer that He received the gift of the Holy Spirit. He dared not begin His public mission without that anointing. It had been promised in the prophetic writings. And now, standing in the Jordan, He waits and prays until the blue above is burst through by the gleams of glory-light from the upper-side and the dove-like Spirit wings down and abides upon Him. Prayer brings power. Prayer is power. The time of prayer is the time of power. The place of prayer is the place of power. Prayer is tightening the connections with the divine dynamo so that the power may flow freely without loss or interruption.

In Luke 5, in a Galilean village, He is moved with the compassion that ever burned His heart. He had healed a badly diseased leper, who disregarded His express command and so widely published the remarkable healing that great crowds blocked Jesus' way in the village and compelled Him to go out to the country. Note what the Master does. A literal reading would be, "He was retiring in the deserts and praying," suggesting not a single act, but a habit over several days or weeks. Being constantly thronged, He had less opportunity to get alone, and yet more need, and so while He patiently continues His work, He also studiously seeks opportunity to retire at intervals from the crowds to pray.

Pressed by duties, by opportunities for service, by the great need around us, we are strongly tempted to give less time to the inner chamber, with the door shut. "Surely this work must be done," we think, "though it does crowd and flurry our prayer time some." "No," the Master's practice here says with intense emphasis. Not work first, and prayer to bless it. But the first place given to prayer and then the service growing out of such prayer will be charged with unmeasured power. The greater the outer pressure, the more jealously He guarded His prayer habit. The tighter the tension, the more time must there be for unhurried prayer.

In Luke 6, "It came to pass in these days that He went out into the mountains to pray, and He continued all night in prayer to God." This is the middle of the second year of His public ministry. Exasperating experiences with national leaders from Judea who had criticized and nagged at every turn, sowing seeds of skepticism had become common. On the day before He selected the twelve who would be leaders after His departure, He preached the mountain sermon. Wearied in spirit by the ceaseless hatred of His enemies, thinking of the serious work of the morrow, He knew where to find rest, and sweet fellowship, and a calming presence, and wise counsel. Turning His face northward, He sought the solitude of the mountain not far off for quiet meditation and prayer. Daylight gradually grew into twilight, and that yielded imperceptibly to the brilliant Oriental stars spraying down their lustrous firelight. And still He prayed, while the darkness below and the blue above deepened, and the stilling calm of God wrapped all nature around, and hushed His heart into a deeper peace. In the fascination of the Father's loving presence, He was utterly lost to the flight of time, but prayed on and on until, by and by, the earth had once more completed its daily turn, the gray streaks of dawn's light crept up the east, and the face of Palestine, fragrant with the deep dews of an eastern night, was kissed by a sun of a new day. And then, "when it was day," how quietly the narrative goes on, "He called the disciples and chose from them twelve." A great multitude of disciples and people came and He healed them all. And He opened His mouth and taught them - power came forth from Him." Is it any wonder, after such a night!

In Luke 9, near the Roman city of Caesarea Philippi, "He was praying alone, the disciples were with Him." He seemed to be drawing the twelve nearer to His inner life, trying to woo them into a love for the fascination of secret prayer. They would need to pray in the coming years when He was gone. He yearned for a closer fellowship with them. And there is no fellowship among men to be compared with fellowship in prayer.

Also in Luke 9, He spends His third recorded full night in prayer. This is the transfiguration scene, but it is Luke who explains that He went up into the mountain in order to pray, and that it was as He was praying as the fashion of His countenance was altered. Without stopping to study the purpose of this marvelous manifestation of His divine glory to the chosen three at a time when desertion and hatred were so marked, it is enough now to note the significant fact that it was while He was praying that the wondrous change came. Transfigured while praying! And by His side stood one who centuries before on the earth had spent so much time alone with God that the glory-light of that presence transfigured his face, though he was unconscious of it. A shining face caused by contact with God! Shall not we, to whom the Master has said, "follow Me," get alone with Him and His blessed Word, so habitually, with open or uncovered face, that is, with eyesight unhindered by prejudice or self-seeking, that mirroring the glory of His face we shall more and more come to bear His very likeness upon our faces? [II

Cor. 3:18]

In Luke 8, He had organized a band of men, sending them out in two's into the places he expected to visit. They had returned with a joyful report of the power attending their work; and standing in their midst, His own heart overflowing with joy, He looked up and, as though the Father's face was visible, spoke out to Him the gladness of His heart. He seemed to be always conscious of His Father's presence, and the most natural thing was to speak to Him. They were always within speaking distance of each other, and always on speaking terms.

In Luke 11, we read "It came to pass as He was praying in a certain place that when He ceased one of His disciples said unto Him, 'Lord, teach us to pray.'" Without doubt these disciples were praying men. He had already talked to them a great deal about prayer. But as they noticed how large a place prayer had in His life, and some of the marvelous results, the fact came home to them with great force that there must be some fascination, some power, some secret in prayer, of which they were ignorant. This Man was a master in the fine art of prayer. They really did not know how to pray, they thought. How their request must have delighted Him! At last they were being aroused concerning the great secret of power. May this simple recital of His habit of prayer move us to make the same earnest request, "Lord, teach me to pray."

In Luke 22, in the large upper room in Jerusalem, He is celebrating the Passover and initiating the new memorial feast. But even that hallowed hour is disturbed by the disciples' self-seeking disputes. With the great patience of great love, He gives them the wonderful example of humility recorded in John 13. Turning to Peter, He says, "Simon, Simon, behold

Satan asked to have you that he might sift you as wheat, but I have prayed for you that your faith fail not." He had been praying for Peter by name! Praying for others was one of His prayer habits, and He has not broken off that blessed habit yet. He is able to save to the uttermost them that draw near to God through Him seeing He ever lives to make intercession for them. His occupation now seated at His Father's right hand in glory is praying for each of us who trust Him - by name? Why not?

On the cross, of the seven sentences He spoke on the cross, three were prayers. Luke tells us that while the soldiers were driving the nails through His hands and feet, and lifting the cross into place, He, thinking even then not of self, but of others, said, "Father, forgive them, they know not what they do."

As the time of the evening sacrifice drew on, near the close of that strange darkness which overcast all nature, after a silence of three hours, He loudly sobbed out the piercing, heart-rending prayer, "My God, My God, why didst Thou forsake Me?" A little later, the triumphant shout proclaimed His work done, and then the very last word was a prayer quietly breathed out, as He yielded up His life, "Father, into Thy hands I commend My spirit." And so His expiring breath was vocalized into prayer.

Adapted from the work of S. D. Gordon, Taken from the Chapter: "Jesus' Habits of Prayer," *Quiet Talks On Prayer*, 1904.

CHAPTER 15

LUKE'S THEOLOGY OF PRAYER

P. Douglas Small

Prayer in Luke-Acts

Luke has been called 'the evangelist of prayer' among the gospel writers.[1] Both Matthew and Mark mention prayer, but not in the way Luke treats the subject. In Matthew, there are abundant mentions of prayer, but Luke's treatment of the prayer is unique. Matthew is the apologist to a Jewish audience. Mark, whose gospel some say is drawn from Peter, is an action narrative. Luke, written to a broader audience including both Jews and Gentiles, presents Jesus as the ultimate man, the son of man, and displays His humanity. He approaches prayer in a more systematic way than either Matthew or Mark. There is content in Matthew not found in Luke (Matthew 6:5-6; 18:19f; 21:22; 24:20), however, Luke has 59 percent more occurrences of prayer terminology than Matthew.[2] Luke's gospel begins with the account of Zacharias, the father of John the Baptist, praying at the altar of incense in the temple (1:10), and it ends, as it were with the answer to that prayer, the blessing of Jesus as He departs the earth (24:51-53). He frames his gospel in prayer.

---

1   W. Ott, *Gebet und Heil. Die Bedeutung der Gebetsparanese in der lukanischen Theologie* (Munchen, 1965), 13; See also: A. Hamman, *La Priere. I. Le Nouveau Testament*, (Tournai: 1959), 144.

2   O. G. Harris, Quoted by D. A. Carson, *Teach Us To Pray*, 58.

The New Age of Prayer

Of all the gospels, it is in the Luke-Acts narratives that we meet the clearest representation of the new age of prayer that comes with Christ.[3] We do not merely pray – because He prayed. The issue is not "Jesus had to pray to survive on earth, and if He had to pray, then where do we stand? How much more do we need to pray?" That may be true, but Luke offers us more than prayer as a desperate survival tactic. God has entered the world, and in the incarnation, He has united himself with man, and launched a new level of communion and fellowship with God not known since the fall of man. He came to the earth to pray. He began His ministry in prayer – and ended it in prayer, on the cross. In His ascension, He opened a highway to heaven, reconciling God to man, through the cross. He is now praying – in heaven. Therefore, prayer represents the present action of the newly redeemed and regenerated human. Christ has entered the most holy place in heaven, and He ever lives to make intercession for us. In one sense, we neither pray nor worship exclusively here on earth. Rather, we also worship in heavenly places. That is, Jesus has entered into heaven, into the throne room with His own blood. And now, in prayer, we enter into heaven after Him, with Him and through Him![4]

The most common Greek term for prayer, used in Luke-Acts forty-one times, is *proseúchomai,* a compound verb. The noun form, *proseuke,* is used twenty-two times.[5] It derives from *prós,* which means "towards or exchange." And also from *euxomai,* which means

---

3   Harvie Conn, *Luke's Theology of Prayer* (Christianity Today, December 22). Much of the material in this section is borrowed and adapted from Conn's incredible article.

4   Harvie Conn, *Evangelism: Doing Justice and Preaching Grace* (Zondervan, 1982).

5   Kyu Sam Han, *Theology of Prayer in the Gospel of Luke* (JETS 43; 2000), 675-693.

"to pray." Literally, it means an exchange between man and God. It means to interact with the Lord by exchanging human desires for His wishes as He imparts faith. Prayer is the context for "divine persuasion." What is often being changed – is us. Our perception. Our desires. Our longings. Our minds and hearts. Prayer is, as the great Christian, E. Stanley Jones would say, "an alignment!" It is not only the context for exchange – but change. Not only for conversation but for conversion.

The term *proseuchomai* occurs eighty-six times in the New Testament, and thirty-five of those occurrences are in Luke-Acts. It is closely related to *pistis* or faith. Faith grows with our deepening roots into and perception of '*the* faith' (Acts 6:5, 6; 14:22, 23; Eph. 6:16-18; Col 1:3, 4; II Thess. 3:1, 2; James 5:13-15; Jude 20). The other term Luke uses is *deesis*, which emphasizes our personal needs in prayer. *Proseuke* is more devotional, more worshipful,[6] and reserved only for God. The term *deesis* is also used of a human request from one man to another.

> **ACCENT**
>
> Charles Duncan was a pastor in Charleston, WV. He had underground stomach surgery and was suffering from peritonitis along with severe complications. He was also in a building program. He prayed, "Lord, let me live and finish that building!" His situation worsened. One night, he thought he had already died. He could see his own body behind him as he traveled to the Valley of Death. On each side of him were gray rocky walls. The sun had set as he entered a canyon with high walls. Suddenly he stopped. An inexplicable noise enveloped him. A voice explained, "This is the voice of the Lord's people praying for you!" These were people, many

---

6   Lindell Harris, "Prayer in the Gospel of Luke" (SWJT 10: 1967), 59-69.

he did not even know, from multiple churches, crying out to God in his behalf. In front of him there appeared a stream of water flowing from a solid rock. He observed a line of people leaving the fountain. A voice said, "Drink. The afflictions of the Lord's people are many, but for every sickness there is a cure." The scene changed again. He was in front of a large white oak with words stenciled into the bark, "You shall return to the road you have been traveling. And the way shall be profitable to you." Immediately, he began to mend. He was convinced, the prayers of God's people pulled him back from death to accomplish his mission.

Lucille Walker, *What To Do When You Pray* (Cleveland, TN: Pathway Press, 1998), 91-92.

Luke opens and closes his gospel with prayer. In Luke 1:10, the people are praying outside the temple prior to the angelic announcement of the birth of John to Zechariah. The last verse of the gospel is, (24:35), "And they stayed continually at the temple, praising God" (NIV). The book of Acts opens as did the gospels, with the 120 waiting on the coming of the Spirit in the Upper Room.

There are two stories at the beginning of both narratives. First, in Luke 1, Zechariah has a private prayer desire fulfilled. He is told by the angel, as he burns incense, that his wife Elizabeth will have a child. Yet, it is unlikely that the prayer of Zechariah in that hour was regarding his wife's barrenness. The people were outside "praying for the redemption of Israel" – and by implication, for the Messiah. They were praying big prayers. But that larger cause fulfilled Zechariah's personal desires. When private prayers are disconnected from kingdom purposes, they often go unanswered. But when we pray 'big picture' prayers, we find our petitions caught up in vigorous answers from heaven.

In Acts 1, the disciples wait, in simple obedience, not knowing what measurable outcome from their discipline might emerge.

They, like Zechariah, are simply burning incense. Suddenly, they are caught up in something larger than themselves. History pivots on the back of their obedience. Fire falls. Zechariah was silenced for God's glory and the confirmation of His will. These disciples, on the other hand, cannot but speak the wonderful works of God, and the resurrection message is confirmed before the nations. Small prayers go unanswered. Big prayers shake nations.

It is in Luke that we learn that Jesus was praying as He was baptized and as the Spirit descended (Lk. 3:21). It is only in Luke that we see the moment of prayer between the healing of the leper prior to the first major confrontation of Jesus with the Pharisees (Luke 5:16). Textually, the inclusion only makes sense as a declaration of the prayer habit of Jesus.[7] Interwoven between the scenes of His life, both positive and negative, are prayer moments.

Luke records nine prayers of Jesus, seven of which are unique to his writings. It is Luke that notes that Jesus spent the night in prayer before He called His disciples (Luke 6:12). It is only Luke that reveals the context of the question, "Who do men say that I am?" as happening in association with Jesus in prayer (Lk. 9:18). It is Luke who informs us that the purpose for going up the mountain when He was transfigured, with Peter and John watching, was to pray (Luke 9:28-29). It is Luke that gives us a note about the so-called 'Lord's Prayer,' one not offered by Matthew, that the prayer model came after He had taken His disciples away with Him to pray, and they requested of Him, "Teach us to pray!" (Luke 11:1). It is from the writings of Luke that we hear the parable of the friend in the middle who intercedes with a neighbor for bread for his indigent friend (Luke 11:5-8). It is Luke that relates the account of the widow who fearlessly haunts the hard-hearted judge until he relents and

---

7   P. T. O'Brien, *"Prayer in Luke-Acts"* (TB 24: 1973), 114; See also, Han, *"Theology,"* 681.

grants her relief from her adversary (Luke 18:1-8). And it is Luke who contrasts the prayer of the Pharisee and the publican.

"The Pharisee is pretending to himself and others that he is thanking God. In reality, in his prayer he only has himself and other human beings in view ... The Pharisee is not talking with God, whereas the publican with his petition for pardon, in awareness of his sin, is seeking to make contact with God."[8]

It is Luke who emphasizes the plea of Jesus to the disciples to pray in Gethsemane (Luke 22:40). And prayer is a prerequisite to their not falling into temptation, a test at least some of them arguably failed to pass with flying colors. The temptation is the entire dark trial into which they are entering, the crucifixion event. Their fate is tied to His. The term Luke uses, *akolouthein,* meaning a technical term, a compound word comprised of a particle of union with *keleuthos* (a road). They are on the same road. To be a disciple, means their fates are now bound together. This is the same term that is used when they left their nets – and followed Him. Only now, will they know the true significance of that decision. His appeal to pray is first for the immediate. All are in danger, not just Him, though they do not yet know that fact. But His prayer also regarded their own destiny beyond the crucifixion and ascension. In the endeavor to which they have been called, only prayer can sustain them.

Prayer – the Difference for Peter

It is Luke who describes the private moment between Jesus and Peter, in which the Lord reveals that He has prayed for Him. Peter's denial is yet to come (Luke 22:31-34). *"I have prayed for you that your faith may not fail" (v. 32).* Satan, Jesus knows by the Spirit, has desired to 'sift' him, or more literally 'to have him.' Evidently, Satan has

8   Oscar Cullman, *Prayer in the New Testament* (Minneapolis, MN: Fortress Press, 1994), 17.

not only laid claim to Judas, but also to Peter. The spiritual warfare swirling around the cross-event is colossal. Satan is not content to see Jesus on the cross, crucified. He desires in one fell-swoop to decimate the disciple band as well by captivating its leaders. Jesus effectively steps between Satan, the accuser of the brethren, and Peter. He does so as intercessor, to interrupt the desire and action of the Evil One. Some have suggested that the plural 'you' in verse 31 extends beyond Peter, and implies all the disciples, noting Peter's representative role. With the defection of Peter, the whole group may be in jeopardy. All may flee. What survives the cross, the advance of the gospel through the church, is on the back of these leaders. The primary targets are Peter and Judas (who you may recall, sat at the last supper in the place of honor),[9] into whom the Evil One entered (Luke 22:3; John 13:27). The goal of Satan was certainly to capture all twelve. The strategy was to do so by the fall or defection of key leaders. Note the prayer of Jesus, *"I have prayed for you, Simon, that your faith will not fail. So when you recover, strengthen the other disciples"* (God's

---

9   Only in retrospect, do we see Judas for the traitor he was. Never, except in retrospect, is there any indication of differentiation – in miracles, teaching, his following or dedication, etc. Judas, when he sat at the seat of honor at the right hand of Jesus on the night of the betrayal, did so without objection from the other disciples. Could it be, that Judas was in the beginning one of the more prominent of the twelve? And that only by his defection, do we see the moments of differentiation more clearly? And only by his defection is he demoted to last on the list? It is true, that Judas is never included in the inner circle – Peter, James and John. Traditionally, he is represented as 'the treasurer' of the group, although there is never any moment when Jesus looks to Judas for an account of funds. The 'money bag' may not be an indication of position, but more of a clue regarding character. In any respect, does it not strike you strange that Judas would sit at the right hand of Jesus, without objection? That no disciple would on the night of the betrayal would say, "Ah! I know who it is – it is Judas!" If indeed, Judas was more prominent among the twelve – then the loss of both he and Peter would have been devastating.

Word). The translations vary. The NIV says, *"And when you have turned back."* The NLT is thus, *"I have pleaded in prayer for you, Simon ... So when you have repented and turned to me again."* The NAS says, *"When once you have turned again."* The old King James, "When thou art converted." The ISV more simply, *"When you have come back."* And the Aramaic Bible in Plain English, *"When you are restored, confirm your brothers."* God's Word Translation reads, *"So when you recover."* Weymouth is more colloquial, but insightful, *"When at last you have come back to your true self, you must strengthen your brethren."*

The 'demand' is meant to stress the perimeters of Satan's activity. His rebellion seems like a wild-fire that will destroy the earth and possibly the universe – but the fire, despite the timber it now chars and the land it claims, is nevertheless contained. There is a fire-break over which it cannot leap. It is hot and intense, but it is, in the larger scope of things, not a challenge to heaven or to the ultimate purposes of God. Even Lucifer is regulated. He too must pray – he must 'ask.' Here he, in characteristic arrogance, 'demands' Peter. God will permit Peter to peer through the doorway of defection under the pressure of his own potential martyrdom. Jesus, simultaneously, will 'pray' for Peter, not that he is exempted *from* the temptation, but that *through it,* he triumphs.

The battle for the souls of the entire disciple band is won on the back of the intercessory prayer of Jesus. One defects – Judas. Another rallies after faltering - Peter. And his stability, his restoration, tied to intercessory prayer, is the key to survival of the apostolic party. O the difference wrought by prayer. No reasoning with Peter on that fateful night could have substituted for the victory won by the prayerful blood, sweat and tears in Gethsemane. No face-to-face exhortation or encouragement would have been the equal of intercessory prayer. This victory had to be won in prayer. If the choice were – Jesus with Peter; or Jesus with the Father, in behalf of Peter – which do we usually assume to be the most efficacious?

Despite His own coming trial, the cross, He was also praying for them. Here, even in the darkest hour of His life, the prayer life of Jesus is bigger than Himself. He prays for His friends. In Luke, we are told that Jesus prayed – three times, bracketed by the admonition to His disciples, *"Pray that you enter not into temptation."* Had I been in that moment, knowing that Peter – and another follower was on the edge of defection – I might have abandoned prayer and resorted to personal one-on-one counseling, exhortation, attempts at encouragement, rational and argumentative intervention, head-to-head confrontation. Jesus does none of those things. He demonstrates that prayer is the more powerful choice, that it is greater than personal argument or influence. Only prayer can save Peter. Jesus prays. Peter sleeps. Thus, Peter falters, but he does not fall. The prayer of Jesus has kept him.

Praying in the Spirit

In Luke, Jesus prays as the prototype of a new era of prayer. He prays in the Spirit (Luke 10:21). Luke is demonstrating that prayer 'in the Spirit' is indispensable for the church. They must tarry for the coming of the Spirit, to be endued, clothed, wrapped in the Spirit, to be empowered with a new capacity of language by the Spirit – in order that they might also pray in the Spirit, following His example.

Jesus does not merely pray for any given situation. His prayers are not so much rooted in this or that moment in time, a reaction to this or that challenge. These prayers transcend time and space. They are eschatological in nature. Cosmic in scope. So, He teaches His disciples to pray, "Thy kingdom come, thy will be done." This is earth shaped by prayer. It is the opening, from earth's side, of a doorway to another world. It is asking God to break into our time-space sphere to right the wrongs, re-center creation by redemption, and fundamentally reorder this earthly sphere. For Jesus, prayer is eschatological activity. The message of John the Baptist is clear, "The Kingdom of God has come!" It is the same message that inaugurates the ministry of Christ. It is the closing message of His ministry, the call to preach the 'gospel of the kingdom.' It is the message about which He speaks to His disciples in the forty days between His resurrection and the ascension. It opens and closes the book of Acts. In Christ, the kingdom of God is inaugurated in the earth. In the church, its expansion continues. And prayer is the means by which the kingdom is mediated here and now.

Prayer – An Eschatological Sign

In the parable of the widow, we have the extraordinary question of Jesus at the end of the story, one that appears to be completely out of context. "When the son of man comes will He find faith in the earth?" The prayer persistence of the widow is an eschatological issue. Faith survives and the kingdom moves forward on the back of persistent prayer. Jesus has come – but the Righteous Judge, God – the Father, has not yet acted on the basis of the cross to utterly redeem the earth and give it as a prize to the Lord. Prayer lives in the tension between the two ages – the kingdom of God has come, but it has not yet fully come! The right of redemption has been accomplished, but the full execution of it has not yet been consummated. We watch and pray. That is, we maintain the vigil of prayer. We assume regularly, and frequently, our positions with regard to the redemptive interest of God, wherever God might have placed us. We pray to the Judge – "get justice for us!"

In the coming of Christ, all that the prophets had longed for was begun. Not consummated, not yet fully manifest, but the work was started. The day of the Lord has dawned. In the early verses of Luke, we find Zechariah, the father of John, the Baptist, burning incense, and praying. Outside, at the

---

ACCENT

"This Christian life is one of constant growth and advancement. To stand still is to die, so we must press onward in order to advance ... if we do not walk in the light, we are liable to lose out ... Humility, too, I think plays a great part in the cost of advancement ... humility is the state or quality of being humble in spirit, freedom from pride and arrogance. If we possess humility we do not think too highly of ourselves and we are modest and unpretending, so let us also humble ourselves ... Exaltation comes when the heart is ready. It is God who lifts up and when we are able to stand God will exalt us ... God does all things well. One reason we are in Bible School is for advancement. We want to learn how to advance so we will be more efficient workers for Jesus in the future. Please pray for me that I may be faithful and always be found working for Him." – A Bible Training School (BTS) student, Eva Mae Whittington (Lefever), Anderson, S. C. Note: BTS is the forerunner to Lee University; and Eva Mae Whittington became Eva Mae Lefevor, of the famed Lefevor Trio, great gospel singers.

Evangel, December 16, 1933; 9.

hour of prayer, the people have gathered. Suddenly, in the holy place, next to the altar of incense, an angel appears (Luke 1:10). The declaration involves the birth of the forerunner, the turning of the hearts of the fathers, a great ingathering – and more. The curse that Malachi warned about will be averted. The Father's heart has turned. He has sent His son. In Luke, at the altar, history turns – in the coming of John the Baptist, the forerunner, and Jesus, the Christ.

As Jesus steps into the baptismal waters, He does so praying. This is not a mere ceremony. This is the moment when heaven will open to accommodate a new level of divine interaction between men and God, not possible since the fall. He emerges from the waters – a symbol of death, as the Ark emerged from the flood waters. Suddenly, the Spirit descends (Luke 3:21). Just as a dove had marked the transition from the earlier pre-flood era (Gen. 8:8), to the time of the patriarchs, now there is another eschatological sign. A new age has dawned. Luke uses the present participle *proseukomenou*, praying, in contrast to the aorist *baptisthentos*, baptized. Here is the point. The baptism was over. It was an event. But Jesus was still praying. And the coming of the Spirit is not in reference to His baptism as much as to His *praying.*[10]

There is arguably a parallel between the prayer at His baptism and that prayed from the cross. The baptism was symbolic and the cross was its fulfillment. At baptism, He died. He laid down His life. He surrendered to the Father's work. He committed himself fully to the Father and to the task at hand. But the full meaning of the baptism, the ultimate implication, is only clear following His death, burial and resurrection. What sustains Him between these two points – the symbolic death and resurrection of baptism; and the literal death and

---

10 John Martin Creed, *The Gospel According to St. Luke* (London: McMillan, 1953), 57.

resurrection, the cross and the empty tomb - is prayer.[11]

From the baptismal waters, Jesus moves to the wilderness for prayer. Prior to the cross, He withdraws to the garden for prayer. His life and mission is lived within these moments. Prayer buttresses His ministry launch and its conclusion. Between the baptism and the wilderness experience, Luke embeds the genealogy of Jesus in his gospel narrative. It seems a bit odd to place it here. Matthew's genealogy reaches back to Abraham, emphasizing the Jewishness of Jesus. Luke, however, goes back to Adam.

The point of Luke's genealogy cannot be missed. Jesus is the new Adam, the last Adam. He is not the second, for there could never be a third. He is the last hope for humanity. He is not merely the Savior of the Jews, but of mankind. He is the "son of Adam, the son of God." He enters the wilderness as one elected by God (Isaiah 42:1). The forty days are a staple biblical numeral – they reference the testing of Israel in the wilderness. But, He will not die there. He will not succumb to temptation, longing for Egypt's bread. He will not test God, as Israel did. He will not bow before the idol nor yet Lucifer. He will regain the right to paradise lost, and do so in behalf of all of humanity. But this victory will be won in one posture, not of the body, but of the heart, the posture of prayer. For forty days, He will pray! Persistently pray. Passionately pray. He will subdue the flesh, making it a servant. Subordinate ego. And keep His spirit unpolluted. He is the new Moses. And around Him, He will gather twelve leaders, twelve witnesses to His work, twelve apostles. But again, this choice is made only after He continued all night in prayer (Luke 6:12). We often seek to undergird our work with prayer. And in that way, we separate the work itself from prayer. The work of Jesus was prayer! And all He did was out of prayer. There is no way to

---

11   Oscar Cullmann, *Baptism in the New Testament* (Naperville, IL: Alec R. Allenson, 1950), 19.

detach prayer from what He did.

Looking ahead, He could see the cross coming. At Caesarea Philippi, He would attempt to initiate His disciples into the radical idea of His coming death and burial, His resurrection and ascension. But, He knew that such a profound shift in their thinking was a matter of the heart. Luke notes that the disclosure came out of a time of prayer (Luke 9:18). Indeed, He had gone up the mountain to pray. We rarely pray with such a weighty eternal perspective. On the occasion of His transfiguration, it is Luke who reveals the contents of the communication with Moses and Elijah – *"His departure, which he was to accomplish at Jerusalem"* (Luke 9:31). Like Frodo with the ring, Jesus and His destiny are irrevocably linked. At every turn, He sees the inevitable. He sees it and feels it when others are oblivious to it.

Pray until you are all broken up with strong crying and tears over a lost and ruined world. Then pray right on until you can rejoice at the thought of the blood of Jesus being sufficient for all who will accept Him.

Evangel, March 15, 1901, 3.

As a result, there is a constant new triangulation – Jesus, the Father, and destiny or the mission, all wrapped in prayer. He moves, under the watchful care of the Father, in the context of a prayerful connection, toward His destiny. His prayer life was not a series of urgent crises-driven-moments. They were not emergency prayers, narrowly focused on some isolated experience. He was moving toward His destiny. He had come to alter the dynamic between heaven and earth, to elevate man to a new position, a new relationship with God. To invite him into the triangle of prayer. So, a new way of praying was born in the process – we too pray now to the Father, of course in the name of Jesus, and by the enabling of the Spirit. And we also pray to the end that we fulfill our destiny, and finish the work of Christ.

The transfigurations of Christ and of Moses are two prayer events that stand together. They are like distant peaks, though seperated by many years, perspective draws them together. On the mountain, after being in the presence of God, the face of Moses had shone so brightly with God's glory that he was forced to wear a veil (Exodus 34:29-35). He, the lawgiver, was the architect of a new era for Israel. They were in their formative season of transition – from a status of slaves to freedom, from bondage to becoming to an independent nation. Moses leads this exodus, it is what he was both born and delivered to do. Now in the New Testament era, Moses, along with Elijah, appear on the Mount of Transfiguration with Jesus as if in a conference. Jesus, in prayer, is transfigured as Moses had been. The stories are bound together. A new age is breaking forth, one that supersedes the old. A new lawgiver is here, greater than Moses. The ultimate prophet has come, the one greater than Elijah. A new exodus is afoot. New fire will fall. This is what Jesus came into the earth to do – to deliver, to save, to establish a new community of witnesses, a new nation, to build His Church, and to inaugurate His Kingdom in the earth.

The balance of relationship and mission must not be missed. Relationship, of course, is permanent. Without it, there is no successful mission; but mission, in the context of history, is no secondary matter. We sadly fail at keeping the balance. Mission is often given preeminence and the result is that we lose God in the attempt to fulfill the thing to which he called us. The triangulation draws constant calibration – God, us and mission, in a context of prayerful dependence.

The Model Prayer

When the disciples asked Jesus to teach them to pray, there were already models for prayer. John had evidently given one or more of these models to his disciples. We know from history, that there were other common prayers utilized in that day.[12] The community at Qumran had prescribed prayers as well, as did the Pharisees. The disciples had been with Jesus long enough to realize that what He was doing, teaching, advocating, did not fit any of the prayer models they knew. In one sense, they were asking, "Give us a model for prayer that is congruent with your message and ministry." Help us learn to pray, like men waiting on and working toward the in-breaking of a new eschatological day. The high point of the prayer is the anticipation of the coming kingdom, tied to the sacredness of 'the Name!' There is a concern for sustenance, until the kingdom fully comes. There is the recognition of the need for on-going reconciliation, with God and men, and the draw upon the grace of God. He is good – He gives us daily bread. He is gracious – He forgives. And there is the recognition of the need to be preserved from the apostasy of the present hour, from the Evil One. He is good, gracious – and He guides, protecting us, delivering us. Only in dependence on Him do we defeat the devil. But in the end, it is the kingdom for which the prayer longs.

Prayer – the Legacy

The entire life of Christ was one of prayer – from the beginning to the end. In the garden, in the final moments of His natural life, He was in the greatest struggle He had yet faced. He perspired. His sweat became bloody. Only Luke revealed the presence of an angel, strengthening Him. On the cross, He prayed. Two of the three last words are prayers, only recorded by Luke (23:34). The writer of Hebrews declares that through His prayer, He is raised from the

---

12 Scribner, *New Testament Theology* (1971), 170.

dead – "He offered up prayers and supplications, with loud cries and tears, to Him who was able to save Him from death" (Hebrews 5:7).

"More compelling than anything Jesus taught about prayer by precept was what He taught by His prayer practice. He depended upon it in the great soul-moving experiences of His life ... whether He needed courage, strength, or fellowship with the Father, prayer was His reliance, His very mood."[13]

The present ministry of Christ is intercession. "He ever lives to make intercession ..." Now, in this present moment, He prays for believers from heaven (Rom. 8:34; Heb. 7:24). He prays that we not fall in the midst of temptation or fail due to weakness. If we sin, He pleads our case before the Father (I John 2:1), joining our repentant plea for forgiveness (I John 1:9). As Christ prays for us and with us in heaven, the Holy Spirit aids our praying on the earth (Rom. 8:26-27).

Our forgiveness in Christ is both legal and forensic. We have been forgiven – all our sin! We are promised, there is no condemnation to those who are 'in Christ' (Rom 8:1). Christ has paid the death penalty for our sin, all our sins (II Cor. 5:21; I Peter 2:24). We will not have to pay a death penalty – for past, present or future sin. There is not another sacrifice for sin.

An inner change has come. We are no longer sinners – but

Dietrich Bonheoffer said, "In the end, there are only two possibilities of encountering Jesus: either man must die or he kills Jesus."

Bonhoeffer, from "Christology," Quoted by Charles Ringma, Seize the Day with Dietrich Bonhoeffer (Colorado Springs, Colorado: Pinion Press; 2000), See entry for January 21.

13 Irwin Ross Beiler, *Studies in the Life of Jesus* (New York: Abingdon-Cokesbury Press, 1936), 181.

saints. We may sin, but we do not practice sin. While there is no longer a death penalty for confessed and forgiven sin, there are still consequences. And while a sin does not mean that God disinherits us as sons, since we now have a legal standing in grace, there are other concerns. Sin still contaminates. It still carries the sting of death. Sinful actions can have deadly consequences. It must be excised. Confession is the means by which we acknowledge before God our awareness of the toxic nature of our actions, of how they offend the holiness of God, of how they violate the essence of who He is and who we are called to be. The Greek word confess is *homologeo*, meaning to say the same thing, in this case, about sin and what God says about it.

CHAPTER SIXTEEN

PRAYER IN ACTS

A WINDOW THROUGH TIME

In some cities, the number of people living in slum-like conditions or sleeping on the streets is half to two-thirds. Seventy-five percent of Calcutta lives in overcrowded housing with 57 percent of families living in one room. An estimated one million live on the streets.

It is the church that first touched the marginalized in culture. Hospitals, schools, orphanages, homes for the needy, care for the dying, ministry to the ailing – all these were begun by the church.

"The first blow against pagan racial and social barriers was struck at the communion table, where master and slave, women and men, Jew and Gentile sat together around a common table and celebrated the same salvation."

Barnabus is often seen in the shadow of Paul. Actually, he is mentioned twenty-two times in Acts. His name means "son of consolation" and points to his gift as a unifier, a healer and agent of reconciliation. He was a man of mercy. It was Barnabus who first took a chance, and believed the conversion story of Paul, introducing him to the apostolic leaders. He gave Paul his first ministerial job at Antioch. It was Barnabus, not Paul, who was named as the leader of that unique apostolic duo. E. Stanley Jones calls the pair, the love and truth apostles. Barnabus was love. Paul was truth. Mercy needs truth; and truth needs mercy.

CHAPTER 16

PRAYER IN ACTS

P. Douglas Small

Someone has said that in the gospels we have what Jesus did in His body on the earth. And in Acts, we have the record of what God does in the body of Jesus, the corporate church. It is still Jesus at work, by the agency of the Spirit, the 'Ghost.' And all that happens is evidence that Jesus is alive, that He has risen from the dead, still working in the earth (Acts 1:11). His followers had seen His life, His example, so they "devoted themselves to prayer." Prayer is the link between the Lord, now interceding in heaven, and His bride partner on the earth. It aligns them. It allies them. It partners them. It informs and empowers them. It is not the apostles that are in charge of the Church. It is the Holy Spirit. And His voice is discerned in prayer – corporate prayer. The church in Acts is a praying church – and we should make the point, that a church that is not a praying church is not an Acts kind of Church. It has departed from the pattern. The triangle of the Church, the leadership of the Holy Spirit and prayer are incontrovertible. Any other formula and you have something other than the pattern of Acts.

In prayer, a replacement for Judas is sought. In prayer, the Holy Spirit descends. On their way to the hour of prayer, the lame man is healed (Acts 3). In prayer, the church gathers strength to face the rising hostility to their message. It is to prayer and the word, that the apostles recommit themselves in the face of division. It is prayer

– 'Behold, he prays!' – that is the first evidence of change in Saul of Tarsus. And into a season of prayer and heart-searching, God sends Ananias, and Saul is filled with the Spirit. It is at the sound of prayer, from the little house of Mary (Acts 12:12), that God sends an angel to deliver Peter from prison to the front door. It is into a gathering or prayer, that God reveals His will for the apostolic team of Barnabas and Saul (Acts 13:1-3).

As in the ministry of Jesus, the church proclaims the message – from city to city. The sick are healed. The dead are raised. Miracles abound. There are dreams and visions. Exorcisms. Angelic activity. The prayer here is not pietistic or primarily devotional. It is tied to the redemptive action of God in history. God has come in Christ. And there continue to be sovereign touching-downs of God. Kingdom manifestations. The kingdom has not fully come. The manifestations are here and there, then and now. But they are in texture and message representative of the same kingdom.

Someone has said, "Prayer has a way of floating away from the center, of becoming peripheral to the heart of things."[1] It is a way of tidying up our busy lives, or cleaning our spiritual glasses for greater clarity, or being renewed for the 'real work.' Daniel Poling has observed that Christianity, when it looks for roots, rarely looks to prayer as the root of reformation. It sees the root as more academic, more ideological, as sociological distress over Rome's excuses. It is always a mistake to minimize the power and role of prayer.

Corporate Prayer in Acts

Acts begins as a prayer meeting. It is into a corporate prayer meeting that the Spirit descends. The book of Acts is decorated with corporate prayer gatherings. They keep regular hours of prayer – the

1 Harvie Conn, *Evangelism: Doing Juxtice and Preaching Grace* (Zondervan Pub. House, 1982), 74.

Holy Spirit comes at 9:00 AM in the morning, an established hour of prayer. Twice the evening hour of prayer, 3:00 PM, is mentioned (3:1; 10:3, 10). Peter also prayed at noon (10:9). And the church interceded at night, perhaps, through the night (12:5-6), as did Paul and Silas (16:25).

Luke-Acts: The Prayer Link

There appear to be deliberate parallels between Luke-Acts.

- Immediately after His baptism, Jesus prays and the Holy Spirit descends on Him(Luke 3:21). Likewise, the first order of business in Acts is prayer (Acts 1:14) before the descent of the Spirit upon them (2:1-4). In Acts 8:15, Peter and John pray for the Samaritans to receive the Holy Spirit. The apostles lay hands on them and the Holy Spirit descends (8:17).

- Jesus prayed before the choice of the Twelve (Luke 6:12); the early church too prays before selecting Matthias (Acts 1:24).

- Jesus, at the point of His death, prays that His enemies may be forgiven (Luke 21:34); Stephen, in the midst of his stoning, cries in a loud voice, "Lord, do not hold this sin against them" (Acts 7:60).

- And as Jesus offered the 'evening prayer', committing His spirit, in the words of the Psalmist, to the Father's care (Luke 23:46), so the first martyr calls upon the Lord Jesus and cries, "Receive my spirit" (Acts 7:59).

The point of Luke is that the disciples, the church is following the pattern of Jesus. They continued their connection to the temple, as He had done (3:1; 22:17; 21:27). They prayed at the breaking of bread, as He had done (27:35). And the praying was not perfunctory. There was a deep commitment to discernment in association with the apostolic sending of Barnabas and Saul, a dedicated season of prayer with fasting (13:1-3f). Peter prostrated himself in prayer before praying for Tabitha (9:40). And when he was in prison, facing death, after the martyrdom of James, one can only imagine the passion involved in prayer (12:5, 12). Paul prayed at Troas, and is pictured in kneeling form after he addresses them (20:36; 21:5). "Prayer is not regarded merely as important, but as an apostolic priority; the seven are chosen so that the apostles will not be distracted from their prayer and their 'service of the word'" (6:2-4).[2]

In Acts 2:42, the new converts are noted to continue in "the prayers." In Acts 4, as threats grow, and the potential for violence intensifies, the church gathered to prayer corporately. And they essentially prayed Scripture, anchoring their plea to Psalm 2. They did not pray to be extricated from harm's way, but rather, that with the escalating potential for danger, they be given boldness. They do not position themselves as powerless victims, but rather, as being targets of anger against Christ. The entire matter is only another opportunity for God to show that He is real and that Jesus is gloriously alive. What faith!

In the Old Testament, there were festival days of prayer loaded with liturgical form. These were 'days' of prayer and spiritual reflection. The pattern of regular times of prayer and the use of prayer forms probably continued into the New Testament era. The Upper Room experience was a formal 'Feast' day (Acts 2); as was Passover and the evening of spontaneous and passionate prayer time in Gethsemane. Further, Peter and John were on their way to the 'hour of prayer' at the Temple when the healing of the lame man occurred (Acts 3f). Jesus is thought to have gone to Jerusalem for as many as three Passovers. Prayer may have been coupled with fixed times and customs, and prayer forms and themes probably informed their praying. Forms threaten authenticity and degenerate to

---

2   M. M. B. Turner, "Prayer in the Gospels and Acts," D. A. Carson, *Teach Us To Pray*, 72.

religion when they are engaged as thoughtless habit. In the monastic era, hours of prayer were prescribed. Today, we know little about extended times of prayer as in the Upper Room. Such multi-day prayer experiences, if embraced, would allow us to detach from the frenzied pace of our world, to celebrate the singular honor deserved by God. They encourage us to enter His rest – to 'come apart' before we come apart. But human nature, being what it is, tends to make even the holy habit, routine and common, then dreary and deadly. Engaged in the habit, without employing the heart, the relationship languishes, leaving the deceptive shell of religion.

Sustained by Prayer

When Peter is imprisoned after the death of James, there is another corporate prayer gathering. The Lord hears the prayers of the church, sends an angel, and releases Peter from prison (Acts. 12:12-17). It is into a corporate prayer and worship event that the Holy Spirit speaks and the apostolic ministry of Barnabas and Saul (Paul), is birthed (Acts 13).

The interjection of prayer moments in Luke's record is clearly a point he desires to make – the church was sustained by prayer. It is the means by which God guides His people. It is the context in which He reveals himself as powerfully present. It is the most important posture of the church to reveal to God its desire to hear His voice and invite His continued intervention. "Peter ... knelt down and prayed" and Dorcas was raised from the dead (9:40). And "many believed in the Lord" (9:42). "Paul visited him and prayed ... and healed him," a reference to the father of Publius (28:8). The result here was a blessed and abundant departure by the apostolic team as they traveled onward to Rome (28:9f). The miraculous was a sign of God's approval. It drew attention to the claims of the risen Christ.

Prayer and the Gospel Advance

One of the greatest miracles in Acts is sociological and theological. It was the embrace of Gentiles into the Church. This was nothing short of miraculous. And the incident was tied to a revelation given to Peter *in prayer*. Cornelius, a devout god-fearer, was said to have '*prayed constantly* to God' (v. 2). In answer to his petition, offered at 3:00 PM, the hour of Jewish prayer, Cornelius was directed by an angel to send for Peter. And Peter, on the following day, at noon, on a roof-top, was given a revelation to accept the overture by Cornelius and respond positively. He went obediently, but also wisely taking witnesses with him. And as he shared with the gathered household of Cornelius, 'the Holy Spirit falls' (10:4). When questioned by his peers, his response was to recount the entire incident and ask, "How could I withstand the Spirit?"

Jewish Christians continued to observe customary hours of prayer (Acts 2:1, 15; 3:1; 10:9; see also 21:20-26). In times of crisis, the church gathered to pray (Acts 4:24-31; 12:5). It was *to prayer and the word* that the disciples felt they should give themselves (Acts 6:5). Paul labored in prayer (Rom. 15:30; Col. 2:1; 4:12). Prayer was a chief feature of public worship. Today, in Pentecostal churches, aside from 'prayer requests' or 'elder's prayer' for personal needs, prayer is virtually neglected (Acts 2:42; I Tim. 2:1-8). Oswald Chambers observed that to "refuse to pray unless it thrills or excites us" and we might add – ingratiates us in some way by meeting some personal desire or request "is the most intense form of spiritual selfishness."[3] Chambers reminds us, "It is the laboring person who makes the ideas of the genius possible."[4]

"The whole of the Pauline and Johannine writings and most

---

3   Leonard Allen, *The Contemporaries Meet the Classics on Prayer* (West Monroe: LA; Howard Publishing Company, 2003), 258.
4   Ibid.

others in the New Testament, present prayer in connection with their theology, but on the other hand their theology is rooted in prayer."[5] Further, "New Testament prayer is rooted in the Old Testament."[6] It borrows the language of the Old Testament, both the prayerful concepts and even the prayers embedded in the text. It borrows Jewish prayer habits. In the letters of Paul, praise and thanksgiving are dominate. These are traceable to the psalms.

Corporate Prayer

In a highly individualist culture, rabidly so, we fail to see the importance of corporate prayer. Corporate sin is not even on our radar screen. Families sin. As do cities. And nations. As well as churches. Individuals can intercede, but only the corporate entity can appropriately rectify the wrong done by the corporate entity. This is why the solemn assembly is such an important concept. It is the act of a corporate body acting before God in its own behalf, asking to be allowed to continue as a distinct entity.

The good news is that we have – for individuals and nations, families and churches, cities and people groups – a covenantal mediator, Jesus Christ. And yet, that does not dismiss either the need for churches to gather to pray and repent, or for cities and nations to do the same. Nor does it negate the need for individuals to pray for others. Indeed, the mediatorial role of Christ is to be replicated by every believer, in behalf of other believers, and even for corporate entities.

Corporate prayer experiences should stretch us to pray beyond ourselves. Prayer connections with other believers can sustain us, grow us, move us to pray in ways and about things we might ordinarily

---

5   Oscar Cullman, *Prayer in the New Testament* (Minneapolis, MN: Fortress Press, 1994), xiv.
6   Ibid..

ignore. Believers belong in a body! Sheep alone don't survive. And we need to pray together, for one another, and do so often. Corporate calls on us to agree, it fosters unity in prayer, it mitigates against our individual wandering hearts. It is the context in which we grow to stand "firm in one spirit" and strive "side by side for the faith" (Phil. 1:27).

Theological Perspective

Turner notes four features of the prayer motif in Acts.

1. The Church stands in continuity with Israel – as 'the Israel of fulfillment.' She is completing Israel's mission. Ancient promises are being fulfilled, and these are inclusive of Gentiles (3:25f; 15:14-19; 28:28; Luke 2:30f).

2. There is a new Christological center to the prayers. Jesus is their Savior (4:12), the very source of life (3:15; 5:31), the grantor of forgiveness, pointing to His new high priestly and judicial role (5:31; 10:42), through His blood (20:27f), and He is recognized in heaven as 'Lord' – who sends forth the Spirit (2:33), and on whose name all must call to be saved (2:17-39). Prayer is not only offered *through* Him, but *to* Him (7:59; 9:10-16). There is a radically new paradigm in prayer. To a man, and through man, a priest – but not one on the earth.

3. Prayer has a new prophetic dimension available to all, by the poured forth Spirit, promised by Joel. All believers may be filled with the Spirit, pray with and by the enabling of the Spirit, indeed, in the Spirit. This is new! The Spirit worked in the Old Testament, His coming in Acts 2 is not new. What is new is that He now operates, for this season, out of and in conjunction with the Office of Christ, the resurrected Lord, to enable the bride partner in fulfilling her mission. By prayer and the Spirit, there is a new order of communion and communication possible never before – not since the fall.

4. "At almost every important turning in the narrative of God's redemptive action we find a mention of prayer." Prayer guides the Church in the critical fulfillment of its mission. [7]

---

7 Turner, 73-74.

CHAPTER SEVENTEEN

SURPRISES IN THE BOOK OF ACTS

A Window Through Time

In the March 15, 1910 Evangel, there is a wonderful and sweet note about prayer, entitled "A Pentecostal Shower." In fact, the simple account of afternoon grace is the lead story. Thursday afternoon was the occasion of a regular prayer gathering for a number of Cleveland women. The report noted that "God has blessedly noticed them at different times, and favored them with Pentecostal showers." On the afternoon in focus, they met on the same street where the editorial office at the Evangel was located. Tomlinson, who probably wrote the article, noted that the sound of the praying women could be heard, their doors being open. He records, that the staff was busy preparing the paper, but he regarded what happened as 'Divine Providence.'

"We were very busy preparing matter for the paper, when suddenly a sound was heard just outside the door, and six of the good sisters filed into our office. Two more soon made their appearance and came into the room reeling under the power of the Spirit. The fire began to spread, and the power began to fall, and a precious refreshing shower fell copiously upon everyone in the room. One shower over, but another followed, and another, and another. Amid prayers, tears, tongues, interpretations and shouts of praise, the glory of God filled the room. A new zeal and courage fastened upon us."

Suddenly, the main thing was no longer the main thing. At times, we need the Lord to interrupt us and remind us that 'the thing' we are doing is connected to something larger. If we lose focus, if we busy ourselves in the minutiae, the mundane, we are diminished. Suddenly reenergized, Tomlinson passionately pens, "The fire must spread. The time is short. The people who are in darkness must hear the message. Hurry! Hurry! We can't spread the gospel and the Pentecostal truth too rapidly. Who will go?" And then he adds a wonderful line, adopted from a parable of Jesus, "Who will not go for the penny? Eleventh hour laborers. Untrained, but full of faith and the Holy Ghost."

Among these early Pentecostals, there was always time – for prayer. Time for divine interruptions. Nothing we do is more important than entertaining God's Presence. One wonders just what the 'headline' for the March 15 issue might have been. A prayer meeting, a refreshing shower, demanded a new headline. What is even more stunning is the simplicity of these early pioneers; their hunger for God; the manner in which they honored and revered moments with the Spirit; their openness to prayer. For them, prayer was not a disruption or a disturbance! The interval that it created gave birth to a refreshing and a new focus for that issue of the publication.

A. J. Tomlinson, Editor, "A Pentecostal Shower," *Church of God Evangel* [Periodical], (Cleveland, TN: Church of God; March 15, 1910; p. 1.

CHAPTER 17

SURPRISES IN THE BOOK OF ACTS

P. Douglas Small

"Beware in your prayers, above everything else, of limiting God, not only by unbelief, but by fancying that you know what He can do. Expect unexpected things 'above all that we ask or think,'" so urged Andrew Murray.

Pastor Joseph Smale led First Baptist Church of Los Angeles in 1905. He was hungry for the kind of revival that was sweeping Wales. In fact, he visited there to meet with Evan Roberts, one of the leaders of that revival movement and to observe the spiritual and social impact firsthand. There, the whole nation seemed to be breathless as a result of a visitation of God. He longed for Los Angeles to experience a taste of what God was doing in the nation where some 100,000 had come to Christ in less than a year. Cultural values had been recalibrated. Crime had fallen. Bars had closed. Foul language had virtually disappeared. A nation had been spiritually renewed.

Smale challenged his church to pray. For fifteen weeks they sought God fervently, but then congregational resistance surfaced. Pastor Smale was forced to resign or abandon his revival quest in that congregation. But he would not give up on the city, so he started a new work. Sadly, that work would also fail as the vehicle for a city-shaking revival. Still, a few among the group he served made their way to prayer meetings that were by then being conducted on Bonnie Brae Street.

And surprise. Revival came there. God's ways are not our ways.

Miles away in Texas, and seemingly unrelated to events in Southern California, William Seymour, the son of a Louisiana slave was also hungry for God. With a badly scarred face and blindness in one-eye from a near fatal bout with smallpox, God had spared him with destiny in mind, and he remained undaunted. His appearance was not commanding. He held no social or educational advantage. In fact, he was arguably decidedly disadvantaged. A black man only one generation removed from slavery, partially blind and marked from his battle with death itself, one that he refused, by the grace of God, to lose – he was resolute.

He knew he needed education. He found the Houston Bible School of Charles Parham hoping to be trained for ministry there. Parham was one of the early theological architects of the holiness-Pentecostal movement. But Parham's racist deference forced Seymour outside the classroom. Parham saw his hunger and allowed him to sit 'outside' and listen, but not alongside the white students. Grace gave Seymour the humility to make spiritual growth more important than personal affirmation.

Surprise again. He wasn't the one outside. No one remembers the students inside that classroom. Even Parham was provided only a sidebar in the historical narrative that would follow. But no one would forget the humble Seymour. He would soon be at the epicenter of an awakening that would shake a deeply racist city, Los Angeles, then America and then the world. God has an extraordinary sense of humor. Most expected someone with Parham's note and prestige, his biblical depth, to preside over the new Pentecost. Surprise! God chooses differently and sovereignly.

With no clue of his destiny, Seymour traveled to Los Angeles to preach in a small holiness church with the idea of becoming its pastor. One sermon and he was locked out of the church. Locked out of his future. Locked out of a new opportunity. Locked out of his first pastorate. Surprise of all surprises. He was being locked in. He would not recognize it on that disappointing day. Anticipating acceptance and a new home at the end of his thousand mile journey, instead, he tasted the bitterness of rejection. Yet, had the church received him, had he settled there – he would have missed the moment God had planned for him. The closed door of the little church was only one side of a larger door, one that opened to the world. Almost immediately, Seymour was involved in the radically integrated house-church prayer gatherings on Bonnie Brae Street. Soon, sizeable crowds demanded another location.

> ## ACCENT
>
> Jewel was a child of five, and the sister of J. H. Walker. Their father was away when Jewel had a deadly epileptic convulsion. J. H. was sent to 'sound the alarm' that alerted the nearest neighbor, a half-mile away. W. A. Capshaw, a Church of God minister had come to the area. Seven doctors examined little Jewel and all with the same conclusion. Medical science had no answer. The seizures increased in frequency and intensity. Bother Capshaw advised, "Well, let's tell the Lord about it!" He prayed, and J. H. Walker recalled, "We watched!" They were members of another church. Capshaw laid his hands on Jewel. He prayed a short prayer- and then, J. H. Walker recalls, he prayed in another language. Jewel never had another seizure. She married H. W. Williams and was a partner in ministry all her life. And Mother and Dad joined the Church of God.
>
> Lucille Walker, *What To Do When You Pray* (Cleveland, TN: Pathway Press, 1998), 147-148.

The little house was packed. With no more room inside, people gathered outside. One neighbor described the scene.

They shouted three days and three nights. It was Easter season. The people came from everywhere. By the next morning there was no way of getting near the house. As people came in they would fall under God's power; and the whole city was stirred. They shouted until the foundation of the house gave way, but no one was hurt.[1]

Seymour's disposition toward prayer would become abundantly evident to all. He prayed in public, more than he preached. And his public leadership evidenced private roots. Oswald J. Smith believed,

"The man who does not spend hours alone with God will never know the anointing of the Holy Spirit. The world must be left outside until God alone fills the vision ... God has promised to answer prayer. It is not that He is unwilling, for the fact is, He is more willing to give than we are to receive, but the trouble is, we are not ready ..."[2]

God had been preparing a vessel. Seymour was ready!

At 312 Azusa Street sat a burned-out, abandoned African Methodist Episcopal Church that had fallen on hard times. No longer a 'house of God' - it was described as a "tumble down shack." But with a rental price tag of $8.00 a month, and overflow crowds on Bonnie Brae Street, it was just the open door the group needed, and it was affordable.[3] Since its days as a church building, it had been a warehouse, a wholesale center, a lumberyard, a stockyard, even a tombstone store. Its most recent usage had been as a stable with cheap rooms for rent on the second floor. On hot days, the building still bore the smell of a stable. The small two-story, rectangular building

---

1   Vinson Synan, *The Century of the Holy Spirit: 100 years of Pentecostal and Charismatic Renewal, 1901–2001* (Thomas Nelson Publishers, 2001). pp. 42–45. ISBN 0-7852-4550-2.

2   Oswald J. Smith, *I Have Walked Along with Jesus: Day by Day Meditations of Oswald J. Smith* (GR Welch Co, 1982). ISBN 0-91964-900-9.

3   Frank Bartleman, *Azusa Street* (Bridge-Logos Publishers, 1980). ISBN 0-88270-439-7.

had a flat-roof, and only measured 40 by 60 feet. It had a clapboard weathered exterior that was whitewashed. It lacked razzle-dazzle. One single gothic-style window at front of the building was the only clue that it had once been a holy place.[4] The first floor ceiling was only eight-feet tall, so there was no platform. As one historian noted, it was not a place for the proud.

The first meeting was held on Azusa Street on April 14, 1906.[5] A throw-away, building and a one-eyed, throw-away man – not surprised? That humble place with its odd mixture of unmatched chairs and plank benches and an equally odd assortment of people who would gather there with the humble Seymour is where God met Los Angeles and much of the world.

Early Wednesday morning, April 18, 1906, after the Los Angeles newspaper had already been printed, San Francisco was virtually destroyed by an earthquake. The Southern California city was jolted out of bed looking for fresh news, but the front page story was about another quake – the one happening on Azusa Street. It was like a sign. The curious city raced to witness the unusual move of the Spirit and there they discovered an amazing display of love between races. And tales of the supernatural. The rich and poor came, all hungry for God. Blacks, whites and a smattering of other internationals, sat together – thirsting for the Spirit. For three years, services were held three times daily and the little building was packed-out, often with hundreds waiting outside! At times, meetings ran non-stop through the day and into the night. These were not preaching meetings. They were more often than not, prayer meetings. Prayer characterized the meetings. Repentance and humility were the orders of the Lord.

---

4   Synan, Ibid.
5   Marshall Allen, "Pentecostal Movement Celebrates Humble Roots." *The Washington Post.* (April 15, 2006). http://www.washingtonpost. com/wp-dyn/content/article/2006/04/14/AR2006041401421.html. Retrieved 2007-05-17.

Ben Jennings, the legendary prayer leader of Campus Crusade observed:

"Prayer and theology [and by implication, preaching/teaching] both deal with God, but from different perspectives. Theology, like a telescope, views the distant stars of His qualities. Prayer, like a space vehicle, moves us among His qualities. Theology studies God and prayer engages Him. Both are adventuresome. Both necessary."[6]

Sadly, the church today receives a veritable non-stop discourse on morality and theology. Sunday after Sunday, we hear 'about' God without engaging God. Theological information provides the material for personal change, but it is by the powerful, inner enabling of the Holy Spirit, in the context of yielded, listening prayer, that information moves to transformation. Sunday after Sunday, millions arrive at the threshold of potential change. Praise teams praise; and preachers preach. And almost everyone leaves as they came. They came close to God. But they never climbed the mountain. Even Pentecostal services are constructed to avoid 'surprises.'

A White-water Ride

The problem with God is that, while He is dependable, He is not predictable. His ways are surprising.

The book of Acts is a white-water ride down the rapids of early church history. It is a Pentecostal wonderland. There are exotic sounds from heaven. There is the rushing wind. Fire. Glory. Open air preaching. Thousands are responding. There is healing in the streets and at the gate of the temple. Boldness, even in the face of death-threats, is exhibited. That is a surprise. This is the same band that a few weeks earlier scattered and hid as Christ was crucified.

---

6   Ben Jennings, *The Arena of Prayer* (NewLife Publications, 1999).

What has happened to them? Surprise! Jesus is not gone - He is back. No longer 'with' them, now, by the Spirit, He is 'in' them. Once limited to one Spirit-filled body, now there are 120 and more being born again every day. In a few days after Pentecost, a lame man is healed - running and leaping through the Temple. The Pharisees and rulers see a ghost. Surprise! Jesus is back and He is healing and preaching again. There is the dramatic intervention by the Holy Spirit on the occasion of the lie told by Ananias and his wife, a judgment intended to protect the integrity of the Church. Here is no-nonsense God. He is in charge. He speaks. He directs. His Church gathers, prays, waits, listens and obeys. He acts. Multitudes respond. He convicts of sin – and people repent. There are miracles – God is alive. And there is more. Dreams and visions come. Special and specific direction by the Spirit is given. Phillip is translated – a magic carpet ride. Wow! Peter, the lead apostle is called to accountability for his involvement in the actions of Spirit! Actions over which he had not control. That was a surprise! His response was "The Spirit told me to go with them … And as I began to speak [to them, at the home of Cornelius], the Holy Spirit fell upon them …" (Acts 11:12, 15). It is clear – this was a surprise to Peter, both his being led to speak to Gentiles; and the action of the Spirit on

---

ACCENT

Early in his ministry, J. H. Walker had a bout of malaria. Chills and fever persisted for weeks. He grew weaker and weaker. His situation grew worse. It appeared that he would die. M. S. Haynes, the State Overseer, along with his wife, drove over two-hundred miles to come and see him, and pray for him. They entered the room and prayed sincerely. Perspiration literally ran from Walker's body. The next morning he woke up, convinced that he was healed. And he was.

Lucille Walker, *What To Do When You Pray* (Cleveland, TN: Pathway Press, 1998), 149.

Gentiles. "It's not my fault," Peter offers a protest. "I was just talking to them. And the Holy Spirit fell on them …" In the Acts Church, it is not men who lead, but the Spirit that leads. And He does not always inform them of what He intends to do. This is the Spirit, the third member of the Trinity. God, Himself. Surprise! In Acts 9, there is another surprise - a voice from heaven and a blinding light that overcomes Saul, the chief-prosecutor and persecutor of the Church, leaving him in the dust and blind. This is theater. Ananias, an unknown, a mere disciple, is then directed to minister to the fire-brand, Saul. He is to go to meet with him, given only an address, by the Spirit. He is to baptize him. And then to induct him into the Church. Not Peter? Not John? Not one of the twelve? Who is in charge here?

These "prayer meetings were the arteries of the early church. Through them, life-sustaining power was derived." As J. B. Johnston reminds us in, *The Prayer Meeting and Its History,* "The prayer meeting is the pulse of the church." It was not man, not an apostolic council that was leading the New Testament Church. It was the Holy Spirit – the *Ghost!* And *'the Ghost'* is full of surprises. The apostles were never in

"Jesus Christ lived in the midst of his enemies. At the end, all his disciples deserted him. On the cross he was utterly alone, surrounded by evil doers and mockers. For this cause he had come, to bring peace to the enemies of God. So the Christian too, belongs not in the seclusion of a cloistered life, but in the thick of foes."

Bonhoeffer, from "Meditating on the Word," Quoted by Charles Ringma, *Seize the Day with Dietrich Bonhoeffer* (Colorado Springs, Colorado: Pinion Press; 2000), See entry for January 8.

charge. Jesus had commanded that they "wait for the Promise of the Father, which, He said, 'you have heard from Me'" (Acts 1:4) The Spirit "will guide you into all truth" (John 16:13). From Him, there would be special revelation, empowerment and comfort. He would convict of sin and convince of righteousness (John 16:8). Christ rules His Church, through the Spirit. And the sword of the Spirit 'is' the Word (Eph. 6:17).

Peter's own personal transformation, his bold empowerment came not by encouragement and affirmation of the band of disciples, not by man, but by the Spirit – what a surprising change! He is a different man after the Acts 2 moment. Afterwards, he spoke without intimidation and with eloquence to authorities (Acts 4:8). There was no more timidity, no more waffling before a fire. He now had the power to be a witness. "Do not pray for easy lives, pray for stronger men! Do not pray for tasks equal to your powers, pray for powers equal to your tasks," Phillips Brooks urges.

When the Church assembled to pray, the Spirit shook the place and enflamed the witness of the entire Church (4:30). They did not pray for exemption from the trial of persecution, but for greater grace by the Spirit. "Look on their threats – and give us boldness." And then they prayed for the hand of God to be stretched forth in a miraculous way, not to reduce their level of risk or extricate them from the

At the 10th General Assembly of the Church of God, Sam C. Perry, preached on Intercessory Prayer. At the close of his message, there was a great manifestation of the presence and power of God. Many saw supernatural tongues 'like as of fire" flashed about. People shouted, wept, screamed, danced, prayed, sang and pen cannot describe the scene.

Minutes of the 10th Church of God General Assembly.

trouble, but to demonstrate that Jesus was alive. And when they had prayed, the Scripture indicates, "they were filled with Spirit!" The Spirit, in His fullness, in their cognizant, awareness of Him was the answer. To be more aware of God, than the threats of evil men alleviates intimidation and emboldens. As Oswald Chambers observes. At such times, "Our true character comes out in the way we pray."

It was not the lie Ananias uttered to Peter, to other leaders, or the Church itself, that was so deadly. He lied to the Spirit, and it was by the Spirit that he was judged (5:3). He did not stand before a tribunal. He did not die at the hands of men. The 'Ghost' was in charge of the Church – including the discipline of its members.

"We are witnesses," the Church confessed, "So also is the Holy Ghost!" (5:32) Theirs' was a partnership, impossible without the Spirit. It was the Spirit that nudged Philip into a chariot and caught him up for a wild ride (8:39). It was the Spirit, after a bewildering vision, who said bluntly to Peter, "Three men are looking for you … doubt nothing" (10:19). It was the Spirit, in the midst of Peter's sermon, who 'fell' on the Gentiles, overcoming them, overwhelming them (10:44). Jewish Christians "were astonished" (10:45). This was not planned. It was not on the program. Who was responsible for this? Surprise. It was *the Ghost* again.

The pattern continues. The prophet Agabus warns of a famine providing helpful intelligence information to believers (11:28). It is the Spirit, not man, not plans, that thrust forth the first missionary team, and they go forth following the Spirit (13:2, 4). P. T. Forsyth reminds us that, "Prayer is the atmosphere of revelation, in the strict and central sense of that word. It is the climate in which God's manifestation bursts open into inspiration."[7]

The final word at the Jerusalem Council was, "It seemed good

---

7   P. T. Forsyth, *The Soul of Prayer* (Regent College Publishing, 1916)..

to the Holy Spirit" (15:28). Their strategy was pray, hear from God, and obey! Our tendency is the opposite. "'We can do nothing,' we say sometimes, 'we can only pray!'" That, we feel, is a precarious second-best. So long as we can fuss and work and rush about, so long as we can lend a hand, we have some hope ..." we seem to think. But that hope is not in the Lord, it is hope in our own acts, out of our own wisdom and strength. If things get worse and "we have to fall back upon God ... Ah, then things must be critical indeed!"[8] Prayer should not be a last resort. It should not be a back-up plan used only in earnest, and at last, in a time of desperation.

The Spontaneous and the Intentional

Looking beyond the surprises, there is another lesson we learn from Acts. It is less obvious. What appears *spontaneous* in Acts, on closer examination, often intersects with the *intentional.* The 120 did not expect a 'sound from heaven or a rushing wind!' They didn't anticipate a fiery cloud reminiscent of the night glory over the wilderness tabernacle. No one predicted that the language barrier would be broken, a strategic reversal of Babel, the sound and sign of a new people, of a new order in the earth. Who, among the ten-dozen souls would have predicted 3,000 converts in one day? Then, growing to 5,000 families, only days later? Andrew Murray writes in *With Christ in the School of Prayer,* "Time spent in prayer will yield more than that given to work. Prayer alone gives work its worth and its success. Prayer opens the way for God Himself to do His work in us and through us. Let our chief work as god's messengers be intercession; in it we secure the presence and power of God to go with us."

Ten-to-twenty percent of Jerusalem's population of some 50,000

---

8   Quote by Arthur John (A. J.) Gossip.

people are now following Jesus. What a reversal. And this is just fifty-days after the brutal crucifixion of Jesus, and His triumphant resurrection, a fact then still denied by the authorities, but now being widely embraced by the multitudes – the 'Ghost' working to demonstrate that Christ was indeed, alive. These signs and wonders, this fire and these tongues - what a surprise! Yet, upon closer examination, we find a group of people who were faithfully obeying, patiently waiting, expecting and hoping. While thousands were filling up the Jerusalem streets for the Feast of Pentecost, this group vigilantly kept watch. For a week, nothing happened. Then there was a "Suddenly." The spontaneous moment intersected with their obedient intentionality.

Bonheoffer would say, "Prayer is not a free-will offering to God ... We are not free to engage in it according to our own wishes. Prayer is the first divine service in the day."

Bonhoeffer, from "Meditating on the Word," Quoted by Charles Ringma, *Seize the Day with Dietrich Bonhoeffer* (Colorado Springs, Colorado: Pinion Press; 2000), See entry for March 24.

The miraculous healing of the lame man in Acts 3 appears to be spontaneous as well, but Peter and John were doing as they customarily did, going to the temple for afternoon prayer. The healing of the lame man intersected with their being intentional and faithful in their own prayer discipline. Likewise, the power moment in Acts 4, in which the place was shaken, also appears spontaneous. But the church had a pattern of intentionally calling a prayer meeting whenever there was a crisis.

What appears as incidental, spontaneous and *delightful* surprises from the Spirit, on examination seem connected to the *discipline* of prayerful obedience. The two always go together. Jesus admonished us to daily go into our closets for prayer. And He promised that the

"God who was in secret," indeed, who "saw in secret," would "reward openly." God, it seems, attends our intentional, quiet, moments – but He doesn't always reveal Himself. He is invisibly present – but then, He watches for moments to reward such tenacity openly! Again, the intentional and the spontaneous get connected by the sovereign action of God.

Prayer – the Subtext

Charles Spurgeon noted, "Prayer itself is an art which only the Holy Ghost can teach us. He is the giver of all prayer. Pray for prayer. Pray till you can pray." We learn to pray – by praying. And by being around praying people. That is why prayer meetings are so important. We 'catch' prayer.

A prayer meeting is the context into which the Spirit descends (Acts 2) – prayer invites God. It signals our desire for an encounter with Him, a longing for His Presence and direction. It is to a prayer meeting at the temple that Peter and John are bound when the lame man is healed at the gate called Beautiful (3:1-10). Prayer is the activity occurring when the place of meeting is shaken and the persecuted saints are emboldened after they are again threatened by authorities, the same powers that had been behind the crucifixion of Jesus (4:24-31). Prayer is the action Stephen takes, when the crowd rejects him and his preaching, and hurls stones at him. Suddenly, the heavens open and he sees Jesus. A persecutor named Saul, listens to the amazing sermon delivered by the articulate young preacher, and then witnesses Stephen's fearless death (6:55-58). In prayer – heaven is opened before Stephen. He dies praying. Prayer is the mission of Ananias when he is sent to meet with Saul. He is to pray over the ready heart of the once hardened man from Tarsus (9:10-19). Prayer is what the church is doing when the angel leads the imprisoned Peter from near death (12:5-19). "The angel fetched Peter out of prison, but it was prayer that fetched the angel."[9] Prayer is the context when apostolic ministry is birthed at Antioch (13:1-3). Prayer is what Paul and Silas do at midnight in the jail at Philippi (16:25-30).

Throughout the book of Acts, we are met with these remarkable surprises, interventions of God - shackles and bondages are broken off. Prison doors fly open (16). Surprised? They were praying. Apostolic ministry is birthed (13). Surprise? No, they were praying. Angels intervene (12). Surprised? That too involved prayer as well. A church split is averted (6) – they committed to prayer. Boldness and the evident power of God vibrates the very place where they gather (4) – they were praying. The fire comes. The crowd gathers. The city is stirred. Thousands come to Christ (2) – they had been praying.

The surprising twists and turns are indeed, unexpected. Remarkable. At times, astonishing. Even startling. But the predictable sub-text is always prayer! Twenty-nine times we find prayer in eighteen of the twenty-eight chapters of Acts. Eight times we see corporate prayer gatherings. The church of Acts prayed – often, and together.

> Prayer can no more be divorced from worship than life can be divorced from breathing. If we follow His impulse, the Holy Spirit will always lead us to pray. When we allow Him to work freely, He will always bring the Church to extensive praying. Conversely, when the Spirit is absent, we will find excuses not to pray. We may say, "God understands. He knows I love Him. But I'm tired ... I'm so busy ... It's just not convenient now ..." When the Spirit is absent, our excuses always seem right, but in the presence of the Spirit our excuses fade away.[10]

---

9   Thomas Watson, *A Divine Cordial* (Sovereign Grace Publishers, 2007), 18.

10   R.T. Kendall and Joy Strong, *By Love Transformed* (Charisma Media, 2006), 152.

Miraculous Community - Fruit and Fire

"It takes us a long time to learn that prayer is more important than organization, more powerful than armies, more influential than wealth, and mightier than all learning."[11] It is by prayer that the character of the Church itself is changed. We connect prayer to the supernatural. But in Acts, there is also a parallel transformational theme in Acts often overlooked. The miracles are obvious. But evident supernatural *fire* is not the only "Wow!" factor. There is also supernatural *fruit*. The rag-tag band of competitive disciples had a tendency to rankle one another, displaying a fierce loyalty to self, prior to Pentecost. In Acts, something has happened to them. Their relationships one to another have been dramatically changed.

First, the character of the conversions themselves is significant. They "*received his word ... were baptized ... continued steadfastly in doctrine (teaching) ... fellowship (community) ... the breaking of bread ... and prayers" (2: 41-42)*. Second, notice the quality of community, "*Believers ... were together (unity) ... they shared with one another ... some sold things and gave to the needy ... they continued daily with one accord ... from house to house ... with gladness and simplicity ... praising God ... finding favor with all the people ... and the Church grew daily!" (2:44-47)*. Behind the visible stream of the miraculous is something more, a love, a fellowship, a selflessness. Suddenly, the whole city wants to be members of this group.

In our age, Samuel Chadwick urged, "There is a marked absence of travail. There is much phrasing, but little pleading. Prayer has become a soliloquy instead of a passion. The powerlessness of the church needs no other explanation ... To be prayerless is to be both passionless and powerless." For the character of the Church to be extraordinary, producing fruit (character, the fruit of the Spirit) and fire (the gifts of the Spirit), required extraordinary prayer.

---

11 Samuel Chadwick, *The Path of Prayer* (Hodder and Stoughton, 1933), 29.

Without supernatural fruit for evidentiary life-transformation, Pentecost is reduced to sensationalism, to signs and wonders, to the making of a carnival side-show with carnival-like pastors and evangelists. Legitimacy, demands fruit with fire. And authentic Pentecostalism demands 'fire' with fruit. The two cannot be separated.

Luke purposely seams the fruit and fire themes together. The power of the Spirit is connected (by context) to this supernatural character! In Acts 4:31, it is easy to emphasize the *'shaking'* – *FIRE;* and miss the *'shaping'* in 4:32-35 – *FRUIT. They were of one heart and soul, freed from things (their stuff now belonged to God!). FIRE: With great power the apostles gave witness to the resurrection of the Lord Jesus, but behind the public blaze of glory is a picture of sharing and caring (FRUIT), as well as the liquidation of assets to finance the first launch of the great commission effort! Here is a caring, sharing community – one that is committed to mission of the Church! And yet they seem to realize, that such a mission requires the evident parallel and powerful work of the Spirit. Their gospel is not mere words.*

The Spirit, through the blazing supernatural, offers a public invitation into Jesus. Yet, equally important, is the supernatural character of the community into which new converts are invited. Without the miracle of character in the community, the flashing fire in the spiritual night is a false promise. Miraculous *praxis* can never take the place of a Christ-like *ethos* in the church. Today, the church lacks both supernatural power and a culture. Advertisement with nothing in stock is always a disappointment. Repeatedly in the first five chapters, the character theme is introduced. Acts is more than a miracle show? So when the blatant violation of character, by Ananias and Sapphira, came like poison into the fresh purity and innocence of the early church, God judged. In a parallel fashion, early after Israel's entrance into the land, when Achan sinned, God judged. The events correspond. So the severe example of judgment underscores that without integrity and a holy core, the Church will fail in their mission.

Surprise! The *fruit* of the Spirit is as supernatural as the *fire*. And God wants us to surprise the secular culture with both.

The late J. Vernon McGee lamented,

> "According to my humble judgment, the greatest need of the present-day church is prayer. Prayer should be the vital breath of the church, but right now it is gasping for air. One of the great Bible teachers of the past said that the church goes forward on its knees. Maybe one of the reasons the church is not going forward today is because it's not in a position to go forward --- we are not on our knees in prayer."[12]

John R. Mott, the great missiologist declared,

> "The Church has not yet touched the fringe of the possibilities of intercessory prayer. Her largest victories will be witnessed when individual Christians everywhere come to recognize their priesthood unto God and day by day give themselves to prayer."[13]

Prayer References

Acts

1. Disciples pray for a successor to Judas (41 words; Acts 1:24-25). Answered, (Acts 1:26).

2. Peter prays for the healing of the lame man (12 words; Acts 3:6). Answered, (Acts 3:7-8).

3. Disciples pray for boldness and power (178 words; Acts 4:24-30). Answered (Acts 4:31-33).

4. Stephen prays for his enemies (13 words; Acts 7:59-60).

5. Paul prays for instruction (12 words; Acts 9:5-6). Answered

---

12 J. Vernon McGee, *J. Vernon McGee on Prayer* (Thomas Nelson, Inc., 2002).

13 John Raleigh Mott, *The Evangelization of the World in this Generation* (Student Volunteer Movement for Foreign Missions, Princeton University, 1905), 189.

(Acts 9:5-6).

6. Peter prays for resurrection of Tabitha (2 words; Acts 9:40). Answered (Acts 9:40-41).

References to prayer (Acts 1:14; 3:1; 6:4; 8:22,24,34; 10:9,31; 12:5; 16:13-16).

Finis Jennings Dake, *Dake's Annotated Reference Bible* (Lawrenceville, GA: Dake Bible Sales, 1963, 1991).

CHAPTER EIGHTEEN

THE EPISTLES AND THE REVELATION

A WINDOW THROUGH TIME

From early September until the following Spring (1940-1941), London was a city of horror as the bombing raids commenced early in what would become WW II. Everything was uncertain. One day, a pair shoes might be left for repair, and the next day the whole shop gone, but in the ruins, the shoemaker sat doing his job. Walls were reduced to powder. Rubble and debris fields increased daily. People lived in what was left of their houses. Raids came by day and night. When the sirens sounded, everyone ran for cover. Rich and poor mingled. The King and Queen made their way through the rubble. Buckingham Palace itself was bombed. But the earliest targets were hospitals, it seemed. A maternity hospital was hit several times. At times, entire structures collapsed around people. One woman bathing her infant had her house hit, all destroyed but her and the little one. Reports read, "Houses are destroyed, casualties are small." In one town, eight bombs fell, and all landed in gardens and open areas. Seaports were raided six to eight times daily. One of the targets of the bombers was Saint Paul's Cathedral, for no other reason than to demoralize. The steeple still towered over the ruin of the city, pointing to sky, like a giant symbol of hope. London, it was said, was one giant circle of overwhelming disaster, except for one corner. The skyline had been obliterated. Even at night, clouds of smoke and yellow flames decorated the horizon, and in the dim light – there was St. Paul's. One report called it, 'an island of God, safe and untouched.'

It was oddly out of place. Londoners declared that if the city were devastated, but the Cathedral still stood, then the city was still the city.

At one point, fourteen hundred fires raged. But the water mains were busted. Firemen could do little more than watch them burn. From London roofs, they could see the steeple – all were encouraged by it. Then came the day, when a huge bomb fell, as other bombs had, with St. Paul's name on it. It landed not on the Cathedral, but near it, burrowing itself into the ground, twelve feet deep. The Bomb Dispatch Squad barreled through the debris filled streets in their little yellow bomb disposal truck. Arriving, they found that the huge projectile was still alive. It was not a dud. Apparently, it was on a time delay. It's detonation would have leveled the Cathedral. Streets were closed. Fire fighters and bomb specialists gathered, and the city held their breath. The bomb, still alive, was digging its way under the Cathedral, burrowing further and deeper minute by minute. Who knew when it would explode? Four young lads, led by Lt. Robert Davies, crawled into the hole to wrestle with the massive bomb – and they did so for 86 hours.

As the four-man team dug, the half-ton bomb burrowed deeper. Gas was seeping down into the area where the men worked, and at times, flames from the ignited gas raced across the surface of the bomb. Time Magazine called it the 'broiling bomb.' Now twenty-five feet underground, they worked under the lights at night, with the flames of the gas fires licking the area around them. Finally, on the third day, George Cameron Wylie shouted, "I've got it!" He tapped his spade against the surface of the bomb and there was clear metallic sound. Men held their breath expecting a flash of light and a deafening sound. There was no time for scaffolding. They created a makeshift harness and begin to pull the bomb to the surface. Twice it slipped from their grip. Twice they had to recapture it. When it was hauled to the surface, it was eight-feet tall. They hoisted it into the cradle on the truck, and prepared to haul it out of the city. Suddenly, one of the lads objected, "You said that we had time to sign the guest book in the Cathedral!" Three did — with a live bomb waiting. If grace had kept them thus far, then grace would allow their names to officially declare, 'We were here!' At Hackney Marsh, the bomb was exploded. It was not a dud. Very much alive, it created a one-hundred foot crater and shattered windows a half-mile away.

In the years prior to the war, St. Paul's had been surrounded by larger buildings, dwarfed and hidden by them. But the raids brought them down, one by one, leaving St. Paul's cross as the towering structure. Londoners would say, "Surely there is something symbolic in that. The confused mass of buildings has gone; the rubbish has gone; but what really matters remains." The humblest and even the irreligious knew the line, "Afloat upon ethereal tides, St. Paul's above the city rides!"

Adapted from, "The City that Wouldn't Die," Margaret Lee Runbeck, *The Great Answer* (Boston: Houghton Mifflin Company, 1944), 111-128.

CHAPTER 18

THE EPISTLES AND THE REVELATION
P. Douglas Small

The Epistles and Prayer

It was in an atmosphere of prayer that the church was born (Acts 1:14; 2:1). And it was sustained in prayer (Acts 2:42; 3:1; 6:4, 6). Prayer is the "sphere of the congregation."[1]

Most of the epistles of Paul begin with a prayer for the church. And they are further decorated with prayers and references to prayer. Prayer is assumed. It's natural. And yet, it is not taken for granted. Paul urges prayer. "Prayer is at the heart of Paul's thinking and practice."[2] He laces prayers into his letters, moving seamlessly back and forth between admonition and intercession, between blessing and thanksgiving. His own practice of prayer shines forth (Rom. 1:19; Eph. 1:16; Phil. 1:9; I Thess. 1:2). He exhorts the churches to practice prayer (Rom. 12:1-2; Eph. 6:18; Phil. 4:6; I Thess. 5:17). The first church in Europe is birthed at a place of prayer.

The prayers of Paul are spontaneous and liturgical. And of course, Paul prayed in the spirit – or 'in tongues.' Paul evidently sang at times, in prayer and communion with God. In Colossians 3:16 and Ephesians 5:19, we have the mention of psalms, hymns

---

1   Raymond Surburg, *The Biblical Doctrine of Prayer* (See: www. confessionallutherans.org/BDOP.doc).

2   David Peterson, "Prayer in Paul's Writings," D. A. Carson, *Teach Us To Pray*, 84.

and spiritual (*pneumatikos*) songs – songs of the Spirit, inspired by the Spirit (I Corinthians 14:15). This at least includes prayer that is a supernatural utterance, using the language of the Spirit – or tongues.

Paul's laces into his epistles 'fixed' prayers – with a liturgical character, especially at the end of his letters. He must imagine that these prayers will be read aloud to the congregation. And thus by proxy, he is praying for them, with them, over them. One of the more beautiful of these liturgical utterances is found in II Corinthians 13:13, where over this congregation where strife has been dominant, he utters a Trinitarian (the essence of unity) blessing, "The grace of our Lord Jesus Christ and the love of God and the fellowship of the Holy Spirit be with you all!" [3]

Paul appears to have set aside regular times for personal prayer – as did Jesus. Andrew Murray reminds us,

> "Of course, mere regularity in such matters does not ensure that effective praying takes place: genuine godliness is so easily aped, its place usurped by its barren cousin, formal religion …"[4]

The dangers of legalism aside, Murray warns, "Unless we plan to pray we will not pray."

Paul prayed for the progress of the faith of believers (II Thessalonians 2:13). He prayed that their love would grow more and more (Philippians 1:9). That they would become stronger as a community (II Corinthians 13:9). He prays 'day and night' that he will get to see them again – this is prayer that is personal, that involves his heart (I Thessalonians 3:10). He is aware of supernatural forces that are at work against him. Twice they impeded his visit to Thessalonica, so now he pleads for prayer support (I Thessalonians

---

3   Oscar Cullman, *Prayer in the New Testament* (Minneapolis, MN: Fortress Press, 1994), 75.
4   Andrew Murray, *Lessons from the School of Prayer,* 20.

2:18). He then gives evidence that prayer counteracts, in some way, the invasive and disruptive work and interference by the Evil One. To the Romans, he asks that they would 'struggle with him in prayer,' no small investment. And this was due to conflicts with Judaizers in Judea. He also worried about the reception he would receive in Jerusalem, and for that he requests prayer. One wonders what kind of reaction might manifest today, if a well-known leader were to transparently plead for a local church to 'struggle in prayer over some issue,' and just what would that struggling look like? Certainly it should amount to more than the yawns that occur in our Sunday morning prayer times.

The power of intercession is that those who pray unite themselves with God and His will. With the coming of the Spirit, believers not only pray 'in the name of Jesus' with direct access to the Father, by the Son, but do so with a new level of confidence and spiritual authority. We pray in the name of *Jesus* – the perfect and sinless man, the ultimate son of Adam. He came as the last Adam to exercise the right to redeem humanity and the earth, to recover the lost dominion of the fallen Adam. In Jesus, we have a standing in righteousness never known before. Man *is,* in Jesus, the noble creature he was created to be. We pray in the name of Jesus, *the Christ* – the anointed One, the Messiah. As such, he inherits all of the accumulated promises of the Old Covenant. He is David's heir, the legitimate King of Israel. We pray in the name of Jesus Christ, *the Lord* – God incarnate, fully man and fully Deity. He has risen from the dead. He is sovereign. Death has no hold on Him. He is enthroned in heaven. And because of Him, we pray. And to Him, we pray. And through Him, we pray. And with Him, we pray. Paul's theology was not only prayer in the name of Jesus, but every deed was also to be done in reference to His name, "Whatever you do, in word or deed, do everything in the name of the Lord Jesus" (Colossians 3:17).

Praying in the Spirit

There is yet another tool. We can also 'pray in the Spirit,' with the enabling of the Spirit, in a collaborative endeavor never known in the previous era (I Cor. 14:14-16). The dreaded throne approached by the high priest only once a year, with blood and fear, has been transformed into a 'throne of grace,' accessible by the weakest believer (Eph. 6:18; Jude 1:20). The early Christians saw themselves as spiritual priests who could pray at any place and any time, with confidence that God would hear them (Heb. 13:15).

For Paul, prayer and the Spirit are seamlessly interconnected. In Paul's theology, prayer would not be possible without the Holy Spirit. "No one can say that 'Jesus is Lord' but by the Holy Spirit" (I Corinthians 12:3). To the Ephesians he urges, "Pray at all times in the Spirit" (3:20), and he expected such

ACCENT

In the early days of the Church of God Evangel, the publication included an abundance of letters. Some were reports. Some were appeals for assistance. Here is a letter from W. F. Bryant, in whose home the Church was reorganized, this time about the work in the mountain area. Bryant noted that the area was full of "hungry hearts" and that a recent trip had resulted in altars full of men and women, humble folks, fathers and mothers. And yet, the dangers were still real. Bryant noted that "the second day of this month an enemy to Holiness burned down their little church cabin ..." In addition, a deacon's house had also been burned down. The mountain region was noted for its isolation and lack of formal training. But with a fresh hunger for God, Bryant observed, in the four years of his ministry in the area, there was now a "flourishing little Sunday School that has been going on for three years. And many," he noted, "have learned to read their Bibles in this time." In the middle of the persecution, the church gathered for prayer. In the midst of the prayer gathering, there came a message from God, a tongue and interpretation, "I will supply all your needs. Trust

Me." It was a simple word, and one they already knew in their heads. But somehow the assurance by the Spirit, in the midst of persecution, gave new confidence. After prayer, the men were "directed by the Spirit to a plot of ground that God laid on our hearts to build on." Acting on faith, they went to see the owner, who after hearing their story, gave them the land. It was an answer to prayer. But then, considering the cost of a building, they again despaired. It would take $150 to $175. "The people," he wrote, "are willing to give all they can in work, but they have no money to buy the material needed." So again they went to prayer. Bryant says, "As we prayed, the saints broke down in tears, and cried so earnestly to God that He would give them a place to worship in, which so deeply touched my heart that I bring this matter to you, believing God will lay it upon our hearts to supply this need." Bryant noted, "He laid it upon my heart while in prayer, to write this piece." In fact, the group appointed Bryant to the building committee. "We want to get this building completed, so as to have it completed by the first of September."

Evangel, July 1, 1901, 4.

prayers to be effective, resulting "infinitely more than we ask and know." Perhaps Luther learned his transparency about requesting prayer for his needs from Paul. You may miss such notes of Paul in a casual read, but when you gather them, you observe a pattern – to the Romans (15:20) he appeals for prayer support, asking them to struggle with him in prayer. To the Thessalonians he appeals, "Pray for us!" (I Thessalonians 5:14), and then more specifically, "Pray for us that the word may go forth and the glorified among you" (II Thessalonians 3:1). To the Colossians he request prayer for an 'open door' to preach the gospel (Colossians 4:2). Paul knows that preaching, reason alone, even coupled with passion is not enough. It must have a spiritual counterpart, and that comes only by prayer. Even the preaching cannot be left to human ability. Pray *"that utterance may be given me in opening my mouth boldly to proclaim the mystery of the gospel"* (Ephesians 6:18). It is neither preached or perceived without the work of the Spirit, connected to prayer.

In Romans 8:12-27 (see also Galatians 4:6), Paul gives us the foundation for prayer in the Holy Spirit, and this is a principle that all true believers can commonly grasp – namely, we are no longer slaves, but sons. The proof is a new intimacy in prayer, by the Spirit, through Jesus Christ, with the Father, whereby we cry 'Abba!' "Because you are sons, God has sent the Spirit of His Son into our hearts, crying 'Abba! Father!'" (Galatians 4:6). "For you did not receive the spirit of slavery to fall back into fear, but you have received the spirit of sonship" (Romans 8:15). Whatever the affect of prayer in the Spirit might be, the core issue cannot be lost, which is our heightened relationship and status. Our newfound identity and intimacy are here. A bold new level of faith and confidence, that not only augments our prayers to heaven, but also our representative role in the earth rises out of such prayer. We are 'heirs' and the very real 'presence' of the Holy Spirit is God's pledge that He will do all He has declared He will do (II Corinthians 1:22; Ephesians 1:14. The Spirit – within us, is a 'guarantee of our inheritance.'

This is not merely a rational argument Paul is making – but a spiritual one. The proof of sonship is not in the head, but in the heart. It is a matter of the Spirit. It is not something we grasp intellectually; it is something we experience transformationally. "Who told you, that you were a son of God?" – Evangelicals will say, "The Bible!" Pentecostal will say, "The Spirit." The correct answer - is both!

In Romans 1, man has an intellectual knowledge of God, and that is not the problem. The descent of man begins when he "glorifies Him not as God," – that is, when he withholds prayerful reverence along with withheld gratitude or thanksgiving, and that is a prayer issue. Man's attempt to 'know God' intellectually, without knowing

God spiritually, reverently, gratefully, worshipfully – is the nexus of the devolution of man, of his descent into depravity. True knowledge of God – knowing God, not merely knowing about God – is possible only through worshipful prayer.

There is more. The Spirit inspires in us the sense of 'Abba!' It is by the Spirit, we utter with new uncommonness the name of God. The Name of God in its original form, *YHWH*, the *Tetragrammaton*, appears hundreds of times in Torah scrolls but is not ever, under any circumstances, pronounced by the reader. Indeed, it would appear that since the destruction of the First Temple almost 2,600 years ago, it has not been pronounced – except by one man, in one specific place and on one specific day each year: that is, the High Priest, in the Second Temple, at one point in the *Yom Kippur* service.[5] Now, the Spirit urges us to call God by the most intimate term – *Abba, Father*. This leap is cosmic. We have moved from a fearful, representative encounter with God, once annually by the High Priest, to an invitation to live in holy space. Indeed, God, the Father, has sent the Spirit of the Son into our hearts, who cries *'Abba, Father.'* The disciples experienced life *with* Christ; we now experience the life *of* Christ, *in* Christ, and *Christ in us* – *by the Spirit*. The spontaneous and native cry, *'Abba, Father!'* is a new energy working in us. It is the 'Spirit of the Son' affirming our relationship with the Father, by the Holy Spirit. Again, this is more than an intellectual posture. And the Holy Spirit also prays – in us, and for us, and with us (Romans 8:16). Tragically, some Pentecostals have exalted the experience, the *affect* in the Spirit, which tends to promote a *pneuma-centric* imbalance. The Holy Spirit Himself, always points to Christ and the Father - *"He will not speak of Himself."*

---

5   Harold M. Kamsler, "A Note On The Prohibition Of Uttering The Name Of God", See: http://jbq.jewishbible.org/assets/Uploads/314/314_ Tetra11.pdf

Intimacy with the Father, and the Son, are possible by the Spirit. He makes His presence known to believers. And it is in the context of His presence that we do our best praying – in a quickened and exercised state. Origen and Chrysostom both see Romans 8:26-27 as an inference to tongues-speech – "Our human languages are incapable of conveying what we want to say to God but the Spirit prays in believers enabling them through tongues to express what is necessary."[6]

This is not a zenith, as some believers seem to think. A 'pledge' after all is just that,

> ### ACCENT
>
> Prayer can no more be divorced from worship than life can be divorced from breathing. If we follow his impulse, the Holy Spirit will always lead us to pray. When we allow him to work freely, he will always bring the Church to extensive praying. Conversely, when the Spirit is absent, we will find excuses not to pray. We may say, "God understands. He knows I love him. But I'm tired ... I'm so busy ... It's just not convenient now ..." When the Spirit is absent, our excuses always seem right, but in the presence of the Spirit our excuses fade away.
>
> ~R. T. Kendall

a 'pledge.' And as real as the sense of the Spirit's Presence might be, we are only at a new threshold of potential. In the shadow of the cross, following Christ, and therefore knowing the Father, means *"the fellowship of his sufferings"* on the way to "being glorified with Him" (Romans 8:17). We are 'already' sons, heir, joint-heirs, but it doth 'not yet' appear what we shall be! To revel in the 'warmth of the Spirit's affirmation of our son-ship is a holy moment no believer should miss. But now the journey begins. With a heightened sense of our new identity, new promises and power, intimate access – we must move from justification, to sanctification. And from sanctification to

---

6   David Peterson, "Prayer in Paul's Writings," See D. A. Carson, *Teach Us To Pray*, 96.

edification. And then to glory. Sanctification is a next step beyond justification. It requires the consecration of our whole being to God in order that we become mature sons, and not bastards. It is both a separation from the world, and a conscious and disciplined pursuit of the Holy. Consecration is our part; sanctification is God's part. We consecrate ourselves to Him, having been justified; and he sanctifies, beginning the process of making us holy and whole. Edification happens in the context of fellowship, not only with other believers, but also with the Trinity itself, in prayer. We should not neglect prayer – stirring one another onward ...

Paul prays to Christ in II Corinthians 12:8. It is the only passage in which his prayer is not directed to God, the Father. That noted, in Romans 10:12, he obverses that it is Christians "who call upon Christ." Christians, Paul acknowledge, talk to Jesus! They pray to Jesus. This should not create a theological meltdown, for Philippians 2:9 became an early Christian formula for confession –

> "*Therefore God also has highly exalted Him and given Him the name which is above every name, that at the name of Jesus every knee should bow, of those in heaven, and of those on earth, and of those under the earth, and that every tongue should confess that Jesus Christ is Lord, to the glory of God the Father.*"

Jesus is not merely the son of God, He is God. As Cullman notes, "Paul can in principle pray without distinction to God or to Christ."[7] There is no competition among the members of the Trinity – prayer is a meeting with the Father, the Son and the Spirit, on the blood-stained ground of covenant promises, by grace in a spirit of faith. We plead the promises, we pray for the in-breaking kingdom of God, on the basis of Scripture, with the enabling of the Spirit, in the name of Jesus, to the Father, who is also 'our father!' We pray. The blood itself pleads. The Spirit prays. Jesus, our advocate and intercessor

7   Cullman, 86.

in heaven prays. Creation is praying, groaning. There are moments when our prayers resonant with prayers prayed before, prayers to which there has been an affirmative, "Yes, but 'not yet,'" and those prayers are held as incense by the elders in heaven. This is really a grand symphony of prayer. Our voice may appear weak and fragile – but in heaven, prayer sounds like thunder, like a Niagara, like a force to be reckoned with. Every voice counts. O, the privilege of prayer.

For Paul, there was no human discourse more valuable than prayer. Not preaching. Not teaching. Not sharing and encouraging. All of those things, as with Christ, flowed out of prayer. And this prayer was enabled by the Spirit, *"For we do not know how to pray as we ought, but the Spirit himself intercedes for us with sighs too deep for words"* (Romans 8:26).

Prayer was never, in either the theology or the practice of Paul, a mere rational exercise. It certainly was not a chat with the inner self. It was a spiritual practice, and for it to be effective, it was necessary at times for the practice to move beyond the inadequacy of the person praying, including their ability to give expression to the working of the Spirit within. So, the Holy Spirit, in such moments enabled 'spirit-speech' (I Corinthians 14:23), what Pentecostals call 'speaking in tongues.'[8] This is not tongues as a sign, or as a gift to the church requiring interpretation. It is a function of the Spirit in personal worship and prayer, in thanksgiving and petition, as well as intercession. Sadly much of the church and the world continues to regard 'tongues-speakers' as irrational, if not mad. Oscar Cullman

---

8   Ibid, 77. Cullman notes, "Whether or not we feel drawn to this overflowing ecstatic phenomenon, which also appears today in so-called charismatic circles, greater attention should be paid to it in the historical accounts of earliest Christianity than is usually the case." Cullman sees tongues as ecstatic. David du Plessis insisted that the tongues were not ecstatic.

notes - " ... the whole of earliest Christianity ... regards it (speaking in tongues) as a quite legitimate gift of the Spirit and he [Paul] thanks God that he himself has this charisma to a greater degree than any others (I Corinthians 14:18).[9] *"If I pray in tongues, my spirit prays,"* of course, by the enabling of the Holy Spirit within. *"What then? Shall I pray in the Spirit, and I shall also pray with the understanding."* In Paul's private world of prayer – the two stood side by side. Prayer, indeed, has a rational element about it. And it has an element of mystery that allows us to express and experience what could not happen either in us or through us, were it not for Spirit-inspired praying.

Paul prays in the Spirit with 'sighs' or 'groans' that cannot be uttered. "The adjective 'inexpressible' is not to be understood as 'wordless', or 'dumb', but as speech that is sacrosanct, akin to what Paul heard when he was transported to paradise. This is in a sense the new *Tetragrammaton* – not unutterable, but not lightly uttered; and when it is uttered, it is revered as spirit-speech." The casual and lightness, even flippant attitude of some classical Pentecostals with regard to 'tongues' is a disregard for the sacredness of spirit-speech, and a failure to understand either its theological or practical implications.

Tongues are fundamentally a sign. They indicate the inauguration of the new age of the Spirit, the new age of prayer, new capacities for language in prayer – 'deep calleth unto deep!' And a new ability for collaboration with the Spirit in intercession is now possible. There is something about 'voiced prayer.' God could have thought the world into existence, instead He spoke it into existence. He is Word, become flesh. Our words are not omnipotent. But 'The Word' is omnipotent, and our words, borrowing His words, are potent. And His *rhemas* prayed, articulated through us, are at times prophetic declarations, in the context of our time-space world, of the intentions of God. They are

9   Ibid, 77-78.

461

Spirit-announcements and pronouncements, though the intercessor, praying by the Spirit, and in the Spirit (tongues), may not have an understanding to the transaction they are prophesying, unless and until, the Spirit gives them understanding. Still, such moments stand as prophetic declarations. The 'sighing' – the tongues, the praying in the Spirit, the groaning in intercession – is a sign that something has begun, but has 'not yet' come to pass. There is a reference point in the past – the coming of Jesus, the descent of the Spirit indicating the enthronement of Christ in the heavens; and a reference point in the future – the second coming of Christ, the ascent of the saints, the marriage of the lamb, the reign of Christ. Prayer 'in the Spirit' lays hold of these two eschological poles and draws them power into some present moment. In the 'not yet fully come kingdom' age, the Spirit prays, he groans for the perfection to come, for the sons of God to be manifest. His groan is a sound that joins the symphony of nature itself (8:22), also longing for redemption and freedom from the curse of the fall. The Holy Spirit has not come to merely engorge our emotions. He is on a mission, namely, the consummation of redemption, the 'glorious eschatological transformation of all things by the Holy Spirit in the new creation" (8:21).[10]

In the New Testament we learn that God treats prayer seriously. He is not dismissive of us when we come to Him. He does not upbraid (James 1:5). We are invited, urged to ask God for things (Matthew 6:11; Luke 11:1-4). And we are informed, that the reason for our lack, is either due to the absence of prayer or perverse prayer - self-centered prayers (James 4:2). We are told that God reserves the best for His children if they persist in prayer (Luke 11:5-13). Further, resisting selfishness, we are not only to ask for ourselves, but also for others. We are taught to bless our enemies (Mt. 5:44). Paul encourages us to pray for all saints (Eph. 6:18; see also James 5:16),

10   Ibid, 79.

and for all people, specifically government leaders (I Tim. 2:1-2).

Prayer appears to be the context in which God moves us from narrow, self-interested praying, to prayers that glorify Him, and by extension, are best for us. In order to *do all* for the glory of God, we must learn to *ask all* for the glory of God. In prayer, we submit our requests, and then submit our will – and that may mean altering our requests. "If it is possible let this happen … nevertheless, not my will but your will be done …" Because Jesus gave himself entirely to the glory of the Father, the Father, in turn, crowned Him with glory.

We are to generally bless and not to curse. And yet, there are at points in Scripture, where imprecatory prayers are admitted. They are found primarily in the Old Testament (Numbers 10:35; Judges 5:31; Psalm 28:3-5; Jeremiah 11:20). Jesus on the cross, dying for humanity, prayed for the forgiveness of His crucifiers (Luke 23:34). As the stones fell on Stephen, he prayed that the Lord would not lay the sin to the account of his attackers (Acts 7:60). Paul spoke a word of judgment against the sorcerer Elymas (Acts 13:6-12). But in all of Scripture, imprecatory prayers consist *of only 65 verses.*

In much of the New Testament, corporate prayer is taken for granted. For example, Paul exhorts the church in Rome, Ephesus, Colossae and Thessalonica to pray for him. The idea of corporate prayer gatherings among believers is assumed (Rom. 15:30; Eph. 6:19; Phil. 1:19; Col. 4:3-4; I Thess. 5:25). Paul spends a great deal of attention in his letter to the Corinthians in providing guidelines for order in their corporate prayer and worship (I Cor. 11; 14). The bottom line is a style and model that edifies the church, and not merely individuals in the church (I Cor. 14:16-17). Some may have difficulty discerning the difference between the two. After all, when individuals are edified, the church is edified; and it is impossible for the church to be edified, without individuals being edified. It is true that the two go hand-in-hand. Indeed, they are conjoined.

Yet, Paul seems focused on corporate moments that are high-jacked by individuals whether for prophetic utterances or simply moments when someone is so carried away in personal rapture, that they become oblivious to the corporate dynamic around them. In

He that is never on his knees on earth shall never stand upon his feet in heaven.

~ Charles H. Spurgeon

such a moment, they are a distraction. They are out of order. They are calling attention to themselves, and away from either Christ or the corporate church. They are individuating.

This principle should not, however, be applied in a legalistic sense. Almost every Pentecostal can cite a moment in their memory, when one individual had a break-through experience that became the catalyst for a revival, the minute in which God broke some wall, saved someone, started a process of reconciliation or a dozen other redemptive actions. Deadness is hardly the goal of Paul. There is a principle here, however, that Pentecostals often ignore – that we are not a group of individuals in the same room worshipping and praying. Rather, we constitute something larger, a corporate entity – one with extraordinary power and privilege, beyond that of any individual. "One chases a thousand, but two put ten-thousand to flight (Deuteronomy 32:30). And "where brothers dwell together in unity" (Psalm 133) – there comes an exponential blessing and anointing, entire regions are potentially affected.

Further, it is not merely the church as a corporate entity that is the focus of New Testament praying. Paul exhorts Timothy to instruct the church, as a church, to pray for kings – and thus governments, and all those in authority. The result of the church engaging, by prayer, the secular government, spiritual authority by prayer interfacing with civil authority affect the social order, "… that we might live peaceable lives." And only so, but the prayers are the essential pre-evangelism labor of the harvest force, *"And that all men might be saved"* (I Tim. 2:1-2, 8).

Prayer itself is the evidence of God at work. Of God consciousness. Of God dependence. Even when it is fleeting and weak, it is still the hope of the earth. It is the indication that a connection between heaven and earth is taking place. We pray because we believe there is a God. And that God is able and willing to save. We pray, because we have some sense that our prayer invites divine intervention that determines historical outcomes and alters the direction of events on the earth. Innate in this hope is the historical fact of God's intervention, and an existential anticipation of mediation. Spontaneous confession of sin, in moments of personal and corporate desperation, are indications in the belief that the God to whom we pray is holy and righteous, and therefore just and fair, and simultaneously impartial. Thus it is necessary for us to be completely honest and forthright about our culpability. biblical corporate prayers are laden with confessions in which people attempt to right themselves before the true God, in which they recollect His faithfulness – both His judgments and mercies. Such prayer expects God to act commensurate with His nature. To do what He has promised to do (Dan. 9; Acts 4:29-30).

The Revelation and Prayer

In the Revelation are diverse forms of prayer – as you find in the Psalms:

1. Doxologies (1:5b-6; 4:9; 5:13; 7:10, 12; 19:1).
2. Acclamations (4:11; 5:9, 12).
3. Attributions (4:8; 15:3-4; 16:5-6, 7).
4. Thanksgiving (11:17-18; 19:7-8).
5. Hallelujahs (19:1, 3, 4, 6).[11]

11 Esther Yue L. Ng, "Prayer in the Revelation," See: D. A. Carson, *Teach Us To Pray*, 120.

465

Author Ng points out the richness of the theological landscape in the Revelation. There God is trinity – there is the trisagion of His thrice holiness: "Holy, holy, holy" (4:8). He is Lord, God, Almighty – another trisagion (4:8). Further, He 'was, is, and is to come' (4:8). He is affirmed as Creator (4:11), thus the link between Genesis and the Revelation is made, the beginning and the end, the first and the last. He is King and Judge (5:13; 6:16; 7:10, 15) as well as the guarantor of salvation (7:10; 19:1). Both God the Father and the Lamb are regarded as worthy of worship (4:11; 5:12). Christ is seen as the Redeemer (1:5b-6; 5:9b-10). He is the Executor of God's plan for humanity (5:9). He is the Bridegroom and the Coming One (19:7-8; 22:17, 20).[12]

In the Revelation, there are twenty-one recorded prayers. And they come from diverse sources:

1. Four prayers are from this world and its inhabitants.

2. Two are from John's own lips (1:5b-6; 22:20), one by the Spirit and the Church and the other from the listener of the book (22:17).

3. Seventeen others are from heaven:
    a. The saints around the throne.
    b. The four living creatures (4:8; 5:14).
    c. The twenty-four elders (4:11; 11:17-18).
    d. The four living creatures and 24-elders together (5:9; 19:4).
    e. Two are by myriads of angels (5:12; 7:12).
    f. One is by the creatures of the universe (5:13).
    g. Another is from the martyrs (6:10).
    h. And one is offered by the 'angel of the water' (16:5-6).
    i. Another by the angel by the altar (16:7).
    j. One by overcomers (15:3-4).

---

12   Ibid, 122-127.

k. Four by the multitudes in heaven (7:10; 19:1-2, 3, 6-8).[13]

In the Revelation, prayer is sung as well as spoken, which has led some to call the Revelation, the psalter of the New Testament. It is a book full of singing! And it is a 'new' song that is being sung (5:9; 14:3; see also the Psalms, which had 'new' songs – 40:2-3; 96:1-2; 98:1; 144:9-10; Isaiah 42:10, 13). At times the prayers are also cried out (5:12; 6:10; 7:10; 16:7; 19:1, 3). The voices blending together are represented as a might stream – many waters and as thunder (14:2; 19:6).[14]

Christensen claimed: "The whole portrayal of the church's struggle finds its culmination in the triumphant prayer and worship of the book of Revelation."[15] In chapters 4 and 5, there is a glimpse into heaven. Preceding those chapters is the dismal news about the sad state of the church (Revelation 2; 3). What follows is the unleashing of war, famine, plague and death in the earth, along with a proliferation of martyrs (6). If we expect such earthly scenes to affect heaven, we are mistaken. There, the music continuously plays. There, angels and elders worship. There living creatures and eventually all of earth joins in worship. The ceaseless prayer and worship in heaven focuses on God's holiness (4:5). It honors Him as the Creator (4:11). It rehearses His redemptive action, His crucifixion and enthronement (5:9-10). It anticipates the consummation of all 'power and riches and wisdom and strength and honor and glory and blessing' (5:12) in Christ. The descriptors compound here – power, riches, wisdom, etc. Nothing will be beyond His reach. All things are committed to

---

13 Ibid, 128-129.
14 Ibid, 129.
15 Christensen, "Prayer," Julius Bodensieck, *The Encyclopedia of the Lutheran Church* (Minneapolis: Augsburg Publishing House, 1966), HI, 1973.

Him. The final prayer-song is a celebration of sovereignty, "To Him who sits on the throne. And to the Lamb, forever and ever" (5:15). Here in these five prayer songs is the cycle of history:

1. The holy God (4:8);

2. Is also the Creator (4:11);

3. And He has redeemed mankind and elevated sinful men to the status of kings and priests, with the promise of the earth itself, remade as a holy kingdom (5:9-10);

4. He is worthy, being alive, yet having been slain. He overcame death – as a 'the Lamb,' the ultimate sacrifice for man (5:12);

5. He is enthroned. The conflict is over. The battle has been won. The Father and the Lamb are forever reunited (5:13).

Here is the whole redemptive story – the holy God, the Creator, is also the redeemer. He was slain, and yet death could not hold Him (5:5-6). He lives, enthroned and one with God.

At first, only the four living creatures are involved (4:8) in singing, then they are joined by the twenty-four elders (4:10). In the next song, the prayers of the saints are loosed in heaven, so heaven and believers on the earth are now praying together. These prayers of the saints are set to music – that is, they are 'music' to heaven. And they are offered at the altar of incense in heaven. We pray, and heaven burns incense. We pray, and heaven sings. Here is the church – on earth and in heaven, bound together, mysteriously, in prayer. Next, angels join their voices in the song – ten-thousand-times-ten-thousand, plus thousands more (5:11). Finally, all of heaven and earth are united in this declarative prophetic prayer (5:13). O the power of prayer. In Revelation 8:2-5, the prayers of the saints are offered on the golden altar in heaven. The angel fills the censor with fire from heaven's altar and cast it into the earth. Suddenly, there are "noises, thunder, and lightning" and the earth trembles. O the power of prayer.

Prayer in the Revelation is presented as an extended liturgical service. The entire framework of the book is prayer. There are glimpses into heaven's worship, into heaven's interaction with prayer. There are shades of Isaiah 6, noting that we are again in the throne-room, and something significant is about to happen, something that transcends the thrones of earthly kings. Hymns are found throughout the book, as are seven beatitudes, thus seven blessings. Here, prayer is not a plea into oblivion, here, prayers are sacred. They preserved. They are sounds from the earth, that when collected in heaven, are like the peels of thunder, like a gathering storm headed for the earth.

Even in the darkest hours of the seeming triumph of the Anti-Christ, prayer lives. There are the prayers of the martyrs (Revelation 6:10). There is the scene of the great multitude of "every nation, tribe, people and language, standing before the throne and before the Lamb ... wearing white robes and holding palm branches ..." (7:9-12). There is the announcement of consummation, "The kingdom of the world has become the kingdom of our Lord and of His Messiah, and He will reign for ever and ever" (11:15). With this announcement, the twenty-four elders fall to their faces and pray, discerning two simultaneous events – the judgment of the dead and the rewarding of the prophets and those who reverence the name of the Lord. Suddenly, the Ark of the Covenant is visible. There are flashes of lightning, rumblings along with peals of thunder, an earthquake and a severe hailstorm follow (11:16-19).

In Revelation 15, there is yet another prayer moment. Those who have been victorious over the beast and its image, over the number of its name, are seen in heaven. They appear with harps and the prayer they sing is a song of both Moses and the Lamb, Jesus. "Great and marvelous are your deeds, Lord God Almighty. Just and true are your ways" (15:3). The song anticipates the moment when Jesus, "King of the nations" will receive His due honor. "Who will not fear you, Lord, and bring glory to your name? ... All nations will come and worship before you" (15:4). Suddenly, the temple in heaven is opened, called "the tabernacle of the covenant law." Jesus, in His great act of love at the cross, has delayed judgment on the earth as long as is possible. Standing behind His death is the law. And also Moses - the lawgiver. Now love itself must demand justice. Righteousness must be engaged, even if it requires wrath. Not only has the innocent Son of God been crucified, but His followers are the victims of the wrath of the beast. Prayer calls for intervention.

The Difference the Cross Makes

In the Old Testament, the covenant of God is tied to an earthly kingdom, the state, responsible for equity, justice, law and order. Holy war is justified. The law is dominant. In the New Testament, we have the full revelation of God in Jesus, the Christ. His earthly life ends at the cross, which we interpret as an act of God's love, of God (John 3:16), in Christ, having come to the earth to die for mankind – the lamb slain from the foundation of the earth (John 1:29, 36; 6:51; 10:17; 16:28; I Timothy 1:15; Hebrews 10:5; Revelation 13:5). But the cross cannot be understood merely as an act of love. There is another factor at work – it is the judgment of God (Colossians 2:14; II Corinthians 5:21). The cross is not merely a matter of love, it is also about truth. "God so loved the world ..." is only half the equation. The other is equally true, that when sin was found not *in* Christ, but 'on' Him, the relationship with the Father and the Son were momentarily severed (Galatians 1:3-5; Hebrews 1:3; I Peter 2:24; Matthew 27:46).

"Not until the supreme exhibition of God's displeasure at sin, demonstrated by the death of His Son upon the cross was it possible for the believer to wait patiently while God's longsuffering permitted the wicked to enjoy his temporary success. Nor was the longsuffering of God properly understood until Jesus came to earth to teach His love to men."[16]

Having seen the cross, can we doubt now the justice of God? *"He who did not spare His own Son, but delivered Him up for us all, how shall He not with Him also freely give us all things?" (Romans 8:32).* The cross is the Father's pledge to redeem the earth and a remnant of mankind. He is first revealed as a lamb, but He will return again as a lion (Revelation 5:4-6). Heaven anticipates the moment.

There is a sound "like the roar of a great multitude." Those seen and heard in heaven are shouting, *"Hallelujah! Salvation and glory and power belong to our God, for true and just are His judgments"* (19:1-2). This moment anticipates the judgment of the great prostitute, the harlot church, "who corrupted the earth by her adulteries" and is responsible for the deaths of martyrs. But there is more. The twenty-four elders and the four living creatures join the moment. They fall down in worshipful prayer and cry out, *"Amen, Hallelujah!"* An amazing thing occurs, urging more praise, *"A voice came from the throne, saying, 'Praise our God, all you His servants, you who fear Him, both great and small!'"* It is as if God Himself, a voice from the throne, urges the intensification of praise.

Ultimately, prayer does not derive from the earth, but from heaven. As Matthew Henry would say, "When God intends great mercy for His people, the first thing He does is to set them a-praying." The response in heaven again sounds like a great multitude, like the roar of a waterfall, like thunder (19:6), *"Hallelujah! For our Lord God Almighty reigns. Let us rejoice and be glad and give Him glory!"* (v. 7) Despite all the beast has done, notwithstanding Lucifer's most valiant attempt, at the end of the efforts of the Anti-Christ and the False Prophet, God is still on His throne and His claim to the earth

16 Gleason L. Archer, Jr. *Survey of the Old Testament Introduction*, 453.

stands. The Lamb has won. Heaven is rejoicing, *"For the wedding of the Lamb has come, and His bride has made herself ready. Fine linen, bright and clean, was given her to wear"* (19:8). Heaven opens and on a white horse is one called *'Faithful and True'* who *'judges and wages war.'* With fiery eyes and multiple crowns on His head, wearing a bloody robe, He goes forth as 'the Word of God' with the armies of heaven following. He is the "King of kings and Lord of lords" (19:11-16).

What must not be missed is that all of these actions throughout the Revelation, the chronicle of God's coming intervention, are in the context of prayer. Prayer seems in some ways to precipitate the action. Prayers are one, seamless with the action. At points, God Himself – or at least 'a voice from the throne' - urges praise and prayer as if they empower the intervention.

In the closing verses of both the book and of the Bible, "The Spirit and the bride" join their voices together, issuing an invitation, *"Come!"* they say. *"Let the one who is thirsty come; and let the one who wishes take the free gift of the water of life"* (21:17). We have now come full circle. We are back at the tree of life (21:19) which is now in the Holy City.

The words actually form a Spirit-inspired word. They proceed from the lips of the Bride. They represent a plea from the true heirs to the earth, an invitation to Christ, the bridegroom, to come. His response to the prayer is, *"Yes, I am coming soon"* (21:20).

Prayer References

Revelation

1. Elders in worship (27 words; Rev 4:11).
2. Angels in worship (22 words; Rev 5:12).
3. All creatures in worship (22 words; Rev 5:13).

4. Martyrs for an end to suffering (22 words; Rev 6:10).

5. Great multitude in worship (13 words; Rev 7:10).

6. Angels in worship (23 words; Rev 7:12).

7. Glorified saints in worship (56 words; Rev 19:1-6).

8. John for the coming of Jesus Christ a second time, 5 words (Rev 22:20).

Finis Jennings Dake, *Dake's Annotated Reference Bible* (Lawrenceville, GA: Dake Bible Sales, 1963, 1991).

SECTION THREE

GLIMPSES INTO THE CHURCH OF GOD HISTORY OF PRAYER

CHAPTER NINETEEN

A History of Prayer
in the Church of God

A WINDOW THROUGH TIME

**Historical Highlights of the
First Twenty-Two Years of the Church of God**
Adapted from a synopsis by Dr. James M. Beaty

1884

Seven years prior to 1884, R. G. Spurling, the son of Richard Spurling, had been licensed to preach by the Pleasant Hill Baptist Church in Cherokee County, NC. Because of the message he preached, charges were brought against him and he turned in his license to preach. Very soon after that, because of the discontent caused by his continued preaching, he asked that his name be removed from the Pleasant Hill Baptist Church membership rolls. Then for two years he dedicated himself to the study of Scripture and church history, with much prayer and fasting.

1886

August 19

The first congregation was organized at Barney Creek with eight (8) members. R. G. (Richard Green) Spurling (1857-1935) preached the message and organized the church. His father, Richard Spurling (1810-1891), an ordained Baptist minister [age: 75] was installed as minister; then R.G. was received as member. Two weeks later, R. G. was ordained and installed as pastor.

The Proposal and Invitation to Membership: 1886

"As many Christians as are here present that are desirous to be free from all man-made creeds and traditions, and are willing to take the New Testament, or law of Christ, for your only rule of faith and practice, giving each other equal rights and privilege to read and interpret for yourselves as your conscience may dictate, and are willing to sit together as the Church of God to transact business as the same, come forward."

Persons who responded:

- Richard Spurling (father) and Barbara Spurling, wife of R. G. Spurling (son)
- John, James and Mary Adeline (Polly) Plemons (with son and daughter)
- Their son and his wife, John Paul & Melinda Plemons
- Their daughter Margaret Plemons Loftis
- And her daughter: Adeline Loftis

Decisions Made Before Dedication

1. **Name:** The name would be 'Christian Union.'
2. **Basis of Participation:** Members would be required to have good Christian character.
3. **Credentials:** The credentials of ministers who joined could be recognized.
4. **Minister/Pastor:** Richard Spurling was selected to serve as the minister.

Action Taken by the New Minister:

Richard Spurling, as the newly elected minister, took charge and

1. Officially and legally organized the group and dedicated it as a church and

2. Received R. G. as a member.

September 2 (Thursday): R. G. (the son) was ordained and installed as the Minister.

Note: Richard (the father) was turned out of Holly Springs Baptist Church immediately, but two months later the charges were dropped. He remarried in 1887 and died in 1891.

1896

Summer

The Great Revival in Shearer School House in Camp Creek, NC, which lasted ten days, was led by William Martin, Joe M. Tipton and Milton McNabb, who were from Monroe Co., TN. and William (Billy) Hamby, Spurling's brother-in-law, who lived in NC. Bryant, and almost certainly Spurling, attended. Over 100 claimed sanctification. Forty people, at one time, were turned out of Liberty Baptist Church. Revival continued after the meeting with W. F. Bryant as the leader. The group was denied the use of the school house. Persecution and fanaticism followed. In the home meetings many began to speak with tongues.

1897

Log church constructed on property donated from Dickson Kilpatrick

The movement came under persecution. First, the log church, which was located across the road from Shearer School House, was set on fire, but rain doused the fire. Then, dynamite was used, but only a portion suffered damage, and it was repaired. Finally, on a Sunday, a group of citizens, with at least one pastor and sheriff among them, tore the building apart, piled the logs high, and set them afire. One-hundred-six people were involved. At the trial, in 1898, the church members themselves pleaded for clemency in behalf of the group. W. F. Bryant's brother was among the persecutors.

1899

Ambrose Jessup Tomlinson (1865-1943) Entered the Picture

From around the time of 1896, A. J. Tomlinson, from Indiana, served as a summer missionary to the remote mountain area. On July 14, 1899, a Friday, he arrived in Murphy, NC, with his family. And on October 16, a Monday, he was in the area of Culberson.

1900

Tomlinson Started a School for Children

The June US Census indicates that two of Bryant's children, Luther and Julius, were living in Tomlinson's home to attend school.

1901

Events in Tomlinson's Life

March 10, Sunday. Twelve children and nine grown workers were living in Tomlinson's home.

March 25, Monday. He participated in 'foot washing' for first time.

April 10, Wednesday. Note in diary: 'No money with 25 mouths to feed.'

June 28, Thursday. The school closes for the summer.

August 18, Saturday. Tomlinson leaves his home, due to persecution. He goes to Maine to attend a convention at Shiloh where he is sick for four days. He reports that he is baptized in water by Sandford. He left Maine on October 6, a Sunday, and arrived back in North Carolina, November 16, a Saturday. He walked most of the way. There were 25 students in school at that time and 14 of those were living in Tomlinson's home.

1902

May 15, Thursday, A New Church Organized

A church was organized in the home of W. F. Bryant in Camp Creek by R. G. (Richard Green) Spurling and R. Frank Porter, a Methodist with Holiness views.

Name: The Holiness Church.

W. F. Bryant is ordained. Spurling is named pastor. There are no new members for one year. In that time, they study the Scriptures.

November (1902) to May (1903)

Tomlinson and family returned to Indiana He worked in secular work.

1903

May 27, Wednesday

Tomlinson leaves Elwood, Indiana to return to Culberson. His wife and family did not come to join him until July 8.

June 13, Saturday

Tomlinson joins the Holiness Church at Camp Creek. So do two deacons and two more members. During the following year, fourteen more members join.

Most of the rest of 1903 and all of 1904 was dedicated to planting and strengthening churches.

1904

December

A. J. Tomlinson moves to Cleveland, Tennessee, to Gaut Street. His family attends Cumberland Presbyterian. The Holiness Church, besides the two or three small groups attended by Spurling, has one congregation in Jones, GA; two in Tennessee – Union Grove and Drygo; and one in Camp Creek, NC.

1906

January 26-27, Friday and Saturday, First Assembly of Churches

The First Assembly was held in Cherokee County, NC, in the home of J. C. and Malissie Murphy. The home is still standing as a memorial to this event. Twenty-one attended. They came from Jones, Georgia; Camp Creek, North Carolina; and Turtletown and Cleveland, Tennessee. Among them were: Belford Abercrombie (Balford Crumby); Johnnie Brown; John Ellison; R. R. Jones; Elder R. G. Spurling; Elder Andrew Freeman (Ordained by Spurling in the Christian Union); Elder W. F. Bryant and his wife Brunetty (Nettie) along with daughters, Agnes and Ella Bryant Robinson; J. C. Murphy, a deacon and his wife, Margaret Malissie Gay Murphy (Maddox, nicknamed, Norma); Theophilus Ellis and Nancy, his daughter; W. M. Coleman, and his mother, Lucy; T. N. Elrod; Alexander Hamby; Sallie Hamby (Wife of Billy, brother of Barbara, and cousin of Alexander); Evangelist M. S. Lemons and Pastor A. J. Tomlinson.

1907

January 9-13, Wednesday - Sunday at Union Grove, Bradley Co. TN.

Second Assembly was held. The name of the organization was changed to Church of God (Jan 11, Friday, 8:30 AM).

1908

January 12, Sunday (Following the close of the Third Assembly)

Tomlinson was baptized in the Holy Spirit with the Bible sign of speaking in tongues while Gaston B. Cashwell, who had been baptized in the Holy Spirit at Asuza Street, was preaching.

CHAPTER 19

A HISTORY OF PRAYER
IN THE CHURCH OF GOD

Dr. James Beaty

Prayer did not start with us and our forebears in the Church of God. Prayer, which is communication with God, goes back to the creation of man. We read in the Word that *"God created man in His own image, in the image of God created He him; male and female created He them. And God blessed them, and God said unto them, 'Be fruitful, and multiply, and replenish the earth, and subdue it: and have dominion...'"* (Gen. 1:27f). And thus began God's conversation with the human race. God speaks to us and tells us about His Will and what we are to do and not to do. And God made it possible that we could speak to Him. That is prayer, talking with God, and it has many forms, which include praise and worship as well as petition and intercession. When we remember that prayer is part of a conversation with God, it should remind us to listen to hear what the Spirit is saying to us.[1]

Pentecostal Prayer

As Pentecostals, our forebears almost always prayed in distinctive ways – first, they prayed "out-loud"; and second, when they prayed the volume was typically "loud"; and third, they lifted their voices audibly, at the same time. They inherited this mostly from the

1   Rev. 2:11, 17, 29; 3:6, 13, 22.

Holiness movement,[2] but it was also found in evangelical revivalism of the early 1800s. In was described in our early history as a sound like that of "the falling of many waters."

"Many prayers were going up to God for the salvation of souls and a general refreshing from the presence of the Lord. At times, we have called for concert prayer, and as eager and precious people fall on their knees and faces, and cry out to God, there is a sound as the falling of many waters."[3]

Let us think about praying out-loud for a moment. To communicate with someone is to speak with them. This implies an audible voice, i.e., a sound that is spoken by the mouth and heard with the ears. We speak and they hear, and then they speak and we hear. This whole process, even in the natural is a mystery and a miracle that is not completely understood, although most of us do it daily and never think of what is really going on.

A conversation begins with an intention in the heart or mind.

---

2   S. B. Shaw, *Touching Incidents and Remarkable Answers to Prayer*, (Grand Rapids: S. B. Shaw), 1893, 133f. Here we find a story of new converts burdened for their neighbors who were against the revival. The Spirit told them to go pray for them. It seemed as we went that we could hardly keep from running; and as soon as we entered the house we fell upon our knees, exclaiming, that God had sent us there to pray. We scarcely realized our surroundings, and do not know how long or loud we prayed; but when we arose from our knees we could see that all in the house were wonderfully affected, and the one who so short a time before was saying bitter things against the Lord and His work, was wringing her hands, and weeping, and saying "What have I done? I did not know that I was so wicked that anybody needed to pray like that for me." Shaw was president of the Michigan Holiness Association. This book had wide circulation among early Pentecostals because it was a collection of testimonies to God's healing power and miraculous answers to prayer. The full text of the book is available on the web. This does not constitute an endorsement of everything in the book.

3   *The Evening Light* and *Church of God Evangel* (Cleveland, TN: Church of God Publishing House, 1910/11/15 [I/18]), 4.

Remember, in the biblical description of the internal workings of the human being, the heart, the inner core of a human being, is where knowing (knowledge), feeling (emotion) and deciding (volition) are done. As Jesus said, *"Out of the heart the mouth speaks"* (Luke 6:45). What comes out of the mouth is always either what we intend, even when people lie, or an indication of what is in the heart. But how is the intent or overflow of the heart turned into words? Physically, and mechanically, this is produced by a bellows - the lungs plus the diaphragm. They force air over the vocal cords which produce varying wave lengths of sound that can be measured. And there it begins to get complicated. How are the intentions of the heart loaded on to these wave lengths? We all acquire, as children, a culturally encoded software program, which we call language. There are many of these in different parts of the world. This is a program for coding and un-coding. And when we pray in tongues, in the Spirit, the Holy Spirit is involved in the coding.[4]

Sound, loaded with meaning, comes out of the mouth. It travels through the air, losing force with the distance as it travels.

> *Thursday, October 30, 1919. the General Assembly service commenced with songs, prayers and praises. After singing, the General Overseer asked the congregation to bow their heads in silent prayer. Then all prayed together - the Lord's prayer.*
>
> Minutes of the Fourteenth Church of God General Assembly, Cleveland, TN; October 29 – November 4, 1919.

---

4   Cf. What Paul says in I Cor. 14: "If I pray in a tongue, my spirit prays (v. 14). I will pray with the spirit, and I will pray with the understanding also: I will sing with the spirit, and I will sing with the understanding also" (vv. 14:15).

Its destination, of course, is another person's ear. It is spoken to be heard. When it reaches the ear, it is channeled into a funnel that brings the sound waves into contact with the ear drum. The incoming sound waves activate vibrations in the ear drum, on the same wave length as the incoming sound waves, and somehow the intention associated with the sound as it was produced is captured and communicated in the brain of the hearer. "Faith comes by hearing!"(Rom. 10:17) What a marvelous process! We are, indeed, fearfully and wonderfully made! (Psalm 139:14).

Our communication with God involves both speaking to God and listening to God speak to us (whether through the Word or through the Spirit). So the Word and prayer go together. One thing we have almost forgotten: the Word was meant to be heard. John wrote, "Blessed is he who reads, and they who hear the words of this prophecy" (Rev 1:3); and Paul said, "Faith comes by hearing and hearing by the Word of God" (Rom 10:17).

ACCENT

George Buttrick asks and answers a rhetorical question. Question: "Can't a man pray without belonging to a church?" Answer: "He cannot pray well or fully until he is a member of some fellowship of prayer."† Private and corporate prayer are conjoined, inseparable! The church cannot be a collection of people who pray – it must be a praying church with people who pray – together!

Spurgeon observed, "The condition of the church may be very accurately gauged by its prayer meetings. So is the prayer meeting a grace-ometer, and from it we may judge of the amount of divine working among a people. If God be near a church, it must pray. And if He be not there, one of die first tokens of His absence will be a slothfulness in prayer!"

~Charles Haddon Spurgeon
George Buttrick, *Prayer*, 283.

Common Prayer

Why do people pray? There are many answers to this question, depending on the enlightenment of the people and the situations in which they find themselves. They may pray because of what God has done for them. They may burst into praise at the sudden realization of the presence and glory of God. They may fall on their faces in supplication when tragedy and disaster happen.

This question should be looked at in the light of the Word. The human being is a finite creature and lives on the edge of eternity. We live both in this material world and in the spiritual world. And we are always just a breath away from the exit of this material world. Since we are finite, we are often up against problems and situations that require more wisdom and more power than we have. We are forced to seek help beyond ourselves. That is why the early members of the Church of God were men and women of prayer. They knew the Lord and they knew that He was their ultimate source of help. They knew that *"every good and perfect gift comes down from above"* (James 1:17) and that, if you did not ask, you could deprive yourself of the blessing, *"You have not, because you ask not"* (James 4:2).

Prayer and Coming to God

The most important point in anyone's life is when that person is made a new creature in Christ Jesus. This is accomplished by hearing God, answering His call and by the transforming power of His Holy Spirit. Hearing the Word of God is a prerequisite to our calling on Him in the name of Jesus. As Paul said, *"How can they call on Him of whom they have not heard"* (Rom 10:14)?

The Holy Spirit, who hovered over the deep, in the creation and the ordering of the earth (Gen. 1:2), also hovers over the re-creation of human beings in the work of the new creation (John 3:5-8). The

Spirit draws the hearer to the Lord – both the Father (John 6:44) and the Son draw (John 12:32) through the Spirit and as the hearer becomes willing and ready to turn *to* God by faith, and *from* idols (they "turned to God from idols" I Thess. 1:9) and *from* sin (i.e., repentance). As the Spirit blows, moves, one is re-created or made a new creature in Christ Jesus (II Cor. 5:17).

This turning in Hebrew is *teshuvah*. It can be illustrated by the process used to change the direction of a sail boat. With the sails set in one position, the boat is directed in one course or bearing. To change direction, the sails must be unfastened from the first position and moved to another, to adjust the direction of the boat. Yet, if the wind dies or there is no wind (the Spirit), there can be no change of direction. Turning necessitates the work of the Spirit.

"Coming to God" involves communication and a connection with God. One must not only confess one's sin and one's need, one must open the heart. Remember, the latch is on the inside: The Lord is at the door knocking (Rev. 3:20). We must say, "Yes, I am a sinner" (I John 1:9). And "Yes, Jesus Christ is Lord, to the glory of God the Father" (Rom. 10:9). Faith is a surrendering of all that we are to Jesus Christ. It dares to believe the promise: "Christ died for me, I am forgiven, I have life, and I am a new creation in Christ Jesus" (Rom. 5:8; John 10:10; 20:31; II Cor. 5:17).

Our forebears understood that the preacher bringing the message needed the anointing of the Holy Spirit and the working of the Spirit to do the work. Only Jesus can save. He is the Savior (Jude 25), and His Holy Spirit is the active force that gives the preacher the inspiration and, at the same time, the Holy Spirit is the one that makes it real in the heart of the hearer, bringing conviction of sin and not only points to Jesus but draws the sinner to Jesus and as he or she yields works the miracle of the new birth.

A Personal Story

Let me share my conversion. It was Sunday night, April 14, 1940, in the little meeting place of the Church of God in Smithfield, NC, a building some twenty-feet wide and only forty feet long. Sister Ida Parrish was the pastor and there were seventeen members. The building sat in the woods, across railroad tracks, and behind the Smithfield Spinning Mill. Charles (Junior) Harrell and I were there that night. The Spirit of God touched our hearts, showed us our sin and pointed us to Jesus. I felt like a ton of bricks was on my shoulder and that I was suspended by the breath of life over hell. We both rushed to the altar, but neither of us knew how to pray because no one was converted in either of our families.

Nevertheless, I prayed - in desperation. All of a sudden, the burden of my soul was lifted and I knew that I was forgiven. Great joy flooded my heart. Several people were around me, praying with me and for me. When the joy of the Lord appeared on my countenance, I heard someone say, "Believe on the Lord Jesus, and He will sanctify you." At the time, I did not know what they meant, but I would soon learn - as a new child of God, the power of God, through the shed blood of Jesus and the power of the Holy Spirit, could and would break every bondage in my life so that I could live in victory, without condemnation, no longer in bondage to old addictions and habits. I would no longer be a servant of sin (Heb. 9:13-14; Rom. 1:16; 6:1-7; 12:1-2).

After a period of rejoicing, the prayer was ended. Sister Parrish encouraged us to tell what God had done for us. I said, "The Lord has saved me and sanctified me. Pray for me." And so did my friend. Then without asking either us or the church members, she said, "Folks, we are going to have church every night this week so that these two young men can receive the Holy Ghost." I was in the ninth grade and Junior was a drop-out, but we were back each night. On Thursday night, the Lord baptized both of us in the Holy Spirit. Somehow, in prayerful seeking, I found myself lying on my back on the floor and speaking in tongues. Down inside there was joy unspeakable (I Peter 1:18). After a certain time the language changed completely; and then, again and again, for several times (Acts 2:4; I Cor. 12:10, 28).

The problem had been in knowing exactly how to yield to the Holy Spirit. I wanted everything to be completely of the Spirit. Later, I learned that the Holy Spirit, contrary to evil spirits, does not invade one's personality, turn off the lights and take over either our personality or abilities (I Cor. 14:32; Lk. 8:29; I Sam. 18:10). We must cooperate and this is stated clearly in the golden text of Pentecost, Acts 2:4, "They spoke as the Spirit gave utterance."

This is what the church needs today – for people to be saved, delivered from the bondage of sin and filled with the Holy Spirit. And we must be intentional about it. We must teach about being baptized in the Holy Spirit. Remember, Jesus is the baptizer, just as He is the Savior and the Sanctifier. We must help new converts, along with those who have not been baptized, to become aware of their need for Spirit baptism, and we should encourage them to seek the blessing.[5] That means, we must make places and times for this to be done.

Prayer and Serving God

The life of the believer is to be a life of love and service. The great commandment (Matthew 22:38) and the one "like unto it" spell out the unconditional nature of our love for God and the obligation to love the "near-one" (our neighbor) as we love ourselves. The Christian life is a life lived in communication with God the Father, God the Son and God the Holy Spirit - *that* is prayer. We are to live in Christ (Acts 17:28); and if we allow Him who saves us to baptize us in the Holy Spirit, we also live in the fullness of the Spirit. The Triune God

---

5   In the early days the 'Baptism in the Holy Spirit' was often referred to as 'the blessing.'

speaks to us through His Word and through His Spirit. The latter may be through nudging and urging us; or it may be crystal clear. And our response is what we call prayer.

The body of the individual Christian is God's temple (I Cor. 6:19-20).

The Triune God dwells within. And He desires and wills to do His work through us. He inspires and nudges us, and we feel that we want to do something for Him, when, as a matter of fact, it is He who wants to do something through us. So often we are not sensitive. We are hard of hearing. We are occupied with "our" agenda.

When we undertake to do something for Him, and find that we are inadequate, we have to turn to Him for wisdom and power. At such times, we neither know *what* to do nor *how* to do it. Early members and leaders of the Church of God learned to be dependent on Him, just as He had said, *"Without me you can do nothing"* (John 15:5). They knew, that unless the Lord watches over the city, the watchmen watches in vain and that unless the Lord builds the house, the laborers labor in vain (Psalm 127:1). So everything had to be bathed in prayer and supported by prayer. Otherwise it was a failure.

> *A church is never more like the New Testament Church than when it is praying.*

Prayer – And Our Denominational Beginnings
The Evangel and Prayer

In March of 1910, when the publication of the *Evening Light and Church of God Evangel* started, the leaders wanted the paper to be a blessing, but they knew it had to be sustained by prayer, if it was to fulfill its purpose. They would declare, "We want the little white-winged 'evangel' to go into every home possible."[6] In the same issue, there was a call for prayer to cover the publication. "While we are scattering the literature we must not forget to pray and ask God to bless the truth, thus given out."[7] The Evangel was born out of prayer and sustained by prayer.

Prayer and Church Planting

Early church ministry, from the beginning, had two dimensions. First, the establishing of new churches; and second, the building up of churches already established. Prayer was needed in both of these activities. What we call revival meetings were instrumental and useful in both areas. We are members, not only of the body of Christ, but also members one of another. We should pray one for the other today, as our forebears did, as we continue to do the task of

ACCENT

As Church of God people traveled to the 2006 General Assembly in Indianapolis, they found the city tense due to a sniper who was randomly shooting cars on the interstate from the vantage of an overpass. Signs urged, "Watch for suspicious overpass activities." The sniper eluded the state police. Two people were dead.

All during the week, Church of God prayer teams walked the area around the convention center. More than a hundred 'prayer-gift packs' were delivered to merchants, the community leaders, to workers in the State Capitol building. One teen prayer team led by Sherry Nicholson was out of the church where Michael Knight serves as pastor. They also went to the State Capitol to pray. There, Tom Walker, founder of the Governor's Prayer Team met them and assisted them, providing a kind of tour. He took them into the small chapel in the Capitol building, and there Tom commented, "My

6 *The Evening Light,* 1910/04/01 (I/3), 2.

7 Ibid. From the beginning every shipment was prayed over before it left the premises.

how those teens prayed!" When they finished, Sherry asked if there was anything specific they could pray for. "The capture of the illusive sniper!" Tom replied. And pray they did. When the prayer time was finished, Tom Walker was convinced, on the very strength of the fervency, that the deed was done. He took the entire team down to the Governor's office to inform him - "It's done! The culprit has been captured" - of course, by faith.

As the team followed Tom into the Governor's secretaries office, and Tom was about to request a moment with Governor Mitch Daniels, the governor himself emerged from his office. Tom reported the fervent prayer time and proclaimed his confidence that the sniper would be apprehended. Governor Daniels, holding his cell-phone in his hand, announced that he had just received the call seconds earlier, "The sniper had been captured."

Even while we pray - indeed, before we pray, the Lord answers.

ministry together or, to put it more correctly, as God does His work through us.

Simultaneous Intercession

Brother M. S. Lemons had gone to South Georgia for a revival. He preached salvation, sanctification and the baptism in the Holy Spirit, as well as offering prayer for the sick and for persons with other problems. Sister Clyde Cotton Haynes wrote a letter to the *Evangel*, which was published in the January 10, 1914 issue. She reported:

> We left Cleveland after Assembly to assist Brother Lemons in a meeting in South Georgia, near Melrose ...

Sister Haynes included in the article a number of revival activities in various places along the journey.

> We joined Brother Lemons in the battle

at Melrose. He arrived during the first service on Saturday night. At the very beginning of the meeting, the Spirit began to weep through us. Brother Lemons preached his first sermon

Sunday morning with tears streaming from his eyes. Awful burdens came upon some of the saints, and they lay prostrate on the floor under them. It was a heart-searching time. Backsliders were reclaimed and some of the saints who were bound got free, and the power began to fall and God did melt hearts with His great white-heated love.

As the glory of the Lord filled the place, some were leaping, dancing, shouting, and speaking in other tongues. As the Holy Ghost played on the organ, a number would be on the floor dancing under the power. Sinners came to the altar crying to God for mercy. The last Sunday night of the meeting while Brother Lemons was preaching, all at once, people began to cry and scream, and arose from their seats all over the congregation, and came rushing to the altar, until the entire front and part of the aisles were filled with seekers. Oh, such a scene as it was can't be described,

ACCENT

Prior to the 1990 Assembly, Doug Small had approached the late Dr. Robert Fisher, member of the International Executive Committee, regarding the possibility of having an early morning prayer room available for those who wished a place to pray at the assembly. Fisher informed him that a morning prayer time had been previously tried at the Assembly decades before, by wonderful men, without success. Small told Fisher – "Even if no one else comes, I need the room!" And that began the morning prayer times at the General Assembly that have now persisted for more than twenty years. In that first year, the prayer meetings were not announced and the site was not well marked. But each day, Dr. Ray Hughes inquired of Brother Small, "How many today?" By the end of the week, hundreds were attending.

In subsequent years, the prayer room has had moments when the crowds simply overflowed the room, and the prayer meeting then spilled out into the adjacent hall.

> At one assembly, when the room was too small, hundreds were turned away on the first morning as they sought a place of prayer, but were not able to be accommodated. Still, this is one of the signs of the spiritual renewal taking place in the denomination. Prayer times have been conducted, with communion, for State Overseers and General Officials just prior to the Assembly.
>
> Each year, someone notes, "This is the best kept secret of the Assembly - the prayer room!"

people crying to God and saints rejoicing.

Brother C. R Curtis, who had been helping in the meeting, was missing this entire service, and when the brethren got to their homes that night he was still missing, and they lighted their lanterns and went out in search for him, and he came to them out of the woods where God had held him in prayer that night while Brother Lemons preached."[8]

No wonder the fire fell in such a mighty way. Prayer is the key that unlocks Heaven's door. Praise God for the victory He gave. The saints were wonderfully blessed and a number of backsliders reclaimed. Eleven received the Holy Ghost. Six were added to the Church, and quite a number healed. We left the dear ones shouting the victory, and preparing to have a Sunday School.[9]

---

8   Editor's Note: This is now commonly called 'simultaneous intercession' – the act of one praying, while another is preaching or ministering. It was common in the partnership of Finney with Daniel Nash. It is pictured in symbolic form in the act of Moses on the mountain in prayer, as Joshua battles the Amalekites. The symbolism is further expanded as Moses tires in intercession, and Aaron and Hur are forced to support him by holding his hands up as the battle proceeds.

9   *Evangel,* 6. For a dramatic story of prayer covering the evangelistic and pastoral ministry see, LaVerne J. Haney, "Praying Through: The Spiritual Narrative of Mother E. J. Dabney," The Journal of the I.T.C., 231-240. The full text is also online. This is not part of our Church of God history but is from the Church of God in Christ, a sister organization.

In the history of the Church of God, it can be said, as Alfred Lord Tennyson wrote in one of his poems, "More things are wrought by prayer than this world dreams of."[10] My wife's mother, Ethel Keener Green, was, along with her husband, a minister of the Church of God. She wrote a lot of statements about prayer in the margins of her Bible. One of those was: "Prayer can do anything God can do." Our people in those days knew that nothing was accomplished without prayer and without God's help.

The Early General Assemblies

At the first assembly in 1906, there were two important measures passed regarding prayer. First, the intent to have a weekly prayer meeting in each local church [11]; and second, for each home to have family devotions, with Bible reading and prayer. [12] It is at this assembly that the character of prayer is noted in the phrase, "strong men wept" and dedicated themselves to "the spread of the glorious gospel of the Son of God."

With the second Assembly in 1907, the practice of opening the morning, afternoon and night sessions with a "prayer service" became the norm. The name of the church was also changed from the *Holiness Church* to the *Church of God*. In the fifth assembly, in 1910, it was decided to start publishing a paper for the church and this was

---

10 From Morte d'Arthur.

11 "It is, therefore, the sense of this assembly that we recommend, advise and urge that each local church hold a prayer meeting at least once a week."

12 "It is, therefore, the sense of this assembly that we recommend and urge that the families of all the churches engage in this very sacred and important service at least once a dry and at a time most convenient to the household and that the parents should see that every child is taught, as early as possible, to reverence God and their parents by listening quietly and attentively to the reading of God's Word and getting down on their knees during the prayer."

done as of March 1, 1910, under the title of *The Evening Light and Church of God Evangel*.[13] From the beginning of the publication, A. J. Tomlinson, as General Overseer, Editor and Publisher, wrote a lot on prayer.[14]

At the sixth assembly in 1911, the General Overseer, after mentioning prospective fields for the up-coming year, said, "With the proper methods, energy and prayers, all these places and more can be reached with the Lord's church this year."[15] At the end of his annual address, the General Overseer delivered a short discourse in which he called attention to the importance of having the church 'in perfect order' according to God's plan. The result was a prayer service. Many were on their faces in prayer. There were many tears, groans, sobs – an "agonizing outcry" and real suffering, desirous of more light, wisdom and knowledge.[16]

Family worship should be regarded by every child of God as a sacred duty and means of grace. Every father and mother who loves Jesus should gather their children around them at least once every day and read a few verses of Scripture and engage in prayer. Every child should be taught to kneel down in sacred reverence to God and our Savior Jesus.

A. J. Tomlinson, Editor, *The Evening Light And Church Of God Evangel* (Cleveland, TN: Church of God; April 15, 1910), 4.

---

13 Our archives have the copies of 1910, but the issues of 1911, 1912, and 1913 are missing. Anyone who has or discovers issues from those years are requested to notify the Pentecostal Research Center (PRC) and to allow the PRC to scan those issues.

14 (1) "Pray," 4/1/1910, (2) "Humble Prayer," 11?15/1910, (3) "Pray! Pray! Pray!" 1/24/1914 and continued 4/10/1914 [A tract of the same name was advertized], (4) "Soul Travail and Prevailing Prayer," 8/18/1917, (4) "Prayer and Work," 5/11/1918, (5) Revival Prayer," 12/14/1918, (6) "Power of Prayer," 3/8/1919, and (7) "Prayer and Faith Will Win," 2/14/1920.

15 Ibid, 4.

16 Ibid, 9.

ACCENT
Church of God Authors - Books related to Prayer

Bevins, Winfield. *Developing a Powerful Prayer Life.* Cleveland, TN: Pathway Press, 2006.

Cutshall, Bryan. *Prayer Ministry Handbook.* Cleveland, TN: Pathway Press, 2005.

Danskin, R. A. *An Exposition of the Lord's Prayer.* Pentecostal Publishing Co., 1930.

Lane, G. W. *The Priviledge of Prayer.* Cleveland, TN, Forwarth in Faith.

Lowery, T. L. (Thomas Lanier), 1929-. *Prayers that Prevail* [Cleveland, TN?] : Lowery Ministries International, 1995.

Martin, Lee Roy. *Jonah and the God of Grace: Lessons in Obedience, Faithfulness, and Prayer.* Cleveland, TN: Pathway Press, 2009.

Small, P. Douglas. *Entertaining God and Influencing Cities.* Kannapolis, NC: Alive Publications, 2008.

— *Five Basic Prayer Principles.* Kannapolis, NC: Alive Publications, 2012.

— *The Great Commission Prayer Guide.* Cleveland, TN: Pathway Press, 2009.

— *Intercession: The Uncomfortable Middle.* Kannapolis, NC: Alive Publications, 2009.

— *Prayer: The Heartbeat of the Church.* Cleveland, TN: Pathway Press, 2008.

— *The Praying Church Resource Guide.* Kannapolis, NC: Alive Publications, 2012.

— *Transforming Your Church into a House of Prayer.* Cleveland, TN: Pathway Press, 2006.

Triplett, Bennie S. *Praying Effectively: Bible Studies in Prayer.* Cleveland, TN: Pathway Press, 1990.

Walker, Lucille. *Lord, Teach Us to Pray: Praying for Results.* Cleveland, TN: Pathway Press, 1986.

Walker, Lucille. *What to Do When You Pray.* Plainfield, NJ: Logos International, 1978.

After the introductory night service at the assembly in 1912, the next morning, "The General Overseer read a Scripture lesson from I Peter 1, and offered prayer to God for guidance and wisdom."[17] In the 1914 Assembly, there is an entry, "Discourse by Sam C. Perry, subject, 'Intercessory Prayer'."[18] This appears to be the first formal message on the subject of prayer delivered at the Assembly. The first message on prayer in which we have a preserved, although condensed record of the text, chronicled in the Minutes, is entitled, "Pray" by John Attey. It was based on I Tim 2:1, and was preached in the 1924 Assembly.[19]

Prayer Conferences

Over the generations, the Church of God has had a strong emphasis on prayer and has held a lot of prayer conferences. A lot of interesting stories could be dug up, all over the world, about marvelous answers to prayer.

In 1986, First Assistant General Overseer Raymond Crowley had a vision to call the church back to prayer.[20] This resulted in the institution of the Prayer Commission, headed up by layman, Al Taylor, and dedicated to enlist the retired ministers of the church to pray for the church and its many ministries. The Prayer Commission's first theme was: "Praying People Spend Time with the Father." A cassette of a sermon on prayer by Crowley was sent to all pastors. For many years the commission met monthly. Drs. John Christopher Thomas and Rickie D. Moore, among others, gave presentations on prayer.

---

17 Ibid, 3.
18 Ibid, 23.
19 Ibid, 33.
20 Information on the Prayer Commission is from an interview with Al Taylor on November 2, 2011.

Prayerborne

In 1987, President Reagan sent the 101st Airborne to Panama. The quick and positive results inspired the Prayer Commission to form *Prayerborne*, which was a prayer emphasis to be led by the retired ministers. During the 1988

General Assembly, retired ministers were invited to a special prayer breakfast, and each was given *Prayerborne Wings*. In every assembly since there has been a special meeting of *Prayerborne*.

Early morning prayer meetings were instituted at the General Assembly in 1990 and that practice continues to the present. In 1992, the church was called to focus on 'Praying for our Pastors'. In 1994, there was a special prayer meeting with leaders from the Church of God and the Church of God of Prophecy. It was a wonderful time of healing for which faculty and students at the Pentecostal Seminary had been praying for several years. Solemn Assembly prayer meetings were also held throughout the denomination in 1995 and on the first day of the 1996 General Assembly. Doug Small developed the Solemn Assembly Manual for use by Church of God congregations. The Prayer Commission called the whole church to a renewed emphasis on prayer under the theme, *"Meet the Son at Sunrise."* This was followed in the next assembly period with *"Follow the Son into the Harvest."* After the 9/11 attack on America in 2001, the Prayer Commission instituted a call to prayer entitled *"Lift Him Up"*. In 2006, World Missions distributed to all pastors a CD entitled: "Praying the Scriptures."

God has led the Prayer Commission to new calls to prayer for the Church of God under various titles. The Executive Committee has given its full support to these varying emphases.

When the two new office buildings at the International Offices were constructed, the Prayer Commission proposed, designed and raised the money to develop the beautiful Prayer Garden that connects the three buildings.

In 2008 the leadership of the Prayer Commission was passed to Dr. Dennis Watkins, the attorney for the International Offices.

Prayer, has to be renewed and passed on to each new generation. This is not just the teaching about prayer but also the practice of prayer. Prayer is the lifeline of our spirituality. Let us pray more, and let us not forget to be in constant communion and conversation with our God and Lord, praying from the heart, praying through the words of Scripture and most of all praying through the Spirit, praying in tongues!

AUTHOR

James M. Beaty, Ph. D.

James M. Beaty, Ph.D., Vanderbilt University, 1963, served as missionary in the Dominican Republic 1949-52 and in Haiti 1946-47 and 1952-59. He was Superintendent of South America (1962-67), taught at Lee College (1967-74), was founder and President of Spanish Institute of Ministry (1974-80), was Academic Dean of the Church of God School of Theology, now Pentecostal Theological Seminary (1980-92) and continued to teach there until 2001.

CHAPTER TWENTY

GENERAL ASSEMBLY PRAYER MOMENTS
- THE FIRST TEN YEARS

A WINDOW THROUGH TIME

The following two chapters are among the most interesting in this whole series. They are snapshots and excerpts of prayer from the earliest General Assemblies of the Church of God. Not every prayer moment is captured here – opening prayers and more 'formal' beginnings and endings to services are not all included, but the stirring moments, the times when prayer seemed the paramount activity – not merely book-ends to the session itself, those are highlighted here.

I must admit, that I have been taken aback by the spontaneous moments of prayer, the easy movement of the whole assembly to their knees, the seamless interface between business – over open Bibles and prayer. They relied on God to reveal His Word to them in the context of the Assembly. These were not debates! These were seasons of exploration over Scriptures by men with teachable and hungry hearts. In reading the early minutes, you cannot help but be struck by the sense that they were caught up in something larger than themselves. They spoke as if they were on a journey, as if God was restoring His apostolic church, and they were a part of that discovery and learning process. It was bigger than them.

CHAPTER 20

GENERAL ASSEMBLY PRAYER MOMENTS
- THE FIRST TEN YEARS

P. Douglas Small, compiler

1906 – 1st General Assembly

The 1906 General Assembly was the first ever, and therefore, historic, though humble. It took place near Camp Creek, Cherokee County, NC, in the Kilpatrick House. J. C. and Malissie Murphy lived there at that time. The humble home is still standing as a memorial to the event.[1] It is located near the current Church of God of Prophecy site known as 'Field of the Woods' which was the home-place of W. F. Bryant. These sites are in the area of Murphy, at the western edge of North Carolina.

At that time there were only five congregations in the 'Christian Union.' Twenty-One persons attended. They came from Jones, Georgia; Turtletown and Camp Creek, North Carolina; and Cleveland, Tennessee. Among them were: Belford Abercrumbie

---

1 At the 8th General Assembly, A. J. Tomlinson would note that this first Assembly took place in the middle of a snowstorm with only 21 persons in attendance (Minutes of the Eighth Assembly, p. 8). Tomlinson would conjecture, "At the time of its birth it was not known whether it [the Church of God] would live or die; but time and evidences prove that it was destined to live and make its mark in the world. Its weak voice was unheard at the start, but it is now assuming such vast proportions that its voice is echoing around the world. It is not too much to say that every state in the Union will hear the voice of this assembly. Canada, South America, Europe, Asia, Africa, and many islands of the sea will hear the sound that goes forth ..." It is doubtful that he could have guessed the far reaching implications of the formative actions.

(Crumby); Johnie Brown; John Ellison; R. R. Jones; Elder R. G. Spurling (the son); Elder Andrew Freeman (Ordained by Spurling in Christian Union); Elder W. F. Bryant and his wife Nettie, along with daughters – Agnes, Ella and
Robinson; J. C. Murphy, a deacon and his wife, Margaret Malissie Gay Murphy (Maddox, nicknamed, Norma); Theophilus Ellis and Nancy, his daughter; W. M. Coleman, and his mother, Lucy; T. N. Elrod; Alexander Hamby; Sallie Hamby (Wife of Billy, brother of Barbara, and cousin of Alexander; Evangelist M. S. Lemons and Pastor A. J. Tomlinson.

The implications of their decisions and the heart of their concerns still bear on the DNA of the denomination. Among the significant measures related to prayer are the following.

Records like the Book of Acts

Each church was advised to keep records, "considering it [record keeping] in harmony with New Testament teaching ..." However, the character of the records that were to be kept has been missed, "The Acts of the Apostles as example." This first assembly anticipated the action of God in the midst of the church. We keep records of business transactions, but rarely do our churches have a record of their spiritual history.[2]

Communion and the Washing of Feet

The second item, which was presented by R. G. Spurling, was

---

2 *Church of God General Assembly Minutes*, First General Assembly (Camp Creek, North Carolina, January 26-27, 1907), 2-3.

that "communion and feet washing" were to be observed among the churches. These ordinances are near the very heart of prayer. Few things come closer than holding the broken bread and the cup, the elements that represent the blood and broken body of the Lord. And the humble act of a brother kneeling while prayerfully and tearfully washing the feet of his brother. Some of the most poignant moments of prayer in my own memory come from moments when prayer and communion; prayer and foot washing intersect. Both provide the context for prayer. And apart from prayer, both symbolic actions dry up.[3]

A Prayer Leader and Prayer Meeting

Alexander Hamby brought forth the issue of prayer meetings. The minutes read,

"It is, therefore, the sense of this assembly that we recommend, advise and urge that each local church hold a prayer meeting at least once a week."

Not only did the assembly recommend a weekly prayer meeting, but they also recommended that each local church appoint a prayer leader.

"Further, that some one in every church, who may feel led by the Holy Spirit or selected by the church, take the oversight thereof [the prayer meeting] and see that such prayer meeting is held regularly and proper order."[4]

Tears and Evangelism

Evangelism was discussed and the minutes read,

"After the consideration of the ripened fields and open doors

---

3   Ibid, 3.
4   Ibid, 3-4.

ACCENT

What Happened at Shearer School House?
Read on August 19, 2011, on the one-hundred and fifteenth anniversary of the revival at Shearer school house.
James M. Beaty, Ph.D.

Here we are, one-hundred and fifteen years after the revival at Shearer School House, asking, "What happened at the School House?" And we could ask, "Why at the School House?" The latter question is more easily answered historically and the answer is this: "The School House was, in most rural areas and in most small towns, the one and only public building in the community and it was used for civic activities, for political events, for religious meetings and for anything that did not offend the public."

To start looking for an answer to the first question, we will look at the evangelists and their message. Three of the evangelists were from just across the line in Tennessee. They were William Martin, Joe M. Tipton and Milton McNabb. They had a fourth colleague in William Hamby, who was a native of Cherokee County, NC. It is interesting to note that McNabb was a cousin to W.F. Bryant and that Hamby was the brother of Spurling's wife, Barbara.

What was the message of these evangelists? First, of course, they preached Jesus Christ as Lord and Savior and proclaimed the good news to the lost. But also, the message that stamped their identity was the message of holiness, i.e., sanctification as a definite second work of grace to deliver the believer from the power and bondage of sin and to make it possible to live a life of victory, without condemnation, for the glory of God. Tomlinson, in his chapter "A Brief History of the Church that is not recognized as the Church of God," which is based on what he had been told, described the message as follows:

They preached a clean gospel, and urged the people to seek and obtain sanctification subsequent to justification. They prayed, fasted and wept before the Lord until a great revival was the result. People became interested, and were stirred for miles around. Quite a large number professed salvation and sanctification through the blood of Christ.

We should note that in the latter half of the 1800s

for evangelism ... strong men wept and said they were not only willing but real anxious to go."

The overt act of prayer is not explicitly mentioned in association with this discussion, but it is difficult to imagine such a scene – 'strong men wept' - without a spirit of prayer.[5]

The Family Altar

Andrew Freeman discussed 'family worship.' The minutes read,

> "It is, therefore, the sense of this assembly that we recommend and urge that the families of all the churches engage in this very sacred and important service at least once a day and at a time most convenient to the household and that the parents should see that every child is taught, as early as possible, to reverence God and their parents by listening quietly and attentively to the reading of God's Word and getting down on their knees during the prayer."[6]

The scope of the discussion is sweeping. The worship of the family is seen as sacred – that is, as having a sanctifying effect on the family and the home. And by extension, on the church. 'Family Worship' was recommended as a daily discipline, with flexibility in reference to the schedule. It is seen as formative, the context in which children learn reverence, and practice the posture of humility in prayer – joining their parents on their knees. Prayer and the reading of the Bible are joined together here. The experience is beyond mere prayer for things – these were intended to be sacred moments for the family to 'worship' together. Prayer was not to be seen as something foreign to daily life, something that only happens 'at church.' Prayerful worship was to run through the home, though life itself. Nothing at church could ever take the place of the site and sound of the family

---

5   Ibid, 4.
6   Ibid, 6-7.

radical holiness began to use the terminology of Acts 2 to refer to second-definite-work sanctification. Some of these evangelists had already been moved by this doctrine and experience and later became associated with the Fire Baptized Holiness Association, which rose to a zenith soon after this and collapsed with the moral failure of its leader, Benjamin Hardin Irwin, in June of 1900. There is still much to sort out about all of this, and I hope that more information and clues will come to light, but one thing is clear. Those who were sanctified at Shearer school house testified of being baptized in the Holy Spirit. At the same time one must acknowledge that there was a mighty move of the Spirit here, but, unfortunately, this was accompanied by a strong wave of emotionalism and fanaticism. There was a lot of unbounded enthusiasm, zeal, emotional expression and possibly speaking in tongues. But both Tomlinson and Bryant, who are writing after the baptism in the Holy Spirit with the initial evidence of speaking in tongues has become the official position of the Church of God, are reluctant to mention that, during the revival, sanctification had been referred to as baptism in the Holy Spirit.

But the two of them refer to speaking in tongues in the wake of the revival, in the meetings held by Bryant. Tomlinson in "A Brief History" wrote, based, of course, on the witness of Bryant:

After the close of the series of meetings, and the three evangelists were gone, the people commenced a Sunday school, and regular prayer meetings were conducted, usually by William F. Bryant, a leading man of the community. The people earnestly sought God, and the interest increased until unexpectedly, like a cloud from a clear sky, the Holy Ghost began to fall on the honest, humble, sincere seekers after God. While the meetings were in progress one after another fell under the power of God, and soon quite a number were speaking in other tongues as the Spirit gave them utterance. The influence and excitement then spread like wildfire, and people came for many miles to investigate, hear and see the manifestations of the presence of God.

And Bryant wrote:†

I was wonderfully saved in the Baptist church when I was fourteen years of age and a member until 1896. Many times I praying together. The lack of humility in the congregation has its roots in the pride and self-sufficiency, the prayerlessness of the home, the absence of knee time. The respect for the reading and preaching of the word in the congregation is learned in the home. A praying church is possible only with praying homes.

The measure continued,

"We recommend further that the ministers and deacons of each church use their influence and make special effort to encourage every family in the church to engage in this devotional exercise every day. And that the deacons ascertain the proper information and make a report of the number of families that have been induced to take up this service during the year, the number that make it a regular practice and those that do not and carry such report to the yearly or general assembly."

The first assembly called for a veritable campaign in behalf of the family altar with accountability. No other measure was treated in quite this way. What if we asked similar questions today, "How many homes have family altar? How many are praying together? How many fathers are praying with, over their families? Where is the Bible being read daily? In what homes are parents and children kneeling together in gratitude for the blessings of God and in ongoing dependence?"

The breadth of the church could be measured by the number of affiliated congregations. But the depth of the church could only be measured by daily, at-home, to-be-like Jesus praying. Our spiritual ancestors knew this. We seem to have forgotten.[7]

1907 – 2nd General Assembly

The Assembly opened on Wednesday, Jan. 9, 1907, at 7 PM with a "song and prayers" followed by the preaching of R. G. Spurling on "the honor of carrying the gospel." On Thursday morning, January

---

7   Ibid, 7.

mentioned to my pastor about getting mad and have malice in my heart. He would say to me, "1 see a higher experience but how to get there, 1 don't know." That would make me hungry for more of God.

In 1896 I began seeking God definitely for an experience that I never had attained to. The spirit within me would cry out, "Give me the blessing like those other few have received." Oh, how I had to consecrate my life, dying out to my own selfish nature and forsaking wife and children, father and mother and all my earthly friends and giving up my Baptist church, in fact, make a clean breast of everything. But, thank God, when I got all on the altar, one Thursday morning, about 9:00 o'clock, I was sanctified while sitting in my saddle on my horse. In that same year many of us received the Holy Ghost.

After we received the Holy Ghost and began speaking in tongues, the persecutions began to arise.

There were over a hundred who were baptized in the Holy Spirit in the Holiness understanding of that terminology and there may have been many of these who were truly baptized in the Holy Spirit in the Pentecostal sense, but Bryant was not one of them. Nevertheless, the 1896 revival in Shearer Schoolhouse inspired, motivated and led to a Pentecostal experience of being baptized in the Holy Spirit and evidenced through speaking in tongues, however, without the full and clear teaching of "Tongues as evidence." That came to the Church of God from Azusa Street. Thank God for what He did here and for his humble servants that were obedient to Him. Amen.

† From *The Faithful Standard* (September, 1922), pp. 6, 20f. Bryant opens telling about the 1896 revival at the Shearer School house.

10, the day began with a prayer service characterized by "the spirit of love to God and one another" and "accompanied with blessings from the Lord." That prayer service was led by W. F. Bryant. When the assembly was called to 'regular order' there was another moment of "united prayer in which the blessing and melting power of the Lord was very sensibly felt."[8]

This assembly had, of all the assemblies, the most intense pattern of deliberate, scheduled prayer. Each morning, a prayer service began the day. The second morning, Friday, January 11, was led by Alex Hamby. After lunch, a second prayer service started the afternoon session. It was led by H. L. Trim and lasted some thirty minutes. That evening, prior to the night service, a third prayer service was held, led by W. F. Bryant from 6:30 – 7:00 PM. On Saturday, January 12, Oscar Withrow led the prayer service. Then the minutes note that "Sister N. J. Lawson spoke briefly on the ministry of prayer." This would have been the first address to the General Assembly on the subject prayer. That afternoon, after lunch, M. S. Lemons led yet another prayer service and gave an exhortation. The assembly concluded on the following morning with an ordination service, communion and foot washing.[9]

1908 – 3rd General Assembly

The Assembly opened with a song and prayer service on Wednesday, Jan. 8 – 1908 at 7:00 PM. R. G. Spurling preached the opening message. On the morning of Thursday, January 9, as at the previous meeting, the day began with a prayer service and then the assembly opened in 'regular order' at 10:00 AM. After lunch, again following the pattern of the previous assembly, a thirty minute prayer session was held to open the afternoon session. It was led by W. F. Bryant. In the evening, prior to the 7 PM service, yet another thirty minute prayer service was held, led by Alexander Hamby.[10]

---

8   *Church of God General Assembly Minutes,* Second General Assembly (Union Grove, Bradley County, TN; January 9-13, 1907), 2. (Pages are unnumbered).

9   Ibid, 6. (Pages unnumbered).

10 *Church of God General Assembly Minutes,* Third General Assembly (Cleveland, TN, January 8-12, 1908), 2-3.

These early assemblies – were prayer meetings. Prayer on prayer!

On Friday, the third day, Jan. 10, 1908, at 8 AM, the day began searching the Scripture together over the issue of marriage and divorce. There is no record of a prayer service. The minutes read, "After hours of discussion and searching of the Scripture and an extra session that lasted until after midnight ... a real decision was never reached." The Assembly put off the matter until the following year.[11]

That afternoon, the question was discussed, "Should Elders give themselves entirely to the ministry of the word and prayer?" In simply language, should they be 'full-time'? It was acknowledged that some "some work ... when not directly engaged in the ministry of the word," but a caution was lifted about being "entangled too much with the affairs of this life."[12]

> ### ACCENT
>
> In the July 1, 1910 issue of the Evangel, there was an announcement about a camp meeting at Hayesville, NC, near Murphy, where the geographical roots of the Church are found. The camp meeting was to begin on a Friday night, August 5, 1910. The field was said to be white unto harvest. Everyone was invited all to come to the mountains to feel "the good cool breeze of the highlands" and for a "drink of mountain water," and better yet, the invitation read, "We expect to drink at the living fountain and feast around our Father's table." At that time, travel by passenger train into nearby Murphy was an option.
>
> *Evangel,* July 1, 1901, 4.

1909 – 4th General Assembly

Unlike previous assemblies, there was no formal morning,

---

11 Ibid, 3.
12 Ibid, 6.

afternoon, and evening pre-service prayer. The minutes read, "After songs, prayer and testimonies," Elder R. G. Spurling delivered the opening sermon. On the following day, Thursday, January 7, the 10 AM service "opened with prayer" but the pre-service given to prayer that had been conducted in earlier years, did not occur. In the afternoon, a "song and prayer" replaced the afternoon season of prayer that had occurred at the second assembly. The primary discussion that afternoon concerned the local church selection of a pastor.

"The church desiring a pastor should earnestly pray for God to give them the person that He, with His infinite wisdom, knows would be the proper one ..."

The Assembly further recommended that they come to agreement regarding their choice "after prayer ... as they feel divinely guided."[13]

On January 8, at 9:45 AM, the session began with "songs and prayer" absent a special prayer service. There is no record of prayer beyond a spontaneous moment later in the assembly.[14]

1910 – 5th General Assembly

The general pattern of the services was "songs, Bible reading and prayer."[15]

1911 – 6th General Assembly

Notice was given, that the number of churches had increased by twenty-seven from thirty-one the previous year, and the number of members had grown to 1850. However, the minutes characterized the report as – "not specially discouraging, yet ... [not] as great as ...

---

13 *Church of God General Assembly Minutes,* Fourth General Assembly (Cleveland, TN, January 6-9, 1909), 1-2 .

14 Ibid, 3.

15 *Church of God General Assembly Minutes,* Fifth General Assembly (Cleveland, TN, January 10-16, 1910).

we hoped." Tomlinson confessed, "I feel that my work as overseer of the churches the past year has been a comparative failure."

Most of us would love to have the failure of an 84.5 percent increase in membership;[16] and an increase of 27 new churches, which represented a growth rate of 87 percent.[17] Tomlinson lamented the fact that he and most pastors were required to find a means of support outside the ministry for their families, and yet the work itself demanded full-time attention. At this early juncture, works had been started in the Bahamas and enquiries had been received from California, Mississippi, Arkansas, Iowa, Indiana, Virginia and Cuba. "With the proper methods, energy and prayers all these places and more can be reached ..." Tomlinson noted.[18]

Tomlinson then spoke of "systematic evangelization ... in every state." The method to which he referred was simple. "We have a number of workers who are not able to preach, but are willing to work ... to do personal work, hold cottage prayer meetings, distribute literature, and give ringing testimonies." The method of cottage prayer meetings would become a critical key in birthing new churches. The message spread by willing hearts and "ringing testimonies." The simple setting of a home, in which neighbors and friends were gathered, heard personal stories of God's active intervention and received the gift of prayer became over the next several decades, a critical tactic in new churches.[19]

On Wednesday morning, January 4, at 9:30 AM, there was a prayer service and Scripture lesson by George T. Brouayer of Chattanooga, Tennessee.[20] These had been conducted in earlier Assemblies.

---

16 The church grew from 1005 members to 1850.
17 The number of congregations grew from 31 to 58.
18 *Church of God General Assembly Minutes*, Sixth General Assembly (Cleveland, TN, January 3-4, 1911), 4-5.
19 Ibid, 5.
20 Ibid, 6.

ACCENT

John Wesley said that there is no such thing as a solitary Christian. The faith must be shared in order to be kept. Christianity is social religion. It becomes dwarfed and blighted when alone; it thrives in numbers. But true to our ruggedly individualistic self-centeredness, we have tried to practice the Christian faith as if it were a home correspondence course in self-improvement. The great heresy in American popular religion is the notion that religion is a private affair, a secret contract between the believer and God.

William Willimon, Quoted in *Christian Quotes* (Holiday, FL: Christian Quotes; February, 2003), 25.

On Wednesday afternoon, January 4, a discussion took place about what the "the glaring 'evening light' … now shining forth after the cloudy and dark day of the dark ages, and the dark day of Protestantism …" Tomlinson spoke of the "noble fathers of The Reformation" who "in the darkness of the time" appeared as honorable and principled men whose writings and accomplishments were impressive. Nevertheless, the position of this group of mountain reformers was that the creeds of the Reformation were never adequate substitutes for the Scriptures, and the reforms, though significant, did not go far enough. They sensed they were a part of a new reformation, a new order of the Church for the last days. The result of this moment led by Tomlinson was a spontaneous season of "groans, cries, tears and sobs." After a season of prayer, they began to sing, *Waiting on the Lord for the Promise Given.* That was followed by another season of "prayers, tears, sobs and cries." Then the Assembly adjourned for the afternoon.[21]

The following afternoon, Thursday, another discussion took place around the subject, "What is the Church of God? Upon what laws is it established? How does it differ from other churches? What

21 Ibid, 7-8.

is its highest tribunal?" The core question had to do with order – with a church that operated in perfect order. And further, the implications of a church out of order. Tomlinson led the discussion, but R. G. Spurling, M. S. Lemons, and George C. Barron were also involved. Then Tomlinson gave concluding remarks, saying, "… that much depends on us setting everything clear and in perfect order that souls who are now being lost can be saved by a church in perfect order." The solemnness of the idea weighed on the Assembly. It "resulted in a service with many on their faces in prayer amid many tears, groans, sobs, and agonizing outcry and real suffering, desirous of more light, wisdom and knowledge." The service was dismissed at 4:30 PM.[22]

On Saturday, January 7-1911, special prayer was offered for R. M. Evans, the church's missionary to the Bahamas.[23]

1912 – 7th General Assembly

The Assembly began with a service on Monday evening, January 8, with an address by F. J. Lee and a sermon by George C. Barron. The next morning at 9:30 AM "songs began to ring out, and with them were mingled prayers and praises." The General Overseer read a Scripture lesson from 1 Peter 1. He then offered his annual address and spoke about "the great need of more pastors, and how the wolves were destroying the flocks on account of the absence and shortage of shepherds." As he shared, the minutes record that "the burden became so great that he had to discontinue the discourse for an interval of several minutes, while the hearers prostrated themselves before God in tears, weeping and intercessory prayers with groanings of the Spirit."[24]

---

22 Ibid, 9.
23 Ibid, 11.
24 *Church of God General Assembly Minutes,* Seventh General Assembly (Cleveland, TN, January 9-14, 1912), 3.

On Wednesday afternoon, January 10, J. W. Buckalew preached on global evangelism,[25] the subject he declared "nearest to my heart." Beginning his remarks, he declared, "I am anxious for the evangelization of the world to be completed, for I want to see Jesus. I realize when this grand gospel is carried to every nation then Jesus will come."[26] It is not clear how pervasive this notion was, namely, that tied to eschatological promise was eschatological condition – the completion of the Great Commission. Buckalew observed, "Someday, when the last message has been preached and the preacher, perhaps weary in body, lays his Bible down, the sky will burst open and the King of kings come riding in, and I want to do my best to hasten that glad hour."[27] When he finished preaching and urging upon the audience the imperative to go "regardless of cost" there was a call to prayer for those "who were willing to go ... at any cost ... [or] send someone else." The minutes say, "The altar was filled with broken hearted men and women who had received a glimpse of the lost world. As they arose from their knees, the Spirit descended in a wonderful way, and in the midst of the rejoicing an old man, about sixty years of age, who had been seeking for his baptism, came leaping over the benches like a sixteen year old boy, talking in tongues."[28]

On Thursday, the business session lasted all day. At one point, the discussion turned to the biblical qualifications of a bishop and the right to ordain. M. S. Lemons was asked to address the measure. Before yielding to Lemons, "The General Overseer called for special prayer that God would give Brother Lemons special wisdom and divine guidance as he discoursed upon the subject, and that he might be able to go beyond all expectations in imparting truth

---

25 He would also preach on an evangelistic message on Saturday night. Thus, he preached twice during the 7th Assembly.
26 *Church of God General Assembly Minutes,* Seventh General Assembly, 13.
27 Ibid.
28 Ibid, 14.

and knowledge."[29] In yielding to Lemons, Tomlinson noted that the government of the Church is not democratic – by popular or majority vote. Nor was it republican, thus representative. Rather, it was Theocratic. And that required that the body must discern God's will in any matter, implying the intersection of prayer, the work of the Spirit and Scripture. Otherwise, the Church is reduced to a mere democratic order comprised of representatives of a larger body. No, the Church itself, must discern. God must decide. It must seem good 'to us ... and the Holy Ghost.' These were high standards.

After Lemons spoke, the Assembly prevailed on Tomlinson to comment. What followed must have been quite remarkable. Tomlinson directed the Assembly to Ephesians 4 and spoke of the five-fold ministry.

> "We have acknowledged the pastors and teachers, etc., but we have failed to acknowledge the apostles ... probably because of prejudice incited by the innumerable failures of those who have called themselves apostles. We have about come to the conclusion that there will be no apostles in the latter days. But in spite of the numerous failures and prejudices that may exist, this office is in the Bible ... We cannot harmonize the Scriptures without taking all, and we can never have a complete church until we acknowledge and have a complete gospel ministry ..."

He was, of course, implying the need for 'apostles.' Tomlinson went on to say he could "not see any one who could fill that office ... but," he announced, "the knowledge is coming, and we must point in that direction." An apostle, Tomlinson noted, would "not only speak as the oracles of God, but they will be in him and then the dead will be raised."[30]

Tomlinson then launched into a brief discourse on the tabernacle in the wilderness. He drew an analogy between the glorious garments

---

29 Ibid, 15.
30 Ibid, 16.

of the high priest and the gravity of wearing them. Wearing them inappropriately, incorrectly, for example, without the sound of bells, brought the death penalty. The higher the office, the weightier the penalty became for inappropriate actions. Ordination was therefore a serious matter.[31]

The minutes say that "during this discourse the power of God fell so forcibly that everyone felt God was in it, and light shined so brilliantly that the Assembly unanimously agreed that a change in our system of ordination be made at once. A committee was appointed to consider the subject and draft a plan to recommend to the Assembly" Even after the committee was named, "The power continued to fall, and the Spirit led all to fall on their knees, and with much groaning and crying, earnest petitions went up to God to reveal His true and perfect plan." The minutes note that the session officially adjourned at 6:00 PM, "… but some of the brethren continued before God exercised by His mighty Spirit and one remained prostrated on the floor before God for about five hours."[32]

---

31 Ibid, 16-17. Note: Tomlinson noted that Paul authorized Titus to appoint (ordain) Elders, but the Elders then appointed, did not have that right. It remained with the office of the Apostle. The point being, that the conferring such a title, and empowering one in such a position was a serious matter. If effect, it might mean placing the holy and fearful garments, though now invisible, upon a novice. As you read the early minutes, it is clear that the church was wrestling with the tension of being free of form and structure, and the implications of retaining order in the context of such liberty. Tomlinson at points spoke to the opposition that he was surely getting, "I know now what you [Tomlinson, some might have said] are aiming at, you want to organize a body like the Catholic Church." His response was "No, we are leaving the type and getting to the real." And the real, he was suggesting, needed principled structure as much as the shadow. "Where did the priests get their authority? Moses gave it to them. Moses is a type of Christ." And he would go on to say, that Christ gave authority to the apostles.

32 Ibid, 17.

This blend of prayer and discussion, searching Scripture in prayerful dependence has sadly been lost. As has the notion that the Church is growing, evolving, that it is on a journey of New Testament restoration.

On Saturday, a special moment took place. The Assembly approved the amalgamation of the Church of God with the Mountain Assembly Churches of God. "We receive your Assembly as a whole … ministers and deacons in their respective positions." Brothers of the Mountain Assembly movement accepted the conditions of union and were invited by the Moderator to come forward and take their places on the rostrum. The Assembly stood to show them honor with hands lifted to God. Spontaneously, they …

> "… all began to pour out their souls … in prayer and praise. Suddenly the Spirit began to manifest His presence, and approved of the union in such a remarkable manner that all were forced to drop on their knees, and with full hearts offered up praise and thanksgiving for the answering of the Savior's prayer, 'That they all may be one.'"

The whole body of churches were formally received by the General Overseer with the Assembly standing, and again, "The Holy Ghost manifested His delight and pleasure in tongues and other manifestations … the right hand of fellowship" was extended and

> "… a spirit of love and unity was manifested that many were pressed to say, 'Oh, how they love each other!' The Assembly while standing began singing, 'Old time religion,' and shaking hands. Tears were in almost all eyes and under the white heat of God's love, all present were melted into one solid mass of love and fellowship. All then kneeled down and were led in prayer by Jonah L. Shelton. 'Behold how good and how pleasant it is for brethren to dwell together in unity.'" Psalm 133.

Sadly, the union was never completed.[33]

---

33 Ibid, 20-21.

ACCENT

At the 8th General Assembly in January, 1913, the problem of the indebtedness of Evangel was discussed, a total of $331.61 was needed. There was brief discussion and the suggestion of a free-will offering. The minutes record, "The whole Assembly knelt before the Lord in silent prayer, after which many came forward with cheerful hearts and shouts of praises to God and laid their offerings of money or pledges on the table until the amount as counted was $334.00. As the announcement was made that the whole amount was raised, a great rejoicing followed and shouts of victory and praises went up to God as all kneeled before Him to render unto Him thanksgiving aid praise for the victory that was won."

On Sunday, January 14, 1912, at 9:30 AM, a model Sunday school was demonstrated. In the middle of the presentation, the minutes record that "a sister was suddenly attacked by the enemy; the saints gathered round her and prayed, and the Spirit manifested Himself in mighty rebuking power."[34] Those in charge of the presentation noted, "A Sunday school should always be ready to stop any part of its service to aid or relieve the suffering." During the model service, there was "prayer by one of the younger members," the first prayer of record by a youngster at any Assembly. This was followed by a "responsive reading" with all the congregation standing, another first.[35]

The Assembly closed with a message by Sam Perry on "The Deeper Life." Perry was one of the early advocates of prayer.[36]

---

34 Ibid, 25.
35 Ibid.
36 Ibid, 26.

1913 – 8th General Assembly

On Wednesday afternoon, special emphasis was again given to the importance of the Sunday School, as at the last Assembly. J. B. Ellis of Alabama City, Alabama was introduced, and spoke to the Assembly on the importance of reaching children. He proposed a partnership between family and church. "Let us discipline them in the home first and then in the Sunday School."[37] His message was met with shouts of 'Amen and Amen!' J. S. Llewellyn followed Ellis with another message, Sunday School in Every Church. When he finished, several arose to vow to have a Sunday School ministry in every church. The minutes record that there were "touching prayers and cries for the little children ..." In the midst of the prayer, one lady begged the group to pray for a Sunday School in her community. Again, another season of tearful prayer followed.[38]

Tomlinson then introduced Spurling whom he called a spiritual father.[39] Spurling preached on 'The Church,' saying that on the Day of Pentecost, the foundation of the church was laid, but in the midst of years, she became a harlot. The Reformation began a process of unfolding truth, of gradual restoration. Spurling spoke of the 'two golden rails' on which the church was to run, and he asserted that they had been covered by creeds and man-made laws. For Spurling,

> *History is a vision of God revealing himself in actions to persons who are sincerely seeking him."*
>
> Arnold Toynbee, Quoted in *Christian Quotes* (Holiday, FL: Christian Quotes; February, 2003), 20-21.

---

37 *Church of God General Assembly Minutes,* Eighth General Assembly (Cleveland, TN, January 7-12, 1913), 36.

38 Ibid, 37.

39 Ibid, 38.

love of God and neighbor were the two golden rails.[40] Spurling finished speaking, and the choir sang, "The Heavenly Railroad" and "The Meeting in the Air." Then Spurling himself sang. The minutes read, "Following this song, the power fell and all were on their feet with uplifted hands, dancing and shouting the praises of God." An interesting note followed, "One played the organ under the power of the Spirit." And "all who were not members and who had fallen in love with the Church and wished to become members were asked to stand up, and about twelve arose."

With the election of A. J. Tomlinson as General Overseer, "the Spirit gave a message which was interpreted as follows, 'The smile of the Lord is upon him.' This so deeply touched Brother Tomlinson that he fell upon his face weeping mightily. The entire Assembly fell upon their faces with weeping and prayers and thanksgivings to God for making the selection in such a marked supernatural way."[41] Tomlinson tearfully accepted the challenge to serve the Church in the office of General Overseer. He requested prayer and wept, as did the whole Assembly. Spurling laid hands on him as he knelt.[42]

In the midst of the General Overseer's address, there were three moments when tongues came with interpretation. The first promised that upon the "rising generation" God would "place great things. The night is past and the day is beginning to shine. Walk in the light."[43] The second message was an admonition to "See that you make all things according to the pattern. Do in all things what I say." The third spiritual exhortation was, "Have your eyes fixed upon God and not on yourselves. I am giving you the truth through my servant. The meek and lowly ones will I give understanding in my

---

40 Ibid, 40.
41 Ibid, 42.
42 Ibid, 47.
43 Ibid, 49.

Word. I'm dealing out my Word to thee, take it to heart and do what I say."[44] After the message, the General Overseer prayed for the congregation. Here is the essence of his prayer, the first prayer recorded in the 'Minutes.'

> God help us to be one heart and soul and become as golden grain with all the chaff and straw taken away, so when the Husbandman comes He can gather us into His garner.[45]

The simple prayer erupted into a "great time of melting and crying all over the house."

These poignant moments, as you will note from reading these Assembly excerpts in this chapter, decorated the early General Assemblies. The remarks reflect not only prayer moments, but the content of prophetic messages. They took seriously the voice of the Spirit. The ministry did not consist merely of a record of sacred business of the church – but it also included what they perceived to be divinely inspired words. They took spiritual gifts seriously. Few of our churches today follow this practice. The 'word of the Lord' may come to the church but is quickly forgotten, treated as decoration, as a badge of our Pentecostal heritage, but not something so significant as to require being written down or remembered. These pioneers evidence profound sensitivity to the mission and the work of the Holy Spirit. Regarding this moment, the Minutes continue, "The Spirit did not seem to be satisfied, so all fell before God again and gave up to weeping and prayer. Then all arose and sang, 'To the fields away.'"[46]

On Friday, just before the Noon break, A. J. Lawson spoke on 'A Biblical Scriptural Money System for the Church.' Among the closing bottom line of his message on tithing and giving was this

---

44 Ibid, 51.
45 Ibid.
46 Ibid, 59.

idea, "The minister ought to be able to give their time to prayer and the ministry of the Word."[47]

On Friday afternoon, J. W. Buckalew was introduced to preach.[48] His message was entitled, 'A Mourning for Pastors.' Buckalew explained that he was an evangelist. "My calling is out in the field to blaze the Way for someone else to come on and feed and nourish the little lambs." The colorful evangelist noted that he often set a church in order, only to return a year or two later to find sick lambs and undernourished sheep causing him "to go down before God and weep over them." He appealed for pastors – indeed, for a restoration of the five-fold ministry in order that the church might be equipped and healthy.

> "If the early church had these orders (of ministries, the five-fold ministry) we need to lie on our faces before God until they are restored to the church today. And until this is done we will hear the bleating of the lambs ... little lambs torn and bleeding ... Oh, that we might weep and pray and get hold of the horns of the altar ..."

It is clear, that the sense of Buckalew and perhaps the entire Assembly, was that prayer was the key to pastors and workers for the harvest. And further, that pastors who dared to preach an uncompromising truth were the key to healthy sheep. Buckalew urged, "We must get the corruption out of the church [even] if it does hurt." Suddenly there were again tongues with interpretation, "Trim up, take out, clean up and the church will prosper." Buckalew charged, "You as pastors are responsible for your flocks ... Preach the Word and have no respect of persons ..."

Another tongue, with the interpretation,

"My children, remember the Word I spoken to you. Submit to

47   Ibid, 62.
48   Buckalew had preached on *Global Evangelism* at the 1912 Assembly.

my Word. Stand by it. Be of good courage and I will bless thee. Go forth! Go forth! Preach my Word in its fullness. I died on Calvary's cross that you might go the clean way."

The preaching and the prophetic words were seamlessly laced together. Buckalew urged, 'My people are destroyed for lack of knowledge!' (Hosea 4:6). It is not the sheep's fault, they would do better if they knew how. Pastors should raise the standard."[49]

The General Overseer remarked at the close of the message, "We are going to pray God to give us strong pastors who will not misconstrue the Word and poison the flock …" The minutes say, "All went down weeping and in prayer before God."[50]

On Saturday morning, at the Eighth Assembly, there was a question and answer session. The movement placed such a strong emphasis on sanctification, that some were evidently teaching that a person was not truly born again until he was 'sanctified.' There was an obvious need for greater precision in theology. A superficial answer was given and the question was deferred. But Buckalew desired to discuss and settle the question immediately. F. J. Lee then rose and again advised deferring the question.

This back and forth exchange was among significant leaders. Suddenly, there was tongue and interpretation. And with it,

> "… the whole Assembly fell upon their faces in weeping and prayer before God. At the close of this season of weeping and prayer the General Overseer said … 'I would rather be in God's order than to settle things ourselves.'"

The Minutes say, "A brother who had never been in our meetings before said: 'I would not take a million dollars for this; to see how the Holy Ghost settles things.' Another, 'I never saw the Holy Ghost

---

49 Ibid, 65.
50 Ibid.

settle things in this way.'"[51]

1913 – 9th Assembly[52]

The Minutes began,

"Several minutes before 7 PM ... the singing began. When the large audience was called to prayer the voices rang out like the sound of many waters."[53]

On Tuesday morning, there was a Scripture lesson by the General Overseer, followed by prayer and his annual address.[54] In the midst of the annual report, the minutes say,

"At intervals during the address, the following messages and interpretations were given: 'I am bestowing upon thee my power, wisdom and strength. The time is now at hand when I will show forth greater power. Believe and search the Word. Be not of doubtful mind. Be not baffled. Be not dismayed. I have many things in store for thee. Press on. Press on.'"

A second word came forth, "I am giving out my Spirit in a mild way, but I am going to pour it out upon thee in greater power. I am going to send this gospel to the end of the earth. Be not discouraged. Press on, press on, my children. The time will fly faster and faster. The time is near at hand for my coming."

---

51 Ibid, 71. One of the items raised regarded a holiness dress code. It was pointed out, there often an equal problem arises from the attempt find a balance, "People sometimes get as proud in going slouchy as others in their vain dress." The question also arose on wearing neckties and collars, a sign of 'worldliness' by some standards. The conclusion to the matter was, "Wear a tie if you want and if not, leave those alone who do. Such things are trivial. There are weightier matters."

52 Two Assemblies were held in 1913. This marked the year that Assemblies were migrated from January meetings to November.

53 *Church of God General Assembly Minutes*, Ninth General Assembly (Cleveland, TN, November 4-9, 1913), 2.

54 Ibid, 3.

M. S. Lemons closed the session with a prayer and song.[55]

On Wednesday morning, November 5, there was a prayer, praise and a song service from 9:30 – 10:15 AM.[56] In the afternoon, there was another prayer and song service from 1:00 – 1:30 PM.[57] Again, on Thursday, November 6, the day began at 9:30 AM with a prayer service.[58] This had been the pattern in the second assembly. The pattern was followed again in the afternoon, from 1:00 – 1:30 PM with a prayer and song service. On Friday, at 9:30 AM, another prayer service – "songs and prayers."[59] And in the afternoon, thirty minutes was again allotted for "song and prayer."[60]

That Friday afternoon, the Assembly wrestled with the question of divorce. The Minutes note after the discussion, that there was a "great time of prayer about divorce and remarriage." Then, the General Overseer urged more prayer "for God to reveal and shed forth more light." This reliance, not on scholarship, but on the Spirit to reveal His will is almost pervasive. This was followed by

> ## ACCENT
>
> At the 9th General Assembly, the body struggled with the issue of marriage and divorce. ""We haven't come to the bottom of this question yet. We haven't come to the place where 'It' seems good to the Holy Ghost and us.' Something has not yet been dug out yet. The outflow of the Spirit is going to settle this." Soon after this moment, the assembly gave themselves in prayer for God to reveal and shed forth the light on His Word. The minutes note, "Wonderful season of prayer. Message in tongues and interpretation: 'I alone

---

55 Ibid, 9-10.
56 Ibid, 10.
57 Ibid.
58 Ibid, 12.
59 Ibid, 14.
60 Ibid.

can make known these things to you. Lay on your faces. I will guide thee to the light. Children, I am going to do this thing. Are you willing to take my Word? Are you willing to follow in my steps? Will you throw away your opinions and take my Word? I will teach thee and bring this to pass shortly.'" Another mighty season of prayer followed. The General Overseer noted his belief that when the matter was settled, there would be weeping. There was more pray and discussion – and then yielding. The Assembly combined discussion/business with sieges of prayer and seeking God.

another "wonderful season of prayer." Then tongues and interpretation,

"I alone can make known these things to you. Lay on your faces. I will guide thee to the light. Children, I am going to do this thing. Are you willing to take my Word? Are you willing to follow in my steps? Will you throw away your opinions and take my Word? I will teach thee and bring this to pass shortly." Following the spiritual manifestation, there was yet "another mighty season of prayer."[61]

The discussion had centered on the innocent party in the matter of a divorce. At this point, the General Overseer made a interesting and passionate plea in behalf of the transgressor. Here was mercy balancing truth.

"Isn't the soul of the transgressor worth as much as the one who has not gone astray? Leave the ninety and nine and go after the one that is lost. Let me discuss this side also."

Again, the Assembly broke out - "much prayer again, talking in tongues and shouting." The General Overseer asked the body,

"Don't you think we have struck something? ... The Spirit is talking to you ... Greater things are to be revealed. When this question is settled there will be weeping and wailing."

61 Ibid, 15.

The Minutes note, "Much prayer again."[62] At this point, J. C. Kelly rose to confess: "I never thought anything would bend me, but my opinions and ideas are gone." Prayer and the Spirit had brought a sense of unity on a controversial matter.

1914 – 10th Assembly

The first service was held on Monday night, November 2, 1914, began with songs and prayers. Z. D. Simpson of Ethelsville, Alabama preached. An uncommon manifestation was reported, called - "Like as of fire" and was witnessed by several as appearing over the congregation.[63]

On Tuesday morning, Nov. 21, the Assembly opened with a Scripture (Isaiah 40:28-31 and 41:1-16) along with remarks by the General Overseer and prayer "that the guiding hand of God direct during the entire Assembly, and that it might surpass all other Assemblies in power and in the settlement of questions."[64] That evening, Tomlinson delivered his annual address. Again, that evening, there was the manifestation of "'Like as of Fire,' and a special manifestation of God's presence and power at the close."[65]

On Wednesday morning, Sam C. Perry gave a discourse on *Intercessory Prayer,* the first message exclusively and specifically focused on prayer at any Assembly.[66]

On Thursday morning, there was a collage of business items – mention of money owed and paid; a call for those needing counsel regarding their field of labor; a discourse by the General Overseer

---

62 Ibid.

63 *Church of God General Assembly Minutes,* Tenth General Assembly (Cleveland, TN, November 2-8, 1914), 3.

64 Ibid.

65 Ibid, 5.

66 Ibid, 23.

> ### ACCENT
>
> At the 10th General Assembly, Sam C. Perry gave the message on *Intercessory Prayer*. At the close, there was a great manifestation of the presence and power of God. Many saw supernatural tongues 'like as of fire" flashed about. People shouted, wept, screamed, danced, prayed, sang and pen cannot describe the scene.

about inculcating doctrine in the hearts and minds of men. It sounds like anything but a fertile spiritual moment. But the Minutes say, "At the close of this discourse the congregation was weeping so they fell upon their faces and gave vent to their pent-up feeling in sobs and cries and prayers." And then another first, "Then a holy silence settled over all." Following this moment, joyful singing provided the opportunity for an offering for the expenses of the Assembly - $83.60.[67]

On Friday morning, there were songs and prayers, and the Assembly held a special prayer for many sick people both present and absent. They prayed over some handkerchiefs and sent to the sick at a distance. This is the first prayer service for the sick and sending of prayer cloths.[68]

On Saturday evening, after the regular service, a special called meeting took place for unfinished business at 10:00 PM. The meeting concluded near midnight with this note, "Call to special prayer for work and workers. Song, doxology and dismissed at 11:46 PM."

On Sunday morning, Sam Perry preached again. The minutes say,

"... at the close of which there was great manifestations of the presence and power of God. Many saw the 'Like as of fire' as it flashed about. People shouted, wept, screamed, danced, prayed,

---

67 Ibid, 25.
68 Ibid, 26.

sang and, pen cannot describe the scene."[69]

In summary, a number of features at this assembly were unusual – the 'like as of fire' manifestation which had been reported in revivals, but never in the minutes at the Assembly. Second, a message on 'intercessory prayer.' Third, silence before God in prayer. Fourth, the singing of the doxology.

1915 – Eleventh General Assembly

On Tuesday morning, following the parade of states, the congregation not only prayed, they knelt and offered prayers and thanksgiving to God.[70] At other points there were also spontaneous moments of prayer.

The above are excerpts from the first ten years of Church of God General Assemblies, with a focus on prayer. It is clear – all they did was around prayer. They did not merely begin sessions and services with a word of prayer; they often began with a prayer service. The whole assembly prayed – fervently, on their knees, and often. Born in prayer, they knew that we could only move forward on our knees, in prayer.

---

69 Ibid, 33.
70 *Church of God General Assembly Minutes,* Eleventh General Assembly (Cleveland, TN, November 1-7, 1915), 13.

CHAPTER TWENTY-ONE

GENERAL ASSEMBLY PRAYER MOMENTS
- THE SECOND TEN YEARS

A WINDOW THROUGH TIME

"The oneness of God's people should be, and surely is the desire of every true believer in Jesus Christ. This oneness has been earnestly sought for, by many professed followers of Christ, at intervals ever since the days of the Apostles. We do not need to say that their efforts in that direction have been fruitless, for it is a well-known fact that scores and hundreds of religious sects have made their appearance since the days of the apostasy." These words are taken from the writings of General Overseer, A. J. Tomlinson. The article goes on to note that the 'great hindrance' is that 'special points of Scripture' all of which came from the sacred lips of Christ, have been made "prominent" while other portions have been "neglected."

Early church leaders believed that law and gospel were too often mixed, and the words of the prophets were not subordinated to the word of the one prophet, Jesus, Moses had predicted, "A Prophet shall the Lord your God raise up unto you of your brethren, like unto me; Him shall ye hear in all things whatsoever He shall say unto you. And it shall come to pass, that every soul which will not hear that prophet shall be destroyed from among the people" (Deuteronomy 18:15:19; Acts 3:22:23). Not only was the word of Jesus to be exalted, but so was the government He brought, "For unto us a child is born, unto us a son is given: and the government shall be upon His shoulder. Of the increase of His government there shall be no end" (Isa.9:6-7).

Daniel also saw one 'like the Son of man' who before the Ancient of days was given "dominion, and glory, and a kingdom, that all people nations and languages should serve Him: His dominion is an everlasting dominion, which shall not pass away and His kingdom that which shall not be destroyed" (Dan. 7:13-14).

Jesus is to be Prophet and King. These early Church of God folks believed that this was not limited to a time after His Second Coming, but a dimension of His kingdom had already been inaugurated. On the Mount of Transfiguration, Jesus had met with the Moses and Elijah. Through Moses came the Law, and of course, Elijah, caught up into heaven in a chariot of fire, was considered the premium prophet. Peter recognized the incredible moment. "Let us make three tabernacles, one for You, one for Moses, and one for Elijah." In truth, Peter was petrified. "A bright cloud overshadowed them: and behold a voice out of the cloud, which said, 'This is my beloved son, in whom I am well pleased; 'Hear Ye Him!'" The Church was to coalesce around Jesus Christ Himself. He was to be the Head of the Church. His prayer was, "that they ALL may be one that they also may be one in us; that the world may believe that thou hast sent me that they may be one, even as we are one: that they may be made perfect in one; that the world may know that thou hast sent me, and hast loved them, as thou hast loved me" (John 17:20-23).

The General Overseer asserted, "What a wonderful thing it would be for all Christians to really be one in answer to the prayer of Jesus." Their conclusion was simple, only by obeying the commands of Christ, the true Governor. Paul urged, "Now, I beseech you, brethren, by the name of our Lord

Jesus Christ, that ye all speak the same thing, and that there be no divisions among you; but that ye be perfectly joined together in the same judgment" (I Cor. 1:10:11).

A. J. Tomlinson, Editor, "The Oneness of God's People," *The Church of God Evangel,* [Periodical], (Cleveland, TN: Church of God Publishing; August 1, 1910), 1-2. Lead article.

CHAPTER 21

GENERAL ASSEMBLY PRAYER MOMENTS
- THE SECOND TEN YEARS

P. Douglas Small

As with the first ten General Assemblies, there remains a strong character of prayer in the meetings. The crowds have increased. The informality, noted in some earlier assemblies, is by necessity gone. But still, there are moments of prayer, snapshots of the group on their knees, scheduled prayer, preaching on prayer. The Church of God, at least in these early years, was a praying church, essentially – a prayer movement.

1916 – Twelfth General Assembly

The 12th Assembly began on a Monday evening. *The Minutes* state that the first thirty minutes were given to "songs, prayers and mighty praises to our loving King." [1]

On Tuesday, November 2, the service began at 9:30 AM with "songs and prayers and weeping and shouting." In addition, the *Minutes* say, "Special concert prayer for the sick" took place and the Assembly proper began at 10:00 AM. [2] This was the second Assembly where special prayer was offered for the sick. This would become a regular feature, particularly in the Lee years.

After the General Overseer spoke briefly from Romans 12, he

---

1   *Church of God General Assembly Minutes*, Twelfth General Assembly (Harriman, TN, November 1-7, 1916), 3.
2   Ibid, 4.

again called for special prayer for the Assembly,

> "That the directing, guiding and protecting hand of God might overrule during the entire Assembly, and that the love of God might predominate in all the deliberations."[3]

'Songs and prayer' generally marked the beginning of each session. After remarks by the General Overseer, all were called to their knees to show gratitude for the great building. After a few moments of kneeling, all were then called to stand upright with bowed heads and in silence while the General Overseer offered the dedicatory prayer. The minutes read,

> "At 9:45 p.m. the last word of the prayer was spoken and all of a sudden the power of the Holy Ghost fell upon the mass of human beings, the brass band struck up the wonderful music and to describe what followed for thirty minutes would be impossible, the shouts, dancing, talking in tongues, music, weeping, and many manifestations of the Spirit of God convinced everybody present that God had accepted the building and filled it with His glory and power."[4]

1917 – Thirteenth General Assembly

The Thursday morning session began has had other Assemblies with a 9:30 AM prayer service – songs and prayers. The official opening was at 10 AM with a Scripture reading from Romans 12. And then the General Overseer prayed:

> Our Father who art in heaven, it is in Thy name we have come here to this Thirteenth Annual Assembly, from the North, East, South and West. Our greetings have been pleasant. Our fellowship has been sweet.
>
> We want to thank and praise Thee because we are followers

---

3   Ibid.
4   Ibid, 3.

of the great Church of God. We thank the good name of our God for ever sending Jesus to establish His Church of which we can be members. We thank and glorify Thee because of Thy special presence. Thy presence was with the apostles and Thy presence is with us. Thou hast been with us for thirteen years and we believe Thy presence will continue with us until Jesus returns.

Our hearts and minds take their flight yonder, and we think of the great assembly by and by where Abraham and Isaac and the blessed old apostles, who followed Jesus and who gave their lives for the great Church of God, will gather together. We are trying to please Thee now, increase our capacity and help us to please Thee more perfectly.

We went to ask Thee to be in all the exercises that may follow in the Assembly. Give us more knowledge and greater ability than we have ever had. Let Thy presence be with all the speakers and give them power through the Holy Ghost.

Lord be with us all the way, every day and hour, and may our fellowship continue to be sweet.

We pray that all the committeemen, and the people and all those who reside in Harriman may feel Thy presence. Oh God, I pray that Thy power may be so great that holiness can be felt, and that everyone will know that God is here.

God bless those that are not members of the Church of God that came to be with us. Help them to feel welcome and in the future to become members.

We want this to be the greatest Assembly we have ever had, not because of our worthiness, but to show the world that Thou art here in mighty power.

We ask all in Jesus' name. Amen.[5]

There is an earlier prayer recorded in the minutes, but not nearly as extensive as is this one. Those with a heritage in the movement will note the phrase – '*the great Church of God.*' It is at one level, a cause

---

5   *Church of God General Assembly Minutes*, Thirteenth General Assembly (Harriman, TN, November 1-6, 1917), 3.

for concern. Pride is such an insidious and at times treacherously invisible thing. And yet, there was a sense among these early leaders that they were a part of something eschatological, something God was doing in the earth through them. That sense of destiny, of corporate purpose and calling, is an invaluable asset. They had a sense that Pentecost reached across the centuries of the church, back to the first century, back to the apostolic era. This was a pervasive idea, not only in the Church of God, but also among movements that sprung from such places as Azusa Street. God, these early Pentecostals felt, was up to something both new and old. The fresh Pentecost, signaled the restoration of the New Testament Church.

There is a precious spirit of dependence on God in this early meetings and a missional concern, that the people of the city in which the Assembly was held, will be impacted by the mere presence of the Church. On the closing night of the Assembly, there was a song service, with prayers and testimonies. And then a healing service and prayers for the sick.[6]

Printed by order of the Council, and included in the *Minutes* was a document titled, 'Instructions and Advices'. The first subheading was 'The World Must Be Evangelized.' The document contained practical advice for pastors and local church leaders. Among the notes were:

- Prayer Time: "All members should be ready to center their minds and prayers on the one thing as a unit when calls for special prayer are made. Each one should feel his or her part of the responsibility, remembering that when one member fails it cripples or dwarfs the body ..."[7]

- Business Sessions: Should begin and end with prayer. Votes should not be the means of deciding a matter, but mutual agreement.

6   Ibid, 45.
7   Ibid, 46.

- Members: "Be ready for vocal prayer when called on or prompted by the Spirit ..."[8]
- Preaching: "Always pray silently for the preacher while he delivers the message."[9]
- Personal Prayer: "Spend as much time as you can in secret prayer. Give yourself all you can to intercessory prayer."[10]
- Caution: "Remember these are the last days and perilous times have come, so it will require much watchfulness and humble prayer on your part to so live and act that you will never bring reproach on the worthy name of Christ and His Church that you so much love."[11]

1918

No Assembly was held due to the Influenza epidemic.

1919 – Fourteenth General Assembly

On Thursday morning, October

We must be ready to allow ourselves to be interrupted by God ... It is a strange fact that Christians and even ministers frequently consider their work so important and urgent that they will allow nothing to disturb them. They think they are doing God a service in this, but actually they are disdaining God's 'crooked yet straight path.'

Bonhoeffer, from "Life Together," Quoted by Charles Ringma, *Seize the Day with Dietrich Bonhoeffer* (Colorado Springs, Colorado: Pinion Press; 2000), See entry for January 17.

8   Ibid, 48.
9   Ibid.
10 Ibid.
11 Ibid.

30, 1919, the General Assembly service began with songs, prayers, and praises – a pre-service as in past years. Then the Assembly proper began at 10 AM.[12]

Silent Prayer

After singing, "the General Overseer asked the congregation to bow their heads in silent prayer ..." This is the first instance of silent prayer. With Tomlinson's Quaker background, this is not strange, but among some Pentecostals today, the idea of 'silence' before God is uncommon.

Corporate Recitation of the Lord's Prayer

Not only does the General Overseer call for silent prayer, but then he leads the congregation in the recitation of the 'Lord's Prayer.' They then sang, and the Overseer asked all to stand and "clap their hands."

Pastoral Prayer by the General Overseer

After reading from Romans, he then offered a prayer. Here is a record of that prayer from the Minutes:

> Dear Father, in the sacredness of Thy presence we bow. Thou hast already overcome us with Thy love.
>
> We thank Thee for the privilege of gathering together again in this Assembly. Some have left us since we met in the last Assembly, but thou hast raised up others to take their places.
>
> Lord, don't let us fail Thee. Help us to keep in the unity of the Spirit. We want to lift up holy hands to Thee. Hold your grip upon us throughout the Assembly. We have no axes to grind, the only thing we want to know, Lord, is Thy will, and we will do

---

12 *Church of God General Assembly Minutes*, Fourteenth General Assembly (Cleveland, TN, October 29 - November 4, 1919), 4.

it faithfully by Thy grace and help. We are making promises to Thee this morning, help us to keep them.

Give us special understanding, wisdom, knowledge, and plenty of white-heated love that will water and bless the world. We thank Thee for the sacredness Thou hast thrown upon us like the dew from heaven which raises and nourishes the plants which are bowed down.

As we continue in the Assembly from day to day we pray that Thou wilt help each speaker to feel his responsibility. Also help each hearer to hear in the same spirit in which it is given out. Help us to be faithful.

Help us to be true. Help Thy servant especially. Then when by and by the trumpet sounds, we may together go up to meet the Lord.[13]

Personal Expression in Prayer

The *Minutes* say,

"Following this prayer, the General Overseer asked the Assembly to yield themselves to the Lord in tears and the melting love of God.[14]

Multiple Prayer Services
– and Fire!

On Thursday afternoon, at 1:30 PM, there was a prayer service prior to the 2:00 PM session.[15] Again on Friday morning, half-an-hour before the 10:00 AM session, another prayer service was held.[16] Again at Noon, the pattern was repeated – at 1:30 PM, special prayer session prior to the 2:00 PM session.[17] On Friday evening,

---

13 Ibid.
14 Ibid.
15 Ibid, 21.
16 Ibid, 24.
17 Ibid, 27.

the *Minutes* read,

> "Song, prayer and testimony service. Ball of fire was seen during testimony service."[18] Songs and prayer services preceded business and regular services quite often, though this was not always the case.

Special Prayer

On Sunday, prayer for the sick was again made available.[19]

Overseers were appointed and special prayer was made for them. In the afternoon, prayer was offered for those who wanted to be sanctified and filled with the Spirit. [20]

On Monday, a letter was read from F. L. Ryder, missionary to South America. He wrote,

> "We shall be mingling our prayers with yours at the throne for His divine guidance in all your deliberations for the re-established and extension of the great and grand Church of God."[21]

The wonderful image of prayers, being mingled together at the One Throne, yet rising from the many places around the world is a glorious picture. The church gathered and the church scattered, united in a prayer meeting, as it were, at the Throne in heaven.

The Minutes contain a synopsis of the Fourteenth Annual Assembly, calling it –

> "... the most wonderful of all

When the vast audience lifted their voices together in prayer, it was as the sound of the rushing of many waters...

–*Minutes of the Fourteenth General Assembly*

---

18 Ibid, 28.
19 Ibid, 30.
20 Ibid.
21 Ibid, 32.

the previous Assemblies. The power and glory of the Lord rested upon the first service and kept increasing until the last. The wonderful manifestations of God's presence and power can never be described by tongue or pen. The heavens were ringing with shouts and praises, and the sweet holy presence of the Lord filled the atmosphere until it seemed we were in very close touch with the heavenly world.

When the vast audience lifted their voices together in prayer, it was as the sound of the rushing of many waters and as they would stand with uplifted hands shouting the praises of the Lord it would remind one of the shouting when the children of Israel marched around the walls of Jericho and blew the trumpets and shouted that great shout of victory that brought those high massive walls of that great city to the ground.

To look out over that large audience with faces shining with the glory of the Lord and feel the sweet fellowship and unity that

Among the number one night was a man with his back and both limbs broken who had not walked without crutches in ten years. When they prayed for him the mighty power of God came down upon him, and he was healed, and left his crutches and ran out of the church house...

-Minutes of the Fourteenth General Assembly

prevailed was indeed a real foretaste of Heaven. Such love and unity we have never witnessed, and the wonderful inspiring discourses delivered by the different ministers of God, under the mighty anointing of the Spirit was food to our souls. It has truly been a time of feasting on the good things on our Heavenly Father's table. The altars were filled with seekers and we have not been able to keep the number of those who were sanctified and filled with the Holy Ghost. Handkerchiefs were sent in to be prayed over for the sick and many requests for prayer and numbers prayed for who were here and wanted healing. God was truly with us and manifested His power to heal those who were sick. Among the number one night was a man with his back and both limbs broken who had not walked without crutches in ten years. When they prayed for him the mighty power of God came down upon him, and he was healed, and left his crutches and ran out of the church house and around outside praising God, and the people following him and looking on at the mighty work of God. Wonderful and convincing messages were given in other tongues and interpreted. Wonderful visions seen, and one evening during the service a ball like as of fire was seen by some coming down and resting on the top of the church house which denotes God's presence. On Sunday morning ... a sister was carried to the platform by the power of the Holy Ghost and raised our General Overseer's hands and united other hands with his to hold them up, thus demonstrating to us in the Church, how we should hold up his hands in this great battle of the Lord in these last days. The mighty power of the Holy Ghost that fell on the congregation and that wonderful scene can never be described. And during this a sister saw a vision of Jesus above the platform ... wonderful manifestations of the presence and power of God, it seems that anyone with their spiritual eyes open can see God's favor and approval ..."[22]

1920 – Fifteenth General Assembly

General Overseer's Prayer

On Thursday morning, there was a Scripture Lesson from Romans 12, and prayer by the General Overseer. Here is a portion of prayer:

Our Father, which art in heaven, we want to humble ourselves,

---

22 Ibid, 44.

before Thee in such a way that we can feel Thy presence ... We thank Thee. for this commodious building, and for the great Church of God. We thank Thee so much that we are bound together with that binding cord of love ...

We are so glad Thou hast accepted our invitation and Thou art already- here. We appreciate that heavenly atmosphere.

(A molting spirit fell upon the entire congregation and there was much weeping before the Lord.)

What few days we are here, we want to sit at Thy feet and learn. We are here to counsel with one another and with God. Lord, we look up to Thee, a body of people desiring to know the truth. We humble ourselves before Thee ..."

Lord, give us ears to hear, eyes to see, and help us to have an eye single to Thy glory ... We are honest seekers of the truth. Give us a fresh revelation of the things of God ... break our hearts while we are here ... Touch the lips of Thy speakers and make them a flame of fire ... Let the fire of God burn out everything which does not belong here ... Give us unity and agreement. Let us, know about Thy laws and government ... (Weeping) ... Thy presence, Thy presence! ..."[23]

> *We can never expect to grow in the likeness of our Lord unless we follow His example and give more time to communion with the Father. A revival of real praying would produce a spiritual revolution.*
>
> *-E. M. Bounds*

Special Prayer Service

Prayer services preceded a number of the sessions. A special prayer service was conducted for the sick. The healing service continued for

23 *Church of God General Assembly Minutes*, Fifteenth General Assembly (Cleveland, TN, November 3-9, 1920), 8.

some two hours. The minutes say, "A large number came forward for healing. Quite a number touched the hem of His garment and were healed. Over three hundred handkerchiefs were anointed to return to the sick." Afterwards M. S. Lemons preached.[24]

Prayer by the General Overseer's Wife

On Sunday afternoon, November 7, there was prayer by the General Overseer's wife, Mrs. A J. Tomlinson.[25]

1921 – Sixteenth General Assembly

Dedication Prayer for the Assembly Building[26]

On November 2, the "great and beautiful Auditorium was formally dedicated to God ..." As the procession proceeded there was "perfect silence in all parts of the building."[27] What is fascinating about this dedication service are the multiple moments of silence.

> At the close of reading, one minute silence with holy reverence to God, then [music] ... As music ceased all stood in perfect silence before God. As the piano sounded loud all were seated ... [When the bishops were seated] ... music ceased and all remained ... in perfect silence before God ... [The music commenced again] ... As the echo from the song died away, there was silence before God ... then prayer by J. S. Llewellyn and perfect silence again. The singers turned their faces to the congregation and sang ... then there was silence again. After silences the singers were

---

24 Ibid, 44.
25 Ibid, 46.
26 David Roebuck, Church Historian, notes that we built the assembly building in Cleveland. It was first used it in 1920 but it had not been finished. The next year, it was dedicated (1921). It was used for Assemblies until 1931. Thereafter, North Cleveland used it for a season, as did the Bible Training School.
27 *Church of God General Assembly Minutes*, Sixteenth General Assembly (Cleveland, TN, November 2-8, 1921), 3.

seated on the front seat. Music by the orchestra from Alabama, followed by perfect silence ..."[28]

Modern Pentecostals are too nervous about silent moments. After remarks by the General Overseer, again, "One minute silence. Prayer by George. T. Brouayer, then one minute silence again ..."[29]

The dedicatory prayer was prayed by the General Overseer.

Our Father in heaven, our eyes are won Thee. We close our eyes so we cannot see the people, but we can see God by faith. We think of Him who made the heaven and the earth and created man in His own image and likeness and for His own glory.

It is our purpose, O God, in life to glorify Thee. We thank Thee more than we can express... We thank Thee because of the many members and those who are our sympathizers that have helped us construct this place where more than 3,000 people can meet to worship God ...

We are so glad we can look into the faces of thousands of those who have the Holy Ghost ... Father, ,we would not forget to thank Thee for this great pile of money; we have never done this before. The great Church of God has a home ... and they come up here once a year to bring an offering to bless God and bless one another and to receive blessings ...

Lord, we have come to stay; no matter how the battle rages: no matter how the enemy roars; no matter what comes; we come with our eyes set upon heaven and upon God ...

The Church of God ... has sprung up almost in a night, causing the people to look on and be amazed. They did not think we could do it, and now they acknowledge it is done. Hallelujah, we are going to give God the glory because the battle is not ours but the battle is God's. Thy servants have labored and toiled, loved and served, and tonight they are enjoying the fruits ... Our hearts are swelling; our souls are enlarging. We wonder, O Lord, what next You are going to do? Thou art a wonderful God! ...

---

28 Ibid, 4.
29 Ibid, 5.

ACCENT

What Happened at Barney Creek?
Read on August 19, 2011,
at the one-hundred and twenty-fifth anniversary of the
organization of Christian Union at Barney Creek.
James M. Beaty, Ph.D.

The first written record of what happened here at Barney Creek was written by Spurling himself, in his 1897 Manuscript. This is in the archives of the Church of God of Prophecy, but only parts of it were publish in *The Lost Link*. This is not so much in a detailed, step-by-step way, but more in the sense of giving the meaning of what it was about.

The first published record was by A. J. Tomlinson in 1913 and was part of his book, *The Last Great Conflict*.[1] It was based on accumulated, oral information received from R.G. Spurling over the years. Tomlinson had joined the church in 1903.

Both documents begin with the two-year period of 1884-86, leading up to Thursday, August 19, 1886. Spurling himself wrote:[2]

During these two years of unparalleled efforts to get the truth, I had taken shelter in the Methodist Episcopal Church until I could know what to do. Now, the matter is forever settled. A church which has not got God's law and government, I cannot serve. To bow to human laws any longer to me was base idolatry.... during the seven years[3] I had been preaching, I thought repentance, faith and baptism was God's law, not knowing that it only brought men to where they could keep God's law. Seeing as I now did, what could I do? If I go to preaching my honest convictions, even my own friends will hiss at me.

But having got nearly a month's schooling in the year 1865, by a little help of my parents, I could read the Bible, and having studied the Scriptures while young. I now was able to be counted a Bible scholar and having taken a wife, who like myself, was a member of the Baptist church, who during these years of trouble, while I was studying, praying and crying, stood unmoved in her church relations... During my troubles she was much humiliated at the thought of my defeat as a minister.

We love You, yes, we love You, Lord. Our hearts love God tonight. Oh, we feel like falling upon our faces as the description given in heaven and saying, "Holy, Holy, Holy! Lord God Almighty! Worthy is the Lamb to open the Book! ..." [30]

On Saturday, November 5, the day began with a funeral service for the infant child of J. B. Ellis. When the Assembly was called to order, there is this note, "All knelt in concert prayer for greater blessings than the day before."[31]

In the afternoon there was a question and answer session.

Question: James says to call for the elders of the church to pray for the sick but we have only twelve and they are usually too far away. What are we to do?

Answer: Get anybody to pray for you that can pray. Many people have just as much power to pray for the sick, as the twelve. This means anybody that is established and has faith in God.[32]

On Tuesday, November 8, at 10:40 AM, the General Assembly dealt with the idea of seventy elders and the length of their terms of service. The staggered term model was somewhat complex. But after its introduction, two notes are worthy of our consideration. First, there was a "prayer of thanks and honor to God for such unity. Many bowed heads to the floor." One of the consistent themes in the early minutes are notes of unity and harmony. A second is the sense that the church was a part of something bigger than themselves, the restoration of a New Testament Church, patterned on biblical truth, and therefore it was not opinion that was to prevail, but Scripture that informed polity issues. Tomlinson would exult, "The way the Lord is opening up His Word to our minds is marvelous. A marvelous spirit has taken hold on us and helps us to settle thing. The spirit that surrounds us allows no dissenting voice. We are certainly walking

30 Ibid, 8-9.
31 Ibid, 37.
32 Ibid, 38.

Meanwhile the Baptists were saying, "Come back and all will be right." *And the* Methodists said, "Stay with us and take the world for Christ and Methodism." These were gigantic temptations to a poor minister of the gospel, almost ready to despair, knowing that the world would frown upon such a one. For I thought if I tell my views, even my own brothers and friends will mock at them....

While praying and studying, I thought of the parable of the great supper and how the servants went and called the people to the supper and no one went, but made their excuses. And the servant went and told his lord of his failure and his lord gave him another mission and did not blame him for his failure. So I knew I could fill my mission and do my duty if no one would heed the truth, I could only go and tell my lord what I had done. So I began to tell the people about God's law and government. I preached what I now saw, and soon found others who saw the fallibility of laws made by men.

Tomlinson wrote the following of these two years:

> About the year 1884, a spirit of dissatisfaction and unrest began to work in the mind of a licensed minister of the Missionary Baptist church by the name of Richard G. Spurling, then living in Monroe County, Tenn.[4] The dissatisfaction arose because of certain traditions and creeds which were burdensome and exceedingly binding on the members.
>
> This humble and sincere servant of God,... began a more careful study of the Bible, and for two years or more spent much time in searching the Scriptures and church history, with a view to a reformation.
>
> After two years or more of careful searching, praying and weeping, and pleading with his church for reform to no avail, he, with others, began to arrange for an independent meeting for a conference and a more careful consideration of religious matters.

But how was August 19, 1886 described in these two sources? First, Spurling wrote:[5]

We formed a Christian Union agreeing to unite upon Christ's law, denouncing all human laws and government and articles of faith. Among this number was an elder softly before the Lord and I am sure we appreciate His presence."[33]

In the same session, the subject of judges was presented before the Assembly. The General Overseer asked, "Is everybody in favor of this office being instituted?" J. S. Llewellyn and M. S. Lemons offered explanations. A motion was offered to adopt the measure – and then, at least in terms of modern assemblies, a strange thing happened. The body prayed – they consulted with God – "to see if this step is right!" The Minutes say, "After prayer, Judges, or Courts of Justice, was unanimously carried."[34]

The 'Constitution' for the denomination was then presented – and accepted unanimously. A note follows:

> The General Overseer said, "In order to show our appreciation of His presence and it seeming good to us and the Holy Ghost, let us all kneel before the Lord and reverence Him."

The minutes say, "All knelt and thanked the Lord. After prayer all stood and praised God while the orchestra was playing!" The General Overseer exclaimed, "Behold What God Hath Wrought!" This sense of 'it seemed good to the Holy Ghost' – the great desire to integrate in all business the searching of Scripture with prayer, discerning the will of God, and 'walking softly' in humble unity to secure God's will is stunning.[35]

1922 – 17th General Assembly

On the morning of Thursday, November 3, the day began with songs and 'concert prayer.' A. J. Tomlinson, General Overseer, read from I Peter 2. It is not known what verses were read, but the chapter begins, "Therefore, rid yourselves of all malice and all deceit, hypocrisy, envy, and slander of every kind." Around the Assembly, accusations were swirling. The persistent theme, "Love – Truth

---

33   Ibid, 56.
34   Ibid.
35   Ibid, 65.

or an ordained minister [this was his father] who served the church until another [this was R.G.] was ordained on (New) Testament authority and qualification.[6]

Tomlinson included more details:

After having taken plenty of time for consideration, the time and place for the meetings was arranged and announced. That day is worthy of remembrance. Thursday, August 19, 1886.

The small company of humble, faithful, conscientious pilgrims met at Barney Creek meeting house, Monroe County, Tennessee.[7] After prayer, a strong discourse was delivered by Richard G. Spurling, emphasizing the need of a reformation.[8] The arguments were full of force and proved effective, and were endorsed by the hearers, so that when the time came for action there was free and earnest response.

The proposition and obligation was simple. We give it below:

As many Christians as are here present that are desirous to be free from all men made creeds (sic) and traditions, and are willing to take the New Testament, or law of Christ, for your only rule of faith and practice; giving each other equal rights and privilege to read and interpret for yourselves as your conscience may dictate, and are willing to set together as the Church of God to transact business at the same, come forward.

In response to this proposition eight persons, whose names are given below, presented themselves and gave to each other the right hands of fellowship....[9]

After having joined themselves together under the above obligation (1) they decided to name the baby organization "Christian Union." (2) They then decided to receive persons into membership who are possessed with a good Christian character, and (3) that ordained and licensed ministers from other churches could retain their same position or office without being re-ordained. (4) By virtue of the office he had held as a faithful ordained minister in the Missionary Baptist church for a number of years, Elder Richard Spurling was duly acknowledged and recognized as their minister, to do

– Unity" was about to be tested. This would be Tomlinson's last Assembly. Sadly, this would be the year of the schism. At the next Assembly, F. J. Lee would preside as General Overseer. And many names so familiar in our early history would disappear from mention in our subsequent history and minutes.[36]

Payer by General Overseer A. J. Tomlinson:

'Our Father who art in heaven, in Thy sacred presence we bow ourselves before Thee. Thou hast told us to humble ourselves under the mighty hand of God and Thou would exalt us in due time. Some time we want to make heaven our home. We want to be exalted as high as heaven. We want to see the great prophets and the great leaders of the past and above all we want to see Jesus, His loving face who gave Himself to redeem us from sin that we might live a righteous life.

We thank Thee for the Holy Ghost which He so wonderfully gives to guide us into all truth and take the things of His and show them unto us. This blessed Spirit has wonderfully revealed unto us His Church. Oh how our hearts feel grateful for this wonderful introduction of His own. We thank Thee because things have been made so plain to us and we have gathered here in this Seventeenth Assembly to expect some advanced revelations, some more of the same kind of truths that have been revealed to us in the past.

Our hearts well up in us this morning in gratitude and thanksgiving for we remember we are taught to make our request known with thanksgiving. Lord, we want to thank Thee because so many are here today. We thank Thee that, in spite of hard times, the brothers and sisters have gathered together from the north, south, east and west to learn more about His precious

---

36 The new building and the acquisition of the printing equipment had placed the general church under an acute financial strain. This was the era in which pastors were being paid out of the general fund, all tithes being sent to headquarters for distribution. A part of the concern was that funds were being used for debt and not appropriately distributed back to the field.

all the business devolved on him as such in the new order. He then having been placed in authority by the body, (1) took his seat as moderator, and by prayer dedicated the infant church of God, imploring His guidance and blessings for it, and that it might grow and prosper, and accomplish great good.[10] (2) An invitation was then given for the reception of members, and they received Richard G. Spurling... The church chose him as their pastor,[11] and had him ordained the next month, September 26, 1886.[12]

In his 1897 Spurling wrote:

So I composed the following poem of encouragement for the little church (tune and chorus: Rock of Ages).[13]

1   Now we set out, sails a breeze,
    Soon we'll pass life's troubled seas;
    Soon we'll gain a better shore,
    There where we shall part no more.

2   Mid[14] life's oceans' roughest gale,
    Then we hoist the greater sail:
    Trusting in our Captain's skill,
    Yield obedience to his will.

3   When the storms shall all have passed,
    And we reach our home at last,
    There with all that happy throng,
    We shall join their glorious song.

May it be true of all of us. Amen.

*See notes as end of Chapter.

Word and the necessary things to know about the great Church of God.

Now, Father, we just want to ask Thee to let Thy presence be with us all the way ... Lord help every one of us to grace this institution by living holy lives and unspotted from the world, and we want to be so united and live such lives before the world that they will see and know that this is the way ..." [37]

---

37 *Church of God General Assembly Minutes*, Seventeenth General Assembly (Cleveland, TN, November 1-7, 1922), 4.

1923 – 18th General Assembly

Among F. J. Lee's Preface to the Minutes of the Eighteenth General Assembly are these words,

> "Many had wondered if the Assembly would be largely attended, and if it would be an enjoyable occasion, but scores have expressed themselves as being agreeably surprised. Some thought Satan might break in and cause friction and disappointment, but thousands of prayers had found their way to the throne, and the dear Lord had graciously come upon the scene. It was marvelous how the sweet, mellow spirit pervaded the whole Assembly, no friction or strife whatever."[38]

The Introductory Remarks describe the first service on Wednesday, October 31. The Assembly opened with the old hymn, 'What a Friend We Have in Jesus.' And then 'When My Name is Called in Glory I'll Be There.' The Minutes read,

> "There came a great wave of glory with much shouting and dancing. Truly God set His seal of approval upon us that He was with us at the very beginning. Oh such shining faces. Truly it could be said, 'The Lord is in His holy temple.' Many saints had been praying during the past year that God might be with us in a marked way and have His way in this Assembly. It can be truly said that it is wonderful for brethren to dwell together in unity. The oil of gladness was poured upon our heads as the distilling of the dew of Hermon. Then a concert prayer as the voice of many waters, was offered for the sick and afflicted, and for the Assembly."[39]

After the state reports on Thursday evening, there is this note:

Many of the states were well represented with a large delegation.

---

38 *Church of God General Assembly Minutes*, Eighteenth General Assembly (Cleveland, TN, November 1-7, 1923), 2.

39 Ibid, 3.

The glory of God could be seen upon their faces, and all had a shout of victory in their souls. Many had come through hard fought battles, but it only made them shine brighter. The banners were very impressive, and were characteristic of the Church in the different states. At times great waves of glory would sweep over the entire congregation, and at other times a spirit of weeping while the representatives were telling of the blessings of the Lord, and of their determination to go out and do more for the Lord than ever before. The love and unity that prevailed is beyond expression; it just can't be told; and all this was in answer to prayer.

There was no preaching at night, as the response from the states continued on into the night service. Service at night closed with uplifted hands and thanksgiving for the blessings of the Lord on the services of the day (amid shouts of praises). Adjourned at 9:30 PM.[40]

On Sunday, November 4, the day began with "songs, prayer and music." Handkerchiefs were anointed and prayed over for the healing of afflicted and diseased bodies. At 10 AM, G.A. Fore preached from Jeremiah 33:3, on prayer. This is the first sermon on prayer in which the content is recorded in the Minutes. It is presented here in abbreviated form:

I presume we all know how to pray, but may learn to pray better. Prayer is communion with our Father in Heaven; and in order to get His attention we must pray from the heart with a sincere desire.

Moses was a man of prayer - a great intercessor whenever Israel got into trouble he would call upon God, and deliverance would come. Abraham was a man of prayer. Joshua was a man of prayer, and prayed until God caused the sun to stand still. Elijah was the praying prophet. You remember how he hid away, and then, appeared before Ahab. This is the secret of success. First, hide away with God, and then appear before the people. God heard and answered prayer for the widow's son and healed

40 Ibid, 15.

him. The prophets of Baal were not praying to the right God; though they lashed themselves, and cried, and cried the answer did not come; but when Elijah began to pray God answered by fire, because he had confidence in God. We must have confidence in God, and know that we are praying for the right thing, then God will answer.

> *Prayer is communion with our Father in Heaven.*
>
> ~ G.A. Fore

When Daniel was cast in the lion's den the jaws of the lions were locked; God sent an angel to lock them in answer to his prayer. The prayer of one man turned a whole nation to God. If it had not been for prayer you and I never would have been saved or filled with the Holy Ghost. When we come to God we must persevere. We must keep going down before God until He hears and answers us. These are the elements of true prayer:

1. *Contrition* - After Saul of Tarsus woke up to the fact that he was persecuting God when he persecuted His saints, he became very contrite and began to pray, and for that reason Ananias was sent to him with a message from the Lord.

2. *Confession* - I have heard men pray when they should have been confessing. Anything wrong in people's lives will hinder their prayers, and God will not hear them until confession is made.

3. *Restitution* - When Jesus told Zacchaeus to make haste and come down, he obeyed and told the Lord that half of his goods he would give to the poor, and if he had taken anything from any man by false accusation he would restore him-fourfold. Jesus then told him that this day salvation had come to his house.

4. *Forgiveness* - An unforgiving spirit will hinder our prayers from going through. The old adage says, "If we can't go over the mole hill God will not come over the mountain." It is a settled fact, if we do not forgive God will not answer us.

5. *Perseverance* - Daniel had to pray twenty-one days before he could get his prayers through to God. Elijah prayed seven times before God sent the rain. Many great men of God have had to pray fervently and earnestly before God would answer. Beloved, let us not get discouraged and give up, but let us keep on praying until God pours down His blessings upon us and others.

> *This is the secret of success. First, hide away with God, and then appear before the people.*
>
> ~ G.A. Fore

6. *Faith* - Jesus said, "Whatsoever ye desire when ye pray, believe, and ye shall receive it." Beloved, if we do not receive, it is because we lack faith.

7. *Unity* - While they were in the upper room praying for the Holy Ghost the power of God came down upon them, because they were all of one accord. When we agree on any one thing it shall be done.

8. *Submission* - While Jesus was earnestly praying in the Garden of Gethsemane He told His Father, "Not my will but Thine be done." We must be willing for God's will and not ours to be done in any matter. We must have a spirit of submission.

Beloved, it is very necessary that we pray, for we are surrounded with evil on every hand, and our enemies are many, our dependence is in God and we must hold on to Him.

At the close of this discourse, all with uplifted hands prayed, thanking God for the privilege of prayer. [41]

On Sunday Evening, C. M. Padgett spoke on the subject, "Pray Though."[42]

---

41 Ibid, 39-40.
42 Ibid, 42.

1924 – 19ᵗʰ General Assembly

General Overseer F. J. Lee called the 19ᵗʰ Assembly, a "great gathering ... one of the greatest in the history of the Church of God ... grand and glorious ... immense." He reported that over 2,000 were in attendance. "There was not the least jar or friction during the entire Assembly." He called the Assembly "a turning point for good ..." [43]

During the Wednesday evening introductory service,

"the auditorium was filled to its utmost capacity ... all present rejoiced to greet each other with a hearty hand shake and a God bless you ... 'At the Cross' was sung by the congregation ... Following this the entire audience fell on their faces and offered thanksgiving to God for the privilege of being present, and also for His grace extended to us during the past Assembly year. After prayer a few more hymns were sung and another mighty season of prayer followed, in which the sick were especially remembered ..."[44]

The Minutes say,

"The evening services were devoted largely to praying for the sick, in which it is said that hundreds were healed. This feature of the evening services was from 6:00 to 7:00 PM after which the regular evangelistic services were held in which many souls were definitely blessed of the Lord."[45]

The business sessions opened with a prayer by F. J. Lee, the General Overseer. Here is that simple prayer:

Heavenly Father, we know that thou art beholding the scene as we stand with bowed heads in thy presence. This is thy people Lord, they have assembled from every corner of the earth, they have come to this place because they love thee, because they

---

43 *Church of God General Assembly Minutes*, Nineteenth General Assembly (Cleveland, TN, October 29 -November 4, 1924), 2.
44 Ibid, 3.
45 Ibid, 7.

want to honor thee and do that which is pleasing in thy sight continually. Some of thy children here have walked part of the way and some of them had to borrow money to come on, but they are here, they would not be denied, their soul is in this great event. Thou didst take care of them on their journey and didst protect them until they were able to assemble in this place.

Father we know that thy smiles are upon us and we pray that thou wilt continue to be with us and direct us in all of our affairs for this is thy work and we want God to help us that we may do everything according to His will.

Give us grace to be submissive and give us the Spirit of humility more and more as we go on with thee. Lead us on to higher heights and deeper depths. Grant Lord that the enemy will have no showing here whatever, but we pray that the Spirit of God will take complete control of the services and that everyone here will realize that God's Holy presence in this place.

We pray thee Lord that sweet fellowship will prevail and that thy children will be submitted to all the will of God. We ask all this in Jesus' name.[46]

On Sunday, November 2, John Attey preached on *"Prayer"* from I Timothy 2. A record of his message is found in the Minutes.

Prayer is a cry or supplication. It is an appeal from the child to the Father. There are two forms of prayer namely: intercessory and supplication.[47] We call your attention to a man who lived a

---

46 Ibid, 9-10.

47 I [Doug Small] often stress prayer as communion with God – and that is the very heart of prayer: oneness, unity, congruence, fellowship, union with God in heart and purpose, the essence of which is worship, and the character of which is love. Because of this relationship, we get to supplicate (offer petitions), and we are in a position to intercede for others. Of course, all of this should be wrapped in a spirit of thanksgiving. It is very possible, that these early men walked in such communion and fellowship with God, that they could not perceive of a day in the church, in which 'petitions' and prayer requests were offered by a people who had restricted prayer only to acquisition, and lacked a heart of devoted passion for God, apart from what he might do for them.

life of prayer. A man who lived close to God; a man whose prayer God heard. His name was Hezekiah. One day he took sick and was about to die, then he turned his face toward the wall and reminded God that he has walked before Him with a true and perfect heart, and that he had done that which was good in His sight.

The Bible tells us that he wept sore. God looked down from heaven and added fifteen years to his life. Beloved, we need more Hezekiah's that are given up to prayer and can reach the throne of grace. As long as we have anything in our hearts that is not in harmony with God, he will not hear our prayer.

> *You can do more than pray after you have prayed, but you cannot do more than pray until you have prayed.*
>
> *~A. J. Gordon*

Another Bible character I want to speak of is Daniel. He, like all other men of God, had his trials and tests. You all remember how the decree was signed by the king, that if any man ask a petition of any god or man for 30 days, save of him, he should be cast into the lion's den, but notwithstanding this decree, Daniel preferred to obey God rather than man.

Humanly speaking it was a dark hour, but we must remember that God will stand by his own when the testing time comes.

When the clouds are hanging low, is a good time to pray.

I believe that God permits things to come our way at times in order to stir us up along the line of praying. In order for our prayers to go through to the throne of God, we must see to it that our lives are clean for I remember that a writer of old said, "If I regard iniquity in my heart God will not hear me. Then again I read where Jesus said, "If ye abide in me, and my words abide in you, ye shall ask what ye will and it shall be done unto you."

It pays to pray. All of us should take more time to pray. We will lose the victory out of our souls if we don't pray. The lengthening of Hezekiah's life was due to his much praying. I am constrained to believe that if we would pray more God would give eternal life to more of the human family. May God help us to live in such close touch with Him that our prayers will be heard.[48]

On Monday, November 3, in the afternoon, there was a sermon by W. M. Rumler on *"Evangelism"* from II Timothy 4. Rumler spoke about working and giving, and then he remarked about the role of prayer in evangelism,

> "Lastly, I will say another good way
> to evangelize the world is for people to pray. Prayer is the main factor in all of our work anyway. Neglect of prayer means powerless sermons and besides, we as ministers, cannot do as we should if we can't have the prayers of the people. I hope the Church of God people will get into the secret of prayer more and more.[49]

1925 – 20ᵗʰ General Assembly

The Assembly opened on a Monday night. The *Minutes* read,

> "From the beginning of this great convocation the presence of the Lord was felt. At the hour indicated on the program the great Auditorium was filled with a happy throng of people whose hearty hand-shakes roved that they were glad: to greet each other, and frequently shouts and praises to God were heard from all over the building. Presently the moderator called the great congregation to order and the chorister announced that good old time hymn, 'In the Sweet Bye and Bye.' This was followed by a few other songs a short testimony service, and a mighty season of prayer." [50]

---

48 Ibid, 33-34.
49 Ibid, 38-39.
50 *Church of God General Assembly Minutes*, Twentieth General Assembly (Cleveland, TN, October 19 -25, 1925), 4.

On Tuesday morning, the General Overseer called on H. L. Trim to offer the opening prayer for the business session. The Minutes offer a record of the prayer:

> Our Father which art in heaven, whom angels and arch-angels adore, we the workmanship of Thy wonderful hand, kneel before Thee just now to offer our prayers and supplication unto Thee, the God of our salvation.
>
> We come before Thee this morning feeling our unworthiness. We know that Thou art a God that hears and answers prayer. We thank Thee for what Thou has done among us, and now we invite Thy presence and ask that Thou wilt have complete charge and control of every one of us. God bless every officer of the Church and honor us with Thy presence and power. Give us the needed wisdom that we may do everything in a way that it will be pleasing to Thee. We thank Thee, oh God, for our General Overseer. We pray that Thou wilt anoint him with power. . Give him special wisdom and overshadow him by Thy mighty power. Bless all the homes that are represented here and bless those that would like to be here but cannot. We pray that the sick may be healed in the name of the Holy child, Jesus.
>
> Take us into a sacred nearness with Thyself and guide Us with Thy unerring Spirit and Thou shalt have the praise![51]

F. J. Lee proceeded to give the annual General Overseer's Address. He noted, "Many times have I been awakened in the dark hours of night meditating and praying over the affairs of the Church."[52] He also offered an insight into the relationship between the Church of God periodical, *The Evangel*, and prayer,

> "While 'there have gone up thousands of prayers from loyal members of the great Church of God, we at the Evangel office have faithfully climbed the stairway to the upper room, here we have gained many victories, handkerchiefs have been sent forth to the suffering, and many have reported healing through this

---

51 Ibid, 6-7.
52 Ibid, 8.

ministry."[53]

Concluding his remarks, he said, ""None of us know what is before us, or how soon our race may be run, therefore it behooves us to watch and pray, live under the drippings of the blood ..."[54]

John L. Stephens spoke on "Tactics for Effective Evangelistic and Pastoral Work" from Proverbs 11:28. Among his comments was the admonition,

> "Many times it will pay us to do the praying and let God do the work, or in other words, some people can be best reached by the way of the throne. If we can move God, He can move the people."[55]

M. W. Letsinger reported on the success of *The Evangel* saying, "... every issue is being prayed over before it leaves the office."[56]

It had become a custom for each State Overseer to give a brief report. In reading the history of those reports, one is struck with the consistent appeal for prayer support by these state leaders. They were apostolic. Some were appointed to a territory where there were few churches, and their role was church planting. Over and over, the appeal to prayer occurs. One speaker after another makes the same earnest appeal. It is clear, they knew their missional success was not in better resources, but in the help of God.

Time or space does not allow for additional years to be explored, at least in this volume. Again, I am overwhelmed by the prayer content in these early years of our Church of God history.

The first twenty years, were truly – years of prayer. The General Assemblies were gatherings of prayer.

---

53 Ibid, 9.
54 Ibid, 13.
55 Ibid, 23.
56 Ibid, 30.

* Endnotes from Accent - What Happened at Barney Creek?

1 This "article" first appeared as part of a chapter in A. J. Tomlinson, *The Last Great Conflict* (Cleveland: R. J. Rodgers, 1913), pp. 126-134. Ten years later it was reprinted as the preface in: *Book of Minutes, A compiled history of the work of the General Assemblies of The Church of God* (Cleveland: Church of God Publishing House, 1922), pp. 7-14.

2 1897 MS, pp. 9-12.

3 R.G., born July 26, 1857, was married to Barbara Melinda Hamby on August 20, 1876, in Cherokee County, NC, about five miles from where he had previously lived with his parents in Turtletown, TN. He became a member of Barbara's church, Pleasant Hill Baptist Church and was licensed for the ministry in 1877. Therefore the seven years are from 1877 to 1884 when he made a break with the Baptist church.

4 According to his death certificate, which was filed by his son, Richard E. Spurling, Richard Green Spurling was born July 28, 1857. This is supported by what his son, Goldberry Pinckney Spurling, wrote in his *Early History of R. G. Spurling*, "Bishop Spurling was born in Whitley County, Kentucky, near Williamsburg, on July 28, 1857." He was married to Barbara Malinda Hamby on August 20, 1876 (date from the Bible), just before he was twenty years old. Shortly after that he was licensed to preach, by her church, the Pleasant Hill Baptist Church in Cherokee County, NC. They returned to Monroe County, TN, soon after that because their first child Goldberry Pinckney Spurling was born in Monroe County on July 13, 1877. In the US Census of 1880 both R.G. and Barbara were 22, "Goldsberry P." was 2 and Sarah E. was 1. On September 5, 1882 another son, Killis G., was born.

Over the course of a few years a mutual dissatisfaction between R.G. and the Baptist churches of the area began to grow. In 1884 he surrendered his license to preach as a concession to this; but their dissatisfaction with his activities continued, so he renounced his membership. In his *Unpublished Manuscript*, dated May 4, 1897, he referred to the years of 1884-86 as follows: "During these two years of unparalleled efforts to get the truth, I had taken shelter in the Methodist Episcopal Church until I could know what to do...Meanwhile the Baptist were saying, "Come back and all will be right." And the Methodists said, "Stay with us and take the world for Christ and Methodism." The version of his son, Pinckney, is as follows: "Bishop Spurling was a member of the Missionary Baptist Church and had a great influence, but about this time some of the Baptist preachers began to get jealous, to try to confuse the people and to ask for Spurling's credentials. But Spurling kept on preaching. Then because he preached without a license, they preferred charges against him. When the church took the vote, the church would not vote against Spurling; but when he saw how they were standing by him, he rose and told them to vote him out and there would be no hard feelings. Then they voted according to his wishes."

5 1897 Ms, p. 12.

6 Christian Union was organized on Thursday, August 19, 1886. The ordained minister was his father, Richard Spurling (1810-1891). R.G. is the one who was "ordained on (New) Testament authority and qualification." This was two weeks later, September 2, 1886. Thus the father was involved for two weeks ("until").

7 The reference to the Barney Creek meeting house raises problems. Christian Union seems to have been organized at the Mill. But wherever you meet that is the meeting house. Pinkney, Spurling's oldest son, who was nine years old in 1886, wrote, "After the organization of the church in 1886, father furnished his own lumber and built a small church house. People would fill this church every meeting and pray. And how God would bless and save! Still it was hard for people to give up their church creeds. But Spurling never became discouraged." A nine-year old would probably remember his father building a place of worship, adjacent to the family mill. In 1889 R.G.'s father sold the mill (with the forty acres) on Barney Creek and R.G. moved to Polk County, where he bought a farm on Shular Creek and took care of a small congregation that he had organized at Piney. In 1893 R.G. moved to Turtletown in Polk County in order to have access to a school for his children (according to Pinckney, "An Early History of Richard Green Spurling," p. 4).

8 It is clear that R.G., not his father, preached the sermon and urged the others to join in.

9 The charter members of Christian Union came from only two families: the Spurlings and the Plemons. • The Spurling family (three persons): Richard (R.G.'s father), and Barbara (R.G.'s wife) were among the first eight and Richard Green Spurling, his son, was received after the "setting in order" by Richard Spurling. (a) Richard Spurling was born on November 10, 1810 in Lincoln County (NC) and married Mary Jane Norman in 1832. Between 1833 and 1849 they had seven children and R.G., the eighth, was born in 1857. Richard's wife, Nancy, died in 1878, eight years before 1886. He was approaching seventy-six on August 19, 1886. (b) Barbara Melinda Hamby Spurling was born in March of 1858 in Wilkes County (NC) and was married to R.G. Spurling on August 20, 1876. She was twenty-eight years of age in 1886. (c) Richard Green (R.G.) Spurling was born July 26, 1857, near Williamsburg, in Whitley County (KY) and had just turned twenty-nine years old. Note: At this point R.G. and Barbara had four children: Pinckney (9 years old), Sarah (7), Killis (almost 4) and Barbara (5 months). • The Plemons family (six persons): John Plemons, Sr., Polly Plemons, Margaret Lauftus, Melinda Plemons, John Plemons, Jr., and Adeline Lauftus. The following information is from the Plemons family via e-mail. (a) John James Plemons, (listed by Tomlinson as John Plemons, Sr.) was born in March, 1815, in Buncombe County (NC)

and died before 1910 in Monroe County (TN). He was married to Mary Adeline Irons ("Polly") on January 1, 1839 in Madisonville, Monroe County (TN) and was seventy-one years old in 1886. (b) His wife, Polly (Mary Adeline Irons), was born in 1805 in Haywood County (NC) and died before 1900 in Monroe County (TN). She was ten years older than her husband and therefore eighty-one in 1886. (c) Their daughter, Margaret Lauftus (Margaret J. Plemons Loftis) was born in 1842 in Monroe County (TN) and married William Loftis (b. 1836) on March 7, 1868. She was forty-four in 1886. (d) Adeline Lauftus (Loftis) was the only child of Margaret, having been born in 1875 and was about eleven years old in 1886. (e) John Plemons, Jr. (John Paul Plemons) was born to John and Polly Plemons on August 5, 1852 in Monroe County (TN). He was married to Ester Melinda Thompson on June 25, 1875 in Monroe County (TN), by Richard Spurling, R.G.'s father. He had turned thirty-four just before the organization of Christian Union in 1886. (f) Melinda Plemons (Ester Melinder Thompson Plemons) born on September 9, 1861 and died in 1913 in Monroe County (TN). She was nine years younger than her husband, John Paul Plemons, and was twenty-five years old in 1886. She is said to have been Cherokee and to have born a total of ten children.

10 After being "acknowledged and recognized", the Elder Richard takes over from R.G., who for the two years previously held no ministerial license at all; and thus it was the father who does the official action of constituting the group a church. From the language used, i.e., "infant church of God," it would seem that both Spurling and Tomlinson saw a direct connection between this and the "Church of God" of 1913, the date this chapter was published.

11 This has to have been an editorial comment of Tomlinson, not something that happened on August 19, 1886, because at that time he was neither licensed nor ordained, which would have been the requirement for being installed as pastor.

12 This was actually September 2, 1886, the date given on R.G.'s handwritten certificate of ordination, signed by his father, Richard Spurling, and on the printed certificate, re-issued later by the Church of God and signed by Tomlinson and Bryant. September 2 (Thursday) was exactly two weeks after the organization of Christian Union on August 19. R.G. was actually installed as pastor on September 2, 1886, following his ordination.

13 Apparently the first two lines of the first verse of "Rock of Ages" were intended to be sung as the fifth and sixth lines of each stanza.

14 The text has "amid" but the meter demands "Mid."

REFERENCE

INDEX

TOPICAL REFERENCES

INDEX

SCRIPTURAL REFERENCES

BIBLIOGRAPHY

Allen, Leonard. *The Contemporaries Meet the Classics on Prayer* (West Monroe: LA; Howard Publishing Company, 2003).

Allen, Marshall "Pentecostal Movement Celebrates Humble Roots." *The Washington Post.* (April 15, 2006) <http://www.washingtonpost.com/wp-dyn/content/article/2006/04/14/AR2006041401421.html. Retrieved 2007-05-17>.

Alliance for Life Ministries, *"America's Christian Heritage, Part II: The Revolution and Beyond"*, <www.alliance4lifemin.org/categori..../ach_part2.htm>, retrieved August 27, 2007.

Andrews, Rex. *What the Bible Teaches About Mercy* (Zion, IL: Zion Faith Homes, 1985).

Aquinas, Thomas. *Summa Theologiae, Vol. 5* (Cambridge University Press, 2006).

Archer, Jr., Gleason L. *Survey of the Old Testament Introduction* (Moody Pub, 2007).

The Assemblies of God, <ag.org/top/Beliefs/topics/charctr_20_reverence_.cfm>.

Baird, Arthur. *The Justice of God in the Teaching of Jesus* (London: S.C.M., 1963).

Bakke, Ray. *A Theology As Big As The City* (Downers Grove, IL: InterVarsity Press, 1997).

Balentine, Samuel. *Prayer in the Hebrew Bible: The Drama of Divine-Human Dialogue* (Overtures to Biblical Theology; Minneapolis, MN; Minneapolis Fortress Press, 1993).

Barr, James. *"'Abba' Isn't 'Daddy' Journal of Theological Studies,* (1988); See also: Geza Vermes, *Jesus in the World of Judaism* (1983).

Bartleman, Frank *Azusa Street* (Bridge-Logos Publishers, 1980).

Barton, David. "Building On Firm Foundations," *Ministries Today, Vol. 30, No. 1* (January/February, 2012: Charisma Media; Lake Mary, FL).

Beiler, Irwin Ross. *Studies in the Life of Jesus* (New York: Abingdon-Cokesbury Press, 1936).

Bernard, *Song of Songs I; Sermon 6.6-9* (Kalamazoo, MI: Cistercian Publications, 1971).

Bevins, Winfield. *Developing a Powerful Prayer Life* Cleveland, TN: Pathway Press, 2006.

Bible Law Course, "Runkel v Winemiller," 4; "Harris & McHenry," 276 (Supreme Court: Maryland; October Term, 1799). <www.moseshand.com/studies/RvW.htm, retrieved August 26, 2007>.

Billheimer, Paul. *Destined for the Throne* (Fort Washington, PA; Christian Literature Crusade, 1975).

Blackaby, Henry and Claude King. *Fresh Encounters* (Nashville, TN: Broadman, 1996).

Bloesch, Donald G. *Essentials of Evangelical Theology, Vol. 2* (New York: Harper & Row, 1979).

Bonhoeffer, Dietrich. *Christology,* Quoted by Charles Ringma, *Seize the Day with Dietrich Bonhoeffer* (Colorado Springs, Colorado: Pinion Press; 2000), See entry for January 21.

— *Ethics,* Quoted by Charles Ringma, *Seize the Day with Dietrich Bonhoeffer* (Colorado Springs, Colorado: Pinion Press; 2000), See entry for January 20.

— *Life Together,* Quoted by Charles Ringma, *Seize the Day with Dietrich Bonhoeffer* (Colorado Springs, Colorado: Pinion Press; 2000), See entry for January 17.

— *Meditating on the Word,* Quoted by Charles Ringma, *Seize the Day with Dietrich Bonhoeffer* (Colorado Springs, Colorado: Pinion Press; 2000), See entry for January 31

— *Psalms: The Prayer Book of the Bible* (Minneapolis: MN; Augsburg Publishers, 1970).

Bounds, E. M. *The Best of E. M. Bounds on Prayer* (Grand Rapids: Baker; 1981).

— *The Weapon of Prayer* (Destiny Image Publishers, 2011).

Bridges, Jerry. *The Joy of Fearing God* (Colorado Springs, CO: Waterbrook Press, 1997).

Brueggemann, Walter. *Great Prayers of the Old Testament* (Louisville/London: Westminster John Knox Press, 2008).

— *The Message of the Psalms* (Fortress Press, 1984).

— *Praying the Psalms,* (Wipf & Stock Pub, 2007).

Brunner, Emil. *The Christian Doctrine of the Church, Faith and the Consummation,* vol. 3, (Philadelphia: Westminster Press, 1960).

Bullinger, E. W. *Word Studies on the Holy Spirit* (Grand Rapids, MI: Kregel Publications, 1985).

Bunyan, John *Prayer* (London: Banner of Truth Trust, 1965).

Calvin, John. *Commentary on the Book of Psalms* (Grand Rapids, MI: 1999).

— *Institutes of the Christian Religion.*

— *The Epistles of Paul to the Romans and Thessalonians, Vol. 8; New Testament Commentaries* (Grand Rapids: Eerdmans, 1980).

Carson, D. A. *Teach Us To Pray* (Wipf & Stock Pub, 2002).

Chadwick, Samuel. *The Path of Prayer* (Hodder and Stoughton, 1933).

Charlesworth, James. *Rule of the Community and Related Documents, Vol.*

1; The Dead Sea Scrolls: Hebrew, Aaramaic, and Greek Texts with English Translations (Louisville: Westminster John Knox, 1994).

Christensen, *Prayer,* Julius Bodensieck, *The Encyclopedia of the Lutheran Church* (Minneapolis: Augsburg Publishing House, 1966), HI, 1973.

Church of God General Assembly Minutes, First General Assembly (Camp Creek, North Carolina, January 26-27, 1907).

Church of God General Assembly Minutes, Second General Assembly (Union Grove, Bradley County, TN; January 9-13, 1907).

Church of God General Assembly Minutes, Third General Assembly (Cleveland, TN, January 8-12, 1908).

Church of God General Assembly Minutes, Fourth General Assembly (Cleveland, TN, January 6-9, 1909) .

Church of God General Assembly Minutes, Fifth General Assembly (Cleveland, TN, January 10-16, 1910).

Church of God General Assembly Minutes, Sixth General Assembly (Cleveland, TN, January 3-4, 1911).

Church of God General Assembly Minutes, Seventh General Assembly (Cleveland, TN, January 9-14, 1912).

Church of God General Assembly Minutes, Eighth General Assembly (Cleveland, TN, January 7-12, 1913).

Church of God General Assembly Minutes, Ninth General Assembly (Cleveland, TN, November 4-9, 1913).

Church of God General Assembly Minutes, Tenth General Assembly (Cleveland, TN, November 2-8, 1914).

Church of God General Assembly Minutes, Eleventh General Assembly (Cleveland, TN, November 1-7, 1915).

Church of God General Assembly Minutes, Twelfth General Assembly (Harriman, TN, November 1-7, 1916).

Church of God General Assembly Minutes, Thirteenth General Assembly (Harriman, TN, November 1-6, 1917).

Church of God General Assembly Minutes, Fourteenth General Assembly (Cleveland, TN, October 29 - November 4, 1919).

Church of God General Assembly Minutes, Fifteenth General Assembly (Cleveland, TN, November 3-9, 1920).

Church of God General Assembly Minutes, Sixteenth General Assembly (Cleveland, TN, November 2-8, 1921).

Church of God General Assembly Minutes, Seventeenth General Assembly (Cleveland, TN, November 1-7, 1922).

Church of God General Assembly Minutes, Eighteenth General Assembly (Cleveland, TN, November 1-7, 1923).

Church of God General Assembly Minutes, Nineteenth General Assembly (Cleveland, TN, October 29 -November 4, 1924).

Church of God General Assembly Minutes, Twentieth General Assembly (Cleveland, TN, October 19 -25, 1925).

Clark, Doug. *Jesus and Women*, <enrichmentjournal.ag.org/200102/024_jesus_and_women.cfm>.

Clements, Ronald E. *In Spirit and in Truth* (Atlanta: John Knox Press, 1985).

Conn, Charles W. *Like a Mighty Army* (Cleveland, TN: Pathway Press, 1977).

Conn, Harvie. *A Clarified Vision for Urban Mission* (Ministry Resources Library, 1987).

— *Evangelism: Doing Justice and Preaching Grace* (Zondervan, 1982).

— *Luke's Theology of Prayer* (Christianity Today, December 22).

Creed, John Martin. *The Gospel According to St. Luke* (London: McMillan, 1953).

Cullmann, Oscar. *Baptism in the New Testament* (Naperville, IL: Alec R. Allenson, 1950).

— *Prayer in the New Testament* (Minneapolis, MN: Fortress Press, 1994).

Cutshall, Bryan. *Prayer Ministry Handbook*, (Cleveland, TN: Pathway Press, 2005).

D'Angelo, Mary Rose. *Journal of Biblical Literature, Vol. 111, No. 4* (Winter, 1992).

Dahood, Mitchell *The Anchor Bible, Vol. 17, Psalms II* (Garden City, N.Y.: Doubleday, 1968).

Dake, Finis Jennings. *Dake's Annotated Reference Bible* (Lawrenceville, GA: Dake Bible Sales, 1963, 1991).

Danskin, R. A. *An Exposition of the Lord's Prayer*, (Pentecostal Publishing Co., 1930).

Day, John N. *The Imprecatory Psalms and Christian Ethics, Bibliotheca Sacra* 159 (April – June 2002):166-186. Copyright by Dallas Theological Seminary. www.dts.edu.

Deffinbaugh, Bob. *Psalm 109: A Prayer for the Punishment of the Wicked.* Accessed online March 11, 2013: <bible.org/seriespage/psalm-109-prayer-punishment-wicked>.

Denton, Michael. *Evolution: A Theory in Crisis* (Bethesda, MD: Adler & Adler, 1985), 328-329; See also, Paul Brand and Philip Yancey, *Fearfully and Wonderfully Made* (Grand Rapids: MI; 1980).

Dickson, David *Commentary on the Psalms* (Minneapolis: Klock and Klock, 1980).

Du Plessis, David. *The Spirit Bade Me Go* (Planfield, NJ; Logos International, 1970).

Dunn, Ronald. *Don't Just Stand There – Pray Something* (Nashville, TN: Thomas Nelson, 1991).

Eastman, Dick. *A Watchman's Guide to Praying God's Promises* (Jakarta, Indonesia: World Prayer Assembly Edition, 2012; Colorado Springs, CO: Every Home for Christ). <www. ehc.org>; <www.globaldayof-prayer.com/downloads/resources/nations/WatchmansGuide.pdf>.

Edwards, Jonathan. *The Select Works of Jonathan Edwards,* vol. 2, Sermon 7 (London: Banner of Truth,1959).

Eichrodt, W. *Theology of the Old Testament,* Vol. 1 (London: S.C.M., 1961).

Evangel, March 15, 1901.

Evangel, July 1, 1901.

Evangel, January 10, 1914 (V/2).

Evangel, December 16, 1933.

The Evening Light, April 1, 1910 (I/3).

The Faithful Standard (September, 1922).

Federer, William J. *American Minute* <www.amerisearch.net/index. php?date=2004-09-17> retrieved August 27, 2007.

Fee, Gordon. *Paul and the Spirit and the People of God* (Peabody, MA; Hendrickson Publishers, 1996).

Ferguson, Sinclair. *Grow in Grace* (Colorado Springs: NavPress, 1984).

Forsyth, P. T. *The Cruciality of the Cross* (London: Hodder & Stoughton, 1909).

Forsyth, P. T. *The Soul of Prayer* (Regent College Publishing, 1916).

Forsyth, P. T. *The Work of Christ* (BiblioBazaar, 2010).

Foster, Richard. from *Celebration of Discipline.* Quoted by, Leonard Allen, *The Contemporaries Meet the Classics on Prayer* (West Monroe, LA: Howard Publishing Company, 2003).

The Founders' Constitution, Vol. 5, Amendment I (Speech and Press): *"Updegraph v. Commonwealth,"* 11; *"Serg. & Rawle,"* 394 (The University of Chicago Press, 1824) <press-pubs.uchicago.edu/founders/print_documents/amendI_speechs30.html>, retrieved August 26, 2007.

Gordon, S. D. Taken from the Chapter: *Jesus' Habits of Prayer, Quiet Talks On Prayer,* 1904.

Gunkel, Hermann. *The Psalms: A Form-Critical Introduction* (Fortress Press, 1967; translation of *Die Religion in Geschichte und Gegenwart* [2nd ed; J.C.B. Mohr (Paul Siebeck), 1930]; and Hermann Gunkel (completed by Joachim Begrich), *Introduction to Psalms: The Genres of the Religious Lyric of Israel* (Mercer University Press, 1998; translation of *Einleitung in die Psalmen: die Gattungen der religiösen Lyrik Israels* [Vandenhoeck & Ruprecht, 1985, 1933]).

Han, Kyu Sam. *Theology of Prayer in the Gospel of Luke* (JETS 43; 2000).

Hanson, A. T. *The Wrath of the Lamb* (Wipf & Stock Pub, 2010).

Harris, Lindell. *Prayer in the Gospel of Luke* (SWJT 10: 1967).

Hassell, E. Keith. *Worship and God's Throne;* The Vision Newsletter (August, 2012); <www.gracefellowshiprusk.com> Grace Fellowship; P.O. Box 260; Rusk, Texas; (903) 683-6550.

Heiler, Friedrich. *Prayer: A Study in the History and Psychology of Religion* (London: Oxford University Press, 1932).

Henry, Matthew. *Commentary on the Bible, I* (Hendrickson Pub, 2008).

Holladay, William. *The Psalms Through Three Thousand Years* (Minneapolis, MN: Fortress Press, 1993).

Huegel, F. J. *Successful Praying* (Minneapolis, MN: Bethany, 1967).

Hurley, James. citing W. Forster, *Palestinian Judaism in New Testament Times.* (London, 1964).

Jennings, Ben. *The Arena of Prayer* (NewLife Publications, 1999).

Jeremias, Joachim. *The Prayers of Jesus* (Philadelphia: Fortress Press, 1978).

Jewish Encyclopedia – Babylonian Captivity. <www.bible-history.com/map_babylonian_captivity/map_of_the_deportation_of_judah_jewish_encyclopedia.html>.

Johnston, J. B. *The Prayer Meeting and Its History* (Scholarly Publishing Office, U of Mi, 2006).

Kaiser, Walter. *Hard Sayings of the Old Testament* (Downers Grove, IL: InterVarsity Press, 1988).

Kamsler, Harold M. *A Note On The Prohibition Of Uttering The Name Of God,* <jbq.jewishbible.org/assets/Uploads/314/314_Tetra11.pdf>.

Kendall, R.T. and Joy Strong, *By Love Transformed* (Charisma Media, 2006).

Kidner, Derek. *Psalms 73-150* (Downers Grove: Inter-Varsity Press, 1975), p. 388. See the chapter, *The Character-Assassin.*

Kirkpatrick, A. F. *The Book of Psalms* (Cambridge, England: University Press, 1906).

Lactantius, *A Treatise on the Anger of God, The Ante-Nicene Fathers, Vol. 7* (Grand Rapids: Eerdmans, 1969-73).

Lane, G. W. *The Priviledge of Prayer,* Cleveland, TN, Forwarth in Faith.

Lane, Tony *The Wrath of God as an Aspect of the Love of God*, which first appeared in Kevin J. Vanhoozer (Ed.) *Nothing Greater Nothing Better: Theological Essays on the Love of God* (Wm. B. Eerdmans Publishing

Company: Grand Rapids, Michigan, 2001). Accessed online, September 7, 2012: <www.theologynetwork.org/christian-beliefs/doctrine-of-god/getting-stuck-in/the-wrath-of-god-as-an-aspect-of-the-love-of-god.htm>.

Lemons, David. *Words Fitly Spoken* (Cleveland, TN: Pathway Press, 1988).

Lewis, C. S. *Christian Reflections* (Wm. B. Eerdmans Publishing, 1994).

Lewis, C. S. *The Lion, the Witch, and the Wardrobe* (Hammondsworth, Middlesex, England: Penguin Books, 1950).

Lewis, C. S. *Reflections on the Psalms* (New York, NY: Harcourt, Brace, and Co., 1958).

Lockyer, Herbert. *All the Prayers of the Bible* (Zondervan, 1990).

Lowery, T. L. (Thomas Lanier), 1929-. *Prayers that Prevail* (Cleveland, TN? : Lowery Ministries International, 1995).

Luther, Martin. *What Luther Says* (St. Louis: Concordia, 1959).

Martin, Lee Roy. *Jonah and the God of Grace: Lessons in Obedience, Faithfulness, and Prayer,* (Cleveland, TN: Pathway Press, 2009).

McClaren, Alexander. *The Psalms, Volume 3* (New York, NY: George Doran Company, 1892).

McGee, J. Vernon. *J. Vernon McGee on Prayer* (Thomas Nelson, Inc., 2002).

McGrath, A. E. *Luther's Theology of the Cross* (Oxford: Blackwell, 1985).

McKenzie, John. *The Book of Psalms* (Grand Rapids: Baker Book House, 1982).

Mepe, R. P. *Spirituality, Dictionary of Paul and His Letters* (Downers Grove, Illinois: InterVarsity Press, 1993).

Morris, Leon. *The Apostolic Preaching of the Cross, 3rd ed.* (London: Tyndale, 1965).

Morrow, A. *The Queen* (The Chaucer Press: Bungay, Suffolk, 1983); J. Morgan, *Debrett's New Guide to Etiquette and Modern Manners: the Indispensable Handbook* (Headline; London, 1996).

Mott, John Raleigh. *The Evangelization of the World in this Generation* (Student Volunteer Movement for Foreign Missions, Princeton University, 1905).

Mueller, George. *George Mueller Quotes.* Online. Internet. oChristian.com. © 1999-2000.

Murray, Andrew. *Lessons from the School of Prayer.*

Murray, John. *Principles of Conduct* (Grand Rapids: MI; Eerdmans, 1957).

Ng, Esther Yue L. *Prayer in the Revelation,* See: D. A. Carson, *Teach Us To Pray.*

O'Brien, P. T. *Prayer in Luke-Acts* (TB 24: 1973), 114; See also, Han, *The-*

ology.

Ott, W. *Gebet und Heil. Die Bedeutung der Gebetsparanese in der lukanischen Theologie (*Munchen, 1965), 13; See also: A. Hamman, *La Priere. I. Le Nouveau Testament,* (Tournai: 1959).

Peels, Henrick. *The Vengeance of God* (Brill, 1995).

Perowne, J. J. Stewart. *The Book of Psalms* (Grand Rapids: Zondervan [reprint], 1976).

Peskett, Howard. *Prayer in the Old Testament Outside the Psalms,* See: D. A. Carson, *Teach Us To Pray* (Grand Rapids: MI; Baker Book House, 1990).

Peterson, David. *Prayer in Paul's Writings,* See D. A. Carson, *Teach Us To Pray*, 96.

Peterson, Eugene. *Answering God* (HarperCollins, 2011).

The Pew Forum on Religion & Public Life / U.S. Religious Landscape Survey. See: *The U.S. Religious Landscape Survey.* Online <religions. pewforum.org/pdf/report2religious-landscape-study-key-findings. pdf>.

Pfieffer, Charles. *Ras Shamra and the Bible* (Baker Book House, 1962).

Pieper, Francis. *Christian Dogmatics* (St. Louis: Concordia Publishing House, 1955).

Pink, Arthur. *The Attributes of God* (Grand Rapids: Guardian Press, 1975).

Plass, E.W. *What Luther Says* (St. Louis: Concordia Publishing House, 1959), II, 1024-1101. See also: Martin Reu, *Lutheran Dogmatics* (Decorah, Iowa: Wartburg Theological Seminary, 1951).

Prayer, *The Reporter, The Importance of Prayer to Nearly Everyone,* (May, 1994).

Rollins, Daniel. *Forward, Ever Forward: A History of the North Carolina Conference of the Pentecostal Holiness Church* (Falcon, NC: North Carolina Conference of the Pentecostal Holiness Church).

Rosscup, James E. *An Exposition on Prayer in the Bible* (5 vols.), Bibliacom.

Rowley, H. H. *The Faith of Israel* (SCM, 1956).

Runbeck, Margaret Lee. *The City that Wouldn't Die, The Great Answer* (Boston: Houghton Mifflin Company, 1944).

— *A Friend of a Friend of His -, The Great Answer* (Boston: Houghton Mifflin Company, 1944).

— *Light in Gestapo Darkness, The Great Answer* (Boston: Houghton Mifflin Company, 1944).

— "The Private Dunkirk" *The Great Answer* (Boston: Houghton Mifflin Company, 1944).

Ryle, J. C. *Practical Religion* (Prisbrary Publishing, 1977).

Sacks, J. *Faith in the Future* (London: Darton, Longman & Todd, 1995).

Scribner, *New Testament Theology* (1971).

Shaw, S. B. *Charlie Coulson, The Christian Drummer Boy, Touching Incidents And Remarkable Answers To Prayer* (Grand Rapids, MI: S.B. Shaw, Publisher, 1893).

— *A Mob Quieted In Answer To Prayer, Touching Incidents And Remarkable Answers To Prayer* (Grand Rapids, MI: S.B. Shaw, Publisher, 1893).

— *Touching Incidents and Remarkable Answers to Prayer*, Grand Rapids: S. B. Shaw, 1893, p. 133f. [3] *The Evening Light* and *Church of God Evangel* (Cleveland, TN: Church of God Publishing House, 1910/11/15 [I/18]).

Sheets, Dutch. *Intercessory Prayer* (Ventura, CA: Regal Books, 1996).

Small, P. Douglas. *Entertaining God and Influencing Cities,* (Kannapolis, NC: Alive Publications, 2008).

— *Five Basic Prayer Principles,* (Kannapolis, NC: Alive Publications, 2012).

— *The Great Commission Prayer Guide,* (Cleveland, TN: Pathway Press, 2009).

— *Intercession: The Uncomfortable Middle,* (Kannapolis, NC: Alive Publications, 2009).

— *Prayer: The Heartbeat of the Church,* (Cleveland, TN: Pathway Press, 2008).

— *The Praying Church Resource Guide,* (Kannapolis, NC: Alive Publications, 2012).

— *Principles of Worship and the Tabernacle of Moses* (Kannapolis, NC: Alive Publications, 1990, 2012).

— *Transforming Your Church into a House of Prayer,* (Cleveland, TN: Pathway Press, 2006).

Smith, Oswald J. *I Have Walked Along with Jesus: Day by Day Meditations of Oswald J. Smith* (GR Welch Co, 1982). ISBN 0-91964-900-9.

Sproul, R.C. *Essential Truths of The Christian Faith* (Tyndale House Pub, 1992).

— *Tabletalk* magazine, "My God, My God, Why Hast Thou Forsaken Me?" (April 1990).

Stanley, Grenz. *Women in the Church: A Biblical Theology of Women in Ministry.* (InterVarsity Press, 1995).

Surburg, Raymond. *The Biblical Doctrine of Prayer (See: www.confessionallutherans.org/BDOP.doc).*

Supreme Court in association with *Holy Trinity Church v. United States,* a case dated February 29, 1892. *Vine & Fig Tree, The Supreme Court*

of the United States, Holy Trinity Church v. The United States 143 U.S.
457, 12 S.Ct. 511, 36 L.Ed. 226 February 29, 1892, members.aol.
com/EndTheWall/TrinityHistory.htm, retrieved August 26, 2007.

Synan, Vinson. *The Century of the Holy Spirit: 100 years of Pentecostal and
Charismatic Renewal, 1901–2001* (Thomas Nelson Publishers, 2001).
pp. 42–45. ISBN 0-7852-4550-2.

Temple, William. *Christus Veritas* (Macmillan, 1925).

Tertullian, *"Against Marcion," Tertullian Adversus Marcionem*, Ed. E. Evans, Vol. 1: 1.27 (Oxford: Clarendon, 1972).

Tomlinson, A. J. Editor, *The Evening Light And Church Of God Evangel*
(Cleveland, TN: Church of God; April 15, 1910).

— *The Last Great Conflict* (Cleveland: R. J. Rodgers, 1913), pp. 126-
134. Ten years later it was reprinted as the preface in: *Book of
Minutes, A compiled history of the work of the General Assemblies of
The Church of God* (Cleveland: Church of God Publishing House,
1922).

— Editor, "The Oneness of God's People," *The Church of God Evangel*,
[Periodical], (Cleveland, TN: Church of God Publishing; August 1,
1910).

— Editor, "A Pentecostal Shower," *Church of God Evangel* [Periodical],
(Cleveland, TN: Church of God; March 15, 1910.

Toynbee, Arnold. Quoted in *Christian Quotes* (Holiday, FL: Christian
Quotes; February, 2003).

Tozer, *The Knowledge of the Holy.*

Triplett, Bennie S. *Praying Effectively: Bible Studies in Prayer,* (Cleveland,
TN: Pathway Press, 1990).

Turner, M. M. B. *Prayer in the Gospels and Acts,* D. A. Carson, *Teach Us To
Pray.*

Voigt, Stephen. *How I learned about the root of law...but not in law school,*
December 22, 2005, <earstohear.net/Separation/rootoflaw.html>,
retrieved August 27, 2007.

Walker, Lucille. *Lord, Teach Us to Pray: Praying for Results,* (Cleveland,
TN: Pathway Press, 1986).

Walker, Lucille. *What To Do When You Pray* (Cleveland, TN: Pathway
Press, 1998).

Watson, Thomas. *A Divine Cordial* (Sovereign Grace Publishers, 2007).

Willimon, William. Quoted in *Christian Quotes* (Holiday, FL: Christian
Quotes; February, 2003).